Modern Communication Systems

Modern Communication Systems

R. F. W. Coates

Lecturer in Electronics
University of Wales

Second edition

M

First edition 1975
Reprinted 1978, 1981
Second edition 1983

Published by
THE MACMILLAN PRESS LTD
London and Basingstoke
Companies and representatives throughout the world

ISBN 0 333 33344 6 (hard cover)
0 333 35832 5 (paper cover)

Printed in Hong Kong

Contents

Preface to the First Edition

This text is intended to cover a two-year course on communication system engineering at B.Sc. level. The subject material is based upon courses which I have taught at both the University of Wales and the University of London.

Chapter 1 concentrates upon the use of Fourier methods in the analysis and processing of waveforms. It provides the mathematical groundwork upon which the rest of the book is based.

The communication channel and the problems it presents to the system designer are studied in chapter 2.

Chapters 3, 4 and 5 are concerned with the various methods of modulating a sinusoidal carrier. Much of the material presented in these chapters is standard and has been well-documented in other undergraduate texts. None the less, I have attempted to introduce modern techniques wherever possible. In particular, I have tended to stress such system implementations as lead naturally to integrated-circuit fabrications. For example, in chapter 4, the principle of frequency discrimination and the desirable features required of a practical discriminator are considered, leading to a description of the Travis discriminator. Instead of following the usual policy and covering the Foster–Seeley and ratio detectors in great detail, the available space has been devoted to introducing that quite-different frequency detector: the phase-locked loop. This system module is now available as an integrated circuit. It is cheap, requires little trimming and involves no transformers. It must, surely, become the major means of attaining frequency detection, even in domestic receivers, in the near future.

The titles of chapters 3, 4 and 5 are 'Envelope Modulation', 'Angle Modulation' and 'Composite Modulation', respectively. Single-sideband systems, being a combined envelope and phase modulation, therefore appear in chapter 5. It is common policy, in most texts, to include them with envelope (amplitude) modulation. I hope that the slightly unusual classification employed here will help the student to appreciate the nature of single-sideband waveforms more clearly.

Digital techniques are discussed in chapters 6, 7 and 8 in greater detail than has been customary in most undergraduate texts. Notwithstanding the small amount of time commonly devoted to these topics, they represent the major growth area in communication system installation at the present time; in particular, digital-data links are becoming an area of great importance. In this respect, I hope that the discussions of both digital coding and data transmission reflect modern practice with reasonable accuracy and provide an indication of trends in the immediate future.

In a text of this nature, space is at a premium and, if the cost of the final work is not to become excessive, some omissions are inevitable. It is with regret, for example, that I have not been able to include descriptions of differential pulse code modulation and delta modulation. The latter system, particularly, is of increasing interest to many engineers. However, it has not yet found extensive practical application in communication systems.

Let me reiterate the function of this book before defending the omission of one major topic. The objective is to teach undergraduates about communication systems. Communications is a vast field; one that is capital-intensive and makes heavy demands on available skilled manpower. The book, then, must attempt to present the principles upon which modern communication system design is based. It must also, perhaps to a lesser extent, present an outline of current practice. A conflict in aims, therefore, tends to arise when we come to consider the suitability of including such subjects as statistical decision theory and information theory. Practice makes it evident that profitable systems are not, in the main, designed as a consequence of the application of the principles which derive from these disciplines.

Thus the techniques used in the design of data modems do not, in practice, derive from decision-making strategies suggested by statistical decision theory. Nor does the use of frequency modulation result from the application of the methods of information theory. It is true that information theory, and in particular Shannon's well-known theorem

$$\text{information transfer} = \text{channel bandwidth} \times \text{transmission time}$$

$$\times \log\left(1 + \text{signal/noise ratio}\right)$$

throws light on the efficacy of the tradeoff between bandwidth and signal-to-noise ratio evidenced by frequency-modulation systems. It is also arguable that Shannon's theorem provides us with upper bounds beyond which we cannot expect to improve the performance of communication systems; perhaps it does. Unfortunately, it is rarely the case that the postulates used in deriving the theorem are all encountered in a real system. Also, most real systems exhibit a performance level well below the Shannon bound. Finally, information theory suggests no way of designing systems so that the bound is approached. Hence its omission in favour of topics of greater practical importance to the young engineer about to seek employment.

Let me conclude by extending my appreciation to the people who have helped me during the preparation of this book, I would like to thank my colleagues, David Armitage, David Everett and Robert Newton for many helpful discussions and for reading and criticising the manuscript with such diligence. For his assistance in preparing and executing the diagrams, particularly some of the more difficult, I would like to thank my father, Stafford Coates, Principal Lecturer, Southampton College of Technology. Finally, thanks are due to my mother, Mollie, and my wife, Gillian, for their support and encouragement during the writing of this book.

October 1974 RODNEY COATES

Preface to the Second Edition

In the short period of seven years since the publication of the first edition of this book, many significant and, in some respects unforseeable, changes in communication system technology have emerged. In particular the 'microprocessor revolution', the rapid escalation in complexity of computing microcircuitry, has provided the communication engineer with powerful, yet flexible and easily implemented processing capabilities. Taken in conjunction with fibre optic and satellite technology and the need to sustain ever-expanding computer data-bases and communication facilities, such capabilities pave the way for a second revolution: the 'information revolution' predicted for the closing decade of this century.

Respecting the pace and nature of communication system developments, I have included a new chapter: 'The Integrated Services Digital Network'. This will I hope provide an orientation for the engineer in a field of some complexity— namely, the structure and organisation of the future international telephony and data-transfer network—which, in social terms, must profoundly affect us all.

In chapters 6, 7 and 8 I have added new material emphasising the importance of digital techniques in the communications industry. Indeed, much of the material included in chapter 6 (in particular, that concerning differential pulse code and delta modulation) had to be deliberately omitted from the first edition, being *at that time* insufficiently important to warrant inclusion. Now, both techniques are essential material for the understanding of the integrated circuit 'CODEC'. This device (described in detail in chapter 6) will, it has been predicted, account for a major proportion of the revenue of the integrated circuit fabrication industry by the end of the present decade.

Changing social attitudes and the volume and sensitivity of commercial information transfer have persuaded me to include in chapter 7 discussions of the use of coding techniques in speech and data communication to achieve security and privacy. In chapter 8, consideration is given to advanced data keying systems and modem techniques. Finally, new material providing a resumé of the significance of fibre optic communications in modern communication networks is to be found in chapter 2.

Despite the inclusion of considerable new material, much has, inevitably, been left unsaid. It is my hope, however, that within the following pages, the engineer will find a helpful overview of this vast, expanding and vitally important field of human endeavour. Finally, I am indebted to Larry Lind for reading and correcting the manuscript and for his many useful suggestions throughout the production of this new edition.

May, 1982   RODNEY COATES

1 The Analysis and Synthesis of Waveforms

Speech is in many ways typical of communication waveforms. When converted into an electrical signal and displayed on an oscilloscope it is seen to have a continuously fluctuating waveshape which is extremely complicated. Faced with the problem of analysing and manipulating a complicated waveform, we naturally look for some 'lowest common denominator', something which allows us to classify all such signals. Then we may be able to isolate categories of signals, or processing techniques, which are of some particular benefit to us. In this first chapter, we shall examine one waveform, the sinewave or *sinusoid*, which is very often used as the basis for analysis and synthesis. It is not the only one which could be adopted but it is the most convenient for our purposes, since it is relatively easy to handle, both mathematically and electronically.

Following from our discussion of the sinusoid, we shall consider the problems of specifying and analysing both periodic and aperiodic waveforms. This will provide us with the essential mathematical groundwork upon which we may base our examination of communication systems and their operation.

We shall also examine the manner in which the content of a waveform may be altered by the process of linear filtering. Finally, we shall consider the determination of power- and energy-density spectra, since these properties tell us how the waveform occupies its transmission bandwidth.

1.1 The Sinusoid

In our investigations into the nature and development of communication systems, we shall repeatedly come into contact with the sinusoidal time function. There is indeed good reason why this should be so. Many natural and physical systems principally contain energy-storage and dissipation elements. Often these elements may be regarded as *lumped* or individual components of the system. When this is the case, we can write first- or second-order differential equations describing the system. When solved, such equations exhibit natural modes of response which are exponential, or damped sinusoidal functions of time.

The sinusoid, as we shall see, is of great value both as a fundamental waveform 'type' from which other, more complicated waveforms may be built up and as a signalling waveform in its own right. We may express the sinusoid as

$$v(t) = A \cos(\omega t + \phi) \quad \text{all } t \qquad (1.1)$$

This equation is a *time domain* mathematical specification of the sinusoid. The phrase 'time domain' is used because the independent variable in the equation is time, t. Notice that t is unrestricted. The condition 'all t' merely states that the sinusoid, as defined, was always 'switched on', so that no transient conditions need be considered. The sinusoid is specified by three parameters: A, the *amplitude*, measured typically in volts or amps; ω, the *angular velocity*, sometimes also referred to by communication engineers as the *radian frequency*, measured in radian s^{-1} and ϕ, the *phase angle*, measured in radians. Note that the radian frequency is related to the period, T, of the sinusoid and to its frequency, f, measured in hertz (Hz)

$$f = \omega/2\pi$$
$$T = 1/f$$

Another important mathematical (not pictorial) representation of the sinusoid is as a rotating *phasor*. In order to facilitate our discussion of the phasor, let us first recollect de Moivre's theorem. That is

$$\exp(j\theta) = \cos(\theta) + j \sin(\theta)$$

We refer to $\exp(j\theta)$ as a *cisoid*, in the same sense that we refer to $\cos\theta$ and $\sin\theta$ as sinusoids. $\exp j\theta$ may be represented on the complex plane as a line of unit length inclined at an angle θ to the real axis; see figure 1.1a. 'cisoid' simply stands for *cos + i sinusoid*. The precise definition of the term 'phasor' depends on the area of application. In circuit theory, the phasor is a complex

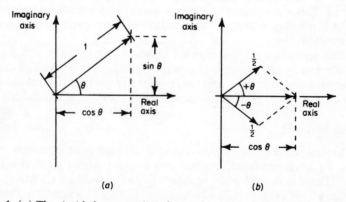

(a)   (b)

Figure 1.1 (a) *The cisoid phasor* $\exp(j\theta)$ *depicted on the complex plane.* (b) *Generation of the sinusoid* $\cos(\theta)$ *as the sum of two cisoids*

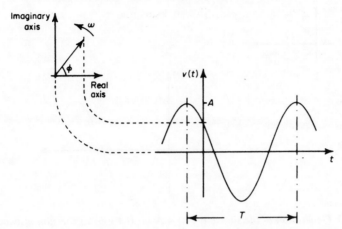

Figure 1.2 Generation of the sinusoid $v(t) = A \cos(\omega t + \phi)$ *as the real part (horizontal projection) of a rotating phasor of length A*

quantity, V, chosen such that

$$\text{Re}\{V \exp(j\omega t)\} = A \cos(\omega t + \phi)$$

It follows that

$$V = A \exp(j\phi)$$

Thus the phasor conveys the essential information regarding amplitude and phase of a fixed frequency sinusoid. Being a complex quantity, the phasor may be depicted on the complex plane as a fixed line of length A, inclined at an angle ϕ to the real axis. The term 'vector' may, in some texts be synonymous with the term 'phasor' defined as above. However, modern usage reserves the former expression for quantities defined spatially, such as electromagnetic fields.

For communication applications, the phasor is defined to be the entire quantity

$$V \exp(j\omega t)$$

This, when represented on the complex plane, consists of a *rotating* line, inclined at an angle ϕ at time $t = 0$, the real part of which generates the sinusoid $A \cos(\omega t + \phi)$ as a function of time. Figure 1.2 illustrates this effect, which is analogous to the familiar process of generation of a sinusoid as the projection onto the horizontal of a uniformly rotating rigid member pivoted at one end.

An alternative definition of the sinusoid makes use of de Moivre's theorem, quoted above. It is easily shown that

$$\cos(\theta) = \tfrac{1}{2}\{\exp(+j\theta) + \exp(-j\theta)\}$$

Figure 1.1*b* illustrates this complex addition, or 'phasor sum'. It follows directly from this relationship that

$$A \cos(\omega t + \phi) = \tfrac{1}{2}A \exp\{+j(\omega t + \phi)\} + \tfrac{1}{2}A \exp\{-j(\omega t + \phi)\} \qquad (1.2)$$

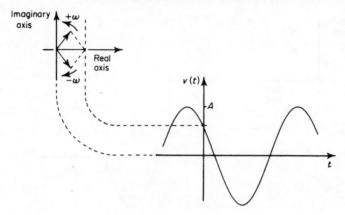

Figure 1.3 Generation of the sinusoid $v(t) = A \cos(\omega t + \phi)$ as the sum of two rotating phasors

This equation describes the phasor sum of two rotating phasors. Their respective rotations are of opposite sense $\pm \omega$ and they start at time $t = 0$ symmetrically disposed about the real axis with initial phase angles $\pm \phi$. Consequently, the imaginary parts of the phasors cancel on phasor addition, generating the purely real sinusoid, as figure 1.3 shows.

We may extend both phasor representations of the sinusoid, figures 1.2 and 1.3, to create *spectral representations* which are of great value in the analysis of systems. Considering first figure 1.2, we see that the phasor itself may be defined in terms of its length, A, initial phase angle, ϕ, and angular velocity, ω. We find it convenient to depict the sinusoid graphically, plotting A and ϕ versus ω. Thus a specific sine wave

$$A_0 \cos(\omega_0 t + \phi_0)$$

for which $A = A_0$ and $\phi = \phi_0$ when $\omega = \omega_0$ is shown in the manner illustrated in figure 1.4a.

In contrast, when we examine figure 1.3, we see that we must spectrally identify two phasors. Because they rotate in opposite directions, we draw a 'two-sided' spectrum encompassing both positive and negative angular velocities. The spectral lines in this case are of length $\frac{1}{2}A_0$ and initial phase angles $\pm \phi_0$; see figure 1.4b.

'Frequency domain' diagrams such as those shown in figures 1.4a and b may be referred to as 'sinusoid-based' and 'cisoid-based' spectra, respectively. Either of these forms may occur in the literature. As might be expected, the cisoid representation tells us no more than the sinusoid representation. Indeed, it merely appears to complicate the issue. While this is a valid argument when we are concerned only with the analysis of simple waveforms, the cisoid representation offers definite advantages when we come to study complex systems and waveforms. In fact its use can make the mathematics very much easier.

Our general sinusoid

$$v(t) = A \cos(\omega t + \phi)$$

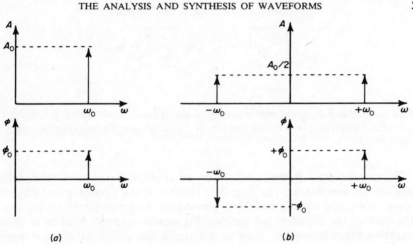

Figure 1.4 *Representation of the sinusoid* $A_0 \cos(\omega_0 t + \phi_0)$ *as* (a) *single-sided sinusoid-based and* (b) *two-sided cisoid-based amplitude and phase spectra*

may be represented in one further, and often very useful, way. Expanding the equation we may write

$$v(t) = X \cos(\omega t) + Y \sin(\omega t) \qquad (1.3)$$

where $X = A \cos(\phi)$ and $Y = -A \sin(\phi)$. We refer to the terms $X \cos(\omega t)$ and $Y \sin(\omega t)$ as the *in-phase* and *quadrature* components of $v(t)$, respectively. Instead of representing the sinusoid in the frequency domain, as in figures 1.4a and b as amplitude and phase spectra, we may alternatively represent it as in-phase and quadrature-component spectra; see figures 1.5a and b.

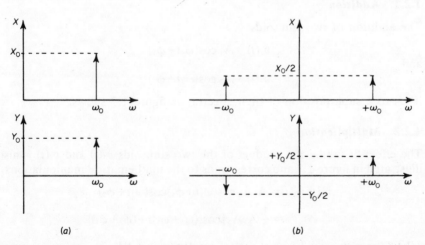

Figure 1.5 *Representation of the sinusoid* $A_0 \cos(\omega_0 t + \phi_0)$ *as* (a) *single-sided and* (b) *double-sided in-phase and quadrature-component spectra*

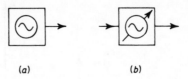

(a)   (b)

Figure 1.6 Block diagram representation of the sinusoidal-waveform generator; (a) fixed frequency, (b) variable frequency or 'voltage controlled oscillator' (VCO)

All our spectra, whether sinusoid-based or cisoid-based have been plotted against an abscissa ω; the angular velocity of the phasor generating the wave. We could equally well have plotted them against frequency, f, and in the case of the cisoid-based spectra this would naturally lead us to define negative frequencies. As long as we recall the origin of the concept of negative frequencies, this form of presentation should cause no problems. In fact, we normally employ a frequency abscissa since it is common practice for communication engineers to work in terms of frequency rather than angular velocity.

Finally, to emphasise the 'functional block' aspect of the communication system, in which we consider the system 'macroscopically', we regard the sinusoid as the output of a *system module*. By this, we mean that it is very often the case that the detailed operation or construction of a system module, or block, is immaterial. There are, for example, many ways of generating sinusoids. We are only concerned that the sinusoid generator should be that system module which has a sine wave at its output; see figure 1.6.

1.2 Operations with Sinusoids

1.2.1 Addition

The addition of two sinusoids

$$v_1(t) = A_1 \cos(\omega_1 t + \phi_1)$$

and

$$v_2(t) = A_2 \cos(\omega_2 t + \phi_2)$$

leads to a superposition of their spectra, as figure 1.7 shows.

1.2.2 Multiplication

The effect of taking the product of the two sinusoids $v_1(t)$ and $v_2(t)$ is also illustrated in figure 1.7 and corresponds to the mathematical manipulations

$$v_1(t)\, v_2(t) = A_1 A_2 \cos(\omega_1 t + \phi_1)\cos(\omega_2 t + \phi_2)$$

$$= \frac{1}{2} A_1 A_2 \left[\cos\{(\omega_2 + \omega_1)t + (\phi_2 + \phi_1)\}\right.$$

$$\left. + \cos\{(\omega_2 - \omega_1)t + (\phi_2 - \phi_1)\}\right]$$

The phenomenon described by these equations is directly analogous to the

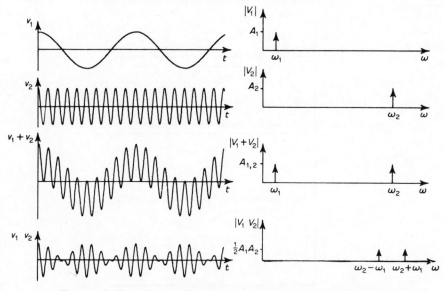

Figure 1.7 Operations with sinusoids: addition and multiplication

'beating' effect which is perceptible to the ear when two acoustic waves, or 'tones' are struck from tuning forks at the same time. The beating, or envelope fluctuation, is most pronounced when the two wave frequencies $(\omega_2 + \omega_1)$ and $(\omega_2 - \omega_1)$ are close together. The envelope fluctuation occurs at a frequency equal to one-half of the *difference* frequency: $\frac{1}{2}[(\omega_2 + \omega_1) - (\omega_2 - \omega_1)] = \omega_1$. This envelope fluctuation is imposed upon a sinusoid at a frequency of one-half of the *sum* frequency: $\frac{1}{2}[(\omega_2 + \omega_1) + (\omega_2 - \omega_1)] = \omega_2$.

The multiplication results in a *frequency translation* of the low-frequency wave $v_1(t)$ so that it is relocated at frequencies $(\omega_2 + \omega_1)$ and $(\omega_2 - \omega_1)$, adjacent to the higher frequency wave. This translation effect we refer to as a *modulation*. Modulation, as we shall see, is of great importance to us as a method of signal processing prior to transmission and also as a fundamental operation in the analysis of the spectral content of signals.

1.3 The Periodic Waveform

A periodic waveform may be defined thus

$$v(t) = v(t + mT) \quad \text{all } t, m \text{ integer} \tag{1.4}$$

where T is an epoch referred to as the *period* of the function $v(t)$. The period is related to the *fundamental frequency*, f_1, by the expression

$$f_1 = 1/T \tag{1.5}$$

The sum of a set of periodic functions $v_1, v_2, \ldots$ with arbitrary amplitudes and shapes but related fundamental frequencies

$$f_n = nf_1 \tag{1.6}$$

will also be periodic, with a fundamental frequency f_1 as figure 1.8 indicates.

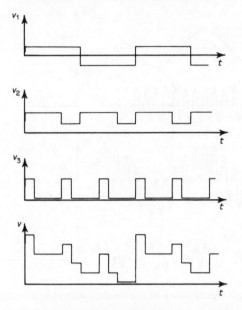

Figure 1.8, The sum of periodic waves with related fundamental frequencies $f_n = nf_1$ is a wave with fundamental frequency f_1

If we choose a convenient set of functions, sinusoids in this case, which are periodic and related in the manner specified by equation 1.6, we may uniquely assemble almost any periodic waveform by suitably adjusting the amplitudes and phases of the component waveforms. In fact, any waveform which is *physically realisable* may be synthesised in this way. 'Physically realisable' simply means that the waveform can actually be created with a suitable physical system, and is not just a convenient mathematical abstraction. For example, a waveform

$$v(t) = \tan(2\pi f t)$$

would contain infinitely high peaks and would possess an infinite discontinuity as it passed through values of its argument $2\pi f t$ equal to odd-integer multiples of $\pi/2$; that is, $\pi/2$, $3\pi/2$, $5\pi/2$ and so on. Because of this it could not be exactly reproduced by a real electronic system in which only finite voltage-excursions may be tolerated.

Although it must be possible to synthesise any realisable waveform as the sum of sinusoids, there are also some non-realisable waveforms which can be constructed in this way. One example, which we shall examine in detail shortly is the square-pulse train. Here, transitions between states occur infinitely rapidly. The waveform cannot, therefore, be exactly reproduced by a physical system, which always involves some form of inertia. It follows that it is not merely the existence of discontinuities which prohibits our synthesising a waveform from sinusoids. The necessary condition, met by the square wave, but not by the 'tan' wave, is that the discontinuities be finite in size.

Another waveform which could not be realised, although it contains no discontinuities and is periodic of period T, is the function

$$v(t) = \sin(1/t)$$

defined over the interval $0 \leqslant t \leqslant T$. Such a function contains an infinite number of maxima and minima, since the sinusoid has a frequency which increases to infinity as t tends to zero. It can be shown that a function $v(t)$ possessing

(1) a finite number of finite discontinuities
(2) a finite number of maxima and minima   } within the period
(3) a finite value to the integral of $|v(t)|$

is capable of synthesis as a suitably chosen sum of sinusoids. This sum is known as a *Fourier series* and the method of choosing it, *Fourier series analysis*. The conditions (1) to (3) are known as the *Dirichlet conditions*. The Dirichlet conditions are of great theoretical importance, although they are rarely responsible for our being unable to synthesise or analyse a waveform. This we might expect, since our interest lies either with realisable waveforms or with 'sensible' abstractions such as the square wave and sinusoid.

We shall now consider the problem of Fourier analysis in detail. It is fairly easy to see how analysis may be achieved electronically, and examining the problem from this standpoint allows us a certain amount of insight into the formal, mathematical approach, which we shall consider shortly.

Given that the periodic waveform is composed of sinewaves, related in frequency as specified above, each component will have the form

$$A_n \cos(2\pi f_1 nt + \phi_n)$$

Applying equation 1.3, this statement may be written in the form

$$X_n \cos(2\pi f_1 nt) + Y_n \sin(2\pi f_1 nt)$$

where

$$X_n = A_n \cos(\phi_n)$$

and

$$Y_n = -A_n \sin(\phi_n)$$

Consider the block diagram, shown in figure 1.9, of a simple electronic spectrum-analyser. The input wave, being presumed periodic and, therefore, the sum of a set of sinusoidal components, will have the form

$$v(t) = X_0 + X_1 \cos(2\pi f_1 t) + \ldots + X_n \cos(2\pi f_n t) + \ldots$$

$$+ Y_1 \sin(2\pi f_1 t) + \ldots + Y_n \sin(2\pi f_n t) + \ldots$$

The result of taking the product

$$X_n \cos(2\pi f_n t)\cos(2\pi f_n t)$$

and subsequently smoothing is illustrated in figure 1.10a. A d.c. level is present at the output of the smoothing circuit which is proportional to X_n. Contrast this with the effect of taking the product

$$X_n \sin(2\pi f_n t)\cos(2\pi f_n t)$$

and smoothing. Now the smoothed output is zero, figure 1.10b.

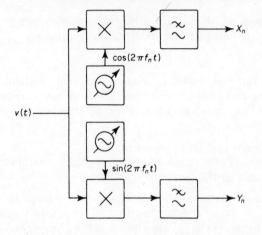

Figure 1.9 A simple electronic spectrum-analyser; the output lowpass filters approximate the operation of averaging by smoothing

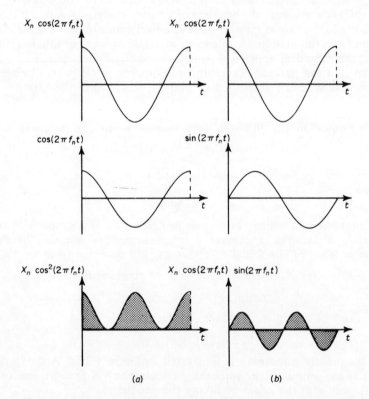

Figure 1.10 (a) Output from the smoothing circuit is equal to the area under the curve which is positive and proportional to X_n. (b) Output from the smoothing circuit is zero, since the area under the curve is zero

In exactly the same way, the product of $Y_n \sin(2\pi f_n t)$ and the second local oscillator output $\sin(2\pi f_n t)$ will yield a zero frequency difference term Y_n at the output of the second smoothing circuit. Thus we may establish the amplitudes of the sine and cosine components of the periodic function in a fairly straightforward manner and, consequently, we have achieved the required waveform analysis.

1.4 Orthogonality

The operation of the spectrum analyser relies on our ability to distinguish between sine terms and cosine terms of particular frequencies by means of the multiplier and filter combination. That is

$$X_n \cos(2\pi f_n t)\cos(2\pi f_n t) = (X_n/2) + \text{double frequency } (2f_n) \text{ terms}$$

whereas

$$X_n \cos(2\pi f_n t)\sin(2\pi f_n t) = \text{double frequency terms alone}$$

Similarly

$$Y_n \sin(2\pi f_n t)\cos(2\pi f_n t) = \text{double frequency terms alone}$$

but

$$Y_n \sin(2\pi f_n t)\sin(2\pi f_n t) = (Y_n/2) + \text{double frequency terms}$$

All the 'double frequency' terms are eliminated by the filter. The effect described by these operations is summed up mathematically in the concept of *orthogonality*. In this context, if two waveforms are orthogonal, the implication is that they contain no shared, or common components. Strictly they are said to be orthogonal in the interval t_1 to t_2 if the integral of their products in that interval is zero

$$\int_{t_1}^{t_2} v_m(t)v_n(t)\, \mathrm{d}t = 0 \quad m \neq n$$

$$\neq 0 \quad m = n$$

Sinusoids in general form an orthogonal set since if

$$v_m(t) = \cos(2\pi f_m t)$$

and

$$v_n(t) = \cos(2\pi f_n t)$$

then

$$\left.\int_{-T/2}^{+T/2} v_m(t)v_n(t)\, \mathrm{d}t = \int_{-T/2}^{+T/2} \cos(2\pi f_m t)\cos(2\pi f_n t)\, \mathrm{d}t \begin{array}{l} = 0 \quad m \neq n \\ = T/2 \quad m = n \end{array}\right\} \quad (1.7)$$

In the following mathematical discussion of the signal analysis procedure, we shall find two other properties of the sinusoid set of importance

$$\left.\begin{array}{l} \displaystyle\int_{-T/2}^{+T/2} \sin(2\pi f_m t)\sin(2\pi f_n t)\, \mathrm{d}t = 0 \qquad m \neq n \\[6pt] \hphantom{\displaystyle\int_{-T/2}^{+T/2}} = T/2 \quad m = n \\[6pt] \displaystyle\int_{-T/2}^{+T/2} \sin(2\pi f_m t)\cos(2\pi f_n t)\, \mathrm{d}t = 0 \qquad \text{all } m \text{ and } n \end{array}\right\} \quad (1.8)$$

1.5   Fourier Series Analysis in Terms of Sinusoids

We have deduced that a periodic waveform may be synthesised from sinusoidal components, provided that the amplitudes of those components are suitably chosen and their frequencies are related in the manner indicated by equation 1.6. They will then be integer multiples of the frequency of the periodic wave itself

$$f_n = nf_1$$

We may summarise this conclusion by writing a *waveform synthesis* equation

$$v(t) = \sum_{n=0}^{\infty} X_n \cos(2\pi f_1 nt) + Y_n \sin(2\pi f_1 nt) \tag{1.9}$$

Here, $v(t)$ is the synthesised periodic wave of frequency f_1. It is formed by the summation of sinusoidal components of amplitude

$$A_n = (X_n^2 + Y_n^2)^{\frac{1}{2}}$$

and phase

$$\phi_n = -\tan^{-1}(Y_n/X_n)$$

so that the nth component may be written as

$$A_n \cos(2\pi f_1 nt + \phi_n)$$

instead of

$$X_n \cos(2\pi f_1 nt) + Y_n \sin(2\pi f_1 nt)$$

The synthesis equation may then equally well be written as

$$v(t) = \sum_{n=0}^{\infty} A_n \cos(2\pi f_1 nt + \phi_n) \tag{1.10}$$

Although the formation of equation 1.9 is a fairly straightforward process, we have yet to find a method of determining the coefficients X_n and Y_n. This may be achieved by applying the orthogonality relations deduced in the previous section. Thus, consider the integral

$$\int_{-T/2}^{+T/2} v(t)\cos(2\pi f_1 nt) \, dt \tag{1.11}$$

This we may write in expanded form

$$\int_{-T/2}^{+T/2} \sum_{m=0}^{\infty} \{X_m \cos(2\pi f_1 mt) + Y_m \sin(2\pi f_1 mt)\}\cos(2\pi f_1 nt) \, dt$$

All terms but the nth in the series, when multiplied by $\cos(2\pi f_1 nt)$ will integrate to zero over the period. The nth term, by virtue of equation 1.7, will integrate to give

$$X_n T/2 \tag{1.12}$$

Thus we derive, from equations 1.11 and 1.12 the first analysis equation

$$X_n = \frac{2}{T} \int_{-T/2}^{+T/2} v(t)\cos(2\pi f_1 nt) \, dt$$

$$= \frac{2}{T} \int_{-T/2}^{+T/2} v(t)\cos(2\pi f_n t) \, dt \tag{1.13}$$

TABLE 1.1 COEFFICIENTS OF FOURIER SERIES

$v(t)$	X_n	Y_n	ϕ_n	A_n
EVEN $v(t)=v(-t)$	Exists for some n	$Y_n=0$	$\phi_n=0$	$A_n=X_n$
ODD $v(t)=-v(-t)$	$X_n=0$	Exists for some n	$\phi_n=+\dfrac{\pi}{2}$	$A_n=Y_n$

A closer inspection of the derivation of this result will show that it is valid for $n=1,\ 2,\ 3,\ \ldots$ but not for $n=0$. If $n=0$, then

$$\int_{-T/2}^{+T/2} v(t)\cos(2\pi f_1 nt)\,\mathrm{d}t = \int_{-T/2}^{+T/2} v(t)\,\mathrm{d}t$$

$$= \int_{-T/2}^{+T/2} \left\{ \sum_{m=0}^{\infty} X_m\cos(2\pi f_1 mt) + Y_m\sin(2\pi f_1 mt) \right\}\mathrm{d}t$$

Now all terms but the first, that for $m=0$, integrate to zero over the period, leaving

$$\int_{-T/2}^{+T/2} X_0\,\mathrm{d}t = X_0 T$$

It follows that we may write

$$X_0 = \frac{1}{T}\int_{-T/2}^{+T/2} v(t)\,\mathrm{d}t$$

and, incidentally, that

$$Y_0 = 0$$

The reader may easily verify the second analysis equation, for $n=1,\ 2,\ \ldots$

$$Y_n = \frac{2}{T}\int_{-T/2}^{+T/2} v(t)\sin(2\pi f_1 nt)\,\mathrm{d}t \tag{1.14}$$

To summarise, equation 1.9 is known as a Fourier series and is a *synthesis equation*. Equations 1.13 and 1.14 are *analysis equations* which enable us to calculate the coefficients of the Fourier series. We may sometimes ease the task of calculating the Fourier series coefficients. For example, if $v(t)$ is an even or an odd function only one of the coefficients need be calculated, as table 1.1 shows.

1.6 Fourier Analysis of a Rectangular-pulse Train

We shall use the methods of the previous section to analyse a rectangular-pulse train. This provides us with a simple example, while allowing us to evaluate a result which will be of importance in our later considerations of sampling and pulse transmission.

Consider the pulse train illustrated in figure 1.11a. This is defined mathematically as

$$v(t)=v_1 \qquad -t_1\leqslant t\leqslant t_1$$
$$=0 \quad \text{elsewhere within its period}$$

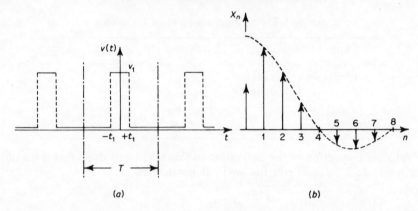

Figure 1.11 Rectangular-pulse train (a) analysed into Fourier series in-phase components, (b) sinusoid-based single-sided spectrum

and

$$v(t) = v(t + mT) \quad \text{integer}$$

First, we observe that this function is even in t, since

$$v(t) = v(-t)$$

Consequently, we need only evaluate the coefficients X_n, and $Y_n = 0$ all n. Then, for $n = 1, 2, 3, \ldots$

$$\begin{aligned}
X_n &= \frac{2}{T} \int_{-T/2}^{+T/2} v(t)\cos(2\pi f_1 nt)\,\mathrm{d}t \\
&= \frac{2}{T} \int_{-t_1}^{+t_1} v_1 \cos(2\pi f_1 nt)\,\mathrm{d}t \\
&= \frac{2}{T} \left[\frac{v_1 \sin(2\pi f_1 nt)}{2\pi f_1 n} \right]_{-t_1}^{+t_1} \\
&= 4v_1 \frac{\sin(2\pi f_1 nt_1)}{2\pi n}
\end{aligned}$$

This expression has a form very similar to the *sinc function* $\mathrm{sinc}(x) = \sin(\pi x)/\pi x$ which is frequently encountered in system analysis. To express the Fourier coefficients in terms of the sinc function, we need only write

$$x = 2f_1 nt_1$$

so that

$$\left. \begin{aligned}
X_n &= (4v_1 t_1/T)\mathrm{sinc}(x) \quad n = 1, 2, 3, \ldots \\
X_0 &= 2v_1 t_1/T
\end{aligned} \right\} \tag{1.15}$$

and

The spectrum then has the form shown in figure 1.11b.

1.7 Fourier Series Analysis in Terms of Cisoids

We have seen, in section 1.5, equations 1.9, 1.13 and 1.14, how the Fourier series equation

$$v(t) = \sum_{n=0}^{\infty} \{X_n \cos(2\pi f_1 nt) + Y_n \sin(2\pi f_1 nt)\}$$

may be constructed by applying the analysis integrals

$$X_n = \frac{2}{T} \int_{-T/2}^{+T/2} v(t)\cos(2\pi f_1 nt)\, dt$$

$$X_0 = \int_{-T/2}^{+T/2} v(t)\, dt$$

$$Y_n = \frac{2}{T} \int_{-T/2}^{+T/2} v(t)\sin(2\pi f_1 nt)\, dt$$

$$Y_0 = 0$$

We may express these equations in a more compact form by rewriting them in terms of cisoids. If we let

$$\left. \begin{array}{l} V_{+n} = \dfrac{1}{2}(X_n - jY_n) \\[2mm] V_{-n} = \dfrac{1}{2}(X_n + jY_n) \end{array} \right\} \quad n = +1, +2, +3 \ldots \qquad (1.16)$$

and

$$V_0 = X_0$$

then

$$V_n = \frac{1}{T} \int_{-T/2}^{+T/2} v(t)\exp(-2\pi j f_1 nt)\, dt \qquad (1.17)$$

This equation requires that n takes on all values, both positive and negative. Recall from section 1.3 that negative values of n in the cisoid argument $(2\pi j f_1 nt)$ correspond to negative angular velocity of the rotating phasor $\exp(2\pi j f_1 nt)$. Recall also that two phasors, one rotating in a positive sense, the other in a negative sense, are needed to construct a sinusoid, thus

$$\cos(2\pi f_1 nt) = \frac{1}{2}\{\exp(+2\pi j f_1 nt) + \exp(-2\pi j f_1 nt)\}$$

Modifying the Fourier series equation to comply with this change of notation

$$v(t) = \sum_{n=-\infty}^{\infty} V_n \exp(+2\pi j f_1 nt) \qquad (1.18)$$

Equations 1.17 and 1.18 are a *generalised* set of equations. They allow us to analyse a waveform into a cisoid-based spectrum.

1.8 Properties of Generalised Fourier Series

1.8.1 Relation to Sinusoid-based Spectra

Providing $v(t)$ is a real function, which for practical purposes we may take it to be, then equation 1.16 relates V_n to X_n and Y_n. Note that the cisoid

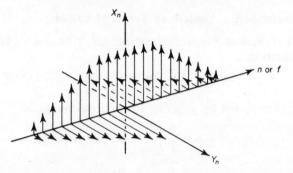

Figure 1.12   Complex conjugate spectral symmetry of a real function of time

spectrum of a function will have complex conjugate symmetry; see figure 1.12.

$$V_n = V_{-n}^* \tag{1.19}$$

and that the X_n and Y_n may be calculated, if only the V_n are known

$$X_n = V_n + V_{-n}$$
$$Y_n = j(V_n - V_{-n}) \tag{1.20}$$

1.8.2   Effect of a Displacement in Time

If $v(t)$ has a Fourier series V_n, then $v(t+\tau)$ has a Fourier series V'_n where

$$V'_n = V_n \exp(2\pi j f_1 n \tau) \tag{1.21}$$

This we may prove in the following way

$$V_n = \frac{1}{T} \int_{-T/2}^{+T/2} v(t)\exp(-2\pi j f_1 n t)\, dt$$

$$V'_n = \frac{1}{T} \int_{-T/2}^{+T/2} v(t+\tau)\exp(-2\pi j f_1 n t)\, dt$$

Let $t+\tau=\lambda$ then $dt=d\lambda$ and

$$V'_n = \frac{1}{T} \int_{-T/2}^{+T/2} v(\lambda)\exp(2\pi j f_1 n \tau)\exp(-2\pi j f_1 n \lambda)\, d\lambda$$

$$= V_n \exp(2\pi j f_1 n \tau)$$

Thus, a time shift of the function $v(t)$ with respect to the origin $t=0$ corresponds to a phase shift of all components in $v(t)$. This may be more clearly appreciated if we examine the sinusoid-based spectra. Applying equations 1.20 and 1.21, we may establish the equivalent expressions

$$X'_n = X_n \cos(2\pi f_1 n \tau) - Y_n \sin(2\pi f_1 n \tau)$$

$$Y'_n = Y_n \cos(2\pi f_1 n \tau) - X_n \sin(2\pi f_1 n \tau)$$

Or, in polar form

$$A'_n = A_n$$

and

$$\phi'_n = \phi_n + 2\pi f_1 n \tau$$

1.9 The Analysis of Aperiodic Waveforms

We have seen how periodic waves may be analysed by deriving their Fourier series and how they may be represented in the frequency domain by line spectra. While the Fourier-series technique is of great practical importance, it is none the less true that almost all communication signals are aperiodic. It may be convenient for us to employ periodic signals in the testing or analysis of systems, since they are relatively easy to generate or handle mathematically, but it must be remembered that they are not informational.

Since we are frequently interested in the nature of informational waveforms, it is important that we find a method for analysing aperiodic signals. We may classify aperiodic signals in three ways

(1) As finite-energy deterministic waveshapes—'pulse waveforms'
(2) As finite-energy random, or partially random, waveshapes—'random pulse waveforms'
(3) As finite-power (and consequently infinite energy) random waveforms—'noise-like waveforms'

In practice, we can only analytically handle waveforms which fall into the first class, producing an algebraic statement of the analysis result. 'Deterministic' simply means specifiable as a straightforward algebraic function. A random waveform cannot be so specified; it is not deterministic and consequently no starting equation exists to be algebraically manipulated to give an equivalent frequency-domain function.

1.10 The Fourier Transform

The principle behind the following derivation of Fourier transform from Fourier series is very simple. We require the spectrum of an isolated finite-duration pulse. First we form a periodic repetition of this pulse, then we calculate its line spectrum. Finally, we let the period of the periodic wave tend to infinity. The spectral-line spacing then tends to zero forming a continuous spectrum which is representative of the isolated pulse.

Let the isolated pulse be $v(t)$

$$v(t) = 0 \quad t_1 \leqslant t \leqslant t_2$$

and with t_1 and t_2 within the range $-T/2$ to $+T/2$, as shown in figure 1.13. We establish a periodic function $w(t)$ of period T, so that

$$w(t) = w(t + mT)$$

for all integer values of m. Then

$$w(t) = v(t) \quad -T/2 \leqslant t \leqslant T/2$$

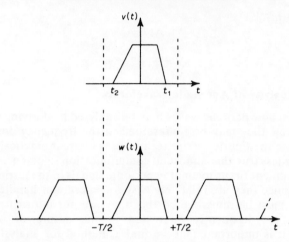

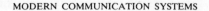

Figure 1.13 *Formation of a periodic function w(t) from the aperiodic function v(t)*

This periodic function is also illustrated in figure 1.13. It has a fundamental frequency

$$f_1 = T^{-1}$$

and its spectrum consequently has a line spacing

$$\delta f = T^{-1}$$

Thus as T becomes large (without altering the pulse shape) δf will become small. We postulate, as the limiting condition as $T \to \infty$, that the spectrum will become continuous; and we express it as $V(f)$. This quantity will be a *spectral density* measured in volt Hz^{-1}, assuming $v(t)$ and $w(t)$ to be voltage waveforms, In contrast, W_n, the line spectrum of the periodic $w(t)$ is a voltage spectrum. Each line is measured in volts. Consider the continuous spectral density sketched in figure 1.14. This approximates to the line

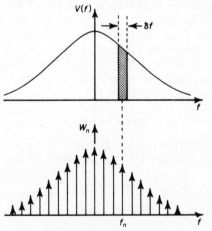

Figure 1.14 *Relationship between the line spectrum W_n and the spectral density V(f)*

spectrum shown, with

$$V(f_n)\,\delta f \approx W_n$$

or

$$V(f_n) \approx W_n T$$

(1.22)

Now

$$W_n = \frac{1}{T}\int_{-T/2}^{+T/2} w(t)\exp(-2\pi\,\mathrm{j}f_n t)\,\mathrm{d}t$$

so that with $w(t) = v(t)$ over the range of integration, it follows that

$$W_n T = \int_{-T/2}^{+T/2} v(t)\exp(-2\pi\,\mathrm{j}f_n t)\,\mathrm{d}t$$

Now, strictly, the approximation, equation 1.22, becomes an equality when we write

$$V(f_n) = \operatorname*{Lim}_{T\to\infty}(W_n T)$$

$$= \operatorname*{Lim}_{T\to\infty}\int_{-T/2}^{+T/2} v(t)\exp(-2\pi\,\mathrm{j}f_n t)\,\mathrm{d}t$$

$$= \int_{-\infty}^{+\infty} v(t)\exp(-2\pi\,\mathrm{j}f_n t)\,\mathrm{d}t$$

Normally, we express this equation in a slightly neater form by replacing f_n with f

$$V(f) = \int_{-\infty}^{+\infty} v(t)\exp(-2\pi\,\mathrm{j}ft)\,\mathrm{d}t$$

(1.23)

This, then, is the Fourier transform which performs analysis. We may construct the synthesis transform by examining the Fourier series synthesis equation

$$w(t) = \sum_{n=-\infty}^{+\infty} W_n \exp(2\pi\,\mathrm{j}f_n t)$$

Now

$$W_n \approx V(f_n)\,\delta f$$

$$= \operatorname*{Lim}_{\delta f\to 0}(V(f_n)\,\delta f)$$

so that

$$w(t) = \operatorname*{Lim}_{\delta f\to 0}\sum_{n=-\infty}^{+\infty} V(f_n)\exp(2\pi\,\mathrm{j}f_n t)\,\delta f$$

$$= \operatorname*{Lim}_{\delta f\to 0}\sum_{n=-\infty}^{+\infty} V(n\,\delta f)\exp(2\pi\mathrm{j}n\,\delta ft)\,\delta f$$

$$= v(t) \qquad -1/\delta f \leqslant t \leqslant +1/\delta f$$

This limiting summation is the definition of an integral, so that

$$v(t) = \int_{-\infty}^{+\infty} V(f)\exp(2\pi\,\mathrm{j}ft)\,\mathrm{d}f$$

(1.24)

1.11 Properties of Fourier Transforms

Fourier transforms have many interesting and useful properties. It is possible to postulate theorems which govern the effect of time and frequency displacements, differentiation, integration and so on. These various theorems are, for completeness, summarised in table 1.2. In general, the proofs of the results quoted in this table can be left to the reader. Should he require assistance, there are many excellent texts on the subject of Fourier analysis. Of these a selected few[7,8,9] are listed in the bibliography.

In the remaining sections of this chapter, the more important results concerning Fourier transform methods, which we shall require frequently in later work, will be discussed in detail.

TABLE 1.2 PROPERTIES OF FOURIER TRANSFORMS

Property	Time Domain	Frequency Domain
Complex Transform	$v(t) = \int_{-\infty}^{+\infty} V(f)\exp(2\pi jft)\,dt$	$V(f) = \int_{-\infty}^{+\infty} v(t)\exp(-2\pi jft)\,dt$
Addition (Superposition)	$v_3(t) = v_1(t) + v_2(t)$	$V_3(f) = V_1(f) + V_2(f)$
Multiplication (Modulation)	$v_3(t) = v_1(t)v_2(t)$	$V_3(f) = \int_{-\infty}^{+\infty} V_1(\lambda)V_2(f-\lambda)\,d\lambda$
		$= \int_{-\infty}^{+\infty} V_1(f-\lambda)V_2(\lambda)\,d\lambda$
Filtering	$v_3(t) = \int_{-\infty}^{+\infty} v_1(\tau)v_2(t-\tau)\,d\tau$	$V_3(f) = V_1(f)V_2(f)$
	$= \int_{-\infty}^{+\infty} v_1(t-\tau)v_2(\tau)\,d\tau$	
Time Scaling	$v(at)$	$(1/|a|)V(f/a)$
	$|a|\,v(t/a)$	$V(af)$
Amplitude Scaling	$av(t)$	$aV(f)$
Time Delay or Shift	$v(t \pm \tau)$	$\exp(\pm 2\pi jf\tau)V(f)$
Differentiation	$\dfrac{dv(t)}{dt}$	$2\pi jfV(f)$
Integration	$\int_0^t v(\tau)\,d\tau$	$(1/2\pi jf)V(f)$
Autocorrelation Function	$R(\tau) = \underset{T\to\infty}{\mathrm{Lim}}\ T^{-1}\int_{-T/2}^{+T/2} v(t)v(t+\tau)\,dt$	
Energy Density Spectrum	$v(t)$ finite energy	$E(f) = |V(f)|^2$
Power Density Spectrum	$v(t)$ finite power	$P(f) = \underset{T\to\infty}{\mathrm{Lim}}\ T^{-1}|V(f)|^2$

Energy Density Spectrum and Power Density Spectrum braced together with $R(\tau)$.

1.12   The Application of Fourier Transforms

Most students, on encountering the Fourier transform for the first time, have difficulty in 'seeing how the transforms are actually done'. Now, the use of transforms does not necessarily imply a need to do them, in the sense of performing an operation to obtain an analytic statement of the transform result. Often we use the concept of a transform as an *aide-mémoire*, or mental shorthand, while considering the processing of signals within a system. The signal itself may be arbitrary. Examples of the use of the transform technique in this way occur throughout the remainder of this book.

Again, some random waveforms, because they cannot be specified as a mathematical equation, are incapable of being analytically transformed to yield a mathematical result.

None the less, there are many functions, both periodic and aperiodic, which are capable of analytic transformation. The transforms of such functions are of value in many physical problems, and tables (of which an example is provided in appendix I) have been compiled.

Given, then, that we shall frequently find it necessary to use transform techniques, it is appropriate that we discuss the actual method of evaluating the transform integrals, equations 1.23 and 1.24, and that we examine the situations in which transform methods may definitely *not* be used.

1.12.1   Evaluating the Fourier Transform

Let us consider the simplest example of a transformation. Suppose we wish to evaluate the Fourier transform of a rectangular pulse

$$v(t) = v_1 \quad -t_1 \leqslant t \leqslant +t_1$$

$$= 0 \quad \text{elsewhere}$$

The first step is simply to insert this function into the integral 1.23. Notice that the integral may be split into three constituent integrals, covering the ranges $t = -\infty$ to $-t_1$, $t = -t_1$ to $+t_1$ and $t = +t_1$ to $+\infty$.

$$V(f) = \int_{-\infty}^{+\infty} v(t)\exp(-2\pi jft)\, dt$$

$$= \int_{-\infty}^{-t_1} v(t)\exp(-2\pi jft)\, dt + \int_{-t_1}^{+t_1} v(t)\exp(-2\pi jft)\, dt$$

$$+ \int_{+t_1}^{+\infty} v(t)\exp(-2\pi jft)\, dt$$

Only in the range $t = -t_1$ to $+t_1$ is $v(t)$, and hence the integral over the range, non-zero. Consequently, we need only evaluate

$$V(f) = \int_{-t_1}^{+t_1} v_1 \exp(-2\pi jft)\, dt$$

From this point onwards, the problem is simply one of evaluating a definite integral, and

$$V(f) = v_1 \left[\frac{\exp(-2\pi jft)}{-2\pi jf} \right]_{-t_1}^{+t_1}$$

$$= \frac{v_1}{\pi f} \left\{ \frac{\exp(2\pi jft_1) - \exp(-2\pi jft_1)}{2j} \right\}$$

$$= \frac{v_1}{\pi f} \sin(2\pi ft_1)$$

This result is sufficient, as it stands, as a statement of the transform of $v(t)$. However, it is common practice to express it in terms of the sinc function introduced in section 1.6. That is, we write

$$V(f) = 2v_1 t_1 \frac{\sin(2\pi ft_1)}{2\pi ft_1}$$

$$= 2v_1 t_1 \, \text{sinc}(2ft_1)$$

Of course, the problem we solved was the simplest we could devise. More complex functions are generally more difficult to evaluate, but all basically require only the evaluation of the integral of the quantity

$$v(t)\exp(-2\pi jft)$$

This integration is often quite difficult, so we tend to consult the work of others by using 'Transform Tables' such as those given in appendix I. Naturally, the tables cannot give every possible transform, so we may need to resort to the shift and scaling theorems quoted in table 1.2. For example, if our rectangular pulse extended not from $t = -t_1$ to $t = +t_1$ but from $t = +t_1$ to $t = +3t_1$, then we could either alter the limits of the integral to t_1 and $3t_1$ and recalculate its value, or we could apply the shift theorem, noting that the new pulse is equal to $v(t-2t_1)$ and that its transform (from the result quoted in table 1.2) must therefore be

$$2v_1 t_1 \, \text{sinc}(2ft_1)\exp(-4\pi jft_1)$$

It is sometimes the case that complex pulses can be broken into abutting sections which are of the form of relatively simple known pulses. Take, for example, the staircase waveform defined by the expression

$$\begin{aligned} v(t) &= 1 & 0 \leqslant t < 1 \\ &= 2 & 1 \leqslant t < 2 \\ &= 3 & 2 \leqslant t < 3 \end{aligned}$$

This waveform we may regard as the superposition (or summation) of three constituent rectangular pulses

$$\begin{aligned} v_1(t) &= 1 & 0 \leqslant t < 1 \\ v_2(t) &= 2 & 1 \leqslant t < 2 \\ v_3(t) &= 3 & 2 \leqslant t < 3 \end{aligned}$$

so that

$$v(t) = v_1(t) + v_2(t) + v_3(t)$$

It follows, by virtue of the superposition principle, that

$$V(f) = V_1(f) + V_2(f) + V_3(f)$$

and all three transforms on the right-hand side of this last equation are easily evaluated by referring to appendix I for the transform of a basic rectangular pulse of unit height extending from $t = -\frac{1}{2}$ to $t = +\frac{1}{2}$ and applying the shift and amplitude-scaling theorems as appropriate.

1.12.2 *Where not to use Fourier Transforms: Non-linearity*

The Fourier series and the Fourier transform essentially embody the principle of superposition. They state that a function is the superposition of its components. Doubling the size of the function will only double the size of each component. Thus they are employed in the analysis of linear systems, where superposition is possible. A non-linear system will not permit superposition. A simple example will suffice to illustrate this. Consider a system element with a transfer characteristic $g(v_1)$. The linear system element will give an output

$$v_2 = g(v_1)$$
$$= kv_1$$

Thus, if

$$v_1 = v_a + v_b$$

then

$$v_2 = kv_a + kv_b$$

and the output of the sum of inputs is the same as the sum of the outputs corresponding to each input considered separately.

A non-linear system, for example

$$v_2 = g(v_1)$$
$$= kv_1^2$$

will produce an output when both v_a and v_b are present at the input which is

$$v_2 = k(v_a + v_b)^2$$
$$= kv_a^2 + kv_b^2 + 2kv_a v_b \qquad (1.25)$$

Applied separately, v_a and v_b give outputs kv_a^2 and kv_b^2 respectively. The sum of these outputs is

$$v_2 = kv_a^2 + kv_b^2 \qquad (1.26)$$

Clearly superposition does not apply, since the two results, equations 1.25 and 1.26, are not the same.

In general, there is no point in attempting to use Fourier methods to solve non-linear system problems. For example, it is usually not possible to use Fourier transforms to obtain the spectra of output waveforms from non-linear devices given an arbitrary input $v(t)$ and an arbitrary transfer function

$g(v)$

$$\int_{-\infty}^{+\infty} g\{v(t)\}\exp(-2\pi jft)\,dt$$

Only when $g(v)$ is a linear function of v can this be done.

1.13   The Delta Function

We shall frequently find it very useful to have recourse to a mathematical concept known as the 'delta function'. The delta function is defined thus

$$\delta(x)=0 \quad x\neq 0$$

$$\int_{-\infty}^{+\infty} \delta(x)\,dx=1$$

This means that, at all points on the x-axis except the point $x=0$, the delta function is zero valued. At the point $x=0$, the amplitude of the delta function is strictly undefined, but may be thought of as being infinitely large. We thus have a unit area, infinitesimally thin impulse at the origin.

The location of the delta function on the x-axis may be altered. An impulse occurring at a point $x=a$ is accommodated by writing

$$\delta(x-a)$$

Then the argument of the delta function $x-a$ is zero only at the point $x=a$.

The size of a delta function may be altered by scaling, so that a delta function of area A is written

$$A\delta(x)$$

Then

$$\int_{-\infty}^{+\infty} A\delta(x)\,dx=A$$

One very important use of the delta function is in providing a means of sampling a value from some other function of x. For example, given a function $f(x)$ the value of that function at a point $x=a$ is determined by the sampling operation defined by the integral

$$\int_{-\infty}^{+\infty} f(x)\,\delta(x-a)\,dx=f(a)$$

This identity, known as the 'sifting integral' is of considerable theoretical value in the analysis of sampled-data communication and control systems.

The delta function is also widely employed in providing a means of specifying the response of linear networks and systems to a wide variety of input signals. This is because a delta function, or impulse, in the time domain has a spectrum which is 'white'—it contains an equal measure of all frequency components. We may show that this is so by evaluating its Fourier transform. Merely inserting

$$v(t)=\delta(t)$$

into equation 1.23 does not help very much of course. We have to use a

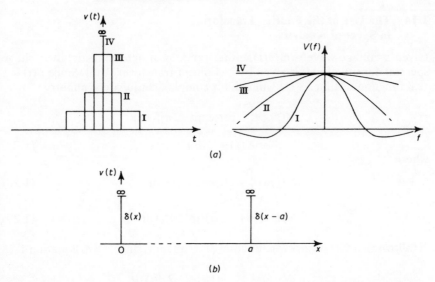

Figure 1.15 (a) The formation of the delta function from a constant-area pulse of gradually diminishing width (curves I to IV) and the corresponding spectral alteration. (b) Representation of the delta function against an arbitrary axis and with arbitrary location

mathematical trick to attain our end. The spectrum of the impulse may easily be found by applying the Fourier transform to a voltage pulse

$$v(t) = \frac{1}{2t_1} \quad -t_1 \leqslant t \leqslant t_1$$

and letting t_1 tend to zero as shown in figure 1.15a. Then

$$\lim_{t_1 \to 0}\{v(t)\} = \delta(t)$$

From the transform tables in appendix I, the Fourier transform of $v(t)$ is

$$V(f) = \text{sinc}(2ft_1)$$

To find the spectrum of the delta function we evaluate, by applying L'Hospital's rule

$$\lim_{t_1 \to 0}[V(f)] = 1$$

and thus we derive the transform pair

$$\delta(t) \leftrightarrow 1$$

In section 1.15 we shall see that the delta function in the frequency domain provides us with a means of representing line spectra corresponding to periodic functions in conjunction with the voltage spectral density of aperiodic functions. To allow us to distinguish between delta functions in the frequency domain and spectral lines, or, indeed, the y-axis of spectral graphs we shall adopt the graphical convention shown in figure 1.15b.

1.14   The Use of the Fourier Transform
in Spectral Analysis

Given a voltage waveform $v(t)$, either random or deterministic, the voltage spectral density of $v(t)$ is given by its Fourier transform, $V(f)$. Since $v(t)$ is a real function of time, $V(f)$ will exhibit complex conjugate symmetry

$$V(f) = \int_{-\infty}^{+\infty} v(t)\exp(-2\pi jft)\, dt$$

$$= X(f) + jY(f) \tag{1.27}$$

where

$$X(f) = \int_{-\infty}^{+\infty} v(t)\cos(2\pi ft)\, dt \tag{1.28}$$

$$Y(f) = -\int_{-\infty}^{+\infty} v(t)\sin(2\pi ft)\, dt \tag{1.29}$$

It follows that $X(f)$ is an even function of frequency, since, from equation 1.28

$$X(-f) = \int_{-\infty}^{+\infty} v(t)\cos(-2\pi ft)\, dt$$

$$= X(+f)$$

since $\cos(-2\pi ft) = \cos(+2\pi ft)$. Similarly, $Y(f)$, from equation 1.29, is an odd function of frequency

$$Y(-f) = -Y(+f)$$

Consequently, $V(f)$ must exhibit complex conjugate symmetry with

$$V(-f) = V^*(+f) \tag{1.30}$$

Often, we find it easier to think in terms of amplitude and phase spectra (rather than the real and imaginary parts of $V(f)$) when considering the structure of a waveform. We may express $V(f)$ in polar form thus

$$V(f) = A(f)\exp\{j\phi(f)\}$$

with

$$A(f) = \{X^2(f) + Y^2(f)\}^{\frac{1}{2}}$$

and

$$\phi(f) = \tan^{-1}\{Y(f)/X(f)\}$$

The amplitude and phase spectra exhibit even and odd symmetry respectively

$$A(-f) = A(+f)$$

$$\phi(-f) = -\phi(+f)$$

1.15   The Use of the Fourier Transform in Determining
the Line Spectrum of Periodic Functions

We have established that the Fourier transform may be used to determine the continuous spectrum of aperiodic functions. However, we often encounter situations where a periodic function or component may be present in a waveform we are studying. To handle such a component we should normally

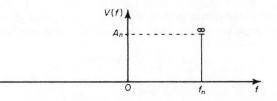

Figure 1.16 Spectral representation of the cisoid $A_n \exp(2\pi j f_n t) \leftrightarrow A_n \delta(f - f_n)$

invoke the methods of Fourier series analysis. This would yield a line spectrum, with line height representing the amplitude of a given spectral component. It is not permissible to superimpose the line spectrum of a periodic function on top of the voltage spectral density of an aperiodic component. This is because Fourier series analysis yields Fourier coefficients which are the amplitudes of the sinusoidal components of the periodic wave. These coefficients are measured in volts. In contrast, the Fourier transform yields a voltage spectral density, measured in volt Hz^{-1} or volt s.

We can easily unify these two forms of spectral analysis by making use of the delta function introduced in section 1.13. In the frequency domain, a delta function

$$A_n \delta(f - f_n)$$

consists of an infinitesimally thin impulse of area A_n located at a frequency $f = f_n$. On a voltage–spectral-density graph, it is areas that denote voltage, ordinates only denote voltage density. As a consequence, if we superimpose the delta function specified above upon the axes on a voltage–spectral-density graph, we obtain the equivalent to a spectral line of length A_n at a frequency f_n on a voltage line-spectrum; see figure 1.16. Since this spectral line is equivalent to the fundamental cisoid building-block, we have a transform pair

$$A_n \exp(2\pi j f_n t) \leftrightarrow A_n \delta(f - f_n)$$

We can now construct the Fourier transform of the other fundamental trigonometric functions. The reader is invited to verify the results quoted in table 1.3.

TABLE 1.3 FOURIER TRANSFORM OF TRIGONOMETRIC
FUNCTIONS

$v(t)$	$V(f)$
$A_n \exp(2\pi j f_n t)$	$A_n \delta(f - f_n)$
$A_n \exp(-2\pi j f_n t)$	$A_n \delta(f + f_n)$
$A_n \sin(2\pi f_n t)$	$-j\dfrac{A_n}{2}\{\delta(f - f_n) - \delta(f + f_n)\}$
$A_n \cos(2\pi f_n t)$	$\dfrac{A_n}{2}\{\delta(f - f_n) + \delta(f + f_n)\}$

General periodic functions may be similarly treated by comparing the delta-function representation with the Fourier-series coefficients thus

$$v(t) = \sum_{n=-\infty}^{+\infty} V_n \exp(2\pi j f_n t) \tag{1.31}$$

from which we establish a spectrum

$$V(f) = \sum_{n=-\infty}^{+\infty} V_n \, \delta(f - f_n) \tag{1.32}$$

Here, $f_{-n} = -f_n$.

1.16 The Use of the Fourier Transform in Describing Linear Filtering

A *linear filter* is a system unit which is capable of modifying the amplitude and phase of certain frequency components in a signal. The modification usually involves the elimination of unwanted frequency bands. However, the term *filter* may also be applied to other operational blocks, such as integrators, differentiators and phase shifters. The term *linear* is applied because, if the input signal to the filter is increased in size by a given factor, the output signal will increase in size by the same factor, without other alteration to its waveshape.

Given a signal $v_1(t)$ with a spectrum $V_1(f)$, unwanted components may be eliminated from $V_1(f)$ by multiplication with a filter *transfer function*, $H(f)$. Thus the spectrum of the filtered signal will be

$$V_2(f) = V_1(f)H(f) \tag{1.33}$$

Application of the inverse Fourier transform will yield $v_2(t)$, the required filtered signal.

Just as the spectra $V_1(f)$ and $V_2(f)$ are, in general, complex, so also is the filter transfer function, $H(f)$. In the next sections, we shall examine some idealised filters for which $H(f)$ is a real function of frequency. None the less, all practical electronic wave filters have a complex transfer function which is often expressed as a gain characteristic, $A(f)$, and a phase characteristic, $\phi(f)$, thus

$$H(f) = A(f)\exp(j\phi(f)) \tag{1.34}$$

The gain and phase characteristics may be calculated from a known transfer function by separating out the real and imaginary parts of $H(f)$

$$H(f) = X(f) + jY(f)$$

and performing the manipulations

$$\begin{aligned} A(f) &= \{X^2(f) + Y^2(f)\}^{\frac{1}{2}} \\ \phi(f) &= \tan^{-1}\{Y(f)/X(f)\} \end{aligned} \tag{1.35}$$

Although we most readily think of the filtering operation as the frequency-domain manipulation, or scaling, of a signal spectrum, we may also regard it as a time-domain operation. Recall from section 1.13 that the Fourier transform of a unit delta or impulse function is a white spectral density of 1 volt Hz^{-1}. Thus if we apply an input signal to the filter

$$v_1(t) = \delta(t)$$

the response, in the frequency domain, will simply be

$$V_2(f) = H(f) \times 1$$

If we denote the Fourier transform of $H(f)$ by $h(t)$ it follows that

$$v_2(t) = h(t)$$

$h(t)$ is, as a consequence, known as the *impulse response* of the filter.

The concept of filtering as a time-domain manipulation is of even greater consequence than this. The frequency-domain manipulation

$$V_2(f) = V_1(f)H(f)$$

corresponds to the mathematical process known as 'convolution'

$$v_2(t) = \int_{-\infty}^{+\infty} h(\tau)v_1(t-\tau)\,\mathrm{d}\tau$$

$$= \int_{-\infty}^{+\infty} h(t-\tau)v_1(\tau)\,\mathrm{d}\tau \qquad (1.36)$$

This is fairly easily demonstrated. We take the Fourier transform of both sides of the convolution integral

$$V_2(f) = \int_{-\infty}^{+\infty}\int_{-\infty}^{+\infty} h(\tau)v_1(t-\tau)\exp(-2\pi\mathrm{j}ft)\,\mathrm{d}t\,\mathrm{d}\tau$$

We next interchange the order of integration

$$V_2(f) = \int_{-\infty}^{+\infty} h(\tau)\int_{-\infty}^{+\infty} v_1(t-\tau)\exp(-2\pi\mathrm{j}ft)\,\mathrm{d}t\,\mathrm{d}\tau$$

and define a new variable

$$\lambda = t - \tau$$

so that

$$\mathrm{d}\lambda = \mathrm{d}t$$

Then

$$V_2(f) = \int_{-\infty}^{+\infty} h(\tau)\int_{-\infty}^{+\infty} v_1(\lambda)\exp(-2\pi\mathrm{j}f\lambda)\,\mathrm{d}\lambda\,\exp(-2\pi\mathrm{j}f\tau)\,\mathrm{d}\tau$$

$$= V_1(f)\int_{-\infty}^{+\infty} h(\tau)\exp(-2\pi\mathrm{j}f\tau)\,\mathrm{d}\tau$$

$$= V_1(f)H(f)$$

On infrequent occasions, particularly when we have to handle the description of communication systems by means of differential equations, we find the time-domain notation representing convolution to be of convenience. We employ the symbol $\otimes$ to denote convolution so that

$$v_2(t) = v_1(t) \otimes h(t)$$

$$= h(t) \otimes v_1(t)$$

We shall not use the convolution integral directly in the calculation of filter or system responses. However, the concept of the 'impulse response' is very important, since it is a defining characteristic for some types of wave filter. It can also provide considerable insight into the behaviour and suitability of a filter for certain kinds of application, as we shall see in the next section.

1.17 Ideal Filters

We shall now examine the response of two kinds of *ideal* filter, those with a *rectangular* (sharp cut-off) amplitude characteristic and those with the more gentle *gaussian* amplitude characteristic.[32] Neither of these two characteristics can be exactly reproduced in practice, although both can be approached quite closely if a sufficiently complicated electronic filter is constructed. The reason for this lies in the nature of their impulse responses. Both classes, as we shall see, exhibit a response to an impulse occurring at time $t = 0$ which starts at time $t = -\infty$. Both, therefore, defy the principle of *causality*, in that their output starts before their input has arrived, an effect which clearly demonstates the futility of attempting an exact 'realisation'. (The principle of causality very simply and reasonably states that an effect must be preceded by its cause.)

Although these ideal filters are not realisable, they are mathematically easy to specify and can be very useful for theoretical work. The rectangular filter may be taken to represent a design target for filtering *analogue* signals to remove unwanted, out-of-band components. It is less useful for processing digital signals, since its impulse response is characterised by severe and sustained ringing. This has the effect of spreading signal energy from any one digit into adjacent digits, causing 'inter-symbol interference'. In contrast, the gaussian characteristic has an impulse response which does not ring at all. It is, therefore, quite a suitable design aim if digital-data waveforms are to be filtered. Of course, the amplitude characteristic cuts off rather too slowly to be of great benefit in filtering analogue signals.

In the remainder of this section, we shall consider the four basic kinds of rectangular characteristic—lowpass, highpass, bandpass and bandstop and compare their properties. We shall then examine the lowpass and bandpass gaussian filters. (The highpass and bandstop gaussian filters are rarely encountered.) All these filters will be assumed to exhibit no frequency-dependent phase shift. The effect of a non-zero phase function, $\phi(t)$, we shall then consider separately.

1.17.1 Rectangular Lowpass Filter

The rectangular characteristic

$$A_0(f) = 1 \quad |f| < f_0$$
$$= 0 \quad \text{elsewhere}$$
$$\phi_0(f) = 0 \quad \text{all } f$$

is shown, normalised, in figure 1.17a. The impulse response may be

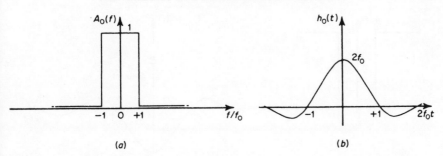

(a)   (b)

Figure 1.17 (a) Amplitude characteristic and (b) impulse response of the ideal rectangular lowpass filter

evaluated by forming the transfer function

$$H_0(f) = A_0(f)\exp(j\phi_0(f))$$

and Fourier transforming

$$h_0(t) = \int_{-\infty}^{+\infty} H_0(f)\exp(2\pi jft)\,df$$

$$= \int_{-f_0}^{+f_0} \exp(2\pi jft)\,df$$

$$= 2f_0\,\text{sinc}(x)$$

where

$$x = 2f_0t$$

The impulse response is illustrated in figure 1.17b and clearly illustrates the severe ringing which occurs when a sharp-cut-off filter is employed. In practice, a very sharp cut-off is not usually necessary and may even be undesirable. This is because a filter which can be realised (that is, actually constructed) will have related amplitude and phase characteristics. The relationship between them is too complex to discuss here, but may be summarised in the following way.

A sharp cut-off always implies phase non-linearity in the cut-off region. Good phase linearity, which is desirable if the filter is not to give rise to distortion of the signals passed through it, can, therefore, only be achieved at the expense of selectivity. Consequently, filter design is always something of a compromise between selectivity and phase linearity.

1.17.2 Rectangular Highpass Filter

The rectangular highpass filter is defined thus

$$A_1(f) = 0 \quad |f| < f_0$$

$$= 1 \quad \text{elsewhere}$$

$$\phi_1(f) = 0 \quad \text{all } f$$

This characteristic is illustrated in figure 1.18a and will be seen to be simply

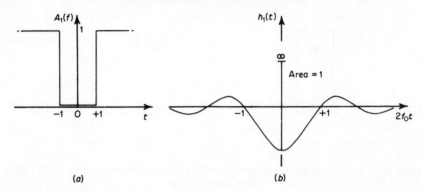

(a)　　　　　　　　　　　　　　(b)

Figure 1.18 (a) Amplitude characteristic and (b) impulse response of the ideal rectangular highpass filter

an inverted lowpass filter. Hence it follows that

$$H_1(f) = 1 - H_0(f)$$

Now, the Fourier transform of $H_1(f)$ gives the highpass-filter impulse response, $h_1(t)$. Applying the superposition principle, and recalling the Fourier transform pair

$$1 \leftrightarrow \delta(t)$$

we see that

$$h_1(t) = \delta(t) - h_0(t)$$

Hence, we may easily illustrate the impulse response of the ideal rectangular highpass filter, figure 1.18b.

1.17.3 Rectangular Bandpass Filter

The bandpass filter is defined by the relation

$$A_2(f) = 1 \quad f_1 < |f| < f_0$$
$$= 0 \quad \text{elsewhere}$$
$$\phi_2(f) = 0 \quad \text{all } f$$

and is illustrated in figure 1.19a. This transfer function may be formed as the sum of the lowpass and highpass transfer functions

$$H_2(f) = H_1(f) + H_0(f) - 1$$

where $H_0(f)$ and $H_1(f)$ have cutoff frequencies f_0 and f_1 with $f_1 < f_0$ so that, by superposition

$$h_2(t) = h_1(t) + h_0(t) - \delta(t)$$

where

$$h_0(t) = 2f_0 \frac{\sin(2\pi f_0 t)}{2\pi f_0 t}$$

and

$$h_1(t) = \delta(t) - 2f_1 \frac{\sin(2\pi f_1 t)}{2\pi f_1 t}$$

Hence

$$h_2(t) = 2f_0 \frac{\sin(2\pi f_0 t)}{2\pi f_0 t} - 2f_1 \frac{\sin(2\pi f_1 t)}{2\pi f_1 t}$$

$$= \frac{1}{\pi t}\{\sin(2\pi f_0 t) - \sin(2\pi f_1 t)\}$$

This expression may be manipulated into a convenient and revealing form if we introduce two new and common filter parameters. These are the filter centre-frequency, f_c, and the bandwidth, B. The centre frequency we define to be the arithmetic mean of the two cut-off frequencies

$$f_c = \frac{f_0 + f_1}{2} \tag{1.37}$$

Such a definition is not uniform in the literature. Many filters have a centre frequency which is defined as the geometric mean of the cut-off frequencies

$$f_c = (f_0 f_1)^{\frac{1}{2}}$$

There is a reason for this. Some filters are symmetrical about f_c only when plotted against a logarithmic frequency-scale. Then an arithmetic mean on the logarithmic axis becomes a geometric mean against a normal linear frequency-scale.

The filter bandwidth is defined as the separation between the cut-off frequencies

$$B = f_0 - f_1 \tag{1.38}$$

It follows from equations 1.37 and 1.38 that

$$f_0 = f_c + \frac{B}{2}$$

$$f_1 = f_c - \frac{B}{2}$$

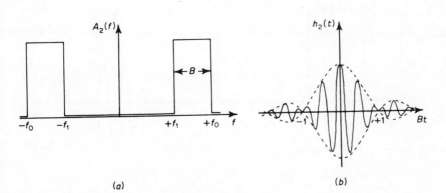

(a) (b)

Figure 1.19 (a) Amplitude characteristic and (b) impulse response of the ideal rectangular bandpass filter

Then

$$h_2(t) = \frac{1}{\pi t}\left[\sin\left\{2\pi\left(f_c + \frac{B}{2}\right)t\right\} - \sin\left\{2\pi\left(f_c - \frac{B}{2}\right)t\right\}\right]$$

Compressing this equation

$$h_2(t) = \frac{1}{\pi t}\sin\left(2\pi \frac{B}{2} t\right)\cos(2\pi f_c t)$$

$$= B\,\text{sinc}(x)\cos(2\pi f_c t)$$

where

$$x = Bt$$

We see that the impulse response, sketched in figure 1.19b, consists of a sinusoid at the filter centre-frequency with a sinc(x) envelope. The rate at which fluctuations of the envelope occur is inversely proportional to the bandwidth of the filter. Thus a narrow filter will exhibit an impulse response which stretches over a long period, encompassing many cycles of carrier.

1.17.4 Rectangular Bandstop Filter

The bandstop filter is defined as

$$A_3(f) = 0 \quad f_1 < |f| < f_0$$

$$= 1 \quad \text{elsewhere}$$

$$\phi_3(f) = 0 \quad \text{all } f$$

and is illustrated in figure 1.20a. Its transfer function may be derived from that of the bandpass filter and is

$$H_3(f) = 1 - H_2(f)$$

Consequently

$$h_3(t) = \delta(t) - h_2(t)$$

This impulse response is shown sketched in figure 1.20b.

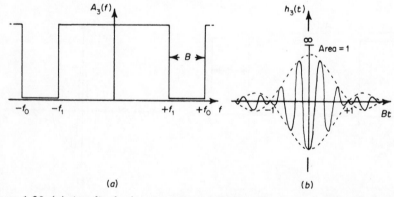

(a)   (b)

Figure 1.20 (a) Amplitude characteristic and (b) impulse response of the ideal rectangular bandstop filter

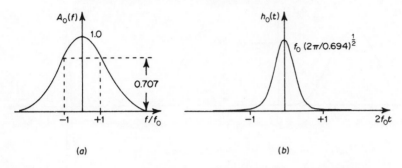

Figure 1.21 (a) Amplitude characteristic and (b) impulse response of the ideal gaussian lowpass filter

1.17.5 Gaussian Lowpass Filter[32]

Here, the definition of the filter is

$$A_0(f) = \exp\{-0.347(f/f_0)^2\}$$
$$\phi_0(f) = 0 \quad \text{all } f$$

This characteristic is illustrated in figure 1.21a. Fourier transformation yields an impulse response which is also gaussian

$$h_0(t) = f_0(2\pi/0.694)^{\frac{1}{2}} \exp(-t^2\pi^2 f_0^2/0.347)$$

and which is shown normalised in figure 1.21b.

Note that, unlike the rectangular filter, the gaussian filter shows no region of very rapid attenuation. The frequency f_0 is referred to as the *nominal cut-off frequency* and defines the point at which

$$A_0(f_0) = (2)^{-\frac{1}{2}} = 0.707$$

That is, the frequency corresponding to an attenuation of 3 dB.

Again, the gaussian filter contrasts vividly with the rectangular filter in that its impulse response shows no ringing whatsoever. For this reason it is well-suited to the filtering of digital data.

1.17.6 Gaussian Bandpass Filter

The gaussian bandpass characteristic is illustrated in figure 1.22a and is defined thus

$$A_2(f) = \exp\left(-1.388\left(\frac{f-f_c}{B}\right)^2\right)$$
$$\phi_2(f) = 0 \quad \text{all } f$$

f_c and B are the centre frequency and nominal (-3 dB) bandwidth of the filter, respectively. Again, as with the lowpass gaussian-filter, the bandpass version does not have regions of rapid attenuation with frequency. Thus at

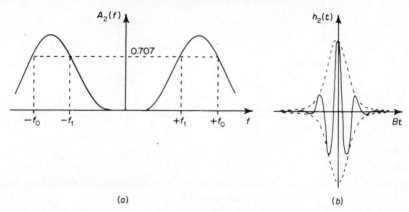

(a)   (b)

Figure 1.22 (a) Amplitude characteristic with $f_0 = f_c + B/2$ and $f_1 = f_c - B/2$ and (b) impulse response of the ideal gaussian bandpass filter

frequencies

$$f_0 = f_c + \frac{B}{2}$$

and

$$f_1 = f_c - \frac{B}{2}$$

the amplitude characteristic has values

$$A_2(f_0) = A_2(f_1) = (2)^{-\frac{1}{2}} = 0.707$$

The impulse response, in this case, is given by

$$h_2(t) = (B/2)(2\pi/0.694)^{\frac{1}{2}} \exp(-t^2\pi^2B^2/1.388)\cos(2\pi f_c t)$$

Again, we see that a shifting of the lowpass transfer function has the effect of modulating the envelope of a sinusoid of a frequency equal to the filter centre-frequency, figure 1.22b. The modulation corresponds to a suitably scaled version of the lowpass impulse response. This is not a perfectly general rule, however. Many bandpass filters do not have characteristics which are simply shifted and expanded versions of a prototype lowpass characteristic. This is particularly true of those filters which are arithmetically unsymmetrical about f_c when plotted on linear frequency-scales.

1.17.7 Effect of a Non-zero Phase Characteristic

In all of the filters described above, the phase characteristic was specified as

$$\phi_k(f) = 0 \quad \text{all } f; \, k = 0, 1, 2 \text{ or } 3$$

The effect of a non-zero phase shift is to produce signal delay. If the phase characteristic is a linear function of frequency a single delayed version of the input signal will be present at the output of the filter. It is this type of phase characteristic that we shall now examine. A non-linear phase shift with frequency produces multiple delayed and attenuated replicas of the input signal and may, as a consequence, give rise to severe signal distortion. This subject is discussed in more detail in section 8.3 since it is very important in the transmission of digital data.

Suppose that we choose to specify the linear phase-characteristic of any of the foregoing filters, thus

$$\phi_k(f) = -2\pi f\tau$$

where τ determines the slope of the phase function. The effect of introducing this phase characteristic is the same as cascading the original filter with a filter of transfer function

$$H(f) = \exp\{j\phi_k(f)\}$$

To find the impulse response of the cascaded pair, we apply the impulse response of the phase-shifting filter $H(f)$ to the prototype, filter $H_k(f)$, and determine the new output. The impulse response of the phase shifter is easily evaluated

$$\int_{-\infty}^{+\infty} \exp(-2\pi jf\tau)\exp(2\pi jft)\,df = \int_{-\infty}^{+\infty} \exp\{2\pi jf(t-\tau)\}\,df$$
$$= \delta(t-\tau)$$

The effect of phase shifting on an impulse occurring at time $t = 0$ is to produce a delayed impulse. The overall effect, therefore is to delay the impulse response of the prototype filter by a time τ as well. Hence, a filter with a characteristic

$$H_k(f) = A_k(f)\exp(-2\pi jf\tau)$$

has precisely the same impulse response as a filter

$$H_k(f) = A_k(f)$$

except for the time delay τ.

1.18 Calculating the Transfer Function of Practical Electronic Filters

A good example of the determination of a filter transfer-function, given an electronic circuit, is provided by the simple 'R–C section' illustrated in figure 1.23, which approximates to the ideal lowpass filter. We may specify the output voltage, V_2, in terms of the input voltage, V_1, by using j-notation. Then

$$V_2 = V_1(1+2\pi jfCR)^{-1}$$

This equation describes the *steady state* behaviour of the circuit. That is, given a sinusoid V_1 at the input, a sinusoid V_2 of the same frequency and calculable amplitude and phase will appear at the output. Since the filter is a linear electrical network, the principle of superposition may be applied. Hence, if we replace V_1 and V_2 with spectral representations $V_1(f)$ and $V_2(f)$ of waveforms $v_1(t)$ and $v_2(t)$ respectively, then since $V_1(f)$ and $V_2(f)$ are

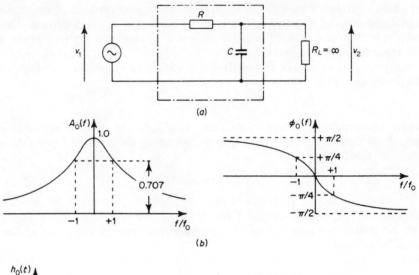

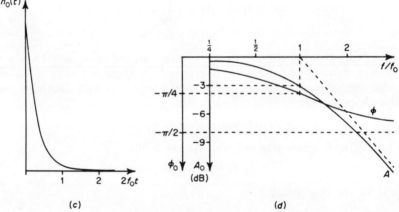

Figure 1.23 (a) The first order RC lowpass filter (b) its amplitude and phase characteristics, (c) its impulse response and (d) Bode plots of amplitude and phase response
plotted against a logarithmic frequency scale

simply the summation of all sinusoidal components in $v_1(t)$ and $v_2(t)$, we may
write

$$V_2(f) = V_1(f)(1 + 2\pi jfCR)^{-1}$$

Comparing this equation with equation 1.33, we see that

$$H_0(f) = (1 + 2\pi jfCR)^{-1} \qquad (1.39)$$

and we have calculated the required transfer function.

As we observed in section 1.16, the transfer function may be expressed,
by means of equations 1.35, in the more readily interpreted form of a gain

and a phase characteristic, figure 1.23b

$$A_0(f) = (1 + (2\pi fCR)^2)^{-\frac{1}{2}}$$
$$\phi_0(f) = \tan^{-1}(-2\pi fCR)$$

These equations are usually written in terms of a *nominal cut-off frequency*, f_0, such that

$$A_0(f_0) = (2)^{-\frac{1}{2}} \equiv -3 \text{ dB}$$

Thus

$$f_0 = (2\pi CR)^{-1}$$

and consequently

$$A_0(f) = (1 + (f/f_0)^2)^{-\frac{1}{2}}$$
$$\phi_0(f) = \tan^{-1}(-f/f_0)$$

Notice that, when f is large

$$A_0(f) \approx f_0/f$$

A curve of (f_0/f) plotted on logarithmic frequency and amplitude scales, as in figure 1.23d, corresponds to a straight line falling with a slope of -20 dB decade^{-1} and intersecting with the frequency axis (that is at 0 dB) when $f = f_0$. The filter amplitude characteristic approaches this line asymptotically with increasing frequency. It therefore provides a convenient aid for sketching log-gain versus log-frequency plots for first-order filter sections.

We may evaluate the impulse response by Fourier transforming equation 1.39 (for example, by utilising the table of transforms listed in appendix I) to yield the result, sketched in figure 1.23c

$$h_0(t) = (CR)^{-1} \exp(-t/CR)$$

Of course, this equation could have been obtained by other means. For example, the impulse places upon the capacitor an amount of charge

$$Q = R^{-1}$$

so that the initial voltage across the capacitor plates is

$$V = Q/C = (CR)^{-1}$$

This initial voltage decays to zero exponentially as the capacitor discharge current flows through the resistor. Although it is probably easier to use elementary circuit theory to solve this particular problem, rather than to determine the impulse response by using Fourier transformation, complicated circuits yield more readily to the latter method.

The impulse response is often written in terms of a *time constant*

$$T_0 = RC$$

so that

$$h_0(t) = T_0^{-1} \exp(-t/T_0)$$

It is frequently the case that a filter transfer function is specified by an equation which determines the *transient* rather than the steady-state behaviour of the circuit. If this is the case, then the 's' operator[10] will almost always be used. In the case of the RC section we find that

$$V_2 = V_1(1 + sCR)^{-1}$$

To obtain the j-notation version of any such function of s, replace s by $2\pi jf$ throughout.

More complex filter structures may be analysed after the fashion of our simple RC lowpass filter. Many texts have been written which treat the complementary problem of filter synthesis (the design of a filter to suit a given application) in great detail. Two books which the reader may find helpful if he wishes to pursue this topic further are given in the bibliography.[11,12]

1.19   Energy-density and Power-density Spectra

Before investigating the derivation and properties of energy- and power-density spectra, let us define the terms *power* and *energy*. When a signal $v(t)$ feeds a load of resistance R, the power dissipation at any time, t, is

$$\frac{v^2(t)}{R}$$

In most theoretical work, the resistance value R is of secondary importance, so that it is common policy to normalise the power dissipation by assuming a standard $1\,\Omega$ load. This is never a serious restriction, since

    (1) denormalisation is easily achieved, when necessary,

    (2) we often work in terms of power or energy ratios measured across the same load value, so that de-normalisation is not even necessary.

We shall adopt this convention, and we shall define the *instantaneous power dissipation* as

$$p_i(t) = v^2(t) \quad \text{volt}^2 \tag{1.40}$$

Electrical power may be converted at a load into a variety of other forms—thermal, acoustic, optical or mechanical. Often it is not the instantaneous power dissipation which is our greatest concern but the averaged, or smoothed, power dissipation. Frequently this is because the load itself imparts some inertia in the conversion of power from the electrical state. For example, a resistance dissipating heat cannot follow rapid fluctuations of the quantity $p_i(t)$, and so tends to impart its own smoothing.

Averaging is performed in many electrical power-measuring instruments in just this way. The technique involves measuring the mean square voltage across a load of known resistance. The mean square voltage is obtained by measuring the thermal output from a standard resistance in parallel with the load by means of a thermocouple. The thermocouple output-voltage is amplified and applied to a suitable meter movement.

Suppose we regard the time origin, $t = 0$, as the start of the measurement interval. Then the averaging process, taking place over a time interval, T, is described by the usual averaging integral, yielding

$$p(T) = \frac{1}{T} \int_0^{+T} v^2(t) \, dt$$

If the waveform is periodic, the averaging interval may be made equal to the period. In most practical situations, irrespective of the nature of the waveform, we attempt to average over as long a time interval as possible. If the waveform is noise-like, the reason for this strategy is fundamental. We need to consider as long a segment of the process as possible to ensure a statistically significant result. We therefore define the *average power* in a waveform $v(t)$ as

$$p_a = \lim_{T \to \infty}\left[\frac{1}{T}\int_0^{+T} v^2(t)\,dt\right] \quad \text{volt}^2 \tag{1.41}$$

Over the time interval, T, the waveform $v(t)$ will yield, to a normalised $1\,\Omega$ load, an *energy* of

$$e(T) = \int_0^{+T} v^2(t)\,dt \quad \text{volt}^2\,\text{s} \tag{1.42}$$

The total energy that the waveform can yield is the integral over all time

$$e_t = \int_{-\infty}^{+\infty} v^2(t)\,dt \quad \text{volt}^2\,\text{s} \tag{1.43}$$

If the waveform has non-zero mean power (for example, any periodic wave or noise-like wave of infinite duration) then the total energy dissipated at the load will be infinite. This is because the total energy is then the accumulation of finite mean power over an infinite time.

We are often particularly interested in the way in which a signal occupies a frequency band. The techniques used for determining band occupancy depend on the nature of the signal. For bounded amplitude, finite-energy signals we employ the concept of the *energy spectral density*, $E(f)$, measured in units of volt^2 s per Hz, or volt^2 s^2. Such signals may be of finite duration or band-limited, or neither, but may certainly not be both time- and band-limited.

If the signal is of finite mean power (for example a sine wave) and, as defined, capable of supplying infinite energy since it is of infinite duration, then the concept of energy density is no longer adequate. We use instead, the concept of *power spectral density*, $P(f)$, measured in units of volt^2 per Hz or volt^2 s.

1.20   Energy Spectral Density' of Finite-energy Pulses

We shall introduce the concept of the energy spectral density of waveforms by examining a simple physical measuring system which could be used to obtain a close approximation to the required spectrum. We may define an energy-density spectrum, $E(f)$, such that $E(f)\,\delta f$ is the total energy in a narrow band at the output of an ideal rectangular bandpass filter of width δf and centre frequency f_n. A hypothetical measuring system is illustrated in figure 1.24. By repeating the basic measurement of the energy at the output of the narrowband filter for a number of different centre frequencies, a graph approximating to $E(f)$ may be drawn. From this graph, we could

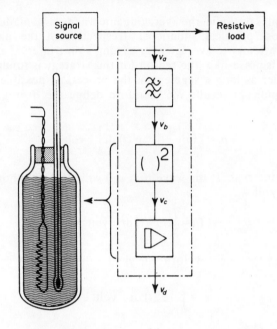

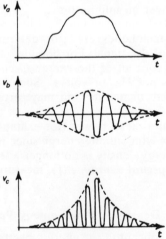

(a)

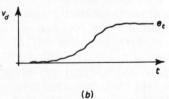

(b)

Figure 1.24 The experimental determination of energy spectral density

estimate the total energy output as

$$e_t = \int_{-\infty}^{+\infty} E(f)\, df \quad \text{volt}^2\, s \tag{1.44}$$

From equation 1.43, we have the alternative expression

$$e_t = \int_{-\infty}^{+\infty} v^2(t)\, dt \quad \text{volt}^2\, s \tag{1.45}$$

We may now derive a simple relationship between $V(f)$, the Fourier transform of $v(t)$ and the energy spectral density $E(f)$. From equation 1.45

$$
\begin{aligned}
e_t &= \int_{-\infty}^{+\infty} v(t) \left\{ \int_{-\infty}^{+\infty} V(f) \exp(2\pi jft)\, df \right\} dt \\
&= \int_{-\infty}^{+\infty} V(f) \left\{ \int_{-\infty}^{+\infty} v(t) \exp(2\pi jft)\, dt \right\} df \\
&= \int_{-\infty}^{+\infty} V(f) V(-f)\, df
\end{aligned}
\tag{1.46}
$$

Comparing equations 1.44 and 1.46, we see that

$$E(f) = V(f) V(-f)$$

From the complex conjugate symmetry property of $V(f)$

$$V(-f) = V^*(f)$$

so that

$$
\begin{aligned}
E(f) &= V(f) V^*(f) \\
&= |V(f)|^2 \quad \text{volt}^2\, s^2
\end{aligned}
\tag{1.47}
$$

Thus the energy spectral density is quite simply related to the voltage spectral density of the finite-energy waveform (normalised to a $1\,\Omega$ load).

It is frequently important for us to be able to estimate the energy distribution of a finite-energy pulse after it has passed through some linear electronic system. The most common such system is the wave filter introduced in section 1.16. We know, from equation 1.47 that the energy spectral density of the input and output signals, $v_1(t)$ and $v_2(t)$ respectively, of the filtering process defined by equation 1.33 are

$$E_1(f) = |V_1(f)|^2$$
$$E_2(f) = |V_2(f)|^2$$

The filtering operation is defined thus

$$V_2(f) = V_1(f) H(f)$$

So that

$$
\begin{aligned}
|V_2(f)| &= |V_1(f) H(f)| \\
&= |V_1(f)|\, |H(f)|
\end{aligned}
$$

It follows that

$$|V_2(f)|^2 = |V_1(f)|^2\, |H(f)|^2$$

In terms of the energy spectral density, we may immediately write

$$E_2(f) = E_1(f) \, |H(f)|^2 \qquad (1.48)$$

and this equation may readily be applied to determine the effect of filtering on the (known) spectrum of the input waveform.

1.21 Energy Spectral Density of the Delta Function

Although we employ energy spectral density for finite-energy pulse-type waveshapes, the delta function or impulse is the exception to this general rule. Although the delta function, introduced in section 1.13, is defined to have unit area, it does not have unit energy. In fact, it has infinite energy. The energy in any voltage waveform is given by the integral

$$e_t = \int_{-\infty}^{+\infty} \{v(t)\}^2 \, dt$$

In the case of the rectangular pulse

$$v = \frac{1}{2t_1} \qquad -t_1 \leqslant t \leqslant t_1$$

the energy transferred by the pulse is

$$e_t = \frac{1}{2t_1}$$

As t_1 increases, therefore, this energy becomes infinite. This agrees with the energy content as assessed from the energy spectral density

$$e_t = \int_{-\infty}^{+\infty} E(f) \, df$$

where

$$E(f) = |V(f)|^2$$
$$= 1 \quad \text{volt}^2 \, \text{s}^2$$

for the impulse, yielding a total energy

$$e_t = \int_{-\infty}^{+\infty} df \rightarrow \infty$$

In practice, we generate impulse-like waveforms which must have finite duration and therefore finite energy. These would correspond to passing an ideal impulse into a system with a necessarily restricted bandwidth. No practical electronic circuit can have an infinite bandwidth.

1.22 Power Spectral Density of Finite-power Periodic Functions

We have seen that the concept of energy spectral density may be employed to allow us to examine the band occupancy or distribution of energy within a given finite-energy signal. Many of the waveforms we commonly work with are not finite-energy processes, as they are defined. That is, the mathematical statement of these waveforms is directed towards analytical convenience, rather than realisability. Almost all periodic functions fall into the category of containing finite mean power. An exception to this general rule is the periodic impulse train, which conveys infinite power. Since all periodic functions are defined to exist for all time, and since the product of mean power and duration yields the energy conveyed, an infinite amount of energy is contained within any periodic function. We know, for example, that the sinusoid has a Fourier transform which consists of a pair of delta functions displaced equally about the origin $(f = 0)$. Since the sinusoid contains infinite energy, we cannot depict it on an energy spectral density graph, since the energy spectrum would then consist of a pair of infinite energy delta functions.

To avoid the problems which arise when we attempt to obtain a measure of the band occupancy of signals by means of energy spectral density we turn to the concept of 'power spectral density'. In much the same manner as we used to define $E(f)$, we specify a power spectral density $P(f)$ such that $P(f_n)\,\delta f$ is the average power in a narrow band δf at the output of an ideal rectangular filter with a centre frequency f_n. A simple hypothetical system for estimating power spectral density may be obtained if we replace the integrator in figure 1.24 with an averaging circuit. This circuit approximates the averaging integral defined in equation 1.41 and may be realised by means of a lowpass filter with an extremely low cut-off frequency.

The power spectral density cannot be calculated from the energy spectral density, since the latter is derived by integrating an 'instantaneous' power spectrum over all time. The resulting function of frequency does not contain information which tells us how the energy was accumulated as a function of time. Nor, indeed, can an instantaneous power spectral density be obtained from an averaged power spectral density, although the reverse would in principle be possible. This is because a loss of detailed information occurs during the averaging process.

The power spectrum of periodic functions may be easily deduced if we have a knowledge of the power spectrum of the sinusoid

$$A_0 \cos(2\pi f_0 t)$$

This sinusoid has an average power obtainable by means of equation 1.41 which is

$$\tfrac{1}{2}A_0^2 \quad \text{volt}^2\,\text{s}$$

The transform of the sinusoid consists of two delta functions at frequencies $+f_0$ and $-f_0$ respectively. Hence we deduce that the power spectral density consists of two delta functions each of area

$$\tfrac{1}{4}A_0^2 \quad \text{volt}^2\,\text{s}$$

Here, the two delta functions have the role of pinpointing locations on the frequency axis

$$P(f) = \tfrac{1}{4}A_0^2\{\delta(f - f_0) + \delta(f + f_0)\}$$

Using this spectral representation we may construct, by using the superposition principle, the power spectral density of any periodic function.

1.23 Power Spectral Density of Finite-power Aperiodic Functions

We cannot apply transform techniques directly to estimate the power spectrum of finite-power aperiodic functions such as noise waves, noise-like signals or carrier waves modulated with noise-like signals. This is because such waves contain a strong random component which cannot be specified in algebraic form. We are forced, as a consequence, to resort to methods of inference. For example, we may have some prior knowledge of the nature of a signal spectrum and a specification of the various stages of processing that it has undergone. Then we can estimate a good approximation to the spectrum. This is the method most commonly employed when we have to handle noise waveforms. Many noise sources produce waveforms which have a power spectral density that is *white*, uniform over all frequencies of interest. An absolutely white spectrum

$$P(f) = N \quad \text{constant; all } f$$

is an impossibility, since then the total power in the waveform

$$\int_{-\infty}^{+\infty} P(f)\, df$$

would be infinite. Consequently, we define an initial source power spectral density thus

$$P(f) = N \quad \text{constant; all } f \text{ of interest}$$

and typically this will be a reasonable approximation over a band of frequencies from a few hundred Hz to tens or hundreds of MHz. (The subject of noise sources is discussed in more detail in chapter 2 and appendix III.)

We have seen, in section 1.20 how the passage of a finite-energy signal through a linear system such as a wave filter results in a predictable modification to the energy spectral density. If the signal applied to the filter is not of finite energy, but of finite power and therefore characterised by a power spectral density $P_1(f)$, then the power spectral density at the filter output, $P_2(f)$, may be obtained by the equivalent relationship

$$P_2(f) = P_1(f) \, |H(f)|^2 \tag{1.49}$$

If, as is often the case when the input signal is a noisewave, $P_1(f)$ is a 'white' spectrum then

$$P_2(f) = N \, |H(f)|^2$$

where N is the input noise power spectral density measured in volt^2 s.

1.24 The Cross- and Autocorrelation Functions and the Correlation Coefficient

We saw in section 1.4 that the orthogonality integral

$$\int_{t_1}^{t_2} v_m(t) v_n(t)\, dt$$

is a measure of the 'alikeness' of the two functions $v_m(t)$ and $v_n(t)$. Specifically, if, when $m \neq n$, this integral is zero, the two functions are said to be orthogonal, or unalike. They then contain no shared Fourier components. If the two functions are not strictly orthogonal, the integral provides some measure of their similarity over the interval $t = t_1$ to $t = t_2$. A positive value of the integral suggests an affinity between $v_m(t)$ and $v_n(t)$. The greater the value, the greater the similarity. A negative value indicates that $v_m(t)$ more closely resembles $-v_n(t)$ than $+v_n(t)$.

There are circumstances, however, when $v_m(t)$ bears a closer resemblance to a delayed version of $v_n(t)$ than to $v_n(t)$ itself. For a variety of reasons which will become apparent in this and the last sections of this chapter, the ability to search for such intricate similarities is of great value to us. A somewhat more general measure of the alikeness between our two waveforms is provided by the integrals

$$\int_{-T/2}^{+T/2} v_m(t)v_n(t + \tau)\, dt$$

and

$$\int_{-T/2}^{+T/2} v_m(t + \tau)v_n(t)\, dt$$

Here, τ is a hypothetical separation, an artificially imposed delay upon one or the other waveform which may be varied to yield a measure of alikeness of the two functions $v_m(t)$ and $v_n(t)$ within the epoch of duration T

$$-T/2 \leqslant t \leqslant +T/2$$

If $v_m(t)$ and $v_n(t)$ are finite-energy waveforms of possibly infinite duration then we may write these integrals in their most general form

$$\left. \begin{aligned} R_{mn}(\tau) &= \int_{-\infty}^{+\infty} v_m(t)v_n(t + \tau)\, dt \\ &= \int_{-\infty}^{+\infty} v_m(t + \tau)v_n(t)\, dt \end{aligned} \right\} \quad \text{volt}^2 \text{ s} \qquad (1.50)$$

$R_{mn}(\tau)$ is referred to as the *cross-correlation function* of $v_m(t)$ and $v_n(t)$. If $v_m(t)$ and $v_n(t)$ are infinite-energy finite-power waveforms, periodic or aperiodic in nature, the cross-correlation integral, equation 1.50, would become infinite at least for some values of τ. Instead, we employ a relationship modified after the manner described in section 1.19

$$\left. \begin{aligned} R_{mn}(\tau) &= \lim_{T \to \infty} \frac{1}{T} \int_{-T/2}^{+T/2} v_m(t)v_m(t + \tau)\, dt \\ &= \lim_{T \to \infty} \frac{1}{T} \int_{-T/2}^{+T/2} v_m(t + \tau)v_n(t)\, dt \end{aligned} \right\} \quad \text{volt}^2 \qquad (1.51)$$

This function is also known as the cross-correlation between $v_m(t)$ and $v_n(t)$. Naturally, we must exercise care in selecting the method whereby we calculate $R_{mn}(\tau)$, choosing the appropriate relationship, either equation 1.50 or equation 1.51, depending on the nature of $v_m(t)$ and $v_n(t)$. It should be noted that the cross-correlation functions of finite-energy and finite-power waveforms are not directly comparable, since they are dimensionally different.

Although the application of the correlation integral to the determination of the alikeness of two different functions is a technique of fairly obvious utility, it is also frequently useful to be able to determine the alikeness of a function to itself, subject to a temporal displacement τ. That is, we apply equations 1.50 or 1.51 to calculate $R_{mm}(\tau)$. It is worth noting that, if $v_m(t)$ is a finite-energy waveform, then

$$R_{mm}(0) = \int_{-\infty}^{+\infty} v_m^2(t)\,dt \qquad (1.52)$$

$$= \text{total energy in } v_m(t) \quad \text{volt}^2\,s$$

If $v_m(t)$ is a finite-power waveform, then

$$R_{mm}(0) = \operatorname*{Lim}_{T \to \infty} \frac{1}{T} \int_{-T/2}^{+T/2} v_m^2(t)\,dt \qquad (1.53)$$

$$= \text{average power in } v_m(t) \quad \text{volt}^2$$

The quantity $R_{mm}(\tau)$ is known as the *autocorrelation function* of the waveform $v_m(t)$. In the next two sections of this chapter we shall see that the autocorrelation function is of importance in providing a method of calculating energy spectral density and, in particular, power spectral density. The latter can often not be calculated directly—particularly if the waveform being analysed is random in nature.

One problem which arises when correlation functions are assessed is the fact that the result, $R_{mn}(\tau)$ or $R_{mm}(\tau)$, is not presented in a normalised form. If the waveforms $v_m(t)$ and $v_n(t)$ were scaled so that they contained only unit energy or power, as appropriate, then a direct comparison of correlation functions of waveform pairs of the same physical type would be possible. Such a normalisation requires that we determine the correlation functions of waveforms

$$\frac{v_m(t)}{\{R_{mm}(0)\}^{\frac{1}{2}}} \quad \text{and} \quad \frac{v_n(t)}{\{R_{nn}(0)\}^{\frac{1}{2}}}$$

Alternatively, we may simply evaluate the *normalised cross-correlation and autocorrelation* functions

$$R_{mn}(\tau)\{R_{mm}(0)R_{nn}(0)\}^{-\frac{1}{2}} \qquad (1.54)$$

and

$$R_{mm}(\tau)/R_{mm}(0) \qquad (1.55)$$

respectively.

From equation 1.54 we may derive a simple normalised measure of the similarity between two waveforms. This is the *correlation coefficient*, ρ_{mn}, which may be expressed as

$$\rho_{mn} = R_{mn}(0)\{R_{mm}(0)R_{nn}(0)\}^{-\frac{1}{2}} \qquad (1.56)$$

This quantity may only take on values within the range

$$-1 \leqslant \rho_{mn} \leqslant +1$$

The range of values which the correlation coefficient may assume may be interpreted thus: if $v_m(t)$ exhibits a likeness to $v_n(t)$, ρ_{mn} will be positive, with its maximum value of $+1$ when $v_m(t) = v_n(t)$. If $v_m(t)$ exhibits a likeness to $-v_n(t)$, ρ_{mn} will be negative, with its minimum value of -1 when $v_m(t) = -v_n(t)$. If $v_m(t)$ and $v_n(t)$ are uncorrelated, they will contain no common spectral components and ρ_{mn} will be zero.

Strictly, both the correlation coefficient and the correlation functions are defined in terms of statistical averages rather than time averages. However, for the majority of situations which the communication engineer has to handle, time and statistical (ensemble) averages are interchangeable.

1.25 The Use of the Autocorrelation Function in Determining Power Spectra

The power spectrum of a finite-power waveform and its autocorrelation function may be shown to be a Fourier transform pair. We shall, for simplicity, omit the subscripts used in the previous section, writing $v(t)$ for the finite-power waveform, $P(f)$ for its power spectrum and $R(\tau)$ for its autocorrelation function. Both $P(f)$ and $R(\tau)$ are real functions with

$$P(f) = \int_{-\infty}^{+\infty} R(\tau)\exp(-2\pi jf\tau)\,d\tau \tag{1.57}$$

and

$$R(\tau) = \lim_{T \to \infty} \frac{1}{T} \int_{-T/2}^{+T/2} v(t)v(t+\tau)\,dt \tag{1.58}$$

$R(\tau)$ is of value in the determination of power spectra for random or noiselike signals for the following reasons

(1) It may be possible to deduce $R(\tau)$ from a knowledge of the statistics of a random process. A very important example of this class of problem is afforded by the random digital-data signal. This waveform is examined in detail in section 1.27.3.

(2) In some situations, the experimental determination of power spectra by means of tuned filters followed by power meters (figure 1.24 with the integrator replaced by a lowpass or 'averaging' filter) may not be advisable. Experimental methods of determining $R(\tau)$ have been devised and can provide a useful, if indirect, alternative.

The experimental determination of correlation functions is also of great value to control engineers since it provides a means of assessing the transfer functions of linear control plant while it is in normal operation.

The transform pair quoted above is often referred to as the Weiner–Khintchine theorem. Its proof is not particularly difficult, but is rather lengthy. The proof may be obtained by a two-part argument. First we establish a necessary result. Suppose that the waveform $v(t)$, aperiodic and of infinite duration, is segmented in the manner shown in figure 1.25 by multiplying it with a window function $w(t)$ to form a finite-energy pulse $v_1(t)$

$$v_1(t) = v(t)w(t)$$

where

$$w(t) = 1 \quad -T/2 \leqslant t \leqslant +T/2$$
$$= 0 \quad \text{elsewhere}$$

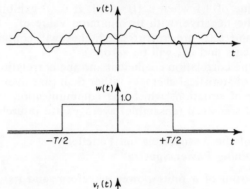

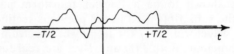

Figure 1.25 The extraction of a finite-energy segment $v_1(t) = v(t)w(t)$ from an infinite-energy waveform $v(t)$ by means of a window function $w(t)$

The energy-density spectrum of $v_1(t)$ will be given by the relation

$$E_1(f) = V_1(f)V_1(-f) \quad \text{volt}^2 \text{ s}^2$$

and the energy contained in a narrow band of width δf centred at the frequency f will be

$$e_1 = E_1(f)\,\delta f \quad \text{volt}^2 \text{ s}$$

Suppose that the average power contributed by this narrow band of frequencies during the interval $-T/2 \le t \le +T/2$ is p_1. Then

$$p_1 T = \text{total energy}$$
$$= E_1(f)\,\delta f$$

However, we may also relate the total power output to the power spectral density $P_1(f)$, since

$$p_1 = P_1(f)\,\delta f$$

Consequently it follows that

$$P_1(f) = \frac{E_1(f)}{T} = \frac{V_1(f)V_1(-f)}{T}$$

If we allow the window function to increase in width, then as $T \to \infty$, $v_1(t) \to v(t)$ and $P_1(f) \to P(f)$. It follows that

$$P(f) = \lim_{T \to \infty} \left[\frac{V_1(f)V_1(-f)}{T} \right] \tag{1.59}$$

The second part of the proof commences with a statement of the inversion transform

$$R(\tau) = \int_{-\infty}^{+\infty} P(f) \exp(2\pi jf\tau)\ df$$

$$= \int_{-\infty}^{+\infty} \operatorname*{Lim}_{T\to\infty} \left[\frac{V_1(f)\,V_1(-f)}{T} \right] \exp(2\pi jf\tau)\ df$$

$$= \operatorname*{Lim}_{T\to\infty} \frac{1}{T} \int_{-\infty}^{+\infty} V_1(f)\,V_1(-f)\exp(2\pi jf\tau)\ df$$

But

$$V_1(-f) = \int_{-\infty}^{+\infty} v_1(t)\exp(2\pi jft)\ dt$$

which, by virtue of our definition that $v_1(t)$ be zero-valued beyond the limits $\pm T/2$ may be rewritten in the form

$$V_1(-f) = \int_{-T/2}^{+T/2} v_1(t)\exp(2\pi jft)\ dt$$

Thus

$$R(\tau) = \operatorname*{Lim}_{T\to\infty} \frac{1}{T} \int_{-\infty}^{+\infty} V_1(f) \left\{ \int_{-T/2}^{+T/2} v_1(t)\exp(2\pi jft)\ dt \right\} \exp(2\pi jf\tau)\ df$$

$$= \operatorname*{Lim}_{T\to\infty} \frac{1}{T} \int_{-T/2}^{+T/2} v_1(t) \left\{ \int_{-\infty}^{+\infty} V_1(f)\exp(2\pi jf(t+\tau))\ df \right\}\ dt$$

Using the shift property quoted in table 1.2 we may write

$$R(\tau) = \operatorname*{Lim}_{T\to\infty} \frac{1}{T} \int_{-T/2}^{+T/2} v_1(t)v_1(t+\tau)\ dt$$

Finally, since $v_1(t)$ is the same as $v(t)$ between the stated limits of integration we may equally well write

$$R(\tau) = \operatorname*{Lim}_{T\to\infty} \frac{1}{T} \int_{-T/2}^{+T/2} v(t)v(t+\tau)\ dt$$

and the required result has been obtained.

1.26 The Use of the Autocorrelation Function in Determining Energy Spectra

The energy spectrum of a finite-energy waveform and its autocorrelation function may be shown to be a Fourier transform pair. As in the previous section, we shall omit subscripts, writing $v(t)$ for the finite-energy waveform, $E(f)$ for its energy-density spectrum and $R(\tau)$ for the autocorrelation function. Again, $E(f)$ and $R(\tau)$ are real functions, with

$$E(f) = \int_{-\infty}^{+\infty} R(\tau)\exp(-2\pi jf\tau)\ d\tau \qquad (1.60)$$

and

$$R(\tau) = \int_{-\infty}^{+\infty} v(t)v(t+\tau)\ dt \qquad (1.61)$$

The proof of these results follows exactly the same line of reasoning as that used in the previous section to relate the autocorrelation function of finite-power waveforms and their power spectra. The results themselves, although of interest in completing the pattern of Fourier manipulations of waveforms, are less often of assistance to us in practical situations than those derived in section 1.25.

1.27 Some Examples of the Calculation and Use of the Autocorrelation Function

To illustrate the use of the results derived in the previous sections, we shall evaluate the autocorrelation function of several frequently encountered waveforms.

1.27.1 *The Sinusoid*

$$v(t) = A_0 \cos(2\pi f_0 t + \phi_0)$$

Since this function is a finite-power waveform, we employ equation 1.58, writing

$$R(\tau) = \lim_{T \to \infty} \frac{1}{T} \int_{-T/2}^{+T/2} A_0 \cos(2\pi f_0 t + \phi_0) A_0 \cos(2\pi f_0 (t+\tau) + \phi_0) \, dt$$

This integral may be evaluated analytically. It requires only the application and manipulation of simple trigonometric relationships to derive the result

$$R(\tau) = \frac{A_0^2}{2} \cos(2\pi f_0 \tau)$$

Notice that, as equation 1.53 requires

$$R(0) = \frac{A_0^2}{2} = \text{average power in } v(t)$$

Furthermore the normalised autocorrelation function

$$R(\tau)/R(0) = \cos(2\pi f_0 \tau)$$

is restricted (as indeed it must be) to values lying in the range -1 to $+1$. It may be interpreted thus: when its value is $+1$, $v(t)$ and $v(t+\tau)$ have been shifted by increments

$$\tau = T_0, 2T_0, 3T_0, \ldots \quad T_0 = f_0^{-1}$$

Thus $v(t)$ and $v(t+\tau)$ must be identical. Shifts of

$$\tau = \frac{T_0}{2}, \frac{3T_0}{2}, \frac{5T_0}{2} \cdots$$

cause $v(t)$ and $v(t+\tau)$ to be in antiphase, with the result that the normalised autocorrelation function is -1. Shifts of

$$\tau = \frac{T_0}{4}, \frac{3T_0}{4}, \frac{5T_0}{4} \cdots$$

cause $v(t)$ and $v(t+\tau)$ to be in phase quadrature and therefore orthogonal. Thus for these values the autocorrelation function is zero.

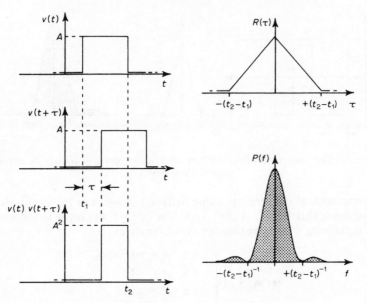

Figure 1.26 The autocorrelation function and energy spectral density of a rectangular voltage-pulse

Determination of the power spectrum is simply a matter of Fourier transforming the autocorrelation function. This may be achieved by consulting the table of transforms listed in appendix I. We find that

$$P(f) = \tfrac{1}{4}A_0^2\{\delta(f+f_0)+\delta(f-f_0)\}$$

1.27.2   The Rectangular Pulse

We shall consider next the autocorrelation function of a finite-energy waveform, the rectangular pulse

$$v(t) = A \quad t_1 \leqslant t \leqslant t_2$$
$$= 0 \quad \text{elsewhere}$$

The autocorrelation function of this pulse may be determined from equation 1.61 by inspection. Consider the waveforms depicted in figure 1.26. $R(\tau)$ is determined by the area beneath the curve $v(t)v(t+\tau)$. As $|\tau|$ increases, this area decreases as a linear function of $|\tau|$. The area falls to zero when $|\tau| = (t_2-t_1)$ so that the function depicted for $R(\tau)$ may be deduced. Again, inspection of the table of results provided in appendix I allows us to obtain the Fourier transform of this function, yielding the energy-density spectrum

$$E(f) = A^2(t_2 - t_1)^2 \operatorname{sinc}^2\{f|(t_2 - t_1)|\}$$

1.27.3   The Rectangular Random-digit Sequence

Our final example is the digital-data waveform depicted in figure 1.27. We assume the digits to be equiprobable. We also suppose that successive digits

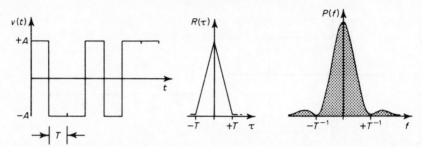

Figure 1.27 The autocorrelation function and power spectral density of a random digital-data signal

are independent. If τ is zero, the value $R(0)$ will be equal to the mean power in the waveform, that is, A^2. A shift such that $|\tau| = T$ will result in independent binary digits being multiplied together in combinations

$$v(t)v(t + \tau)\begin{cases} A \times A = +A^2 \\ A \times -A = -A^2 \\ -A \times A = -A^2 \\ -A \times -A = +A^2 \end{cases}$$

These combinations will occur with equal probability and will average to zero, so that $R(\pm T)$ will be zero. Between $\tau = 0$ and $|\tau| = T$, the same argument that was applied to determine the autocorrelation function of the isolated rectangular pulse may be applied, so that we derive the autocorrelation function shown in figure 1.27. Fourier transformation yields the power spectrum

$$P(f) = A^2 T \operatorname{sinc}^2(fT)$$

Note that although the form of the autocorrelation function of the isolated rectangular pulse and that of the random digit sequence are the same, the units are different. The transform of the autocorrelation function yields in the first case an energy spectrum and in the second, a power spectrum.

1.28   Fourier Transforms: A Credibility Gap?

Having, hopefully, carefully followed the foregoing discussion on the derivation and application of the Fourier transform method, the student may begin to experience misgivings. For example, he may correctly suppose that he cannot actually create an ideal rectangular pulse. That would obviously imply circuitry with infinite bandwidth which, pragmatically, will be rejected as an unreasonable presumption. Even worse, the Fourier transform might be thought to lend mathematical credence to the concept of non-causal filtering because an ideal rectangular transfer function can, in fact, be shown to produce a sinc-shaped impulse response starting at $t = -\infty$. After all, can you have it both ways? Surely either non-causal filtering is wrong or Fourier transforms make mistakes.

    To resolve these and other paradoxes we should, perhaps, recall that the basic transform method might best be thought of not as an engineering utility but *as an abstract mathematical mapping* between two arbitrary domains of convenience.

This viewpoint may be easier to appreciate if we write the Fourier transform pair in less problem-specific notation. Thus we might attempt to express transformation between α- and β-domains by writing $f(\alpha) \Leftrightarrow F(\beta)$. Since these domains are abstract, we may readily conceive of whole ranges of *definable functions of infinite extent* or infinitesimally short discontinuity which we should baulk at, were we asked to create them as aspects of 'reality'. One such, might be the delta function. No problems arise in its abstract definition. Place units of volt.seconds upon its area and time on its abscissa and the delta function purports to convey infinite energy!

If, then, we accept that the transform pair is, in essence, an abstract notion then no question of physical reality arises and establishing transform pairs becomes simply an exercise in pure mathematics. For example, the transform pair rect $(\alpha) \Leftrightarrow \text{sinc}(\beta)$ assumes the philosophical significance of a geometrical proposition and has as little, fundamentally, to do with the physical 'realities' of engineering as might a postulate abstracted from Euclid. Problems only arise when the engineer *presumes* equivalence between abstraction and reality and thereby ascribes dimension to that which is, in essence, dimensionless. Thus if 'rect(α)' is given units of **voltage** and α is given units of **time**, then 'sinc(β)' will necessarily have dimensions of **volt.seconds** and will be a spectral density and β will be a frequency measured in **reciprocal seconds**. Do not blame Fourier if you cannot *make* the rect-function, or if your channel will not support the bandwidth demanded by the sinc-spectrum. You put the units there; there was nothing wrong with his transform pairs. In fact, as long as this distinction between abstraction and reality is borne in mind, the tutorial value of 'idealised' functions is unimpaired and the extreme usefulness of transform procedures based upon cisoid orthogonality is reaffirmed.

Problems

1.1   Figure 1.3 illustrates the generation of a wave $A_0 \cos(\omega_0 t + \phi_0)$ as the sum of two phasors. Sketch in a similar manner the generation of the sinusoid $A_0 \sin(\omega_0 t + \phi_0)$ determining first its equivalent expression as a phasor sum.

1.2   For purposes of comparison, sketch the spectra of the two waves specified in question 1.1. Use spectral representations plotting amplitude and phase as functions of frequency and also representations plotting the in-phase and quadrature components as functions of frequency. In both cases take (as in section 1.1) the function $\cos(\omega t)$ as the basis for phase reference.

1.3   Sketch spectra corresponding to the following functions

   (a) $A_0 \cos(\omega_0 t) + B_0 \sin(\omega_0 t)$
   (b) $A_0 \cos(\omega_0 t) B_0 \sin(\omega_0 t)$
   (c) $A_0 \cos(\omega_0 t) B_0 \cos(\omega_0 t)$
   (d) $A_0 \sin(\omega_0 t) B_0 \sin(\omega_0 t)$

In what important particular does the spectrum of (b) differ from those of (c) and (d)?

1.4   Suppose that functions of period 2π: csq(x) and ssq(x) are defined over the interval $-\pi \leqslant x \leqslant +\pi$ such that

$$csq(x) = sgn\{\cos(x)\}$$
$$ssq(x) = sgn\{\sin(x)\}$$

where the sgn function is defined thus

$$sgn(y) = +1 \quad y > 0$$
$$= -1 \quad y < 0$$

Sketch these functions and note that they are square waves with the appearance of 'hard limited' sinusoids. Confirm that they both obey the definition of periodicity, equation 1.4.

1.5   The functions $csq(x)$ and $ssq(x)$ could be used as synthesis functions for the construction of any given periodic waveform, v. A typical synthesis equation would be

$$v(t) = \sum_{n=0}^{\infty} X_n \, csq(2\pi n f_1 t) + Y_n \, ssq(2\pi n f_1 t)$$

Comment on the possibility of forming an analysis equation to determine the coefficients X_n and Y_n. How is this operation affected by the orthogonality properties of the set of functions $csq(nx)$ and $ssq(nx)$? (*Hint* Are the functions in this set, in general, orthogonal? Can you find a single example of functions within the set which are not orthogonal?)

1.6   If the functions in the set $csq(nx)$ and $ssq(nx)$ are not orthogonal, does this raise the possibility that synthesis of a waveform may take place in more than one way? (The reader intrigued by speculations as to the possibility of spectral analysis based upon other functions than sinusoids may be interested to learn that a 'square-wave-like' set of functions—'Walsh functions'—can be used for just this purpose.[9])

1.7   By comparison with the result given in section 1.6 show that the function $csq(2\pi f_1 t)$ may be analysed to yield a Fourier series

$$v(t) = (4/\pi) \sum_{n=0}^{\infty} (-1)^n (2n+1)^{-1} \cos\{2\pi(2n+1)f_1 t\}$$

Show, by applying the shift theorem quoted in section 1.8.2 that the Fourier series corresponding to the function $ssq(2\pi f_1 t)$ is

$$v(t) = (4/\pi) \sum_{n=0}^{\infty} (2n+1)^{-1} \sin\{2\pi(2n+1)f_1 t\}$$

1.8   The differential of a sawtooth wave is a function of ssq form. Show that the Fourier series of the sawtooth is the integral of the Fourier series of the ssq function and is given by the relation

$$v(t) = -(2/f_1 \pi^2) \sum_{n=0}^{\infty} (2n+1)^{-2} \cos\{2\pi(2n+1)f_1 t\}$$

Comment on the linearity of the operation of integration. Why is linearity of importance in being able to deduce Fourier series of functions after the manner suggested by this question? (*Hint* The material in section 1.12 may throw some light on these latter considerations.)

1.9 Prove the amplitude and abscissa scaling theorems quoted in table 1.2. (*Hint* While the first of these theorems is not difficult to prove, the second is a little less obvious. Attempt to find the transform of $v(at)$ by substituting $\lambda = at$ and replacing t and dt in the transform integral as appropriate.)

1.10 Prove the shift theorem quoted in table 1.2. (*Hint* In this case, try substituting $\lambda = t + \tau$ and then, again, eliminating t and dt in the transform integral.)

1.11 Determine the transform of the staircase waveform used as an example in section 1.12 both from first principles and by means of the transform tables in appendix I. The two answers should, of course, be the same!

1.12 Verify the transform of the gaussian pulse given in appendix I working from first principles. (*Hint* Proceed by writing down the transform equation and combining the exponential terms. The argument of the exponential term will have the form $-(at^2 + bf)$, with a and b constants. Force this into the form $-(t + cf)^2$, with c a constant. Let $\lambda = (t + cf)$ and rewrite the integral. Integrate, noting that $\int_{-\infty}^{+\infty} \exp(-x^2)\,dx = \pi^{\frac{1}{2}}$.)

1.13 Determine from first principles the Fourier transform of the rectangular-pulsed sinusoid

$$v(t) = A\cos(2\pi f_0 t) \quad -T/2 \leqslant t \leqslant +T/2$$

checking your answer by referring to the results listed in appendix I.

1.14 Determine from first principles the Fourier transform of a unit-step function

$$u(t) = 1 \quad t \geqslant 0$$
$$= 0 \quad t < 0$$

Does this function implicitly obey the requirements for transformability?

(*Hint* Start by obtaining the transform of a pulse for which the Dirichlet conditions, section 1.3, for $T \rightarrow \infty$, are obeyed, such as $u(t)\exp(-at)$, a positive, and let $a \rightarrow 0$, determining the transform of $u(t)$ in the limit.)

1.15 Which of the following waveforms exhibits a power spectrum, and which an energy spectrum, and why?

(a) The pulsed sinewave defined in question 1.13.
(b) White gaussian noise.
(c) A voltage impulse. (*Hint* Work from first principles starting with a narrow rectangular pulse whose height is inversely proportional to its width.)
(d) A continuous sinusoid

$$v(t) = A\cos(2\pi f_0 t) \quad \text{all } t$$

(e) A waveform composed of the sum of the continuous sinusoid defined in (d) above and the pulsed sinewave defined in (a) above.
(f) A waveform composed of the sum of a continuous sinusoid and white gaussian noise.

1.16   Can you obtain a measure of the power in a white gaussian noisewave? Can such a waveform exist in real life? What about the continuous sinusoid, considered in the same manner?

1.17   For the pulsed sinusoid defined in question 1.13 what is the effect on the energy spectrum of increasing

    (a) the pulse width T
    (b) the pulse amplitude A
    (c) the frequency of the tone burst, f_0

Sketch your answer carefully, paying attention to detail, such as the effect on points where the energy spectrum is zero valued, or has a maximum.

1.18   What, dimensionally, is the difference between an energy spectrum and a power spectrum? Do these two functions have the dimensions of power and energy respectively? Suggest two finite-energy functions and two finite-power functions other than those listed in question 1.15 above.

1.19   For the pulsed sinusoid of question 1.13, show, by referring to the results presented in appendix II (Integral Relationships), that the area beneath the spectrum remains invariant if T is increased while A remains constant. Hence show that the Fourier transform of the sinusoid

$$v(t) = A \cos(2\pi f_0 t) \quad \text{all } t$$

is

$$V(f) = (A/2)\{\delta(f+f_0)+\delta(f-f_0)\}$$

1.20   A periodic wave has the general spectrum

$$V(f) = \sum_{n=-\infty}^{+\infty} V_n\, \delta(f-f_n)$$

where

$$f_{-n} = -f_{+n}$$

Answer the following questions.

    (a) What is V_n, how is it obtained and in what units is it measured, if $v(t)$ is measured in volts?
    (b) What is $\delta(f-f_n)$ and what is its significance?
    (c) In what units is $V(f)$ measured? The units of $V(f)$ and those of V_n are different. How do you explain this difference, and what part does $\delta(f-f_n)$ play in keeping the equation dimensionally correct?

1.21   Show that, if $v(t)$ is real, and if we write

$$V(f) = X(f) + j\,Y(f)$$

then

$$X(f) = \int_{-\infty}^{+\infty} v(t)\cos(2\pi ft)\, \mathrm{d}t$$

$$Y(f) = -\int_{-\infty}^{+\infty} v(t)\sin(2\pi ft)\, \mathrm{d}t$$

Show that $X(f)$ is an even function and $Y(f)$ an odd function of frequency. Comment on the statement made above '... $v(t)$ is real...'.

1.22   Parseval's theorem states that

$$\int_{-\infty}^{+\infty} \{v(t)\}^2 \, dt = \int_{-\infty}^{+\infty} |V(f)|^2 \, df$$

Taking as your example a rectangular pulse, demonstrate the validity of this theorem. (*Hint* One of the results in appendix II (Integral Relationships) may be of assistance in answering this question.)

1.23   If a signal consists of sinusoidal components thus

$$v(t) = \sum_k A_k \cos(2\pi f_k t + \phi_k)$$

show that its mean square value is given by the expression

$$\frac{1}{2} \sum_k A_k^2$$

How does this result relate to Parseval's theorem, quoted in question 1.22?

1.24   The performance of many filters is usefully characterised by an 'impulse response'. However, the impulse is a strictly unrealisable entity. One reason for its being unrealisable is that it is an infinitely high voltage-spike. A second reason is connected with its energy content. What is this second reason?

Because we cannot apply impulses to determine experimentally the response of filters, we often turn to 'step-response' testing. The input is the unit step, $u(t)$, defined in question 1.14. How is the step response of a linear filter related to the impulse response? Why is it important that the filter be *linear*?

1.25   A filter has a step response

$$v(t) = \exp(-6284t)$$

Sketch this response and determine and sketch the impulse response. What kind of filter does this step response characterise and what is its cut-off frequency.

1.26   Given the power spectrum of the continuous sinusoid

$$v(t) = A \cos(2\pi f_0 t) \quad \text{all } t$$

what will be the power spectrum of the continuous sinusoid

$$v(t) = A \sin(2\pi f_0 t) \quad \text{all } t$$

and what, by deduction, will be its autocorrelation function. (*Hint* Does a power spectrum or autocorrelation function convey phase information? Is either quantity uniquely related to a given time function, $v(t)$?)

2 The Information Source and Communication Channel

In its most basic form, a communication system consists of an information source and an information sink connected by a channel. Often, the information-bearing waveform is of a nature which makes it incompatible with effective transmission through a given channel. Then the complementary operations of modulation and demodulation are invoked to yield a signal that is compatible with effective transmission.

Both the information source and the channel present constraints on the design of the overall communication system. Ideally, by carefully selecting the modulation method, we should be able to maximise the rate of information-transfer per unit of channel bandwidth, subject to whatever signal corruption is encountered in the channel. Unfortunately it must be admitted that such a maximisation operation is simply not possible, being as yet beyond our mathematical and technological capability. Certainly attempts have been made to place the theory of communication on a formal mathematical footing. For example, much effort has been devoted to the development of information theory and modulation theory but these disciplines have made relatively little impact on the design of real communication systems.

It is because of this situation that advances in communication system design have retained a closer correspondence to the state of electronics technology at large, rather than to far-reaching theoretical precedent. In short, it is often possible to justify and refine a system design by applying theoretical methods. It has rarely been the case that theory has predicted a major area of development.

In this chapter we shall investigate the nature and properties of information waveforms, the communication channel and the operation of modulation.

2.1 The Primary Information Source

A convenient idealised model of the primary information source in a communication system consists of a module delivering a random, or partially

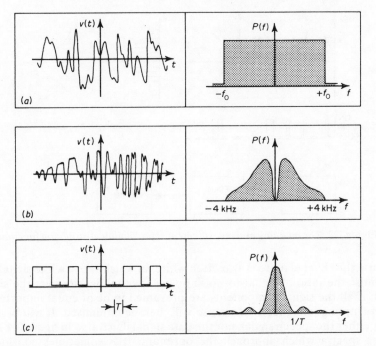

Figure 2.1 Information waveforms and their spectra. (a) White noise-like signal; (b) speech signal; (c) random digital-data waveform

random waveform of infinite duration and finite mean power. We cannot realise such a source, if only because any experimental or practical system must deliver a waveform of finite duration. None the less, the model is of value in that it closely approximates all the practical information sources in which we shall be interested.

Since such a model involves a signal which is of finite mean power, the energy that it is capable of delivering to a load is infinite. Consequently, the concept of *power spectral density*, $P(f)$, must be applied as a method of characterising the band occupancy of the output waveform. Because the mean power of the signal must be finite, it follows that $P(f)$ must be band-limited. Normally we find that $P(f)$ is *baseband* in nature, with most of the signal power concentrated at relatively low frequencies. That is

$$P(f) \to 0 \quad \text{as} \quad f \to \infty$$

Figure 2.1 illustrates several typical information waveshapes, together with their power spectral densities. Both the noise-like signal and the speech waveform are classified as analogue processes, because their waveforms can take on any amplitude value. In contrast, the data waveform is typical of digital processes, in that only two amplitude levels corresponding to the binary numbers 0 and 1 are permitted. Data waveforms are produced by computing and telegraphy systems as primary information-bearing signals.

It is generally considered that a channel is most economically used when the information waveform has a *white* or *uniform* power spectral density. This is

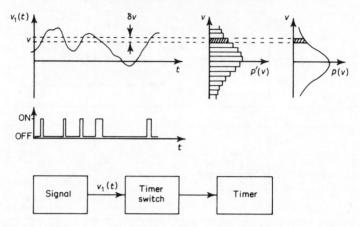

Figure 2.2 *The meaning and measurement of probability-distribution functions*

because the channel noise is also often white, in which case a white signal will maximise the ratio of signal-to-noise power spectral density over the signal band. If all the signal components are presumed to be of equal importance, the corrupting influence of the noise will then be minimised. It will be seen that neither the speech signal, nor the data signal illustrated in figure 2.1 have power spectra which approach the optimum. It is sometimes considered worthwhile to pass the information-bearing waveform through a filter designed to 'whiten' the signal spectrum before transmission, thereby improving the signal-to-noise ratio after detection.

It is worth noting that, although the power spectrum provides a useful means of categorising signals, it cannot be used uniquely to identify any given signal: waveforms of radically different superficial appearance may all have identical power spectra. This is because, in assessing the power spectrum of a signal, either theoretically or by experiment, phase information is lost.

Another very useful method of characterising a signal which we have not so far considered is the amplitude *probability-distribution function*, PDF; this quantity we denote $p(v)$. The PDF is a measure of the probability that a waveform $v_1(t)$ lies between voltage levels v and $v + \delta v$ when δv tends to zero. Its nature may be understood by considering the hypothetical PDF measuring system illustrated in figure 2.2. As the diagram shows, an electronic timer measures the length of time during which the source waveform $v_1(t)$ lies between voltages v and $v + \delta v$. From this measurement, the ratio of 'on' to 'off' time of the timer switch can be calculated. This ratio is the probability that the waveform $v_1(t)$ lies between the prescribed voltage levels. By repeating the experiment for many different values of v, a histogram which approximates to $p(v)$ may be constructed. The accuracy of the approximation improves as the voltage level separation decreases, although too small a separation would lead to a prohibitively lengthy experiment and, because of the presence of noise within the measuring system, might lead to increased experimental inaccuracy as δv approached the noise level.

The amplitude PDF of a waveform, it must be stressed, is *not* related to the power spectral density or to the Fourier transform of that waveform.

Normally we think of a noise-like signal, such as is shown in figure 2.1, as conveying the greatest amount of information. Noise-like waveforms are characterised by an amplitude PDF of a special kind, known as a *gaussian distribution*. The gaussian distribution is defined thus

$$p(v) = (2\pi p_a)^{-\frac{1}{2}} \exp(-v^2/2p_a) \tag{2.1}$$

where p_a is the average power (strictly the mean square voltage) in the noise-like signal. This distribution is illustrated in figure 2.3.

On an intuitive basis, it is not surprising that the gaussian distribution typifies both highly informational analogue signals and also highly corrupting noisewaves. A signal with a high information content cannot be predictable. Conversely, a predictable waveform is non-informational. It is largely because of this inherent 'randomness' (to the recipient, if not to the sender) that the analogue signal often matches so well to the gaussian PDF.

The gaussian distribution is often encountered in nature, usually as the statistical description of a variable which results from the interaction of many independent events. An example is afforded by the process of generation of 'thermal noise', which we shall discuss in greater detail in the next section. This waveform originates in the agitation of electrons by thermally excited atoms in a resistor. Many electrons, all moving independently and randomly, produce across the resistor a small noisewave with gaussian statistics.

Actually, a formal proof of the hypothesis that a highly informational signal must have gaussian statistics is possible. The proof places one constraint on the waveform, however, requiring that it be *unbounded*. This simply means that $v(t)$ must be able to accept all values in the range

$$-\infty \leqslant v \leqslant +\infty$$

Just as we think of an unbounded signal as having the greatest informational capacity when its distribution is gaussian, so also we think of an unbounded gaussian noisewave as offering the greatest corrupting influence,

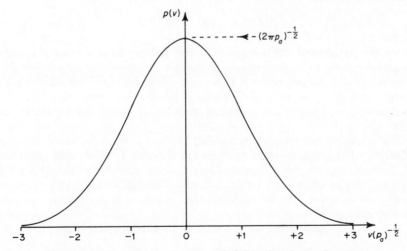

Figure 2.3 *Normalised gaussian probability-distribution function*

at least for analogue, as opposed to digital, signals. Certainly it is reasonable that the 'worst-case' noise would have a very similar appearance to the signal it was to corrupt, simply because it would then be very difficult to tell them apart.

Other kinds of distribution function occur from time to time in the study of communication systems. We shall not find it necessary to delve very deeply into the formal mathematics of probability theory, even though this subject is of great importance to the communication engineer in permitting him to predict noise performance. Should the reader require further information on this subject, several of the texts[1,2,13] listed in the bibliography will supply it.

2.2　The General Properties of Communication Channels

Just as there are many types of information signal, all with different characteristics, so there are many different types of channel. We shall take the channel to include everything following the 'modulator', which prepares the information signal for transmission, and preceding the 'demodulator' or 'detector', which reconstitutes it. Thus it may include, in addition to the physical medium which actually conveys the signal, transmitter and receiver hardware which can introduce additional signal impairments. The 'best' channel, from our point of view, would be linear in its voltage-transfer characteristic, so that an input voltage v_1 would be related to an output voltage, v_2, according to a law

$$v_2 = kv_1 \tag{2.2}$$

Additionally, it should produce no attenuation distortion or phase distortion of the signal spectrum. That is, with a channel transfer characteristic

$$\frac{V_2(f)}{V_1(f)} = A(f)\exp\{j\phi(f)\} \tag{2.3}$$

we should hope that

$$A(f) = 1 \quad \text{and} \quad \phi(f) = 0$$

within the signal band. As it happens, none of these characteristics of the ideal channel are likely to be encountered in practice. Often non-linearity derives from those stages of signal processing in a receiving equipment which precede the actual operation of detection. Attenuation and phase distortion may result both from the receiving equipment and from the medium separating the transmitter and receiver.

The effect of non-linearity is twofold. It may, obviously, cause *amplitude distortion* of the signals passed through the channel. Typically this might take the form of clipping (amplitude limiting) of the transmitted signal. This can be quite a serious problem when certain kinds of communication system are employed, notably those which rely on amplitude fluctuations of a carrier wave to convey the information.

A second problem arises when a number of different signals are present in a non-linear channel. Since the non-linear transfer characteristic can be expanded as a power series, it generates at its output products of the input signal components. These products give rise to a phenomenon known as *cross-modulation*, because the product theorem, section 1.2.2, may be applied to yield component sum- and difference-frequencies. These new spectral components overlap the transmitted spectral components and cannot be removed by filtering.

Another natural and unavoidable phenomenon that we have to contend with in the design of a communication system is channel noise. Noise is usually a problem because it places a lower limit on the signal power inserted into the channel. We usually prefer not to utilise a higher transmitter power than is absolutely necessary because the higher the power the more costly is the transmitter equipment. As a result, much effort has been devoted to the design of systems with some inherent noise immunity.

The sources of noise are many and varied. Some of the most important sources of electromagnetic noise which arise outside the electronic parts of a communication system, and are therefore beyond control, are solar and stellar radiation, lightning discharge and other atmospherics and arcing contacts in electrical machinery. Within the electronic parts of the communication system we find noise sources which may, to a certain extent, be controllable. Appendix III indicates how the careful choice of circuitry and selection of components can minimise the contribution of thermal, shot and other noise occurring within the electronic system. Thermal noise occurs because electrons are moved within a metallic resistance of value $R\,\Omega$ by the random thermal agitation of atoms. Its mean square value at temperature T Kelvin, and over a single-sided bandwidth B Hz is given by

$$\langle v^2 \rangle = 4kTBR$$

Shot noise is encountered in amplifying devices and is caused by the discrete nature of electron flow and other charge-transfer processes. The current does not behave as a continuous fluid, but as a stream of particles with known statistical properties. The mean square random perturbation caused by shot noise, given a mean current flow I is

$$\langle i^2 \rangle = 2IeB$$

In these expressions, k is Boltzmann's constant ($\cong 1.38 \times 10^{-23}$ J K^{-1}) and e is the charge on an electron ($\cong 1.6 \times 10^{-19}$ C).

Both thermal and shot noise exhibit a power spectral density which is white to frequencies of hundreds of megahertz and present a gaussian-amplitude probability-distribution function. Impulsive noise is also spectrally white, but is of non-gaussian distribution. It is extremely difficult to define statistically, and its effects on a given communication system can usually be determined only by means of 'field trials'. Unfortunately it is the most commonly encountered type of noise in line communication systems within the switched telephone-network and is particularly deleterious to digital communication systems.

In the next sections of this chapter we shall discuss the nature of the propagation medium itself. We shall restrict our attention to electromagnetic propagation through the atmosphere and through free space, guided wave propagation along transmission lines and optical communication by means of light-guides (fibre-optic cables). Since these media sustain the bulk of information transfer, we shall not consider the various other experimental media (taken in the context of long-haul communication applications) such as waveguide or acoustic systems.

One serious problem which our discussion of baseband signal sources and channels brings to light is the incompatibility of the signal with the concept of electromagnetic propagation. By this we infer that the baseband signal must be transmitted across free space and one way of achieving this is to employ electromagnetic propagation. Unfortunately, very low frequency signals do not propagate well, and also require extremely large antennae systems. To alleviate this problem we employ the techniques of modulation, which serve to relocate the signal spectrum at a high frequency where the problems of achieving propagation are not so great.

2.3   Electromagnetic Propagation Through the Atmosphere[16]

In considering the propagation of radio waves through the atmosphere, we shall examine only the gross behaviour of the medium. Both radio waves and light are electromagnetic wave motions, although the latter has much the higher frequency. Consequently, they share the same basic properties of straight-line propagation, reflection, refraction, diffraction and scattering. The spatial scale on which these phenomena take place is, however, different by many orders of magnitude.

For our purposes, the atmosphere may be regarded as being divided into two principal regions of interest. These are the troposphere, the region closest to the earth's surface and extending to a height of about 10 km and the ionosphere, lying above the troposphere and extending from about 50 km to 500 km.

Depending on the nature and location of the antennae and the frequency of the signal a variety of different propagation modes can exist for the electromagnetic transmission of information through the atmosphere, of which the most important are

(1) line-of-sight propagation
(2) ground- or surface-wave diffraction
(3) ionospheric reflection
(4) forward scattering

Line-of-sight propagation occurs at all frequencies whenever the transmitter and receiver antennae are so located as to be visible, one from the other. This mode assumes its greatest importance at frequencies in excess of 30 MHz, however, since then the ionosphere presents a 'window' to electromagnetic radiation and will not sustain a long-range reflected wave.

For frequencies up to about 10 GHz, attenuation is low, so that relatively small transmitters can be conveniently employed to cover ranges of the order of tens of kilometres. This has the attendant advantage that geographical separation may be used to permit different transmitters to operate on the same frequency allocation, thereby extending the usage of the electromagnetic spectrum very considerably.

At about 10 GHz, absorption of energy from the propagated wave rises rapidly because of the spin resonance of water molecules present in the atmosphere. This causes signal attenuation and can present problems in the transmission of signals at frequencies in excess of 10 GHz. Since frequencies of the order of 10 to 50 GHz are employed in 'pole hop' line-of-sight microwave relays, deep fading caused by rainstorms passing between antennae can give rise to troublesome reception conditions. At even higher frequencies absorption takes place because of other molecular resonances.

The presence of rainstorms in the vicinity of line-of-sight links can lead to another interesting effect if the signal frequency is sufficiently high. In the super high frequency region (SHF—3 to 30 GHz) and above the refraction of waves within the body of the rainstorm can be quite pronounced. This can lead to a situation in which components of the received wave have travelled along paths of different length, being bent towards the receiver antennae within the rainstorm. Because the received signal-component path lengths differ, so also do the phases of the sinusoidal components contained therein. When added together these components may, because of the relative phase differences involved, sum destructively, resulting in a partial cancellation of the received signal. This effect is known as multipath transmission and, as far as line-of-sight systems are concerned, may be minimised by employing two parallel paths separated by a suitable geographical distance. Since heavy rainstorms in temperate climates are usually very localised, it is improbable that both links will be out of service simultaneously.

The surface-wave mode is caused by the diffraction of electromagnetic waves around the surface of the earth. In this respect the mode of propagation is not dissimilar to the effect whereby we hear acoustic waves around corners. We cannot see the sound source because the wavelength of light is too small to permit diffraction to the degree which would be required. The surface-wave mode will usefully sustain information transfer at frequencies below 1.5 MHz although long-range transmission is usually restricted to frequencies below 500 kHz. Long-range propagation in the region above 500 kHz is usually achieved by making use of ionospheric reflection.

Reflection occurs in the ionosphere because of the presence of ionised molecules. The ionisation is caused by a variety of natural radiations of which the most important are solar emissions. Because the molecular density of the ionosphere is low, recombination of the ions takes place slowly. Consequently the ionosphere has, as a whole, conductive properties. Furthermore the effective 'refractive index' of the medium is not uniform. At very low levels in the ionosphere, where the molecular density is high and recombination rapid, the conductivity is relatively low. The same is true of the very high regions, because the molecular density is so low that very few molecules exist to be ionised. An oblique radio wave, entering the ionosphere, may be diffracted in such a manner that it is bent back into the lower atmosphere. As it happens the amount of bending decreases with increasing signal frequency, so that a frequency will be encountered, depending on the angle of propagation, at which the signal is not reflected in this way. In general, ionospheric reflection is only useful at frequencies within the high frequency band (HF—3 to

30 MHz). Spurious physical conditions may permit operation at frequencies up to 50 MHz, although such a condition of operation is unreliable, being prone to deep fading.

One significant advantage of ionospheric reflection is the possibility of obtaining propagation beyond the visual horizon at frequencies well in excess of the upper range of ground-wave propagation. This may be accomplished by means of a single 'hop' from transmitter to receiver, or by 'multiple hops' resulting from reflection of the downward signal from the earth's surface, which is a conductor, albeit rather a poor one. The range of a transmitter thus tends to be governed by the height of the reflecting ionospheric layers. In general the high radiation levels from the sun during daylight produce intense ionisation right through the ionospheric region. At night a high ionised layer exists, so that long-distance propagation takes place most readily after dark.

At frequencies between about 100 MHz and 10 GHz, another technique may be employed, particularly in terrain which prohibits the installation of the many antennae needed for normal line-of-sight working. This technique is known as tropospheric-scatter propagation and makes use of an effect whereby over-the-horizon propagation may be obtained by forward scattering in the troposphere. It is usually necessary to design the transmitter antennae to radiate a highly directional, very powerful signal. The receiver antennae must also be highly directional and, because troposcatter systems are prone to multipath propagation and hence deep fading, the receiver organisation may embody the principle of 'diversity'.

Diversity is the duplication of receiver (and sometimes also transmitter) hardware in much the same manner as was described above, as a means of compensating for multipath propagation in line-of-sight links. One technique, known as space-diversity detection, requires that two or more antennae be supplied at the receiving station. These antennae are separated by distances of several hundred metres, so that the signals received by each are largely uncorrelated, in so far as transmission paths and hence depth of fade are concerned. The receiver outputs are then averaged to yield a signal with a statistically reduced depth of fade.

Another diversity technique is to separate the transmitted information on two carriers of different frequency and then to receive these carriers on antennae at nominally the same location. This method is known as frequency diversity.

A method of obtaining high-frequency long-distance communication which has assumed great importance during the past decade is the use of communication satellites. The first communication satellites were passive in nature: large metallised balloons which were allowed to inflate when in orbit around the earth. Highly directional antennae were then used to bounce signals off the surface of the balloon. The reflected signals were detected by receivers with high-gain low-noise antennae. Current practice is to employ active satellites which act in much the same manner as microwave relay stations. These employ solar-cell batteries to provide a power source. Retransmission is always at a different frequency to reception by the satellite.

Since they can be designed to handle signals in the ultra high frequency (UHF—300 MHz to 3 GHz) and SHF bands, they are potentially capable of handling a considerable quantity of information and already form a viable alternative to submarine cable for intercontinental telephone and television communication.

2.4   The Transmission Line as a Communication Medium

Next, we examine the properties of transmission lines as they affect the communication of information. In so doing, we shall restrict our attention only to those features of the transmission line that will be of direct concern to us. The subject of transmission lines is a study in itself of such breadth as to defy inclusion in a single chapter.

Transmission lines act to convey electromagnetic energy, the energy fields being guided by and localised in the vicinity of the line. Furthermore, they always involve the use of two conductors connecting source to load. Since this is so they can, in principle at least, handle baseband signals. In practice, a.c. coupling of other circuits within the line system may eliminate or distort low-frequency signal components, but this is the result of system organisation and design rather than a fundamental physical limitation of the line itself. In this respect, transmission lines differ from waveguides, in which d.c. levels cannot be sustained, since there is no return conductor. For waveguides, both upper and lower frequency limits exist.

Both waveguides and transmission lines operate, none the less, by setting up guided electromagnetic waves. Performance may be described for both these systems by the application of Maxwell's equations governing electromagnetic wave motion. Indeed this is the usual method of analysing waveguide operation. Transmission lines are most often analysed by applying circuit theory methods, and it is this approach which we shall adopt, since it yields convenient line transfer-functions with predictable effects on different signals and modulations. We shall not attempt to derive similar results for waveguide systems. Most waveguides operate at frequencies greatly in excess of the propagated carrier bandwidths so that their performance may be characterised as typically narrow-band in nature, giving rise to little attenuation within the signal band. Thus the waveguide operates very much as an ideal channel, as far as modulated sinusoidal carriers are concerned.

The physical structure of transmission lines plays an important role in determining their electrical properties. For example, on 'local' telephone circuits—those which connect the subscriber to his local exchange—it is frequently the case that suspended open-wire pairs are used. The wire is either copper, copper-clad steel or aluminium alloy and is insulated from the supporting poles by ceramic bobbins. The wire-pair separation is usually about twelve inches. Typically such a circuit will exhibit the following electrical properties

Capacitance between conductors	$0.01~\mu F~mile^{-1}$
Conductor resistance	$3–10~\Omega~mile^{-1}$
Leakage conductance between conductors	$1~\mu mho~mile^{-1}$
Inductance	$3~mH~mile^{-1}$

These parameters, which are known as the *primary electrical parameters*, will vary slightly with prevailing weather conditions. Consequently, for long-distance telephone connections, 'trunk' circuits connecting exchanges, bunched twisted-conductor pairs are employed. Here the wires are individually insulated with paper or polyethylene and are twisted together to reduce crosstalk between pairs. Many such wire-pairs are bunched together and the bunch itself is sheathed in plastics. A layer of steel wire or tape armouring may be laid onto this first plastics sheath to provide resistance to mechanical damage, the armouring being itself sheathed with a further layer of plastics. Typical primary parameters for such cable are

Capacitance between conductors	$0.1\ \mu F\ mile^{-1}$
Conductor resistance	$30-300\ \Omega\ mile^{-1}$
Leakage conductance between conductors	$0.1-100\ \mu mho\ mile^{-1}$
Inductance	$1\ mH\ mile^{-1}$

For applications requiring extremely wide bandwidth, the considerably more expensive coaxial cable is used. Here, the two conductors consist of a central copper core surrounded by a copper sheath separated from it by a dielectric. The dielectric may be solid polyethylene or air. In the latter event, the correct spacing between the sheath and the central core is maintained by means of thin polyethylene discs at intervals of a few centimetres. The sheath of copper may be woven from fine wire strands. This is the usual method of construction if a solid dielectric is employed. If an air dielectric is used, an outer conductor of copper tape is preferred. The entire assembly is then sheathed in plastics for both electrical and mechanical protection.

Depending on the nature of the excitation and the medium in which the wave is to propagate, guided-wave structures may sustain a number of different 'modes' of oscillation. The mode concept may be aided by the following simple analogy. A plucked string will normally vibrate at its natural frequency, with a node at each end; this is the principle 'mode' of oscillation. If the string is damped at its midpoint, at the instant at which it is plucked and is then allowed to vibrate freely, the first harmonic of the natural frequency will be set up. This is a second 'mode' of oscillation. Many other modes may also be set up, providing only that the frequency of oscillation which is initiated is compatible with the existence of nodes at the ends of the string.

Waveguides are usually capable of sustaining a great number of modes of oscillation and care is usually required to ensure that they only operate in their 'dominant mode'. Transmission lines, on the other hand, usually only enter higher modes of oscillation when excited at extremely high frequencies, so that non-dominant mode formation presents no problems.

One important difference between waveguides and transmission lines lies in their frequency of operation. In the main, waveguides are used to connect UHF and SHF antennae to other system units. As yet they are not employed in long-haul communications applications, although there is interest in the use of circular waveguides in extremely high-capacity communication links. Coaxial cables are employed at rather lower frequencies, extending typically to tens or hundreds of megahertz.

2.5 The Physics of Line Operation

The physical structure of a transmission line suggests that the line will possess certain electrical properties. It is obvious, for example, that the line will exhibit a resistance to current flow. Likewise, because the medium separating the two conductors is never a perfect dielectric, it will also exhibit some conductance, permitting a current leak to occur between the line conductors. Again, it is fairly obvious from the physical nature of the line that a capacitance will exist between the conductors. Finally, as with any conducting wire, each cable in the line pair will exhibit self-inductance.

Although we may associate these electrical properties with the transmission line, the line itself differs from a normal electrical circuit in one very important respect. That is, its electrical properties are *distributed* in nature. This means that we cannot think of the transmission line as a simple *LCR* circuit with a transfer function specified by the methods described in chapter 1. However, we can consider an infinitesimally short section of the line in this manner and by applying the methods of differential calculus we may determine transfer characteristics which describe the attenuation and phase shift of the line in exactly the same manner as the transfer function of a filter.

The transfer function of the transmission line, in contrast to that of the lumped-component filter must be specified in terms of one additional parameter, the length of the line from the source to the point of inspection. To aid our calculations, and to comply with standard practice, we further specify the fundamental electrical properties of the line in terms of impedances per unit length.

Figure 2.4 shows how an infinitesimally short section of the transmission line may be represented by means of lumped components. Given that the length of the line so represented, δx, does tend to zero, it follows that the

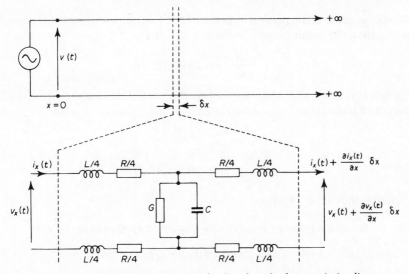

Figure 2.4 *The equivalent circuit of a short length of transmission line*

leakage current between the conductors will be sufficiently small that it can be neglected for loop voltage calculations so that

$$v_x(t) = \left[L \frac{\partial i_x(t)}{\partial t} + R i_x(t) \right] \delta x + v_x(t) + \frac{\partial v_x(t)}{\partial x} \delta x$$

In a similar manner the voltage drop along this section of the line will be negligible in the calculation of node currents, so that

$$i_x(t) = \left[C \frac{\partial v_x(t)}{\partial t} + G v_x(t) \right] \delta x + i_x(t) + \frac{\partial i_x(t)}{\partial x} \delta x$$

Simplifying, we find that

$$L \frac{\partial i_x(t)}{\partial t} + R i_x(t) = - \frac{\partial v_x(t)}{\partial x} \tag{2.4}$$

$$C \frac{\partial v_x(t)}{\partial t} + G v_x(t) = - \frac{\partial i_x(t)}{\partial x} \tag{2.5}$$

We require a differential equation in $v_x(t)$ in order to establish a transfer function in $V_x(f)$. This we may obtain by differentiating these equations and substituting appropriately. It is a straightforward exercise in partial differentiation to obtain the result

$$C \frac{\partial^2 v_x(t)}{\partial t^2} + G \frac{\partial v_x(t)}{\partial t} = \frac{1}{L} \frac{\partial^2 v_x(t)}{\partial x^2} + \frac{R}{L} \frac{\partial i_x(t)}{\partial x}$$

Further substitution of the second equation given above eliminates the extreme right-hand term

$$\frac{\partial^2 v_x(t)}{\partial x^2} = LC \frac{\partial^2 v_x(t)}{\partial t^2} + (RC + LG) \frac{\partial v_x(t)}{\partial t} + RG v_x(t)$$

We may express this equation in terms of the Fourier transform $V_x(f)$ of $v_x(t)$ by recalling the result quoted in table 1.2, namely

$$\frac{dv(t)}{dt} \leftrightarrow 2\pi j f V(f)$$

this result is still valid when applied to the partial derivatives of $v_x(t)$ with respect to time. Thus

$$\frac{\partial v_x(t)}{\partial t} \leftrightarrow 2\pi j f V_x(f)$$

$$\frac{\partial^2 v_x(t)}{\partial t^2} \leftrightarrow (2\pi j f)^2 V_x(f)$$

It follows that we may write

$$\frac{\partial^2 V_x(f)}{\partial x^2} = (2\pi j f)^2 LC V_x(f) + 2\pi j f (RC + LG) V_x(f) + RG V_x(f)$$

$$= (R + 2\pi j f L)(G + 2\pi j f C) V_x(f)$$

If for convenience we let

$$(R + 2\pi j f L)(G + 2\pi j f C) = \gamma^2 \tag{2.6}$$

we then have a simple second-order differential equation in x

$$\frac{\partial^2 V_x(f)}{\partial x^2} = \gamma^2 V_x(f)$$

which has a general solution

$$V_x(f) = A(f)\exp(-\gamma x) + B(f)\exp(+\gamma x)$$

where $A(f)$ and $B(f)$ are parameters determined from the boundary conditions. We know that, as $x \to \infty$, $V_x(f) \to 0$, so that $B(f)$ must be zero. Hence

$$V_x(f) = A(f)\exp(-\gamma x)$$

$A(f)$ we may find simply by inserting the condition $x = 0$, so that

$$V_0(f) = A(f)\exp(0) = A(f)$$

Thus the general solution for the transmission line is

$$V_x(f) = V_0(f)\exp(-\gamma x)$$

which yields a transfer function

$$H_x(f) = \frac{V_x(f)}{V_0(f)}$$

$$= \exp(-\gamma x) \tag{2.7}$$

Returning to equation 2.6, we find on expansion that

$$\left.\begin{array}{ll} \gamma = \alpha + j\beta & f > 0 \\ \quad = \alpha - j\beta & f < 0 \end{array}\right\} \tag{2.8}$$

where

$$\alpha = \left[\frac{1}{2}\left[\{(R^2 + 4\pi^2 f^2 L^2)(G^2 + 4\pi^2 f^2 C^2)\}^{\frac{1}{2}} + (RG - 4\pi^2 f^2 LC)\right]\right]^{\frac{1}{2}} \tag{2.9}$$

= attenuation per unit length of the transmission line
   expressed in nepers (one neper equals 8.686 decibels)

and

$$\beta = \left[\frac{1}{2}\left[\{(R^2 + 4\pi^2 f^2 L^2)(G^2 + 4\pi^2 f^2 C^2)\}^{\frac{1}{2}} - (RG - 4\pi^2 f^2 LC)\right]\right]^{\frac{1}{2}} \tag{2.10}$$

= phase shift per unit length of the transmission line measured in radians

These expressions are somewhat cumbersome. We shall see in the next five sections how they may be simplified to describe the performance of transmission lines operating under typical conditions.

2.6 The Terminated Line

In the previous section we analysed what was, effectively, a semi-infinite line. The line was assumed to be of infinite length from the source in the direction of positive x, and this assumption was invoked when we deduced that the boundary condition $B(f)$ was zero as the result of progressive energy drain as the voltage waveform passed along the line. Naturally, no real line can be

semi-infinite. It must be terminated at some point in a load, and the load will
have some impedance, Z. In fact, the equations for the semi-infinite line hold
for a terminated line, provided the terminating impedance is selected with
care. Restating equation 2.4

$$-\frac{\partial v_x(t)}{\partial x} = Ri_x(t) + L\frac{\partial i_x(t)}{\partial t}$$

Applying the Fourier transform

$$-\frac{\partial V_x(f)}{\partial x} = (R + 2\pi jfL)I_x(f)$$

But

$$V_x(f) = V_0(f)\exp(-\gamma x)$$

so that

$$\frac{\partial V_x(f)}{\partial x} = -\gamma V_0(f)\exp(-\gamma x)$$
$$= -\gamma V_x(f)$$

and hence

$$\gamma V_x(f) = (R + 2\pi jfL)I_x(f)$$

so that

$$\frac{V_x(f)}{I_x(f)} = \frac{R + 2\pi jfL}{\gamma}$$
$$= \left(\frac{R + 2\pi jfL}{G + 2\pi jfC}\right)^{\frac{1}{2}} \tag{2.11}$$

This result gives us the impedance of the line at any point x. Note that its
value is independent of x and consequently provides a secondary line constant
which we denote Z_0 and refer to as the *characteristic impedance*. If we
terminate the line at any point in its characteristic impedance, then, to signals
progressing along the line, no discontinuity will exist at the point of termination and the line will behave exactly as a semi-infinite line at all points up to
the load location. Energy which would have been dissipated in the distributed
resistance and conductance of the semi-infinite line will now be dissipated by
the resistive component in the terminating impedance. The voltage across this
impedance and the current passing through it will be exactly the voltage $v_x(t)$
and the current $i_x(t)$ which would have been present at the same point on a
semi-infinite line.

If the line is not terminated by a load of value equal to the characteristic
impedance, reflections are set up which travel back down the line to the
source. If the source impedance is also not equal to the characteristic
impedance, further reflections will occur, contaminating the propagated
signal very severely. We shall only consider the performance of lines which
are correctly matched to both source and load. This is standard practice in
telecommunication engineering and wherever possible is particularly closely
adhered to for line communication systems.

The reader might imagine that matching with a complex impedance Z_0 as
given by equation 2.11 would be extremely difficult. In general this would
indeed be true, but normal operating conditions, as we shall see, result in the
characteristic impedance becoming predominantly resistive with an easily
determined value.

2.7 The 'Lossless' Line

If the transmission line has no energy-dissipation components, so that $R = G = 0$, then it is easily shown from equations 2.9 and 2.10 that $\alpha = 0$ and $\beta = 2\pi f(LC)^{\frac{1}{2}}$. Consequently, the line transfer-function is

$$H_x(f) = \exp(-2\pi jfx(LC)^{\frac{1}{2}})$$

As we have seen in section 1.17.7, such a transfer function imposes only a delay on the waveform, so that

$$v_x(t) = v_0(t - t_g x)$$

where

$$t_g = (LC)^{\frac{1}{2}} \quad \text{s distance unit}^{-1}$$

We refer to t_g as the *group delay*. It is related to the velocity of propagation of the signal

$$u_g = t_g^{-1} \quad \text{distance unit s}^{-1}$$

and u_g is known as the *group velocity*. (Sometimes the term 'envelope' is used instead of 'group'.) Figure 2.5 illustrates the propagation of a baseband signal pulse along a lossless transmission line.

It can be shown[1] that group delay is related to the phase characteristic of a line or a lumped linear network in the following way

$$t_g(\omega) = \frac{d\beta(\omega)}{d\omega}$$

For the lossless line, $t_g(\omega)$ is independent of frequency, because the phase characteristic is a linear function of frequency.

Strictly, the group velocity defines the speed of propagation of a narrow-band pulse (see for example question 1.13, with $f_0 \gg T^{-1}$) or wavepacket. Generally, the group velocity will depend upon the centre frequency of the pulse spectrum. If the signals being handled by the transmission line are, themselves, inherently narrow-band modulated radio-frequency-carrier

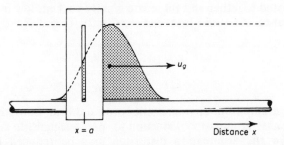

Figure 2.5 Propagation of a voltage pulse along a lossless transmission line. The pulse may be visualised as a lamina free to slide along the transmission line at the propagation velocity u_g. No change in pulse shape or height will occur, since the line is lossless. The fluctuation of voltage at any point $x = a$ on the line may be visualised as a function of time by imagining a card to be superimposed upon the 'model' as depicted above. If the slit is located at the required inspection point, the height of the lamina showing through it will describe the function of time alone, $v_a(t)$

waves, then the line will only impose a delay upon the demodulated information signal. This delay will be equal to the group delay at the carrier frequency;
no waveform distortion will be incurred, even if the group velocity is not
independent of frequency. In contrast, if a baseband signal, such as the pulse
waveform illustrated in figure 2.5, is inserted into a line which has a
frequency-dependent group delay, then the different parts of the signal
spectrum will propagate at different speeds. This causes the frequency
components to separate spatially as the pulse moves along the line and
consequently its shape will alter with distance—a phenomenon known as
signal dispersion. Dispersion causes severe degradation to signals for which
waveform *shape* is important. Digital signals fall into this class, whereas
speech signals remain intelligible after transmission through a line system
with a quite severely non-uniform group-delay characteristic. We refer to the
signal corruption imposed by a line which is dispersive as *phase-* or *group-
delay distortion*.

It is interesting to note that the propagation of a steady-state sinusoid of
radian frequency ω_0 follows the same general pattern, with peaks of voltage
'rolling' down the line, much as waves may be shaken along a piece of rope.
The velocity of any one peak is u_p and is derived from the phase characteristic
as

$$u_p = \left(\frac{\beta(\omega_0)}{\omega_0} \right)^{-1}$$

u_p is referred to as the *phase velocity* of the line. The corresponding *phase
delay*, t_p, is given by $t_p = u_p^{-1}$. In the case of the lossless line, $u_p = u_g$ so that, for
example, a carrier and its 'sidebands', which contain the transmitted informa-
tion, will propagate with the same velocity. The distinction between phase
velocity and group velocity, then, is that the former describes a steady state,
and the latter a transient condition.

2.8 Multicore Telephone Cable

Multicore telephone cable exhibits low dielectric loss and, because the cable
pairs are twisted together and therefore closely packed, low inductance and
high capacitance. At audio frequencies, $G \ll 2\pi fC$ and $R \gg 2\pi fL$, with the
result that

$$\alpha \approx \beta \approx (\pi fCR)^{\frac{1}{2}}$$

and

$$Z_0 \approx (1-j)(R/4\pi fC)^{\frac{1}{2}}$$

Notice that the amplitude characteristic is non-uniform. Consequently, multicore cables cause attenuation distortion to speech signals. In section 2.9, we
shall see how the attenuation distortion may be reduced by artificially
increasing the line inductance. Although the phase characteristic is non-linear
and therefore dispersive, it does not cause severe degradation to speech
signals, since the human ear is relatively insensitive to phase distortion. It is
particular damaging to digital signals, however, and methods of 'phase
equalisation', used to linearise the overall channel phase-characteristic (see
section 2.10) are applied to reduce its effects.

2.9   The Distortionless Line

The main reason for the poor attenuation characteristic of multicore telephone cable is the relatively low inductance of the wire pairs, in comparison
with the shunt capacitance between the two conductors. Indeed, if we assume
that R and G are non-zero, we may calculate the minimum attenuation, α, by
differentiating with respect to L, the line inductance. It can be shown that α is

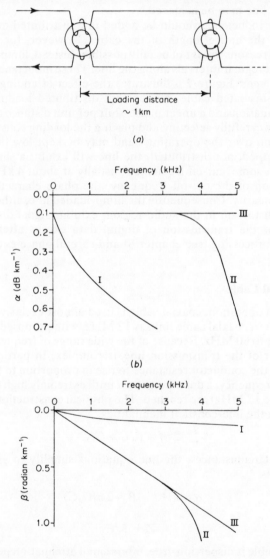

*Figure 2.6 The effect of loading on transmission-line performance. Curve I: unloaded
twisted-pair cable; curve II: lumped loading; curve III: distributed loading*

minimised when

$$L = \frac{CR}{G}$$

Substitution of this value yields the secondary line constants

$$\alpha = (RC)^{\frac{1}{2}} \quad \beta = 2\pi f(LC)^{\frac{1}{2}}$$

We see that, by increasing L until it has the value specified above, a distortionless line may be achieved.

Ideally, the inductance should be added in a distributed manner; that is, evenly along the entire length of the cable. However, for economic and technological reasons this is not usually possible. Instead, lumped inductances are inserted at regular intervals along the line. These inductances are referred to as *loading coils*. Figure 2.6 illustrates the effect of adding inductance to polyethylene-insulated cable. Notice that distributed loading results in a uniform attenuation and a linear phase-shift per unit distance as a function of frequency. By carefully selecting and placing the loading coils within the line the attenuation over the operating band may be kept low but because the loading is lumped, not distributed, the line will exhibit a sharp increase in attenuation at some 'cut-off frequency', usually at about 4 kHz.

In the region of the cut-off frequency, the phase characteristic exhibits severe non-linearity. Consequently the lump-loaded line, although free from attenuation distortion in the audio region, exhibits signal dispersion and is unsuitable for the transmission of digital data except after suitable pre-transmission processing (see chapter 8) and careful phase equalisation (section 2.11).

2.10 Coaxial Cable[17]

For wideband operation, coaxial cable is used almost exclusively. The bandwidth of modern coaxial cable links is 12 MHz, with proposed developments indicating use to 60 MHz. Because of the wide range of frequencies involved, the behaviour of the transmission line is complex. In particular, the 'skin effect' causes the conductor resistance to rise in proportion to the square root of the signal frequency, a dominant effect until extremely high signal frequencies (far above 12 MHz) are reached. The physical construction of the coaxial line results in the line-constant inequalities

$$2\pi f \gg R/L \gg G/C$$

Under these circumstances, the line equations simplify to yield the secondary constants

$$\alpha = kf^{\frac{1}{2}} \quad \beta \approx 2\pi f(LC)^{\frac{1}{2}}$$

and

$$Z_0 = L/C$$

Thus such a cable is dispersion-free, offers small attenuation per unit distance (but implicitly requires attenuation equalisation) and, from the nature of its physical construction, results in a characteristic impedance of the order of 50 to 75 Ω.

2.11   Repeaters and Equalisers

In the previous sections we have investigated the limitations of practical cable systems. Irrespective of the nature of the signal distortion that may be caused by the cable, a progressive attenuation with distance will occur. Furthermore noise will be added, so that the signal-to-noise ratio will progressively degrade with distance from the signal source. To some extent, this effect can be combated by the inclusion of *repeater amplifiers* spaced at suitable intervals along the line (see section 9.1).

If the transmission is analogue in nature, such as an audio-band voice-telephony signal, the repeater must have a linear amplification law and will, therefore, amplify signal and line noise equally. Consequently however frequently repeaters may be spaced along the line the signal-to-noise ratio at the end of a long line may become intolerably low.

Because analogue signal repeaters result in a worsening of signal-to-noise ratio, there has been a general move towards pulse code modulation telephony, in which the analogue transmission is coded in digital form. The repeaters can then be made to reconstruct and retime the original digital signal, completely eliminating both line noise and the adverse effects of band-limiting on the pulse shape as seen at the repeater input. Such repeaters are referred to as being 'regenerative' in nature.

Attenuation and phase distortion can arise within a variety of ancillary equipment, as well as within the lines themselves. Even those lines described in the previous section as being in some way inherently distortion-free will, when installed, be a part of a system presenting to the user both kinds of distortion, in some measure.

The process of correcting deviations of the practical channel characteristics $A_a(f)$ and $\phi_a(f)$, from the ideal, specified in section 2.2 is referred to as *equalisation*. Attention has to be paid to the correction of attenuation distortion in analogue-signal links, in which the preservation of signal waveshape by ensuring phase linearity is not of the greatest importance. In contrast, digital links require careful phase equalisation to ensure the preservation of the digit waveshape.

To achieve equalisation, we attempt to find networks with transfer functions $A_e(f)$ and $\phi_e(f)$ such that $A_e(f)\exp\{j\phi_e(f)\}A_a(f)\exp\{j\phi_a(f)\}$ approaches as closely as possible to the ideal. We may equalise in this way either before transmission through the channel, pre-distorting the signal spectrum which is transmitted, or afterwards, correcting distortion incurred during transmission.

Often, the equalisation networks employed are passive and time-invariant in nature. However, because of the possibility that signal paths through a large communication network may be changed during transmission, this is by no means always the case. Thus in many modern high-speed data-transmission systems, *adaptive* equalisers are employed. These are active networks, often digital in nature, which monitor the channel characteristics and automatically vary the equalisation characteristic as the channel characteristic changes.

A limit to the equalisation bandwidth (that is, the bandwidth over which equalisation is attempted) is set by the noise levels encountered within the channel. Usually, the gross effect of a transmission line is to attenuate high-frequency signal components. When the most severely attenuated of such components have fallen to a power level which is comparable with that of the system noise, attempts at equalisation will result in an unacceptably low signal-to-noise ratio.

2.12 Optical Communications[62]

In the foregoing sections of this chapter, we have discussed the properties and uses of transmission lines. Wire-based line plant has, for reasons of economy and convenience, been the dominant factor in determining the evolution of the telephony network throughout its history. However, at the time of writing, the telecommunication industry may be regarded as having arrived at a crossroads of extreme significance. We now enter an era in which the emphasis will lie not on wire-based but on *optical* line-plant systems, utilising glass-fibre light-guides. This transition to optical communication has profound implications so far as network structuring is concerned, primarily because light-guide systems effectively remove bandwidth constraints on the choice of modulation format. Consequently, even in trunk applications, classical bandwidth-efficient modulation procedures (employed to 'frequency multiplex' many users on a single physical carrier) will be superseded by digital 'time multiplexed' schemes. The 'integrated services digital network', as we shall see in chapter 9, offers massive advantages in message routeing and the provision of advanced subscriber facilities. These advantages can most conveniently be provided by means of integrated digital switching circuits under computer control. In the future, the impact of optical-fibre systems will be felt *throughout* the network, from the subscriber loop (which connects the user to the local exchange) through urban and intercity connections to trans-oceanic cable connections. Fibre-optic systems exhibit, in addition to increased bandwidth, the following further advantages over wire-based communication systems.

(1) Freedom from crosstalk and electromagnetic interference, conferring a quality benefit in adverse environments. This benefit is manifest in substantially increased repeater spacing (by about an order of magnitude) over typical requirements for wire-based systems, where spacings of 1 or 2 km are commonplace. It should, perhaps, be noted that wire-system digital transmission involves the use of signal amplitudes of several volts which are thus greatly in excess of 'thermal' noise levels at the detector. By contrast, optical systems operate with detected photon fluxes which are sufficiently small to make gaussian noise, rather than general and perhaps poorly characterised line impairments, a matter for concern. For these two competing systems, the factors determining repeater spacing are thus somewhat different in 'kind'.

(2) Elimination of frequency-dependency (and temperature-variability of frequency-dependency) conferring a benefit in the elimination of line-loading and complex transfer function equalisation.

(3) Reduced cost as the 'per user, per kilometre' price of light-guide cable falls below that of copper-wire cable.

(4) Probable reduced long-term maintenance owing to the chemical and mechanical properties of the glass-based optical system.

The most significant fibre-optic cable parameters relate to cable loss. Attenuation, caused by the presence of material inhomogeneities, has been reduced over the decade to 1980 by some three orders of magnitude. Current practical attenuation figures of about 1 to 5 dB km^{-1} (depending upon glass properties and operating frequency) are now competitive with the attentuation figures for wire-based cables. However, from the system viewpoint, the critical parameter of repeater spacing is, for other reasons, much improved for optical links, as we have already seen. Figure 2.7 illustrates the loss-spectrum typical of transmission through high-quality silica-glass fibre, doped with germanium to improve its optical properties. The loss curve is lower-bounded by Rayleigh scattering loss caused by material contaminants and inhomogeneities and by infrared absorption loss. Other loss mechanisms, attributable to the presence of hydroxyl ions trapped in the fibre, give rise to the resonance peaks in the experimental loss curve. A loss-minimum is observable at 1.3 μm wavelength (2.3 x 10^{14} Hz) within the near infrared band which extends from 0.78 μm to 3 μm (the visible light spectrum extends from red at 0.78 μm to violet at 0.4 μm).

A second loss component, known as 'microbending loss', is caused by the unintentional introduction of small ('millimetre') radius bends in the fibre. Such loss can be virtually eliminated by suitable mechanical design of the cable system.

Another important optical-fibre characteristic is *dispersion*, which causes different light frequencies to travel with differing group velocities (a phenomenon evident, for example, in the dissociation of light into its colour-spectrum by a glass prism). This effect is clearly deleterious to pulse-shape in the transmission of extremely broadband (high-rate) signals and would lead to unacceptable waveform degradation. It may be minimised by appropriate fibre design and appears not to be a dominant problem in the installation of state-of-the-art light-guide systems. In this context, 'fibre design' relates primarily to the precise control of *doping profile* across the fibre diameter. Doping profile governs refractive index and consequently determines mode paths for the different modal states which can be

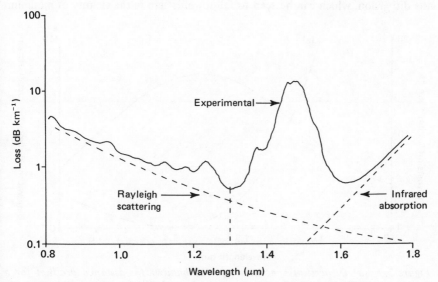

Figure 2.7   Loss-spectrum for germano-silicate glass single-mode fibre

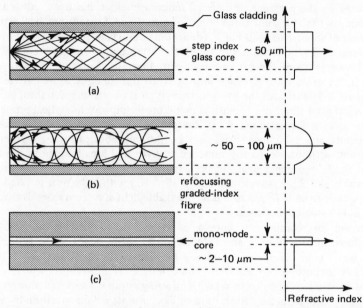

Figure 2.8 Light-guide mode formation. (a) Large core diameter relative to light wavelength results in multimode propagation. (b) Parabolic grading acts as a refocusing structure. (c) A small core diameter results in single-mode propagation

propagated, as figure 2.8 shows. Typically, a narrow-core, step-refractive-index fibre grading would be used to establish a profile suitable for single-mode transmission.

Figure 2.9*a* illustrates (for the same fibre type as was characterised in figure 2.7) the dispersion, which can be seen to fall towards zero in the vicinity of minimum

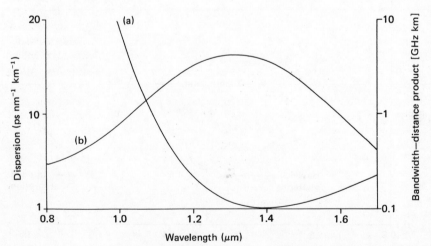

Figure 2.9 (a) Dispersion spectrum and (b) bandwidth–distance product for a germano-silicate single-mode fibre

loss. Pulse spreading caused by dispersion is thus seen to be minimised by restricting pulse bandwidth. Furthermore, spreading increases with distance. Consequently, system bandwidth effectively decreases with increasing fibrelength, is maximised at minimum group-delay and is characterised as a bandwidth–distance product, as figure 2.9*b* indicates.

Two optical source technologies are currently used: gallium arsenide (GaAs) light-emitting diodes (LEDs) and injection lasers. The technical attributes of these alternatives are compared in table 2.1. It should be noted that neither source can be *coherently* modulated (that is, modulated in amplitude or phase, or both, with reference to some absolute value of phase). This is because, even for the laser, the 4 nm spectral width, representing as it does, a fractional bandwidth of 0.5% at 0.8 μm, implies a carrier bandwidth in excess of 10^{12} Hz even before modulation is attempted. Modulation is thus essentially the power control of a noise-like carrier, power being fluctuated in sympathy with the modulating signal.

The critical parameter determining effective available source bandwidth is the optical pulse risetime, typically in the low nanosecond region. Source bandwidth is thus constrained to some few hundreds of megacycles. The higher power output of the injection laser, together with its superior conversion efficiency and better coupling properties (it generates relatively few modes and thus loses proportionately less power when coupling into a single-mode fibre), taken in conjunction with its poor linearity, make it most suitable for long-haul (up to $\sim$ 60 km) digital applications. The LED, by contrast, is adequate for medium-haul ($\sim$ 10 km) digital or short ($\sim$ 1 km) videoband (5 MHz) analogue links. It should be noted that the performance requirements on analogue and digital links are distinctly different. The former place heavy dependency upon high signal-to-noise ratio (typically in excess of 40 dB). The latter can operate at low bit-error rates at substantially smaller signal-to-noise ratios (of the order of 10 dB); thus, in a transmission context which is not, itself, bandwidth constrained, they are to be preferred. In other words, whenever possible it is better to digitise, rather than transmit raw analogue signals, in an optical communication context.

Optical detection is performed by means of a photodiode. Two types are used: the *p-i-n* diode and the avalanche diode. The term '*p-i-n*' signifies a three-layer structure, in which a lightly doped *p*- or *n*-layer (the '*i*-layer') is sandwiched between more heavily-doped *p*- and *n*-type layers. The avalanche photodiode, reversed-biased into the avalanche region where secondary breakdown can occur during optical stimulation, provides a photomultiplication capability and hence higher detection sensitivity. Of these two devices, the high linearity of the *p-i-n* diode makes its use mandatory for high-quality analogue links. Otherwise, the avalanche photodiode offers preferable performance, although the requirement for a high supply voltage, to ensure bias into the avalanche region can introduce logistical problems in system development. Good performance figures in respect of response time, low dark-current and good quantum efficiency (the ratio between generated electron–hole pairs and incident photons) are consistently obtained with silicon devices, which are suitable for wavelengths of 0.8–0.9 μm. However, silicon devices exhibit a rapidly diminishing response for wavelengths in excess of 0.9 μm. To accommodate applications making use of the attenuation minimum at 1.3 μm, referred to above, germanium-based devices, which exhibit good long-wavelength sensitivity, are being developed.

Overall system performance may be gauged in terms of *transmission margin*.

We presume that the optical system transmits binary data. Binary 'zero' is represented by zero photon flux incident upon the detector. Binary 'one' is represented by a mean incident photon flux of M photons per T second-long digit. Quantum theory tells us that a photodiode will generate (per T seconds) N electron–hole pairs from the M photons (with $N \leqslant M$ assuming no detector gain) according to a Poisson distribution

$$Q(n) = \frac{M^N \exp(-M)}{N!}$$

If a binary 'one' is transmitted, and detection of that fact is accomplished if at least one electron–hole pair is released during the T second digit period (the theoretical minimum required for detection), then the probability of *failure* must simply be $Q(0) = \exp(-M)$. It is frequently the case that an error rate of 1 in 10^9 transmitted digits is used to indicate performance of the optical link. Then $Q(0) = 10^{-9}$, and we find that $M = 21$. We therefore note that an exceptionally low error rate of 1 in 10^9 is indicated, provided that at least 21 photons reach the detector photodiode per transmitted binary 'one'. Such an argument provides an upper bound to system performance. It ignores detection efficiency and the contribution of dark-current noise; it also takes no account of the comparative performance of subsequent detection circuitry. The combined effect of such additional factors serves to increase the required photon flux for a 10^{-9} error rate to perhaps $M = 200$ for an avalanche diode, with a gain of 100 or to about 20 000 for a unity-gain *p-i-n* diode.

The energy per photon is given as (hf) Joules, where h is Planck's constant $(6.62 \times 10^{-34} \text{ J s})$ and f is the optical transmission frequency. The peak transmitted power is thus Mhf/T or $MhfR$ where R is the digit rate. Applying this formula, and assuming $f = 2.3 \times 10^{14}$ Hz, corresponding to transmission at the minimum loss wavelength of 1.3 μm, we find that the required received power is as plotted on figure 2.10. Superimposed upon this graph are typical output domains for LED and injection lasers, taken (in part) from table 2.1. (At high digit rates, thermal effects within the optical source force a lowering of average output power.) Thus a system configured using a LED source and a *p-i-n* diode detector, operating at 4 Mb s^{-1} may be expected to yield (for an error rate of 1 in 10^9) a transmission margin 'A' of about 35 dB. With a fibre loss of, say, 1 dB km^{-1}, this margin will have reduced to zero at 35 km, at which distance regeneration and retransmission will be necessary if the error rate is not to degrade.

2.13 Modulators

The system block that will be of major interest to us in the following chapters is the *modulator*. A modulator is a device which operates on an input *carrier* waveform $v_c(t)$ with a *modulating* waveform to provide some related output waveform. The operation is functional, in that

$$v_o(t) = f\{v_m(t), v_c(t)\} \tag{2.12}$$

where $f(\ \ )$ represents some non-linear function of the two variables $v_m(t)$ and $v_c(t)$. By 'non-linear', we mean that doubling either input does not merely double the output.

Almost always, the carrier waveform is either sinusoidal, square or an impulse

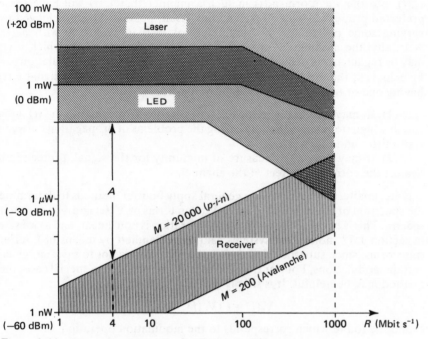

Figure 2.10 Transmission margin for the optical fibre system

TABLE 2.1

Property	GaAs LED	Injection Laser
Typical power to fibre	0.1–10 mW	1 mW–100 mW (substantially higher at low duty cycle)
Transfer linearity	Excellent	On–off nonlinearity
Conversion efficiency (electrical: optical into cable)	0.025% (many modes launched)	0.25% (few modes launched because of lasing action, so coupling efficiency high)
Peak emission wavelength	800–1000 nm	800–1000 nm
Spectral width	30–60 nm	4 nm typically
Lifetime	10^7 h	Variable: to 10^6 h at best; 10^4 h typically
Risetime	2–10 nS	1 nS

train. On occasion, noise-like carriers have been employed, mainly in experimental systems. A case in point would be the modulation of the power output of an infrared or optical source as has been discussed in the previous section.

The broad purpose of modulation is to insert the information contained in

$v_m(t)$ into the waveform $v_o(t)$ in such a manner that $v_o(t)$ will have some preferred properties which $v_m(t)$ did not, itself, possess. This is achieved by varying some parameter, or parameters of $v_c(t)$ in sympathy with $v_m(t)$. Naturally, the modulation process must produce a signal from which $v_m(t)$ may be regained in a *demodulation* process. Assuming that demodulation can be achieved, the modulation operation will result in the output signal $v_o(t)$ having one or both of two important properties

(1) It may spectrally relocate the baseband information $v_m(t)$ at a suitably high frequency, thereby easing the problems of propagation between transmitter and receiver.

(2) It may provide a measure of immunity for the signal, protecting it against the corrupting effect of the channel.

Note, finally, that we cannot in general apply Fourier methods to determine the spectrum of the modulated wave $V_o(t)$ in terms of $V_m(t)$ and $V_c(t)$ or their spectra. This is because the modulation operation is non-linear, and as we saw in section 1.12, non-linear systems cannot be handled by means of Fourier transforms, since superposition does not apply. This is not to say that, given certain modulations, Fourier transforms may not be used; in special cases the method may be helpful. It is simply that a general expression

$$V_o(f) = F\{V_m(f), V_c(f)\}$$

cannot be found which corresponds to the modulation operation

$$v_o(t) = f\{v_m(t), v_c(t)\}$$

2.14 Sinusoidal Modulation

We have, as our specification of the sinusoid, the equation

$$v(t) = A \cos(2\pi ft + \phi)$$

When we perform a sinusoidal modulation, we vary one or more of the parameters of $v(t)$ in sympathy with a modulating signal $v_m(t)$. In order that we may establish a coherent theory of modulation, it is necessary that we should discuss in some detail the implications of allowing $v(t)$ to have time-varying parameters. In its most general form, we may express the modulated wave as

$$v(t) = A(t)\cos\{\theta(t)\} \qquad (2.13)$$

where both $A(t)$ and $\theta(t)$ are as yet unspecified functions of the modulating signal.

Equation 2.13 has a phasor representation, figure 2.11, which consists of a rotating member of length $A(t)$ making an angle $\theta(t)$ with the abscissa. Since this phasor is rotating, it will have an angular velocity $\dot{\theta}(t)$. In the case of a completely *unmodulated* sinusoid, since $\theta(t) = 2\pi ft + \phi$ it follows, as we might expect, that $\dot{\theta}(t) = 2\pi f$. We may conveniently think of the quantity $\dot{\theta}(t)/2\pi$ as a time-varying frequency and as a consequence we refer to it as the *instantaneous frequency* of the wave $v(t)$. Furthermore, we regard the instantaneous frequency as being composed of some fluctuation about a fixed value, much as a general time waveform is composed of a fluctuation about a 'd.c.

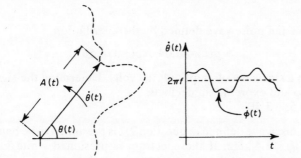

Figure 2.11 The general modulated sinusoid $v(t) = A(t)\cos\{\theta(t)\}$

level'. To this end, we write

$$\frac{\dot{\theta}(t)}{2\pi} = f + \frac{\dot{\phi}(t)}{2\pi} \tag{2.14}$$

so that, when we integrate to obtain $\theta(t)$, we obtain

$$\theta(t) = 2\pi f t + \phi(t) \tag{2.15}$$

In so defining the sinusoid, we see that the frequency, f, is not a parameter that may be varied as a function of a modulating signal. Instead, frequency variation corresponds to a fluctuation of $\dot{\theta}(t)/2\pi$ and hence of $\dot{\phi}(t)/2\pi$. We shall discuss the implications of this, and the nature of both frequency and phase modulations at greater length in chapter 4.

We have, then, a general sinusoid with time-varying parameters

$$v(t) = A(t)\cos\{2\pi f t + \phi(t)\} \tag{2.16}$$

from which we may isolate the three basic classes of modulation summarised in table 2.1.

TABLE 2.2 THREE BASIC CLASSES OF MODULATION

Case	Condition	Practical Examples
Envelope Modulation	$A(t) = g_1\{v_m(t)\}$ $\phi(t) = $ constant	'Product' modulation Conventional amplitude modulation
Angle Modulation	$A(t) = $ constant $\phi(t) = g_2\{v_m(t)\}$	⎰ Phase modulation ⎱ Frequency modulation Frequency modulation with pre-emphasis
Composite Modulation	$A(t) = g_1\{v_m(t)\}$ $\phi(t) = g_2\{v_m(t)\}$	⎰ Single sideband Asymmetric sideband Independent sideband Vestigial sideband Compatible single sideband ⎱ Single-sideband FM

Problems

2.1   A gaussian noisewave defined by the distribution

$$p(v) = 0.04 \exp(-0.005v^2)$$

is added to a sinewave of amplitude 10 volts. Determine the signal-to-noise power ratio and express it in decibels.
(*Answer* 0.5, −3 dB)

2.2   The noisewave defined in question 2.1 is presumed to be band-limited to the range $|f| < 3.4$ kHz. If the spectrum is presumed white in this range, determine the value of the noise-power spectral density.
(*Answer* 0.03 volt^2 Hz)

2.3   A channel has a transfer function

$$H(f) = \frac{1}{2}\{1 + \cos(\pi f/f_0)\} \quad |f| < f_0$$
$$= 0 \quad \text{elsewhere}$$

Sketch this transfer function and state its effect on signals passing through it.
   Show that the channel may be represented by a parallel bank of filters

$$H(f) = H_a(f) + H_b(f) + H_c(f)$$

where

$$H_a(f) = \frac{1}{2} \quad \text{all } f$$

$$H_b(f) = \frac{1}{4}\exp(+j\pi f/f_0)$$

$$H_c(f) = \frac{1}{4}\exp(-j\pi f/f_0)$$

Show that the effect of the channel is to pass an attenuated replica of any input signal, plus two echoes.

2.4   Distinguish clearly between the kinds of distortion introduced by (a) a linear channel with a non-ideal transfer function and (b) a non-linear channel with an ideal transfer function.

2.5   State two important reasons for utilising modulation to prepare a signal for transmission. Is the modulator a linear device, in general, and is its operation capable of specification as a transfer function as would be the case with a linear filter?

2.6   Show that a transfer function $H(f)$ will act upon a white noise source of power spectral density η to yield a power spectral density

$$P(f) = \eta |H(f)|^2$$

How would you determine the mean square noise-voltage (that is, the total noise power) at the output of the transfer function $H(f)$?

2.7   It is sometimes useful, in assessing the performance of communication systems to have recourse to the concept of the ·noise-equivalent bandwidth',

B_N, of a filter. The noise-equivalent bandwidth is the bandwidth of an ideal rectangular filter which would yield an output-noise power spectral density that was white and conveyed the same noise power.

Gaussian noise of uniform spectral density η is applied to a first-order RC lowpass filter. Show that the spectral density of the output noise is

$$P(f) = \eta\{1 + (2\pi fCR)^2\}^{-1}$$

and that the total noise power is $\pi\eta CR$ volt^2. Hence show that the noise-equivalent bandwidth is $\pi CR/2$ Hz.

2.8 A phase detector, used as the first stage of a frequency demodulator, exhibits at its output a noisewave of uniform spectral density η within the range $|f| \leq B/2$. The phase detector is followed by a differentiator which is used to convert the phase detector to a frequency detector. Determine and sketch the noise spectrum at the differentiator output and calculate the total noise power as a function of B. (*Hint* First obtain the transfer function of the differentiator from table 1.2.)

2.9 A narrow-band process is one for which $f_c \gg B$ where f_c is the nominal band-centre frequency and B is the nominal bandwidth. Such a process may be regarded as a sinusoid

$$v(t) = A(t)\cos\{2\pi f_c t + \phi(t)\}$$

or, alternatively, this expression may be written as

$$v(t) = x(t)\cos(2\pi f_c t) + y(t)\sin(2\pi f_c t)$$

(a) Determine $x(t)$ and $y(t)$ as functions of $A(t)$ and $\phi(t)$, and vice versa.

(b) Discuss the statement: '$A(t)$ and $\phi(t)$ will be slowly varying fluctuations, relative to the fluctuations of the wave $v(t)$'.

(c) Discuss the statement: '$x(t)$ and $y(t)$ must be independent baseband processes of bandwidth $B/2$'.

2.10 An envelope-modulated carrier

$$v_c(t) = \{A_c + v_m(t)\}\cos(2\pi f_c t)$$

modulated with a sinusoid

$$v_m(t) = A_m \cos(2\pi f_m t)$$

has a spectrum consisting of a carrier δ-function plus a symmetrical pair of sideband δ-functions spaced a distance f_m on either side of the carrier. Show this to be the case and hence show, by analogy, that the most rapid fluctuations of the envelope of the general narrow-band process defined in question 2.9 will be of period

$$T \approx 1/B$$

2.11 If the narrow-band process described in question 2.10 is simply the noisewave in a typical communication channel, then $v(t)$ will have a gaussian distribution. It is also the case that $x(t)$ and $y(t)$ will have gaussian distributions. If the power in $x(t)$ and $y(t)$ is

$$p_x = p_y = p$$

calculate the average power in $v(t)$.

3 Envelope Modulation

We have defined the general modulated sinusoid, in section 2.14, as

$$v(t) = A(t)\cos\{2\pi f_c t + \phi(t)\}$$

The amplitude and phase terms are some functions of the modulating signal $v_m(t)$, as yet undefined, so that

$$A(t) = g_1\{v_m(t)\}$$
$$\phi(t) = g_2\{v_m(t)\}$$

There are three principle reasons for modulating a sinusoidal carrier

(1) To relocate baseband information so that it is spectrally adjacent to the high-frequency carrier. This frequency translation makes electromagnetic propagation much easier. Both transmission power and antenna size may be reduced as the carrier frequency is increased.

(2) To provide the capability of frequency division multiplexing many baseband channels.

(3) To increase the transmitted signal (that is, the modulated carrier) redundancy, thereby gaining a measure of immunity to the signal corruption introduced by the channel.

In this chapter, we shall examine the class of modulations in which only $A(t)$ is varied, and then linearly in sympathy with the modulating signal so that

$$A(t) \propto v_m(t)$$

$$\phi(t) = \text{a constant}$$

This class we refer to as *linear envelope modulation*. In its most general form, linear envelope modulation is defined by the equation

$$v(t) = (kv_m(t) + c)\cos(2\pi f_c t + \phi_c) \tag{3.1}$$

where k, c and ϕ_c are constants.

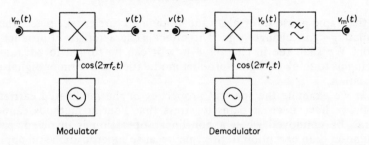

Figure 3.1 The product modulator. $v_m(t)$: modulating signal; $v(t)$: modulated carrier

3.1 Product Modulation

The envelope modulation, equation 3.1, has its simplest form when $k = 1$ and $c = 0$. If we choose to regard the carrier as phase reference, then we may set ϕ_c to be zero as well, so that

$$v(t) = v_m(t)\cos(2\pi f_c t) \tag{3.2}$$

This equation we shall take to define *product modulation* of a sinusoid by a modulating signal $v_m(t)$.

We may commence our examination of product modulation by defining the system block which performs the modulation operation. This block is simply a multiplier, figure 3.1. Next we shall consider the operation in the time domain, figure 3.2. The time-domain waveform corresponding to the modulator output can be seen to be a sinewave with a time-varying envelope. The zero crossings, which loosely define the 'frequency' of the modulated carrier are unchanged by the modulation process, so that no 'frequency' modulation is taking place. At points A in figure 3.2 it will be

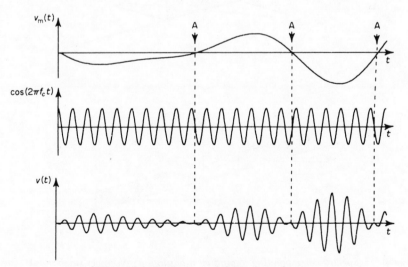

Figure 3.2 Product-modulation waveforms

seen that rapid phase reversals of the modulated carrier take place when the modulating signal changes sign. This effect is characteristic of product modulation. We shall see in chapter 8 how it can be turned to advantage in allowing us to think of digital-product modulation as a form of digital-phase modulation.

Next we examine the spectral properties of the modulated carrier. Although we have been at pains to stress that Fourier methods cannot, in general, be employed when a non-linear operation is involved, product modulation is an exception to this rule because superposition still applies.

Suppose that the modulating signal $v_m(t)$ and the modulated carrier $v(t)$ have Fourier transforms (that is, voltage spectra) $V_m(f)$ and $V(f)$ respectively. Then, as we shall show shortly, it follows that

$$V(f) = \frac{1}{2}\{V_m(f-f_c) + V_m(f+f_c)\} \qquad (3.3)$$

The frequency translation defined by this equation is illustrated in figure 3.3. Notice that the baseband spectrum is sketched as having complex conjugate symmetry. Notice also that the modulated carrier occupies twice the bandwidth of the baseband signal. Another feature of the modulated carrier spectrum should also be apparent. The two halves of the spectrum above and below the carrier convey the same information. The spectrum exhibits gross redundancy—a feature which, as we shall see in section 3.10, can be turned to our advantage when we consider the noise performance of linear envelope-modulation systems. We refer to the two halves of the

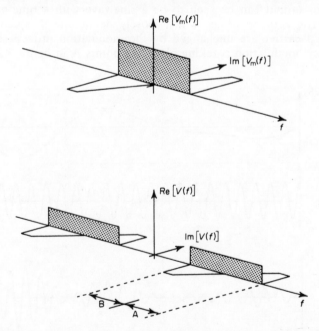

Figure 3.3 Spectra corresponding to product modulation; A: upper sideband, B: lower sideband

modulated carrier spectrum as the 'upper and lower sidebands' of the signal. By deleting one or the other of these by means of a suitable filter, we may form a non-redundant 'single-sideband' waveform. Such waveforms are extensively employed in voice communication systems and we shall consider them in detail in chapter 5. They are not suitable material for this chapter, however, since the deletion of one sideband results in the generation of a modulated carrier in which both amplitude and phase are functions of the modulating signal: a *composite modulation*.

Another feature of the product-modulated wave is apparent from either figure 3.3 or from equation 3.3. Although a carrier wave $\cos(2\pi f_c t)$ is used in the generation of $v(t)$, no component of this wave other than that which results from the d.c. level in $v_m(t)$, if any, is present in the modulated carrier. For this reason the product-modulated carrier is sometimes referred to as a suppressed carrier amplitude-modulated wave. The fact that a 'suppressed carrier' is involved in the modulation process is sometimes depicted on sketches of spectra relating to the modulated carrier by a broken δ-function (see, for example, figure 5.10).

The proof of equation 3.3 is not particularly difficult. We have first the Fourier transform integral

$$V(f) = \int_{-\infty}^{+\infty} v(t)\exp(-2\pi jft)\,dt$$

However, $v(t)$ is defined by equation 3.2 as

$$v(t) = v_m(t)\cos(2\pi f_c t)$$
$$= \frac{v_m(t)}{2}\{\exp(2\pi jf_c t) + \exp(-2\pi jf_c t)\}$$

so that

$$V(f) = \frac{1}{2}\int_{-\infty}^{+\infty} v_m(t)\{\exp(2\pi jf_c t) + \exp(-2\pi jf_c t)\}\exp(-2\pi jft)\,dt$$
$$= \frac{1}{2}\int_{-\infty}^{+\infty} v_m(t)\exp\{-2\pi j(f - f_c)t\}\,dt + \frac{1}{2}\int_{-\infty}^{+\infty} v_m(t)\exp\{-2\pi j(f + f_c)t\}\,dt$$

If, now, we let

$$\lambda_1 = f - f_c$$
$$\lambda_2 = f + f_c$$

Then

$$V(f) = \frac{1}{2}\int_{-\infty}^{+\infty} v_m(t)\exp(-2\pi j\lambda_1 t)\,dt + \frac{1}{2}\int_{-\infty}^{+\infty} v_m(t)\exp(-2\pi j\lambda_2 t)\,dt$$
$$= \frac{1}{2}\{V_m(\lambda_1) + V_m(\lambda_2)\}$$
$$= \frac{1}{2}\{V_m(f - f_c) + V_m(f + f_c)\}$$

If we make the assumption that the carrier frequency is sufficiently high, and the bandwidth of the baseband function $V_m(f)$ is sufficiently low that the shifted bandpass functions $V_m(f - f_c)$ and $V_m(f + f_c)$ do not overlap in the region of zero frequency, then we may express the power spectrum $P(f)$, of the modulated carrier $v(t)$ in terms of the power spectrum, $P_m(f)$, of the modulating signal $v_m(t)$.

$$P(f) = \frac{1}{4}\{P_m(f + f_c) + P_m(f - f_c)\} \qquad (3.4)$$

The assumption quoted above is not a very restrictive one, since it is almost always the case that modulated carriers are 'narrow-band' processes or at least have minimal spectral overlap at zero frequency.

Before proceeding with a discussion of the detection of product-modulated waves, it is worth noting that the modulation operation

$$v(t) = v_m(t)\sin(2\pi f_c t) \qquad (3.5)$$

generates a spectrum

$$V(f) = \frac{1}{2j}\{V_m(f - f_c) - V_m(f + f_c)\} \qquad (3.6)$$

The proof of equation 3.6 is virtually identical with that quoted above for equation 3.3 and can therefore be left to the reader to complete. We shall find this result of particular use to us when we come to consider the generation of single-sideband waves in chapter 5.

3.2   The Detection of Product-modulated Waves

The modulation operation defined by equation 3.2 may easily be reversed to yield once more the modulating signal. Figure 3.1 shows how this may be accomplished. The modulated carrier is passed into a second multiplier and the product

$$v_o(t) = v(t)\cos(2\pi f_c t)$$

is taken. The wave $v_o(t)$ contains a mean value which follows $v_m(t)$, plus components at twice the carrier frequency. The mean value, being a baseband process, may be extracted by lowpass filtering.

Formally, this conclusion may be substantiated thus

$$v(t) = v_m(t)\cos(2\pi f_c t)$$
$$v_o(t) = v_m(t)\cos^2(2\pi f_c t)$$
$$= \frac{1}{2}v_m(t) + \frac{1}{2}v_m(t)\cos\{2\pi(2f_c)t\}$$

so that the output from the lowpass filter is, indeed, directly proportional to $v_m(t)$.

The detection process requires that the 'local oscillator', the source of the wave $\cos(2\pi f_c t)$ at the demodulator, be in frequency and phase lock with the modulator oscillator. We could discuss the implications of a loss of lock at great length. However, this is a rather sterile study since the product-modulation process is not widely used for analogue-signal communication. This is largely because of the severe detected-signal degradation which results from a loss of lock. Should the reader wish to pursue this aspect of the system performance further, the appropriate results will now be quoted. If the local oscillator produces a signal $\cos(2\pi f_1 t + \phi_1)$ the detector will deliver an output proportional to

$$v_m(t)\cos\{2\pi(f_c - f_1)t\}\cos(\phi_1)$$

which is an attenuated baseband-signal with a superimposed sinusoidal amplitude-fluctuation at the difference frequency $(f_c - f_1)$. This fluctuation will cause, assuming a relatively small frequency separation, slow, deep fades and these cannot be combatted by any form of automatic gain-control within the receiver because they fade to zero amplitude.

None the less, product modulation is employed in three important areas. First, it is employed as a functional block within transmitter or receiver systems. Then the modulation/demodulation operations can be performed with precision because a single master oscillator will be locally available to drive all modulators. One example of this kind of application is encountered in the generation of single-sideband waves by the phase-shift method described in section 5.2. Second, product modulation is encountered in 180° phase-shift keying of a carrier by a data waveform. We shall discuss this application in more detail in section 8.6. Suffice it to say that an accurate reference certainly is needed at the receiver to permit coherent detection of the received binary-digit waveforms and that great care is taken to ensure that this reference is available. Third, it is encountered as a *subcarrier* modulation in broadcast stereophony. In this instance a 'pilot tone' at the subcarrier frequency is also transmitted and provides the means of establishing a coherent local oscillator signal for product demodulation of the modulated subcarrier at the receiver.[45]

3.3 Conventional Amplitude Modulation

We have discussed product modulation, the simplest form of envelope modulation, in the preceding sections and have arrived at the conclusion that, for broadcast pruposes, the resulting demodulate can be rather unreliable. We turn next to examine 'conventional amplitude modulation', and we shall see that, not only is the detection system very much simpler than that required for product modulation, but also it does not suffer from the same deep fading which results from the lack of a phase- and frequency-locked local oscillator. These factors make the system very attractive for large-scale commercial use.

We may define conventional amplitude modulation in terms of our general linear envelope modulation, equation 3.1, as

$$v(t) = \{v_m(t) + A_c\}\cos(2\pi f_c t) \tag{3.7}$$

We define a *modulation index*, m, thus

$$m = \frac{\text{r.m.s. value of } v_m(t)}{\text{r.m.s. value of unmodulated carrier}} \tag{3.8}$$

Such a definition allows us to specify a typical operating value for the modulation index even when the modulating signal is 'noise-like'. Many texts define the entire modulation operation in terms of a sinusoidal test-modulating signal. As we shall see in section 3.6, such an approach fits in

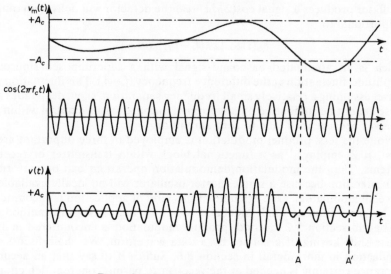

Figure 3.4 Conventional AM *waveforms*

perfectly well with our more general definition, even though it does not describe a very realistic transmission condition.

Figure 3.4 illustrates the form of the modulated carrier when $v_m(t)$ is noise-like. We could certainly demodulate such a waveform by applying the product detector described in the previous section. However, if we do, we are bound by exactly the same restrictions on frequency and phase stability of the local oscillator.

Examination of the amplitude-modulated carrier in figure 3.4 indicates that we may recover the information in the waveform by detecting its envelope. This we may achieve by means of the rectifier and lowpass-filter circuit shown in figure 3.5. The lowpass filter simply performs a smoothing operation on the rectified waveform.

Note that, provided

$$v_m(t) \geqslant -A_c$$

envelope detection will detect the received signal quite adequately without reference to either the frequency or the phase of the received carrier

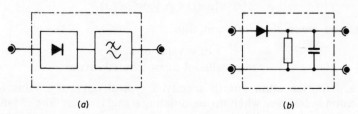

         (a)   *(b)*

Figure 3.5 (a) *The envelope detector as a system block-diagram and* (b) *as a simple electronic-circuit implementation*

component. If the condition specified above is not met, for example within the region AA' in figure 3.4, the phase reversal which typifies the process of product modulation becomes apparent. The envelope detector then rectifies the demodulate, folding it upwards about the line corresponding to the condition

$$v_m(t) = -A_c$$

Such a rectification is subjectively appreciated by the recipient of a communication as severe distortion. To prevent its occurrence, we choose such a value of modulation index as to make this condition of modulation extremely unlikely. For example, if the modulating signal were truly noise-like, then a value of modulation index of 0.67 would result in distortion of this kind occurring for less than 0.25 per cent of the transmission time.

3.4 Band Occupancy of Conventional AM

By expanding equation 3.7, we see that $v(t)$ is the sum of a product-modulated wave

$$v_m(t)\cos(2\pi f_c t)$$

plus a carrier component

$$A_c \cos(2\pi f_c t)$$

Applying equation 3.3 it follows that the spectrum of $v(t)$ has the form shown in figure 3.6 and is given by the relation

$$V(f) = \frac{1}{2}\{V_m(f - f_c) + V_m(f + f_c)\} + \frac{1}{2} A_c\{\delta(f - f_c) + \delta(f + f_c)\} \qquad (3.9)$$

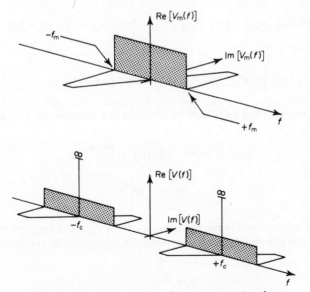

Figure 3.6 Spectra corresponding to conventional AM

Normally, with the modulation index below unity, the carrier would be relatively large. If the modulation index is increased to a value in excess of unity, however, we approach the product-modulation condition of operation and the carrier component becomes small. Product-modulated waves are sometimes injected on purpose with a small carrier component to provide an accurate phase and frequency reference for demodulation.

If the maximum frequency component in the modulating signal, $v_m(t)$, is f_m then by inspecting the spectra in figure 3.6, we see that the required channel bandwidth for the modulated carrier must be

$$B = 2f_m$$

3.5   Transmission Efficiency in Envelope Modulation

We may define the transmission efficiency, η, of a modulation system as the ratio of the transmitted power actually conveying intelligence, p_s, to the total transmitted power, p_t. Thus

$$\eta = \frac{p_s}{p_t}$$

The total transmitted power will be the integral of the power spectral density, $P(f)$, of the modulated carrier

$$p_t = \int_{-\infty}^{+\infty} P(f) \, df$$

By applying equation 3.9 and, as in section 3.1, assuming the carrier to be a narrow-band process, $P(f)$ may be found to be

$$P(f) = \frac{1}{4} \{P_m(f - f_c) + P_m(f + f_c)\} + \frac{1}{4} A_c^2 \{\delta(f - f_c) + \delta(f + f_c)\} \qquad (3.10)$$

Noting that

$$\int_{-\infty}^{+\infty} P_m(f) \, df = \{\text{r.m.s. value of } v_m(t)\}^2$$

and that this integral is unaffected by a frequency translation, and also that, from equation 3.8

$$\{\text{r.m.s. value of } v_m(t)\}^2 = \frac{m^2 A_c^2}{2}$$

it follows that

$$p_t = \frac{m^2 A_c^2}{4} + \frac{A_c^2}{2}$$

The first term is the power in both sidebands. If we choose to regard the power in just one of the sidebands as all that is necessary to convey the information, then

$$p_s = \frac{m^2 A_c^2}{8}$$

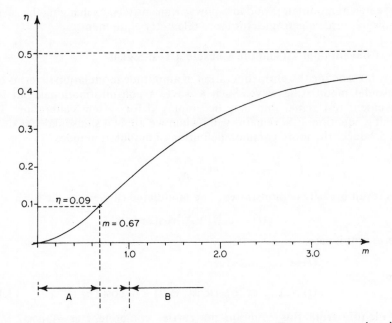

Figure 3.7 Transmission efficiency in envelope modulation. Region A: normal working range for envelope detection, assuming a noise-like modulating signal. In region B envelope detection would result in distortion

and hence

$$\eta = \frac{m^2}{2(m^2+2)}$$

A plot of transmission efficiency versus modulation index is shown in figure 3.7. Obviously as m becomes small, then since the sideband power also becomes small, so does the efficiency. Most of the transmitted power is wasted in generating the relatively large carrier component. At the other extreme, as m becomes very large, the efficiency rises towards a maximum value of 50 per cent. The carrier is now entirely suppressed and the modulation is purely multiplicative.

If we choose the 'reasonable' value of modulation index of 0.67, so that relatively little distortion occurs in envelope detection, the efficiency is approximately 9 per cent. This is the price we must pay for ease of detection and detector simplicity. In the case of commercial broadcast transmission, the penalty is not severe. The transmitter has access to a good source of power, and the expense of heavy-duty transmitting equipment is offset by the very large audience that can be reached. Other applications might preclude the use of conventional AM, however. A good example would be the transmission of information from a space probe or an earth satellite. Here the power available is limited by the number of solar cells or batteries provided, and these in turn are limited by the launching-rocket payload capability. Since the designer will wish to obtain as much data from his spacecraft as possible, he will employ very efficient modulators and low-power transmitters, exchanging the saving in power-source electronics for more telemetry equipment.

3.6   Conventional AM and the Sinusoidal Test Signal

Many texts define the entire operation of amplitude modulation in terms of a sinusoidal modulating wave. Such a wave is non-informational, but is a convenient test signal that may be employed for system calibration. The defining equation, 3.8, remains valid when we apply a sinusoidal test signal and produces the more common definition of modulation index

$$m = \frac{A_m}{A_c}$$

This result is easily demonstrated. The modulated carrier has the form

$$v(t) = \{v_m(t) + A_c\}\cos(2\pi f_c t)$$

where, in this case

$$v_m(t) = A_m \cos(2\pi f_m t)$$

Thus

$$v(t) = A_m \cos(2\pi f_m t)\cos(2\pi f_c t) + A_c \cos(2\pi f_c t) \qquad (3.11)$$

We identify from this equation the carrier component as $A_c \cos(2\pi f_c t)$. Consequently we may calculate modulating signal and carrier r.m.s. values as $(2)^{-\frac{1}{2}}A_m$ and $(2)^{-\frac{1}{2}}A_c$. Inserted into equation 3.8, these values yield the equation quoted above.

The spectrum of the envelope-modulated sinusoid defined by equation 3.11 may be deduced either from equation 3.9, or by applying a simple trigonometric argument. We shall adopt the latter procedure here. Expanding the product-modulation term in equation 3.11, we have

$$A_m \cos(2\pi f_m t)\cos(2\pi f_c t) = \frac{1}{2} A_m[\cos\{2\pi(f_c + f_m)t\} + \cos\{2\pi(f_c - f_m)t\}]$$

The terms

$$\frac{1}{2} A_m \cos\{2\pi(f_c + f_m)t\} \quad \text{and} \quad \frac{1}{2} A_m \cos\{2\pi(f_c - f_m)t\}$$

are, respectively, the upper and lower-sideband components of the modulated carrier respectively. They produce (see table 1.3) pairs of spectral lines thus

$$\frac{1}{2} A_m \cos\{2\pi(f_c + f_m)t\} \leftrightarrow \frac{1}{4} A_m[\delta\{f + (f_c + f_m)\} + \delta\{f - (f_c + f_m)\}]$$

$$\frac{1}{2} A_m \cos\{2\pi(f_c - f_m)t\} \leftrightarrow \frac{1}{4} A_m[\delta(f + (f_c - f_m)\} + \delta\{f - (f_c - f_m)\}]$$

The carrier component in equation 3.11 transforms to yield the pair of spectral lines

$$\frac{1}{2} A_c\{\delta(f + f_c) + \delta(f - f_c)\}$$

The value of modulation index may be calculated from measurements made on an oscilloscope display of the modulated waveform. From equation 3.7, we see that the *envelope* of $v(t)$ is

$$v_m(t) + A_c$$

which has maximum and minimum values

$$a = A_c + A_m$$

and

$$b = A_c - A_m$$

respectively. Solving these equations for A_m and A_c and substituting in the relation we have derived for the modulation index, given sinusoidal modulation

$$m = \frac{a - b}{a + b}$$

Further insight into the process of envelope modulation, which will be of value for the purpose of comparison when we come to examine narrow-band frequency modulation, can be obtained by considering the phasor representation of conventional amplitude modulation. The components forming the modulated carrier are obtained by expanding equation 3.11

$$v(t) = \frac{1}{2} A_m \cos\{2\pi(f_c + f_m)t\} + \frac{1}{2} A_m \cos\{2\pi(f_c - f_m)t\} + A_c \cos(2\pi f_c t)$$

If we take the carrier phasor to be the phasor of reference, we may consider it to remain fixed and erect at all instants of time. Relative to the carrier phasor, the sideband phasors will rotate with angular velocities $+\omega_m$ and $-\omega_m$. The phasor sum of the carrier and the two sidebands describes the *envelope* of the modulated carrier, figure 3.8. By allowing the carrier phasor

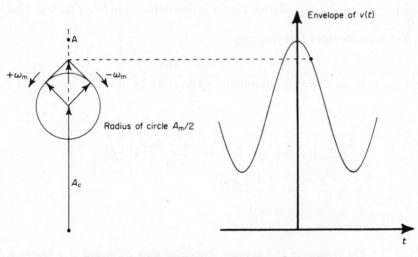

Figure 3.8 Phasor representation of conventional AM

to rotate, instead of remaining fixed, the endpoint of the phasor sum would inscribe, within the envelope, an amplitude-modulated sinusoid. With $\omega_c \gg \omega_m$, this sinusoid would execute many cycles to each cycle of modulation.

3.7   System Implementation: Modulators

3.7.1   Amplitude Modulators and Mixers[18,19,20]

In this section we shall discuss the principles of envelope modulator and 'mixer' design. The term 'mixer' is commonly applied to the low-power amplitude modulators used very frequently in radio receivers to translate a radio-frequency spectrum to a lower band, the 'intermediate frequency' band. The reason for doing this is to make the filtering amplifiers in the receiver easier to design and cheaper to construct than the equivalent radio-frequency versions.

The basic operation of product modulation may be performed by applying the sum of the modulating signal and unmodulated carrier to a square-law device with a transfer function

$$v_2(t) = \{v_1(t)\}^2$$

Then, with

$$v_1(t) = v_m(t) + \cos(2\pi f_c t) \tag{3.12}$$

it follows that

$$v_2(t) = \{v_m(t)\}^2 + \frac{1}{2}[1 + \cos\{2\pi(2f_c)t\}] + 2v_m(t)\cos(2\pi f_c t)$$

In this wave, the first and second components are at frequencies respectively much lower and much higher than the carrier frequency (assuming that the carrier frequency itself is much greater than the baseband-signal bandwidth, as would normally be the case). They can therefore be eliminated by bandpass filtering, so that the modulation system is that depicted in block form in figure 3.9.

Any second-order non-linearity

$$v_2(t) = a_0 + a_1 v_1(t) + a_2 \{v_1(t)\}^2$$

will generate an envelope-modulated wave, since by inserting equation 3.12

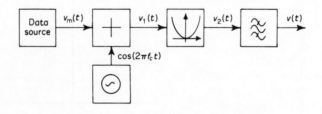

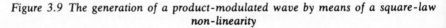

Figure 3.9 The generation of a product-modulated wave by means of a square-law non-linearity

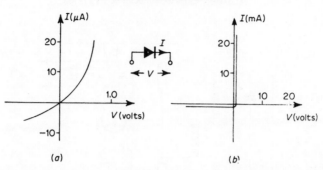

Figure 3.10 (a) The semiconductor diode characteristic corresponding to a small signal, or power-series law and (b) corresponding to a large signal, or piecewise-linear law

we find that

$$v_2(t) = a_0 + a_1 v_m(t) + a_1 \cos(2\pi f_c t) + a_2 \{v_m(t)\}^2$$
$$+ \frac{a_2}{2} [1 + \cos(2\pi(2f_c)t)] + 2a_2 v_m(t)\cos(2\pi f_c t)$$

The output from a bandpass filter following the non-linearity is a wave

$$v(t) = \{a_1 + 2a_2 v_m(t)\}\cos(2\pi f_c t)$$

which corresponds directly with the form of a conventional AM wave, equation 3.7.

Unfortunately, devices with perfect second-order non-linearities are rare. Non-linearities in general, however, are quite easy to come by. These fall into two broad categories

(a) Power-law non-linearities (characterised by a smooth curve) which have the general form

$$v_2(t) = a_0 + a_1 v_m(t) + a_2 \{v_m(t)\}^2 + a_3 \{v_m(t)\}^3 + \dots$$

(b) Piecewise-linear non-linearities.

It is often the case that the power-law non-linearity characterises the 'small-signal' behaviour of a device, whereas the piecewise-linear non-linearity characterises its 'large-signal' behaviour. To provide an illustrative example of this, consider the diode $p-n$ junction law

$$i = i_s\{\exp(eV/kT) - 1\}$$

A typical device characteristic is sketched in figure 3.10 for both small- and large-signal behaviour.

If we choose a suitably small signal swing we may expect a second-order equation to provide a good fit to any smooth curve. (Given an extremely small signal swing, even a first-order curve would be a good fit to a given function, providing the function contains no discontinuities. Differential calculus is based on this principle.)

It follows that the power-law curve corresponds most closely to low-level *Mixer* operation, rather than large-signal modulation prior to transmission. A

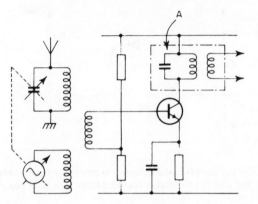

Figure 3.11 *A small-signal superheterodyne receiver mixer and first intermediate-frequency amplifier stage. Block* A *provides bandpass filtering at the intermediate frequency*

typical circuit employed for this purpose is shown in figure 3.11. The small amplitude radio-frequency signal picked up by the antenna is summed with a small signal generated by the local oscillator. The oscillator, which is usually an integral part of the first stage of transistor amplification, has a frequency which is variable in sympathy with the tuning frequency of the antenna resonator. Thus the difference frequency between the local oscillator and the incoming radio-frequency signal is maintained constant. The transistor is biassed into a non-linear region of operation and provides gain. Consequently the collector voltage is a modulated sinusoid at the difference, or 'intermediate', frequency. This signal is passed to the 'intermediate frequency' amplifier—a bandpass amplifier with a centre frequency equal to the difference frequency and a bandwidth just sufficient to pass the two sidebands of the modulated difference-frequency sinusoid. The intermediate-frequency amplifier usually consists of several stages of tuned, transformer-coupled transistor amplification. This method of achieving highly selective bandpass filtering of the incoming radio-frequency signal is known as *superheterodyne* reception.

It is useful, before passing on to examine the use of piecewise-linear approximations in the development of modulators, to examine the effect of applying too large an input signal, $v_1(t)$, to the non-linear device. Suppose, for example, that as a result of making just this mistake, we cause the curve to be most closely approximated over our larger signal range, by a third-order equation

$$v_2(t) = a_0 + a_1 v_1(t) + a_2 \{v_1(t)\}^2 + a_3 \{v_1(t)\}^3$$

If now we insert equation 3.12 into this expression and gather terms, we arrive at an equation of the form

$$v_2(t) = \{A_0 + B_0 v_m(t) + C_0 v_m^2(t) + D_0 v_m^3(t)\}$$
$$+ \{A_1 + B_1 v_m(t) + C_1 v_m^2(t)\}\cos(2\pi f_c t)$$
$$+ \{A_2 + B_2 v_m(t)\}\cos(2\pi 2 f_c t)$$
$$+ \{A_3\}\cos(2\pi 3 f_c t)$$

Here the coefficients A_0, A_1, ... are all functions of the coefficients a_0, a_1, a_2 and a_3. The second term, which consists of an envelope-modulated carrier, contains a component

$$C_1 v_m^2(t)\cos(2\pi f_c t)$$

which contributes, on demodulation, a signal proportional to the square of the modulating signal, and therefore gives rise to distortion. Note that the distortion cannot be removed by filtering; all we can do to reduce it is to decrease the input signal strength applied to the non-linearity until the signal range is such as to encompass, effectively, only a second-order law.

The piecewise-linear (large-signal) law may be employed to obtain conventional amplitude modulation in a variety of ways. If we take as our model the diode characteristic sketched in figure 3.10, we may construct a simple modulator after the fashion of figure 3.12.

The first step in the modulation process is the summation of the analogue-data waveform $v_m(t)$ and the carrier waveform $\cos(2\pi f_c t)$ to form the input waveform $v_1(t)$ which is applied to the non-linearity. The excursions of the modulating signal are arranged to be rather smaller than the amplitude of the carrier. If this is not the case gross distortion of the modulating signal will be evident, on detection. The non-linearity effectively rectifies $v_1(t)$ forming the waveform $v_2(t)$ from which the conventional AM wave $v(t)$ may be extracted by bandpass filtering.

A very simple circuit which might be developed into a practical modulator operating in this manner is shown in figure 3.13. Here i_1 and i_2 are the carrier

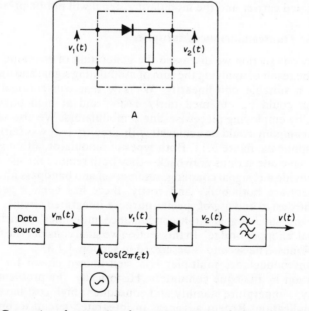

Figure 3.12 Generation of conventional AM *using a piecewise-linear non-linearity. The circuit shown in inset* A *obeys a law:* $v_2(t) = v_1(t)$ *when* $v_1(t) > 0$. *Otherwise,* $v_2(t) = 0$

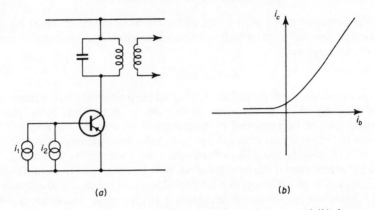

(a)   (b)

Figure 3.13 (a) A class C tuned-collector transistor modulator, and (b) the non-linear transistor-characteristic

and modulating-signal current waveforms. These current waveforms feed the modulating transistor. The transistor is biassed for class C operation so that it is switched off when the sum of i_1 and i_2 is negative and operates virtually linearly when the sum of i_1 and i_2 is positive. Operation is therefore 'large-signal'. The collector circuit is tuned to the carrier frequency and serves to isolate the modulated carrier components about the carrier frequency.

This type of modulator circuit is only suitable at small values of modulation index. To obtain a deep modulation, it is necessary to cascade two or more such stages. If this is not done, the linear relationship between the envelope of the modulated carrier and the modulating signal will not be preserved.

3.7.2   *The Transconductance Multiplier*

In the previous section we discussed the generation of envelope-modulated waves as the result of applying the sum of modulating signal and unmodulated carrier to a suitable non-linearity. We saw that conventional amplitude modulation could be obtained fairly easily, and at high power-levels if necessary, by employing piecewise-linear modulators. We also saw that low power-level mixing could be achieved with circuitry that was fairly economical of components, figure 3.11. Both types of modulator, although simple in principle, have one serious drawback—they both require the use of transformers to provide a.c. signal coupling, summation and bandpass filtering. Since transformers are both bulky and costly, there has been a general trend towards the design and use of special-purpose integrated circuits making use of either the small-signal 'transconductance multiplier' principle, or the large-signal 'chopper bridge'. In this section we shall consider the first of these two techniques. The second is described in section 3.7.3.

The transconductance multipler is a well-known circuit for high-speed multiplication in analogue computers. Historically, the problems of circuit complexity, temperature stability and consequent high cost have limited its field of application. Recent advances in integrated-circuit technology have resulted in the development of complex linear circuits in which precise control of component values is possible. This, together with the close thermal tracking of components placed on the same substrate, has allowed manufacturers to reproduce the analogue transconductance multiplier very cheaply as an integrated-circuit chip. The device has the additional very desirable features that transformer coupling is not required, and that the multiplier output, being a true product, does not need to be bandpass filtered.

The heart of the transconductance multiplier is the differential transistor amplifier shown in figure 3.14a. The important features of this circuit are as follows

(1) The input signal swing is small and fluctuates about the level v_b.

(2) The collectors of the transistors act as current sources. This means that the current issuing from each will not fluctuate with changes in load resistance (no resistors are shown in figure 3.14a because this transistor pair will be used to feed two more such pairs). It does not mean that the collector currents do not themselves fluctuate, only that such fluctuations as result because of the applied input signal are independent of changes of load. This is because the transistor is a device with an output impedance which is relatively large in comparison with the load values chosen to be operated in conjunction with it.

(3) The currents issuing from the collectors have the same bias value, corresponding to the condition $v_1 = 0$, or balanced operation, of $i_e/2$.

(4) The collector current fluctuations, which are in antiphase, vary in sympathy with the fluctuations in v_1 and are proportional in magnitude to i_e.

(5) It follows that the circuit performance may be summarised by the relations

$$i_{c_1} = +k_1 v_1 i_e + i_e/2$$
$$i_{c_2} = -k_1 v_1 i_e + i_e/2$$

where k_1 is a constant of proportionality, and

$$i_{c_1} + i_{c_2} = i_e$$

If, next, we apply the collector currents i_{c_1} and i_{c_2} to two more differential amplifiers, as figure 3.14b indicates, the following relations will be found to exist

$$i_{c_3} = +k_2 v_2 i_{c_1} + i_{c_1}/2$$
$$i_{c_4} = -k_2 v_2 i_{c_1} + i_{c_1}/2$$
$$i_{c_5} = -k_2 v_2 i_{c_2} + i_{c_2}/2$$
$$i_{c_6} = +k_2 v_2 i_{c_2} + i_{c_2}/2$$

Solving, we find that

$$i_{c_3} + i_{c_5} = 2k_1 k_2 v_1 v_2 i_e + i_e/2$$
$$\propto v_1 v_2$$

By simply implementing this equation electronically, we arrive at the basis for an integrated circuit which may be used either as a mixer, or if its output is fed

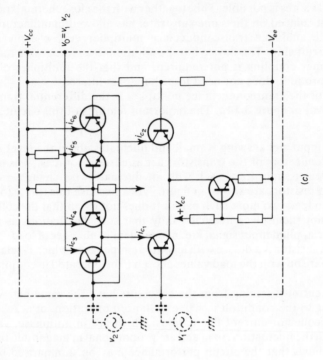

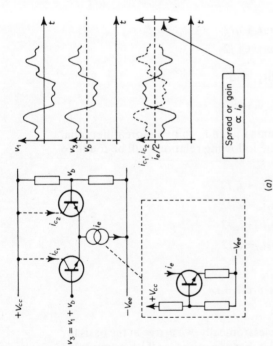

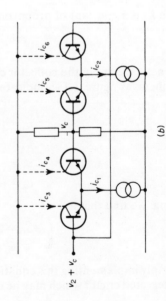

Figure 3.14 An integrated-circuit transconductance modulator: (a) the differential transistor amplifier, (b) the first stage of development of the multiplier and (c) the basis for a practical implementation

to a suitable high-frequency power amplifier, a high-quality product modulator. By suitable injection of a carrier component prior to power amplification a conventional AM wave may be generated.

Provided that it is used in the small-signal mode, the transconductance multiplier is capable of 'four-quadrant' operation. This means that it will deliver a correct product when v_1 and v_2 are either positive or negative. If we attempt to run the multiplier in the configuration sketched in figure 3.14c in a large carrier-signal mode, to obtain the sharp-edged 'chopper-modulated' waveform which characterises this type of modulation, we find that the device will yield only two-quadrant operation. This is because, with a large carrier swing, the two upper differential transistor pairs operate as switches, and are either 'hard ON' or 'hard OFF'. As a consequence, the collector currents i_{c_1} and i_{c_2} are either blocked, or pass straight through the collectors of those of the upper transistors which happen to be in the 'hard ON' state. Thus the negative half-cycles of carrier do not appear in i_{c_3} and the positive half-cycles do not appear in i_{c_4}. The problem can be resolved by generating the sum

$$i_{c_3} + i_{c_5} - i_{c_4} - i_{c_6}$$

This can be achieved very easily by feeding the collector currents i_{c_4} and i_{c_6} into another collector resistance of the same value as that fed by i_{c_3} and i_{c_5} and differencing the two resulting output voltages by applying them to another differential pair. In the next section we shall see how we may arrive at this same basic integrated-circuit configuration as the logical development of the traditional 'diode ring modulator'.

3.7.3 Ring Modulators[18]

In this section we shall discuss the development of modulators and mixers based upon signal processing by means of square-wave carriers. Let us consider a function of period T defined thus

$$\text{csq}(2\pi f_c t) = +1 \quad -T/4 < t < +T/4$$
$$= -1 \quad \text{elsewhere within the range } -T/2 < t < +T/2$$

This function is analogous to the sinusoid $\cos(2\pi f_c t)$ and may be regarded as a hard limited version of that waveform. We may generate a conventional amplitude-modulated wave by applying a csq carrier in the modulator block diagram shown in figure 3.12, in place of the sinusoidal carrier generator. The process of formation of such a modulated carrier in this way is shown in figure 3.15. Of particular importance to us is the pre-filtered waveform, $v_2(t)$, which, by inspection, contains a modulated csq carrier, an unmodulated csq carrier and a component proportional to the modulating signal. This last component and the harmonics in the csq components are eliminated by the bandpass filter. The general form of the wave $v_2(t)$ before filtering, by inspection, is

$$v_2(t) = v_m(t)\text{csq}(2\pi f_c t) + k_1 v_m(t) + k_2 \text{csq}(2\pi f_c t) \quad (3.13)$$

where k_1 and k_2 are constants. By choosing from different combinations of $\pm v_m(t)$ and $\pm\text{csq}(2\pi f_c t)$ we may eliminate the second and third terms in this expression. These terms represent, respectively, the csq carrier and the modulating-signal components at the output from the non-linearity. Their

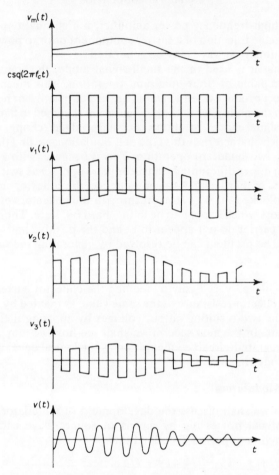

Figure 3.15 Generation of conventional AM *by means of a csq carrier*

elimination before the filtering process is of significance in that it implies that we may be able to design a large-signal modulator, operating on a switching principle, without the need for a filter and hence bulky and expensive inductive reactances. This in turn means that the circuit would be suitable for integration. The modulated carrier generated by such a modulator is still of the basic 'csq' form. As it stands, this is unsuitable for propagation, but is quite suitable for many signal-processing applications.

The elimination of the second and third terms in equation 3.13 is most easily grasped by inspection of typical system waveforms, figure 3.16, which indicates that four-quadrant modulation may be obtained if we form the sum

$$\frac{1}{4}(v_a - v_b + v_d - v_c) = v_m(t)\text{csq}(2\pi f_c t)$$

This sum, in which the csq carrier is suppressed, may be implemented by the

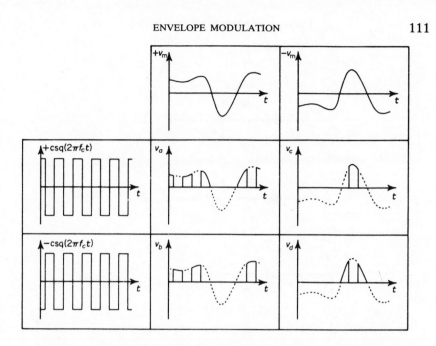

Figure 3.16 System waveforms for four-quadrant chopper modulation

system illustrated in figure 3.17, from which the classical 'diode ring modulator' follows directly as perhaps the simplest and most obvious practical implementation. In fact, the carrier, v_c, is usually applied as a sinusoid, if only because the transformer T_2 may then be tuned to resonate at the carrier frequency, to provide a suitably large amplitude to switch the diodes. The action within the bridge of the carrier is still that of a 'csq' switching waveform. If this modulator circuit is required for transmission purposes, or a narrow-band modulated sinusoid is needed, then the output transformer, T_3 may also be tuned to resonance at its secondary terminals. It should be noted that if this is done the resulting waveform is a product modulation in which the sinusoidal carrier is suppressed.

A considerable improvement in performance may be obtained by replacing the diode bridge in the ring modulator by a switching transistor-bridge. Such transistor bridges as the one illustrated in figure 3.18 are commercially available as integrated circuits. Because all the transistors are fabricated on the same substrate, close temperature-tracking of the transistor parameters is possible. This minimises carrier and signal leakage through the bridge to the output transformer. This circuit configuration provides a close link between the discrete-component diode-ring modulator and the entirely-integrated 'chopper' modulator.

Transformers T_1 and T_3 incorporated in both the transistor and diode bridge modulators essentially serve the purposes of phase splitting and signal summation respectively. As figure 3.19 indicates, they may be replaced by differential transistor amplifiers. The entirely integrated large-signal modulator is then easily deduced, in its prototype form, by comparing circuit functions and suitably redrawing the transistor bridge after the fashion of

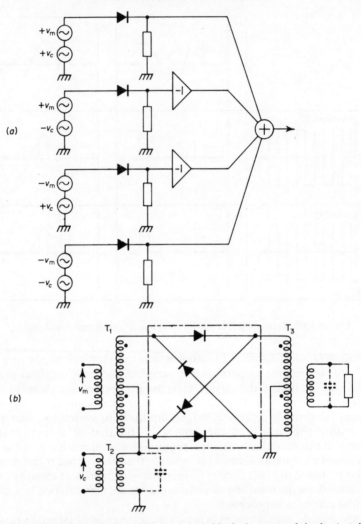

Figure 3.17 Switching diode-modulators. (a) A block diagram of the basic 'chopper modulator' and (b) the diode 'ring modulator'

figure 3.20. The reader will notice the many similarities between this circuit and the transconductance modulator circuit shown in figure 3.14c. It will also be noticed that the chopper modulator can be used for small-signal transconductance modulation and is consequently the more flexible circuit design. However, since the chopper modulator is rather more complex, it tends to be more expensive to incorporate in a system, although it must be admitted that, with integrated-circuit technology, it is not so much complexity as popularity which finally determines cost.

We have seen that, by virtue of their design, the modulators depicted in figures 3.14c, 3.17, 3.18 and 3.20 operate to produce a product-modulated wave in which the carrier term is suppressed. Because of the intrinsic

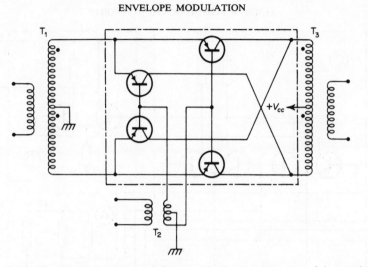

Figure 3.18 The transistor-ring modulator, with the transistor ring fabricated as an integrated circuit

symmetry of the manner in which they function, these circuits are often referred to as *balanced modulators*.

3.8 System Implementation: Demodulators

The demodulator for product-modulated waves is, as we have seen, a product modulator itself. Consequently, we need only concern ourselves with the detectors employed for conventional amplitude-modulated signals: 'envelope detectors'.

The simplest, and by far the most common implementation of the envelope detector consists of a half-wave rectifier followed by a smoothing circuit,

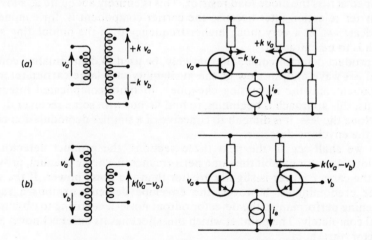

Figure 3.19 (a) Phase splitters, and (b) signal differencers

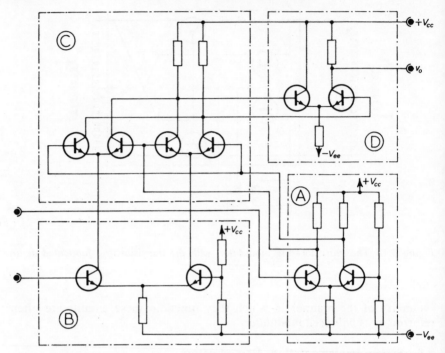

Figure 3.20 An integrated-circuit prototype for a transistor-bridge modulator. A, B: input-signal phase splitters; C: transistor bridge; D: differencing amplifier

figure 3.5. Normally, the smoothing circuit merely consists of a capacitor strapped across the diode load resistor. This is entirely adequate as a lowpass or carrier-rejection filter because the carrier component is, for commercial broadcast AM, at a very much higher frequency than the modulating signal which is to be extracted.

A product detector could, alternatively, be used to demodulate a conventional AM wave and, in view of the availability of a large carrier-reference component and the increasing cheapness of quite complicated integrated circuits, this approach is beginning to find favour with some receiver designers. None the less, it is difficult to conceive of a simpler demodulation circuit than the envelope detector.

As we shall see in the next three sections, the product detector and envelope detector exhibit the same performance in a noisy channel, provided that the carrier power is slightly greater than the noise power. If the noise power predominates, however, the envelope detector exhibits a rapidly worsening performance, the detector output noise-level rising to obscure the signal completely. The point at which this effect has its onset is known as the detector 'threshold'.

3.9   The Effect of Noise in the Detection of Envelope-modulated Waves

During transmission, the modulated carrier will become corrupted by channel noise. This noise may take several forms, of which the most common are

(1) Cross-talk, or co-channel noise arising because adjacent broadcast channels have spectra which overlap the spectrum of the signal being detected.
(2) Impulse noise, such as is caused by lightning discharge or commutator arcing in electrical machinery.
(3) Gaussian noise, both natural and artificial.

We choose to examine the third of these, since it provides us with a fairly standard and reproducible test of the performance of detectors.

First let us consider the nature of the noise in more detail. We suppose that it has a white power spectrum. This is very frequently the case in practice since, even if the total noise environment is non-white, the narrow-band nature of the pre-detection filters in the receiver makes the relatively narrow band of noise which enters the detector to all intents and purposes white. In a modern communication receiver, designed for professional use, the pre-detection filtering will be carried out by one or more intermediate-frequency amplifiers. The current trend is towards the use of monolithic quartz filters within the intermediate-frequency amplifiers, so that they are extremely selective. Even in domestic receivers, the use of ceramic resonators, as opposed to the more conventional single- or double-tuned intermediate-frequency transformers, is gaining ground. Although not quite so selective as the quartz filters, these still give a remarkably fast cut-off beyond the passband. As a consequence, we may feel justified in assuming that the pre-detection filters closely correspond to the ideal rectangular filter introduced in chapter 1. It follows that the noisewave applied to the detector will have a power spectrum of the form illustrated in figure 3.21a.

Such a bandpass noisewave could be synthesised in the following way. We require two independent baseband noise sources delivering gaussian noisewaves $x(t)$ and $y(t)$, figure 3.21b. These are used to modulate in-phase and quadrature oscillators at the carrier frequency. This yields a bandpass noisewave of the most general form

$$n(t) = x(t)\cos(2\pi f_c t) + y(t)\sin(2\pi f_c t) \qquad (3.14)$$

Furthermore, if the noise power in each of the baseband waves $x(t)$ and $y(t)$ is p_n volt^2, then

$$\left.\begin{aligned}
p_n &= \operatorname*{Lim}_{T\to\infty} \frac{1}{2T} \int_{-T}^{+T} x^2(t)\,dt \\
&= \operatorname*{Lim}_{T\to\infty} \frac{1}{2T} \int_{-T}^{+T} y^2(t)\,dt
\end{aligned}\right\} \qquad (3.15)$$

The power in the noisewave $n(t)$ may be evaluated by expressing it first in

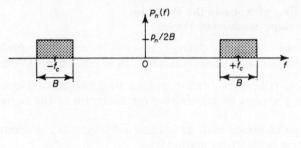

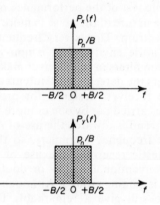

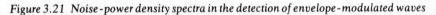

Figure 3.21 Noise-power density spectra in the detection of envelope-modulated waves

polar form

$$n(t) = \{x^2(t) + y^2(t)\}^{\frac{1}{2}} \cos\{2\pi f_c t + \phi(t)\}$$

where

$$\phi(t) = \tan^{-1}\{y(t)/x(t)\}$$

It follows that

$$n^2(t) = \{x^2(t) + y^2(t)\}\cos^2\{2\pi f_c t + \phi(t)\}$$

$$= \frac{1}{2}\{x^2(t) + y^2(t)\}[1 + \cos\{4\pi f_c t + 2\phi(t)\}]$$

Performing the integration

$$\operatorname*{Lim}_{T\to\infty} \frac{1}{2T} \int_{-T}^{+T} n^2(t)\,\mathrm{d}t$$

we find that the power in the noisewave $n(t)$ is simply p_n volt^2, the contribution from the double-frequency carrier term averaging to zero.

3.10 Signal-to-noise Ratio at the Output of the Product Demodulator

The product-modulated carrier, as we saw in section 3.1, may be expressed as

$$v_m(t)\cos(2\pi f_c t)$$

The sum of noise and carrier, the waveform applied to the detector is then, from equation 3.12, given by

$$\{v_m(t) + x(t)\}\cos(2\pi f_c t) + y(t)\sin(2\pi f_c t)$$

The detector multiplies this wave with the local-oscillator output, which is the wave $\cos(2\pi f_c t)$. Thus the detected waveform is

$$\{v_m(t) + x(t)\}\cos^2(2\pi f_c t) + y(t)\sin(2\pi f_c t)\cos(2\pi f_c t)$$

$$= \frac{1}{2}\{v_m(t) + x(t)\} + \text{high-frequency terms}$$

After lowpass filtering, the detector output may be written as

$$v_o(t) = v_m(t) + x(t)$$

We know that the output signal power is

$$p_s = \lim_{T \to \infty} \frac{1}{2T} \int_{-T}^{+T} v_m^2(t)\, dt$$

and that the power in the noise component, $x(t)$, is defined in equation 3.15 to be p_n. We also know that the channel-noise power is p_n, this result having been derived in the previous section. Finally, the modulated carrier power is given by the integral

$$\lim_{T \to \infty} \frac{1}{2T} \int_{-T}^{+T} v^2(t)\, dt = \lim_{T \to \infty} \frac{1}{2T} \int_{-T}^{+T} \frac{1}{2} v_m^2(t)\{1 + \cos(4\pi f_c t)\}\, dt$$

$$= p_s/2$$

It follows that the output signal-to-noise ratio, s, may be written in terms of the carrier-to-noise ratio, p, as

$$s = p_s/p_n$$

$$= 2p$$

Figure 3.22 illustrates the detection performance of this law. It should be noticed that the product demodulator offers an improvement in signal-to-noise ratio as the result of the detection operation of $+3$ dB. This improvement is obtained at the expense of requiring twice the baseband bandwidth through which to transmit the modulated carrier. The reason for the improvement may be explained in non-rigorous terms as follows.

During the detection operation the demodulation of the upper and lower-sideband components to baseband results in the summing of sideband-component amplitudes. This applies to both signal and noise components within the transmission band. However, the signal components are related in phase whereas the noise components at any two frequencies $(f_c \pm f_n)$ have independent phase terms. Thus the demodulated-signal components double

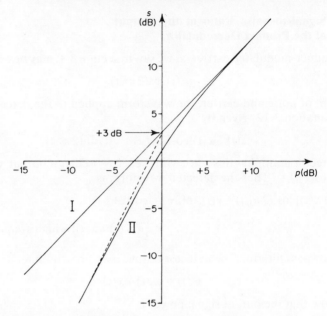

Figure 3.22 Envelope modulation: detector-noise characteristics. Curve I: *product detector; curve* II: *envelope detector*

in amplitude relative to the demodulated-noise components. The signal at baseband has a power increase by a factor of four, in comparison with the noise, which exhibits a power increase by a factor of two. Consequently, the signal acquires an advantage of $+3$ dB over the noise during demodulation.

3.11   Signal-to-noise Ratio at the Output of the Envelope Detector

The received and noise-corrupted carrier for this detection system has the general form

$$\{v_m(t) + A_c\}\cos(2\pi f_c t) + x(t)\cos(2\pi f_c t) + y(t)\sin(2\pi f_c t)$$

If we write, for compactness

$$v_m \equiv v_m(t)$$
$$x \equiv x(t)$$
$$y \equiv y(t)$$

then this equation may be expressed in the form

$$(v_m + A_c + x)\cos(2\pi f_c t) + y \sin(2\pi f_c t)$$

The envelope of this wave, which is the output of the envelope detector, is simply

$$\{(v_m + A_c + x)^2 + y^2\}^{\frac{1}{2}} \tag{3.16}$$

Two conditions of operation are amenable to further analysis

(1) Input carrier-to-noise ratio very high, so that both x and y are much less than the carrier amplitude A_c. To simplify the analysis of this condition we also assume that the modulation index is small, so that v_m is much less than A_c.

(2) Input carrier-to-noise ratio very low, so that both x and y are much greater than the carrier amplitude.

Since both x and y are noisewaves with a gaussian distribution, it follows that, however large the signal-to-noise ratio, these variables will, on occasion, assume very large values. The reader will appreciate that condition 1 specified above refers to a most typical, rather than a guaranteed operating state for a high carrier-to-noise ratio.

Continuing with our analysis of the envelope detector, we expand equation 3.16 to yield the detector output signal v_o

$$v_o = (A_c^2 + v_m^2 + x^2 + y^2 + 2A_c v_m + 2v_m x + 2A_c x)^{\frac{1}{2}} \tag{3.17}$$

Under the stated condition 1, we may write this expression in a form suitable for expansion by the binomial theorem. First, we divide throughout by A_c^2

$$v_o = A_c\{1 + (v_m/A_c)^2 + (x/A_c)^2 + (y/A_c)^2 + 2v_m/A_c + 2v_m x/A_c + 2x/A_c\}^{\frac{1}{2}}$$

Rejecting the second-order terms, which are small under the conditions of operation quoted above, we may express the detector output as

$$v_o = A_c\{1 + 2(v_m + x)/A_c\}^{\frac{1}{2}} \tag{3.18}$$

Because the term

$$2(v_m + x)/A_c$$

is itself much less than unity if the carrier-to-noise ratio is large it follows that we may employ the binomial theorem to simplify equation 3.18 further, so that

$$v_o = A_c + v(t) + x(t)$$

We are only interested in the effect of the noise on the information; that is, in the waveform

$$v_o = v(t) + x(t)$$

This result is identical to that which we derived in analysing the product detector so that the same performance graph applies to the envelope detector, providing that the carrier-to-noise ratio is large and the modulation index is fairly small.

If we turn now to the stated condition of operation 2, we may rewrite equation 3.17 in the form

$$v_o(t) = (x^2 + y^2)^{\frac{1}{2}}\left(1 + \frac{A_c^2 + v_m^2 + 2v_m A_c + 2v_m x + 2xA_c}{x^2 + y^2}\right)^{\frac{1}{2}}$$

again we may employ the binomial theorem to expand and simplify this expression, thus

$$v_o(t) = (x^2 + y^2)^{\frac{1}{2}} + \left(\frac{(A_c^2/2) + v_m A_c + xv_m + xA_c}{2(x^2 + y^2)^{\frac{1}{2}}}\right)$$

Now we see that the signal term v_m is always multiplied by a noise term of some form. Consequently the signal is entirely suppressed, and the detector output consists only of noise. This effect of complete takeover of the detector by the noise is manifest when x and y are much larger than A_c. This in turn occurs most frequently at very low values of carrier-to-noise ratio. At intermediate values, the effect is present for a proportion of the transmission time determined by the noisewave being actually, as opposed to statistically, much larger than the carrier. Consequently, we observe a deterioration of the performance of the detector. A typical plot of signal-to-noise ratio for an envelope detector is shown in figure 3.22. A slope of 2 may be found for the detection curve below the threshold by applying advanced mathematical methods. This corresponds to a square-law fall-off. The actual threshold location depends upon the diode law, but usually occurs at a carrier-to-noise ratio of about unity, or zero decibels.

Although, as we remarked in section 3.10, the envelope detector may be, and sometimes is, replaced by a product detector—in which case the threshold effect would not present a problem—it must be admitted that without further signal processing, at a carrier-to-noise ratio of zero decibels, the output signal-to-noise ratio of 3 dB is all but unusable. The fact is that for the great majority of users of domestic AM receiving equipment, the carrier-to-noise ratio never approaches the threshold value, so that the problem does not arise.

Problems

3.1 Derive equations to illustrate the effect of loss of phase and frequency-lock during product detection of a product-modulated sinusoid by assuming a local oscillator signal

    (a) $\cos(2\pi f_c t + \phi)$
    (b) $\cos\{2\pi(f_c + \Delta f)t\}$

Discuss your results, explaining why product modulation is not used to convey information in practical radio-communication systems.

3.2 Show that, if a product-modulated wave is applied to a square-law non-linearity, a component at twice the carrier frequency may be extracted and further processed to yield a phase and frequency-locked local-oscillator signal. State the further processing which is required and draw a suitable system block-diagram. If the transmitter and receiver are moving rapidly with respect to each other, Doppler frequency shifts will occur. How well will your system cope with such an effect?

3.3 An envelope-modulated wave is defined by the equation

$$v(t) = \{10 + 3\cos(2\pi 10^3 t)\}\cos(2\pi 10^7 t)$$

Identify the amplitude and frequency of the unmodulated carrier and the modulating signal. Determine the modulation index, the power in the two sidebands and the total power in the carrier.

3.4   For the envelope-modulated wave defined in question 3.3, calculate the transmission efficiency both from first principles and by using the result derived in section 3.5.

3.5   An envelope-modulated carrier is defined by the equation

$$v(t) = \{10 + 3\cos(2\pi 100t) + 4\sin(2\pi 200t)\}\cos(2\pi 10^6 t)$$

Sketch the modulating signal, and the general shape of the modulated carrier. Write down an expression for the modulating signal and determine its mean square value. (*Hint* Refer to question 1.23 for guidance on the latter point.) Determine the modulation index and state whether envelope detection will be possible without distortion.

3.6   Carefully sketch the frequency spectrum of the amplitude modulation defined in question 3.5 taking care to identify the phase relationships of the various components in the upper and lower sidebands. Sketch also, to scale, the power spectrum of the specified wave.

3.7   What is a superheterodyne receiver and how does it differ in operation from a tuned radio-frequency receiver? Determine the value of the local-oscillator frequency if a 98 MHz radio-frequency signal is to be translated to an intermediate frequency of 10.7 MHz?

3.8   A square-law device is proposed as a detector for a conventional amplitude-modulated signal. Show that its output contains a term proportional to the modulating signal. What further processing is required to isolate this component?
   Show that a distortion term is present and indicate how it is best minimised. Contrast the operation of the square-law detector with that of an idealised piecewise-linear (or large signal) rectifier detector.

3.9   Explain why phase coherency of the sidebands during product detection leads to a +3 dB advantage in output signal-to-noise ratio over input signal-to-noise ratio. How does envelope detection differ from product detection in its behaviour in the presence of noise?

3.10   A sinewave of amplitude 4.2 volts is modulated with another sinewave of amplitude 2 volts and frequency 100 Hz. This second sinewave may be considered representative of the maximum modulating-signal frequency within the particular system under consideration. The modulated sinusoid is immersed in white gaussian channel-noise of spectral density 0.1 volt^2 Hz^{-1}. Show that the system as specified operates below the threshold for envelope detection and determine the input signal-to-noise ratio applied to the detector.

3.11   If for the system described in question 3.11, the threshold is taken to be the point of intersection of the asymptotes

$$s = 2p$$

and

$$s \propto p^2$$

and is taken to occur at a value of $p = 0$ dB, determine the system output signal-to-noise ratio.

3.12 Prove that, if

$$v(t) = v_m(t)\sin(2\pi f_c t)$$

then

$$V(f) = (1/2j)\{V_m(f - f_c) - V_m(f + f_c)\}$$

Sketch the spectrum of $V(f)$ if

$$v_m(t) = A_m \cos(2\pi f_m t)$$

What change occurs if

$$v_m(t) = A_m \sin(2\pi f_m t)?$$

4 Angle Modulation

In the introduction to chapter 3, we stated that modulation of a sinusoidal carrier was employed to effect a spectral relocation of baseband information. We saw that linear envelope-modulation, defined by the relation

$$v(t) = \{kv_m(t) + c\}\cos(2\pi f_c t + \phi_c)$$

also provided a small improvement in noise immunity. When the carrier is immersed in gaussian noise, we find that the signal-to-noise ratio at the detector output is 3 dB higher than the carrier-to-noise ratio at its input. This improvement is only obtained at the expense of additional transmission bandwidth, since the spectrum of the modulated carrier occupies twice the bandwidth of the spectrum of the baseband modulating-signal.

As it happens, we can substantially improve upon this detection performance if, instead, we employ angle modulation. Angle modulation involves maintaining a constant carrier-amplitude and allowing the phase term $\phi(t)$ to fluctuate in proportion to the modulating signal. Not only does angle modulation improve upon the detection performance of linear envelope-modulation, albeit at the expense of an even greater channel bandwidth, it is also immune to channel non-linearity. This is because the information is conveyed not in the envelope, which remains constant, but in the *zero crossings* of the carrier, the time instants at which $v(t)$ is zero. Consequently, any amplitude distortion introduced by the channel, which would seriously corrupt an envelope-modulated wave, has no effect on the detectability of an angle-modulated wave.

Because of these properties, angle-modulation systems are widely employed for high-quality links handling both analogue and digital data—but only when bandwidth is not at a premium. Since transmission quality is obtained by trading bandwidth for noise immunity, it is usually the case that angle modulation is confined to relatively high carrier-frequencies. The reason for this is twofold. At low frequencies, the radio spectrum is heavily loaded with traffic. At higher frequencies (in the VHF band and above, at frequencies in excess of 30 MHz) not only is there less traffic, but the propagation mode is *line-of-sight* and consequently of relatively short range. Hence, providing their geographical separation is sufficient, many transmitting stations may share the same frequency allocation, conveying different local information. Line-of-sight propagation is enforced because the ionosphere has a *microwave window* and will not reflect very-high-frequency carriers.

As we shall see in chapter 8, digital data is used to angle-modulate very-low-frequency carriers for line-transmission purposes. This can result in the relatively inefficient use of the line in comparison with the performance that would be obtained if envelope modulation were used. However, angle modulation offers the advantages of a communication scheme that is both robust and economical.

4.1 The General Angle-modulated Sinusoid[21]

The general modulated sinusoid was defined in section 2.14 by the relation

$$v(t) = A(t)\cos\{2\pi f_c t + \phi(t)\}$$

where

$$A(t) = g_1\{v_m(t)\}$$

and

$$\phi(t) = g_2\{v_m(t)\}$$

The angle-modulated sinusoid is defined by restricting the amplitude term to be time-invariant

$$A(t) = A_c$$

Current practice requires that we need only consider linear relations between $v_m(t)$ and $\phi(t)$, of which the simplest is

$$\phi(t) = k_1 v_m(t) + c \tag{4.1}$$

This equation allows us to define the condition of operation known as *phase modulation*. For simplicity, we may, without unduly restricting our analysis, set the constant c to zero. Then

$$v(t) = A_c \cos\{2\pi f_c t + k_1 v_m(t)\} \tag{4.2}$$

The coefficient k_1 is a 'modulator constant', specified in units of radian volt^{-1}. It defines the extent of phase excursions of a hypothetical electronic phase-modulator circuit. In practice, it is a quantity which may be determined, for a real modulator, by experiment as we shall see in section 4.6.

We might be tempted to define 'frequency modulation' as the variation of the parameter f_c in sympathy with the modulating signal. To be absolutely accurate, this is certainly not the case, although under conditions of operation which cause the 'frequency' fluctuations imposed by $v_m(t)$ to take place very slowly, it is the superficial appearance presented by the modulated carrier.

When we discussed the nature of the general modulated sinusoid in section 2.14, we saw that our concept of frequency as the reciprocal of the period (the distance between adjacent zero crossings of the same sense) was quite inappropriate when the phase of the sinusoid was permitted to be time-variant. This loose definition of frequency is basically incorrect.

Let us return to the phasor representation of the modulated sinusoid first introduced in section 2.14. This representation is illustrated in figure 4.1. We

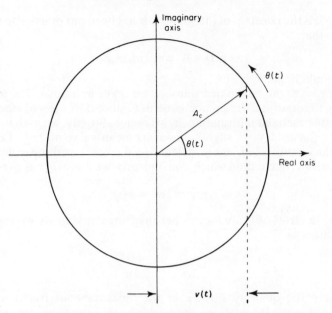

Figure 4.1 Generation of the angle-modulated carrier $v(t) = A_c \cos\{\theta(t)\}$

think of the phasor as a rigid, rotating member of length A_c making an angle θ with the real axis. Since the phasor rotates, θ is time-variant, $\theta(t)$. The sinusoid is generated as the real part of the phasor (the horizontal projection of the rotating member) so that

$$v(t) = A_c \cos\{\theta(t)\}$$

The rotation of the phasor is further defined by its angular velocity, which is the derivative of the total phase angle $\theta(t)$, that is $\dot{\theta}(t)$ radian s^{-1}.

In this respect, angular rotation is the direct analogue of linear motion, with

$$\theta(t) \equiv x(t)$$
$$\dot{\theta}(t) \equiv \dot{x}(t)$$

$x(t)$ and $\dot{x}(t)$ being, respectively, the displacement and velocity of a particle constrained to move along a straight line.

For an *unmodulated* sinusoid, the angular velocity is constant

$$\dot{\theta}(t) = \omega_c$$
$$= 2\pi f_c$$

where f_c is the frequency of the sinusoid as we should conventionally define it. By integrating the angular velocity, we may obtain the total phase angle and hence specify the unmodulated sinusoid in full.

$$\theta(t) = \int \dot{\theta}(\tau)\, d\tau$$
$$= 2\pi f_c t + \theta(0)$$

Here, $\theta(0)$ is the constant of integration. It has been our practice to write $\theta(0)$ as ϕ_c, so that

$$v(t) = A_c \cos(2\pi f_c t + \phi_c)$$

as we should hope.

In the case of the *modulated* sinusoid, we argue as follows. The phasor will continue to rotate at a 'frequency' close to f_c, since the object of modulation is to relocate baseband information in this region. Strictly, we wish to make the angular velocity deviate slightly about its mean value of $2\pi f_c$. Let us then regard the quantity $2\pi f_c$ as equivalent to a d.c. level, and superimpose upon this a small a.c. fluctuation which, conveniently, we may write as $\dot\phi(t)$. Then

$$\dot\theta(t) = 2\pi f_c + \dot\phi(t)$$

Thinking in terms of frequency rather than angular velocity we may rewrite this equation as

$$\frac{\dot\theta(t)}{2\pi} = f_c + \frac{\dot\phi(t)}{2\pi}$$

We regard the quantity $\dot\theta(t)/2\pi$ as the 'instantaneous frequency' of the rotating phasor. Integrating, to establish the equation for the angle-modulated carrier, we find that

$$\theta(t) = 2\pi f_c t + \phi(t)$$

so that

$$v(t) = A_c \cos\{2\pi f_c t + \phi(t)\} \tag{4.3}$$

The connection between equations 4.2 and 4.3 is immediately apparent. The latter defines a *phase-modulated* wave provided that

$$\phi(t) = k_1 v_m(t)$$

It is less obvious that, defining $\phi(t)$ in a different manner, equation 4.3 also describes 'frequency modulation'. We have arrived at the conclusion that when a wave is angle-modulated it is only correct to discuss the properties of the wave in terms of 'instantaneous frequency'. We define *frequency modulation* to be the fluctuation of the instantaneous frequency in sympathy with the modulating signal.

$$\frac{\dot\theta(t)}{2\pi} = k v_m(t) + c$$

Retaining the convention used above, we let

$$c = f_c$$

and rewrite this expression as

$$\dot\theta(t) = 2\pi f_c + k_2 v_m(t) \tag{4.4}$$

so that, integrating, we obtain the total phase angle

$$\theta(t) = 2\pi f_c t + k_2 \int_0^t v_m(\tau)\, d\tau$$

It follows that

$$v(t) = A_c \cos\left\{2\pi f_c t + k_2 \int_0^t v_m(\tau)\, d\tau\right\} \qquad (4.5)$$

Again, we have a phase-modulated wave with

$$\phi(t) = k_2 \int_0^t v_m(\tau)\, d\tau$$

but one in which the instantaneous frequency is linearly related and directly proportional to the modulating signal. The phase term is also linearly related to $v_m(t)$—integration is a linear mathematical operation.

The constant k_2 in equations 4.4 and 4.5 is, like k_1 in equations 4.1 and 4.2, a modulator constant. Its units are radian s^{-1} volt^{-1} and it may be determined experimentally for real modulators by means of the method outlined in section 4.6.

Having defined the phase- and frequency-modulated sinusoids mathematically we should like to examine their properties in the time domain. To simplify this task, we reiterate the very common constraint that the modulated carrier be narrow-band. This amounts to demanding that the 'd.c. component' in the instantaneous frequency, that is, the parameter f_c, is much greater than the fluctuation amplitude, or 'a.c. component', $\dot\phi(t)/2\pi$. In fact this constraint is not a condition implicit in the definition of either phase or frequency modulation. It is applied only to make visualisation of the phasor or time-domain operations easier. Another constraint is that the bandwidth of the modulating signal be much less than f_c. Then fluctuations of instantaneous frequency occur slowly, over many hundreds of cycles of carrier. Consequently, the period of each cycle will very closely approximate to the

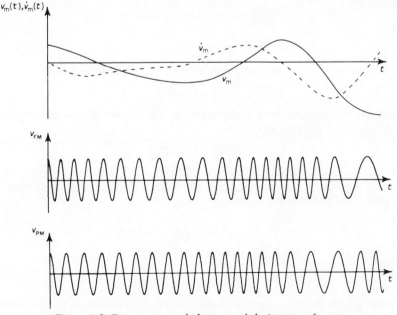

Figure 4.2 Frequency- and phase-modulation waveforms

reciprocal of the instantaneous frequency. Since the instantaneous frequency is proportional to the differential of the total phase angle

$$2\pi f_c t + \phi(t)$$

it follows that adjacent zero crossings of the modulated carrier will group together for high values of $\dot{\phi}(t)$ and become spaced apart for low values. Thus if the wave is 'frequency modulated' (and narrow-band) its apparent frequency, estimated in the non-rigorous manner as equal to the reciprocal of the distance between adjacent zero-crossings of the same sense, will fluctuate in sympathy with the modulating signal. In contrast, if the wave were phase-modulated the 'frequency' would fluctuate in sympathy with $\dot{v}_m(t)$. In both cases the amplitude of the wave will remain constant at a value A_c. Figure 4.2 illustrates typical phase- and frequency-modulated carriers as functions of time.

4.2 The Problem of Spectral Analysis

Having described the angle-modulated wave in the time domain, we naturally wish to investigate its properties in the frequency domain. Specifically, we should like to estimate or calculate $V(f)$, the Fourier transform of $v(t)$, since this quantity will lead to a determination of the carrier power spectral density $P(f)$. The power spectrum will, in turn allow us to predict the carrier bandwidth and hence determine the necessary channel bandwidth required if the wave is to be conveyed without severe band limiting. Before we embark upon this task, it is useful to examine the general problem of spectral analysis for angle-modulated waves more closely.

We have that

$$v(t) = A_c \cos\{2\pi f_c t + \phi(t)\}$$

where

$$\phi(t) = g_2\{v_m(t)\}$$

To be completely general, we could rewrite this equation as

$$v(t) = f\{v_m(t)\}$$

where $f(\ \ )$ is a highly non-linear function. Ideally, we should like to be able to determine a parallel equation

$$V(f) = F\{V_m(f)\}$$

where $F(\ \ )$ was inferred, or calculated from $f(\ \ )$. Indeed, we were able to achieve just this in the previous chapter when we deduced the spectrum of a product-modulated wave

$$V(f) = \frac{1}{2}\{V_m(f - f_c) + V_m(f + f_c)\}$$

from the defining equation

$$v(t) = v_m(t)\cos(2\pi f_c t)$$

Now, any modulation process (including product modulation) is inherently non-linear. Those modulations in which the *envelope* is linearly related to the modulating signal and in which the phase term ϕ is constant do at least permit *superposition* to be applied. To appreciate the implications of this statement, suppose that

$$v_m(t_2) = v_m(t_1)$$

It does not follow that, for a product-modulated wave

$$v(t_2) = v(t_1)$$

since $\cos(2\pi f_c t_2)$ may have quite a different value to $\cos(2\pi f_c t_1)$. Consequently the modulation is strictly a non-linear operation. However, suppose that

$$v_i(t) = A_i(t)\cos(2\pi f_c t)$$

and that

$$A(t) = \sum_i A_i(t)$$

Then if

$$v(t) = A(t)\cos(2\pi f_c t)$$
$$= \sum_i A_i(t)\cos(2\pi f_c t)$$

it follows that

$$v(t) = \sum_i v_i(t)$$

Thus even though the modulation is non-linear, superposition still applies and consequently Fourier methods can be employed. That is, if we determine the spectrum for a sinusoidal modulating-signal, we may infer its spectrum for any other modulating signal by decomposing that signal into the sum of its constituent sinusoids, employing as appropriate either Fourier series or Fourier transform methods to achieve this.

In contrast, if we write

$$v_i(t) = A_c \cos\{2\pi f_c t + \phi_i(t)\}$$

and form the sum

$$\phi(t) = \sum_i \phi_i(t)$$

then it is immediately apparent that

$$A_c \cos\left\{2\pi f_c t + \sum_i \phi_i(t)\right\} \neq \sum_i A_c \cos\{2\pi f_c t + \phi_i(t)\}$$

Hence superposition does not apply, Fourier methods may not be used and the search to specify the function $F(\ )$ from a knowledge of the function $f(\ )$ is a fruitless one.

4.3 A Quasi-linear Spectral Analysis

We have seen that a general relationship prescribing $V(f)$ as a function of $V_m(f)$ does not exist. However, under one restricted set of conditions, a very simple linear relationship does exist between $V(f)$ and $\Phi(f)$, the Fourier transform of $\phi(t)$.

Since we have constrained $\phi(t)$ to be a linear function of $v_m(t)$ it is by no means difficult to express $\Phi(f)$ in terms of $V_m(f)$ to determine spectra for specific phase or frequency modulations.

First let us examine the defining equation

$$v(t) = A_c \cos\{2\pi f_c t + \phi(t)\}$$

We may expand this to yield

$$v(t) = A_c \cos(2\pi f_c t)\cos\{\phi(t)\} - A_c \sin(2\pi f_c t)\sin\{\phi(t)\}$$

We know that both $\cos\{\phi(t)\}$ and $\sin\{\phi(t)\}$ may be expanded as power series

$$\cos(\phi) = 1 - \frac{\phi^2}{2!} + \frac{\phi^4}{4!} - \frac{\phi^6}{6!} + \cdots$$

$$\sin(\phi) = \phi - \frac{\phi^3}{3!} + \frac{\phi^5}{5!} - \frac{\phi^7}{7!} + \cdots$$

It follows for small values of ϕ, $|\phi(t)| \ll 1$, that

$$\cos\{\phi(t)\} \approx 1$$

and

$$\sin\{\phi(t)\} \approx \phi$$

Thus

$$v(t) \approx A_c \cos(2\pi f_c t) - A_c\phi(t)\sin(2\pi f_c t) \qquad (4.6)$$

We shall examine the effect of larger values of ϕ shortly. Notice that the second term in this expression corresponds to a product modulation. Since this is so, it is an easy matter to write down the spectrum of the general angle-modulated wave for small phase deviations as

$$V(f) = \frac{1}{2} A_c[\delta(f - f_c) + \delta(f + f_c) + j\{\Phi(f - f_c) - \Phi(f + f_c)\}] \qquad (4.7)$$

If the carrier is phase-modulated, then with

$$\phi(t) = k_1 v_m(t) \qquad (4.8)$$

it follows that

$$V(f) = \frac{1}{2} A_c[\delta(f - f_c) + \delta(f + f_c) + jk_1\{V_m(f - f_c) - V_m(f + f_c)\}] \qquad (4.9)$$

This spectrum is illustrated in figure 4.3. The power spectrum, again assuming narrow-band conditions ($f_c \gg B$) is given as

$$P(f) = \frac{1}{4} A_c^2[\delta(f - f_c) + \delta(f + f_c) + k_1^2\{P_m(f - f_c) + P_m(f + f_c)\}] \qquad (4.10)$$

where $P_m(f)$ is the power spectrum of $v_m(t)$. If equation 4.10 is compared with equation 3.10 it will be seen that both have the same form and would, indeed, by identical if $k_1 = A_c^{-1}$. Thus although AM and narrow-band PM are quite different time-waveforms, their power spectra are of identical form.

Inspection of the spectra shown in figure 4.3 shows that the signal band-width is determined by the relation

$$B = 2f_m$$

As we increase the phase deviation so that the condition $|\phi(t)| \ll 1$ no longer applies, more of the power terms in the series expansions of $\cos \phi$ and $\sin \phi$

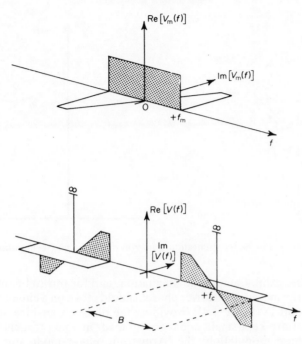

Figure 4.3 Spectrum of narrow deviation phase-modulated wave; $B = 2f_m$

given above become significant. Since multiplication in the time domain is equivalent to convolution in the frequency domain, the result is a spreading of the power spectrum so that, when $\phi(t)$ is no longer small the transmission bandwidth is substantially greater than that required for the various envelope modulations: $B \gg 2f_m$. Indeed, if $\phi(t)$ is large, all terms in the expansion must be included and $B \rightarrow \infty$. However, the convolution process tends to retain most of the carrier power in a band adjacent to the carrier so that, for practical purposes, the modulation scheme is still narrow-band, despite having small components at frequencies remote from f_c.

An interesting comparison exists between the phasor representation of the generation of conventional AM (figure 3.8) and the phasor representation of the generation of phase modulation in the manner described by equation 4.6. In the latter case, the product-modulated component has a carrier in phase quadrature with the larger, main-carrier phasor. Comparison of figures 3.8 and 4.4 shows that in the first instance, at time $t = 0$, the endpoints of the phasors start from point A and move in opposite rotational sense with angular velocities $+\omega_m$ and $-\omega_m$, so that their sum has a locus which passes through the point A perpendicularly.

In the second instance—the generation of phase modulation—the sidebands again rotate in opposite sense but they start at time $t = 0$ at the point B. Their sum has a locus which passes horizontally through point B. Notice that the horizontal locus through B results in the modulated carrier exhibiting a small amplitude-fluctuation. A fixed amplitude, phase-modulated carrier should

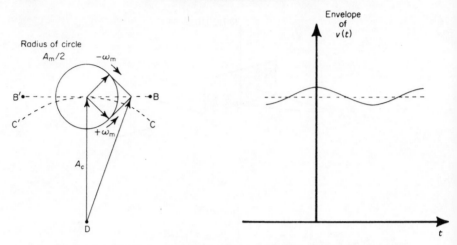

Figure 4.4 Phasor representation of narrow deviation phase-modulation

not, of course, exhibit amplitude fluctuation, and for this to be the case, the endpoint of the modulated carrier phasor should move on a circular locus CC' about the point D (figure 4.4). Providing the phase excursions of the modulated carrier are kept small, equation 4.6 leads us to a practical method of obtaining phase modulation: the 'Armstrong phase modulator', which is described briefly in section 4.7.2.

4.4 A Quasi-static Spectral Analysis

We have considered in the previous section the quasi-linear analysis of angle-modulated waves which is applicable when the amplitude of the modulating signal and consequently the excursions of the phase function $\phi(t)$ are very small.

Another very simple method of estimating *power spectra* for angle modulation, known as *quasi-static analysis*, may be employed when the bandwidth of the modulating signal is small in comparison with the fluctuations of instantaneous frequency. The quasi-static method involves the same approximation that was employed in section 4.1 when we discussed the time-domain representation of the angle-modulated wave. That is, we choose to apply it only when the fluctuations of instantaneous frequency occur sufficiently slowly that the 'instantaneous frequency' and the 'zero-crossing-count frequency' are virtually interchangeable quantities. Basically, the method requires that we regard the modulated carrier as a moving δ-function. Sometimes the rather graphic phrase 'moving finger in the frequency domain' is used to describe the carrier. The moving finger slides along the frequency axis in sympathy with the modulating signal. The overall effect is very similar to considering the modulator as a mechanistic system consisting of a variable-frequency sinewave oscillator, the dial of which is rotated through an angle proportional to the modulating-signal amplitude at any given instant of time.

We shall consider first the spectral analysis of a frequency-modulated wave, and then discuss the application of the method to phase modulation. To see

how the model of the modulating process described above allows us to predict
the power spectrum, recall that $P(f)$ may be experimentally obtained by
measuring the mean power at the output of a narrow bandpass filter centred at
a frequency f_1. If the mean power is p_a and the filter bandwidth δf, then

$$P(f_1) \approx \frac{p_a}{\delta f}$$

The approximation improves as δf becomes small. Next, consider figure 4.5.
The proportion of time during which the moving finger resides in the narrow
band δf at the frequency f_1 is equal to the proportion of time during which the
modulating signal resides in an equivalent narrow strip δv at a voltage v_1. It
follows that the power spectrum will be proportional to the amplitude
probability-density distribution of the modulating signal and must be suitably
scaled so that

$$\int_{-\infty}^{+\infty} P(f)\, df = \frac{1}{2} A_c^2$$

The procedure involved in determining $P(f)$ for a modulating signal of
specified distribution function is most clearly demonstrated by an example.
Let the signal frequency modulating a sinusoidal carrier be a gaussian

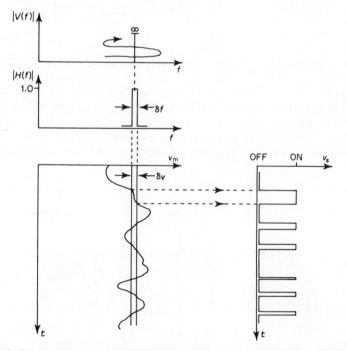

Figure 4.5 Quasi-static spectral analysis. v_s is the switch voltage applied to trigger an
electronic timer to measure the probability that v_m lies in the narrow strip δv and hence
that the frequency-domain δ-function lies within the range of the bandpass filter (see also
figure 2.2)

noisewave of power p_s with a distribution

$$p(v_m) = \frac{1}{\sqrt{(2\pi p_s)}} \exp(-v_m^2/2p_s)$$

The quasi-static method implies that the power spectrum will also be gaussian. We define a peak carrier deviation, Δf, which could be thought of as the result of clipping $v_m(t)$ to ensure the practical requirement that both it and the deviations of the carrier were bounded. We also define an r.m.s. carrier deviation f_σ. Since the general gaussian distribution has the form

$$p(x) = \frac{1}{\sigma\sqrt{(2\pi)}} \exp(-x^2/2\sigma^2)$$

where

$$\sigma = \text{r.m.s. value of } x$$

we may deduce a carrier power spectrum, by analogy, which has the form

$$P(f) = \frac{1}{4} A_c^2 \frac{1}{f_\sigma\sqrt{(2\pi)}} [\exp\{-(f-f_c)^2/2f_\sigma^2\} + \exp\{-(f+f_c)^2/2f_\sigma^2\}] \quad (4.11)$$

A common choice of the ratio of peak to r.m.s. carrier deviation in analogue FM systems is

$$\frac{\Delta f}{f_\sigma} = 3 \quad (4.12)$$

so that

$$P(f) = \frac{1}{4} A_c^2 \frac{1}{\sqrt{(2\pi)}} \frac{3}{\Delta f} [\exp\{-4.5(f-f_c)^2/\Delta f^2\} + \exp\{-4.5(f+f_c)^2/\Delta f^2\}]$$

$$(4.13)$$

This ratio of Δf to f_σ ensures that the carrier deviation is clipped by the bounds $f_c \pm \Delta f$ for approximately 0.1 per cent of the time. The distortion which arises as the result of this small probability of exceeding the bound is held to be negligible. The general form of the power spectrum is shown in figure 4.6.

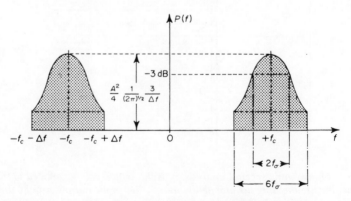

Figure 4.6 Power spectrum of a carrier frequency-modulated with gaussian noise: quasi-static analysis

Spectral analysis of a phase-modulated wave can be inferred in the following way. A phase modulator can be formed by preceding a frequency modulator with a differentiator. If we can either calculate or estimate the probability-density distribution of the differential of the modulating signal, we can deduce the power spectrum. To use, once again, the example of a noise-like modulating signal we note that since a differentiator is a linear filter, the signal at its output will also be gaussian. If the input noisewave has a white spectrum, the output noisewave will be 'coloured'. However, the spectral shape of the modulating signal is not of importance in a quasi-static analysis. We need only to know the *power* in the noisewave at the differentiator output.

In section 1.23 we saw that the power spectrum at the output of a linear filter with a transfer function $H(f)$, given an input-power spectrum $P_1(f)$ is

$$P_2(f) = |H(f)|^2 \, P_1(f)$$

If we assume a white modulating signal of power p_s and bandwidth f_m, then

$$P_1(f) = \frac{p_s}{2f_m} \quad \text{volt Hz}^{-1} \quad -f_m \leq f \leq f_m$$

The differentiator, from table 2.1, has a transfer function

$$H(f) = 2\pi j f$$

so that

$$P_2(f) = \frac{p_s}{2f_m} 4\pi^2 f^2 \quad -f_m \leq f \leq f_m$$

$$= 0 \quad \text{elsewhere}$$

The total power in the output wave is given by the integral

$$\int_{-f_m}^{f_m} P_2(f) \, df = \frac{4\pi^2 f_m^2 p_s}{3}$$

Since the output wave from the differentiator is gaussian, so also will be the power spectrum of the phase-modulated wave. The maximum carrier-deviation of the phase-modulated wave is given by the ratio

$$\frac{\Delta f_{PM}}{\Delta f_{FM}} = \frac{\text{r.m.s. of derivative of modulating signal}}{\text{r.m.s. of modulating signal}}$$

or

$$\Delta f_{PM} = \Delta f_{FM} \left(\frac{4\pi^2 f_m^2}{3} \right)^{\frac{1}{2}} \tag{4.14}$$

Consequently, a phase modulator produces a carrier spectrum which has a width dependent on both the modulating-signal amplitude and its bandwidth.

4.5 Band Occupancy of Angle-modulated Waves

In the previous sections we have seen that for small phase-deviations, a quasi-linear spectral analysis may be used to estimate the carrier spectrum bandwidth. Given a baseband modulating signal of bandwidth f_m the carrier bandwidth is

$$B = 2f_m \qquad (4.15)$$

As the phase deviation increases, the bandwidth of the modulated carrier becomes substantially larger than this value. For very large phase-deviations we can apply the quasi-static spectral analysis and we then find that

$$B = 2\,\Delta f \qquad (4.16)$$

where Δf is the *peak carrier deviation*.

We may take the ratio $\Delta f / f_m$ to be a 'universal constant' for all angle modulations and we shall denote this constant by the symbol m, referring to it as the *modulation index* or *deviation ratio*. We shall see why this is permissible in the next paragraph, but for the moment let us take the result on trust. The bandwidth specification derived for the quasi-static case may be written as

$$B = 2mf_m$$

and applies only when m is large, since this constraint implies that f_m must be much less than Δf, or that sweeps of instantaneous frequency take place slowly. The quasi-linear result applies when the modulation index and hence the amplitude of fluctuation of both instantaneous frequency and its integral, the total phase angle, are small. Thus

$$\begin{aligned} B &= 2f_m \qquad m \ll 1 \\ B &= 2mf_m \qquad m \gg 1 \end{aligned} \qquad (4.17)$$

We may unify these two equations by writing

$$B = 2f_m(m + 1) \qquad (4.18)$$

and this result empirically determines the required channel bandwidth for any given modulation index. This general formula is known as Carson's rule, after its innovator, and is widely accepted as a criterion of band occupancy for all angle-modulation systems in which the modulating signal is analogue in nature, rather than digital.

In order to derive Carson's rule, which in itself is a very important criterion in the design of angle-modulation communication systems, we used the fact that the quantity

$$m = \frac{\Delta f}{f_m} \qquad (4.19)$$

was a universal constant for such systems. Naturally, we must be able to justify such a sweeping statement. We employ the concept of 'modulation index' because it allows us to think in terms of a *normalised* modulation operation. Any results that we obtain which are in terms of this normalising variable, rather than Δf and f_m we may subsequently denormalise to suit any particular cases of operation that are of interest to us. We are at present concerned essentially with spectral analysis. What conditions, we may ask, lead us to a set of spectra of the same detailed 'shape' or 'form' with, as the only permitted differences between members of this set, a possible frequency-scale or amplitude-scale expansion or contraction? As table 1.2 states, a time-scale expansion by a factor k leads to a frequency-scale contraction also by a factor

k, together with an amplitude scaling of $1/k$

$$v(t) \leftrightarrow V(f)$$

$$v(kt) \leftrightarrow \frac{1}{k} V(f/k)$$

If $v(t)$ is our angle-modulated carrier, a time-scale expansion to give $v(kt)$ must also involve a time-scale expansion of $v_m(t)$ to $v_m(kt)$. This will result in a frequency-scale contraction, the highest frequency component in $v_m(kt)$ being kf_m. In the same way, the phase term in the carrier $\phi(t)$ will become $\phi(kt)$ with a differential $k\dot{\phi}(t)$. The maximum instantaneous frequency must therefore also increase by a factor k to preserve the *shape* of both time- and frequency-domain processes. We see that all modulated carriers in which the ratio, for a given modulating waveform shape, of Δf to f_m is kept constant will have spectra of the same shape. The band occupancy, suitable scaling included, will be the same for all.

In the next section we shall see that the sinusoidal test signal provides a simple example of just this phenomenon—although the test signal itself is quite unrepresentative in many respects of typical modulating waveforms, which tend to be noise-like in appearance.

4.6   The Sinusoidal Test Signal

In the earlier sections of this chapter we found it necessary to specify modulator constants k_1 and k_2 for phase and frequency modulators respectively. The estimation of these constants is often of value in the assessment of practical systems. It may sometimes be possible to achieve modulator calibration by means of a static test. That is, we apply a voltage displacement to the modulator input and measure the resulting change in either ϕ or $\dot{\phi}$ from its rest position. Such a test may prove difficult or unreliable for a variety of reasons. One simple technical obstacle that can render the static method unworkable is the presence of a.c. coupling at the modulator input. Again, a dynamic calibration may produce different values of k_1 or k_2 than would be obtained by means of a static calibration because the 'a.c.' and 'd.c.' equivalent circuits of the modulator are not the same. Furthermore, the measurement of a phase difference by a direct method is inherently difficult, even allowing that an ambiguous result may occur if the phase difference is greater than 2π radians.

To avoid these problems, we may utilise a dynamic test procedure involving a sinusoidal modulating signal. This is because the sinusoid creates a discrete line-spectrum of predictable form, with properties inherently suitable for the measurements we wish to make.

Let the modulating signal, then, be

$$v_m(t) = A_m \cos(2\pi f_m t)$$

Then the frequency-modulated wave may be written as

$$v(t) = A_c \cos\left\{ 2\pi f_c t - \frac{k_2 A_m}{2\pi f_m} \sin(2\pi f_m t) \right\}$$

Differentiation of the total phase angle yields the instantaneous frequency

$$f_c + \frac{k_2 A_m}{2\pi} \cos(2\pi f_m t)$$

Since the maximum and minimum values of $\cos(2\pi f_m t)$ are ± 1 it follows that the peak carrier-deviation is

$$\Delta f = \frac{k_2 A_m}{2\pi} \tag{4.20}$$

Consequently we may write the modulated carrier as

$$v(t) = A_c \cos\left\{ 2\pi f_c t - \frac{\Delta f}{f_m} \sin(2\pi f_m t) \right\}$$

$$= A_c \cos\{2\pi f_c t - m \sin(2\pi f_m t)\} \tag{4.21}$$

The reader may care to verify for himself that precisely the same equation is obtained when the wave is phase modulated. Coincidentally, if the modulating signal is a sinewave, the modulation index also specifies the maximum phase deviation. This is not generally the case, however. For the phase-modulated carrier, we arrive at an equation which is the equivalent of equation 4.20

$$\frac{\Delta f}{f_m} = k_1 A_m \tag{4.22}$$

If we expand equation 4.21 in the usual way, we find that

$$v(t) = A_c \cos(2\pi f_c t)\cos\{m \sin(2\pi f_m t)\}$$

$$+ A_c \sin(2\pi f_c t)\sin\{m \sin(2\pi f_m t)\} \tag{4.23}$$

This leaves us with the problem of handling the terms

$$\cos\{m \sin(2\pi f_m t)\}$$

and

$$\sin\{m \sin(2\pi f_m t)\}$$

As it happens, both of these quantities are equivalent to trigonometric series. To provide a general statement of the results we need, we write

$$\cos\{m \sin(\psi)\} = J_0(m) + 2\{J_2(m)\cos(2\psi) + J_4(m)\cos(4\psi) + \ldots\} \tag{4.24}$$

$$\sin\{m \sin(\psi)\} = 2\{J_1(m)\sin(\psi) + J_3(m)\sin(3\psi) + \ldots\} \tag{4.25}$$

Here, the quantities $J_k(m)$ are known as 'Bessel functions of order k, of the first kind'. Bessel functions, like trigonometric functions (cos, sin, etc.) are tabulated. That is to say, tables of values of $J_k(m)$ have been calculated by means of digital computers and are available in handbooks of mathematical functions.[29] Figure 4.7 illustrates the first four orders of Bessel functions against an abscissa which is the argument, m.

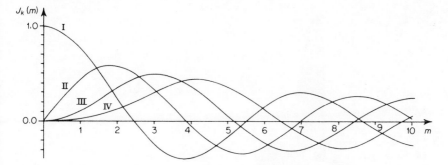

Figure 4.7 First four orders of Bessel function of the first kind: $J_k(m)$. I: $J_0(m)$; II: $J_1(m)$;
III: $J_2(m)$; IV: $J_3(m)$

Rearranging equations 4.23, 4.24 and 4.25, and using the identity

$$J_n(m) = (-1)^n J_{-n}(m) \qquad (4.26)$$

we find that

$$v(t) = A_c \sum_{n=-\infty}^{+\infty} J_n(m)\cos\{2\pi(f_c + nf_m)t\} \qquad (4.27)$$

Fourier transforming, we obtain the spectrum

$$V(f) = \frac{1}{2} A_c \sum_{n=-\infty}^{+\infty} J_n(m)[\delta\{f - (f_c + nf_m)\} + \delta\{f + (f_c + nf_m)\}] \qquad (4.28)$$

which yields a power spectrum

$$P(f) = \frac{1}{4} A_c^2 \sum_{n=-\infty}^{+\infty} J_n^2(m)[\delta\{f - (f_c + nf_m)\} + \delta\{f + (f_c + nf_m)\}] \qquad (4.29)$$

On examination of equation 4.29, we see that the power spectrum consists of spectral lines disposed symmetrically about the carrier component at the frequency f_c. The line spacing is equal to the frequency, f_m, of the modulating signal. Figure 4.8 depicts the effect of changing the modulation index by increasing the carrier deviation Δf and maintaining a constant modulation frequency. At low values of modulation index, only the carrier and the first pair of sidebands are significant. All other sidebands are of vanishingly small amplitude. This is as we should expect from the quasi-linear analysis described in section 4.3. As the modulation index rises, more and more sidebands become significant in their contribution to the form of $v(t)$. This means that the required transmission bandwidth must become larger than the width

$$B = 2f_m$$

and confirms Carson's rule, stated in the previous section.

To return to our initial problem of devising a method of calibrating angle modulators, the reader will notice, on closer inspection of figure 4.7, that, at certain particular values of modulation index, the carrier amplitude falls to zero. Thus figure 4.7 indicates a first zero when m is about 2.4 and a second

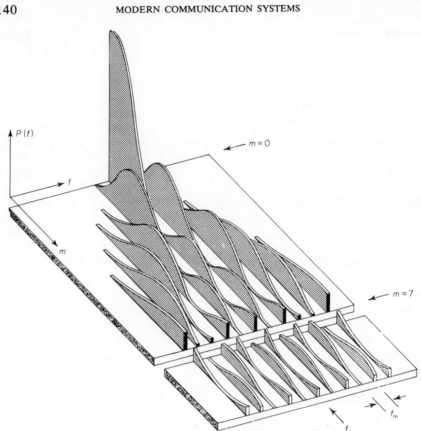

Figure 4.8 Power spectral density for frequency modulation. Linear scales of modulation index, frequency and power spectral density have been used. Notice that, as modulation index increases, so also does the band occupancy of the spectrum. The heavily shaded ends of the laminae at the cut $m = 7$ illustrate the magnitudes of the spectral components at that value of modulation index

zero when m is about 5.5. Likewise, all the sidebands exhibit zeros as m is increased. If we use a wave analyser to isolate one suitable spectral component, say the carrier, and apply a known-frequency sinusoidal modulation, its amplitude may be adjusted from an initial value of zero to such a value as causes the carrier component to decrease to zero for the first time. We then know that m is 2.4 and we can estimate, from m and the modulating frequency, the carrier deviation

$$\Delta f = m f_m$$

Since a precise measurement of the amplitude of the modulating sinusoid is not difficult, we can also estimate, by means of equation 4.20, the modulator constant

$$k_2 = \frac{2\pi \, \Delta f}{A_m} \tag{4.30}$$

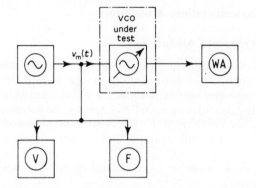

Figure 4.9 Voltage-controlled oscillator calibration. WA: wave analyser, used to determine the Bessel zeros; F: digital frequency-meter, to measure f_m; V: digital voltmeter, to measure A_m

(A phase modulator can be calibrated in the same way, except that we employ equation 4.22, not equation 4.20, for the last step in the calculation.)

Figure 4.9 illustrates a typical test circuit. Suppose, for example, that $f_m = 4.158$ kHz and that a first carrier zero is obtained when $A_m = 3.46$ volts. Then with $m = 2.4$, we calculate

$$\Delta f = 2.4 \times 4158$$

and, from equation 4.30

$$k_2 = \frac{2.4 \times 4158}{3.46}$$

$$= 2890 \text{ Hz volt}^{-1}$$

By suitably extending this method, a detailed calibration of the modulator may be effected, indicating, for example, linearity of deviation with modulating signal amplitude. To facilitate such studies, the values of the first few zeros of the carrier and the first sidebands are given in table 4.1. It is worth noting that the first carrier disappearance occurs at a deviation of precisely 1 kHz when the modulating frequency is set to 416 Hz. A corollary to this observation is that a deviation of k kHz occurs in conjunction with a modulation frequency of $k \times 416$ Hz.

TABLE 4.1 ZEROS OF CARRIER AND FIRST SIDEBANDS

Zero Point	Modulation Index Carrier	1st SB
First	2.405	3.832
Second	5.520	7.016
Third	8.654	10.173

4.7 System Implementation: Modulators

4.7.1 Direct Frequency Modulators

One intuitively obvious method of obtaining frequency modulation, which stems from a quasi-static appreciation of the nature of the modulated carrier, is to cause the natural frequency of an oscillator to fluctuate in sympathy with the modulating signal. Numerous and ingenious variations on this theme have been employed in both instrumentation and communication circuitry. However, a simple example will serve to demonstrate the principles involved.

Figure 4.10a shows a simple LC oscillator circuit, the oscillator frequency being given by the law

$$f_0 = (4\pi^2 LC)^{-\frac{1}{2}} \tag{4.31}$$

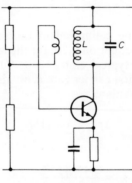

(a)

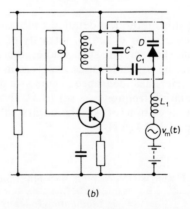

(b)

Figure 4.10 (a) A simple LC oscillator circuit. The transformer secondary (the left-hand winding) is connected to ensure positive feedback at high gain. This results in a self-sustaining oscillation. (b) Frequency modulation by means of a varactor diode, $D + C$ is the entire capacitance within the hatched enclosure. C_1 and L_1 act as blocks to low- and high-frequency signals respectively

If either L or C is made voltage variable

$$L = L(v_m)$$

or

$$C = C(v_m)$$

then it follows that f_o will also fluctuate. Of course, f_o will not, in general, be linearly related to fluctuations of v_m. However, the basic law, equation 4.31, contains no discontinuities, so that, for suitably small signal-swings we may expect the frequency deviation to respond linearly. Differentiating equation 4.31 with respect to C, for example, yields a slope value

$$\frac{df_o}{dC} = -\frac{f_o}{2C}$$

so that the fractional change in f_o is directly proportional to the fractional change in C, providing the fraction is sufficiently small—a condition entirely compatible with the narrow-band nature of most modulation processes. That is

$$\frac{df_o}{f_o} = -\frac{dC}{2C}$$

The same basic relation holds if we modulate the inductance value

$$\frac{df_o}{f_o} = -\frac{dL}{2L}$$

The two methods most frequently employed to obtain a voltage-variable reactance involve the use of either the 'varactor' diode principle or a 'reactance device'. The varactor diode is a specially fabricated $p-n$ junction which operates in the following way. The diode is reverse-biassed to set up a depletion layer at the junction. Superimposed upon the bias voltage is a small modulation component. Since the depletion-layer width depends on the magnitude of the reverse bias, the modulation component causes this width to fluctuate. Being free from charge carriers, the depletion layer acts as a dielectric, and the $p-n$ junction is therefore a small capacitance (usually in the range 10 to 100 picofarads) of voltage-variable dielectric width. Thus the capacitance of the varactor diode will vary with the modulating signal. A typical circuit configuration for a modulator employing a varactor diode is shown in figure 4.10b.

The reactance device is somewhat more involved in its mode of operation. Figure 4.11a illustrates a prototype circuit for a voltage-variable reactance based upon the reactance device principle. In the past, vacuum tubes have been designed to have characteristics which are particularly suited to this application. However, field-effect transistors (FET) have similar characteristics to reactance tubes and in many applications might be employed as a more convenient alternative, being compatible in their power-supply requirements with the semiconductor devices now favoured in most modern communication circuitry.

The circuit function may be understood from figure 4.11a. The FET gate voltage is the sum of the bias voltage and a sinusoidal contribution derived from the carrier component applied across the reactance terminals AA'. The

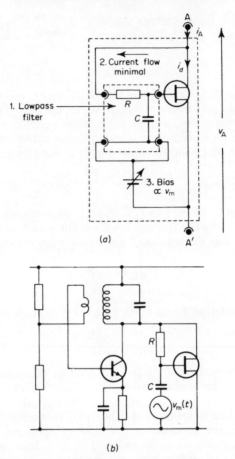

Figure 4.11 Reactance-device modulation: (a) the voltage-variable reactance circuit;
(b) the modulator, incorporating the voltage-variable reactance

bias voltage is proportional to the modulating signal v_m and it is presumed that fluctuations of v_m take place much more slowly than fluctuations (cycles) of the carrier. The sinusoidal contribution at the gate of the FET is effectively obtained by lowpass filtering the carrier component through the RC network. If the time constant of this network is chosen to be large in comparison with the carrier period (that is, its nominal cut-off frequency is much smaller than the carrier frequency) the carrier component appearing at the gate of the FET will be severely attenuated and will suffer a phase shift of very nearly $\pi/2$ radians. The FET drain-current is given by the relation

$$i_d = -g_m v_g$$

where g_m is the device transconductance. It follows that i_d will be in antiphase with v_g and hence in phase-quadrature with the applied voltage v_A. By a suitable choice of component values, the current through the RC filter and bias system can easily be made negligible in comparison with i_d so that

$$i_A \approx i_d$$

It follows that i_A and v_A will be in phase-quadrature and that, as a consequence, the entire circuit between terminals AA' is a reactance.

The reactance is voltage variable by means of the bias voltage because the FET has a non-linear transconductance characteristic. Specifically

$$i_d \propto v_g^2$$

The transconductance is given by the partial derivative

$$g_m = \left[\frac{\partial i_d}{\partial v_g}\right]_{v_d} \propto v_g$$

Hence a linear relationship exists between g_m and v_g. As the slowly varying modulation component in v_g alters, so also does g_m and consequently i_d. Since the ratio between i_d and v_A varies, the value of the reactance also varies, and in proportion to the modulating signal.

It must be stressed that the reactance circuit depicted in figure 4.11a only produces a voltage-variable reactance. To modulate the centre frequency of an oscillator, it is necessary to strap this circuit across the tank circuit of the oscillator, after the manner of figure 4.11b.

Many extremely linear low-frequency (below 10 MHz) modulators have been developed from sawtooth generator circuits. Recently, this type of modulator has found extensive application in voltage-controlled oscillator and phase-locked loop integrated circuits. The principle of operation is very simple. A linear voltage-ramp may be generated by the constant current charging of a capacitor. If the current direction is reversed when the ramp attains some predetermined voltage, a discharge ramp with exactly the same magnitude of slope will result. Recharge is restored when the discharge ramp falls to some predetermined minimum voltage. A circuit schematic for such a modulator is shown in figure 4.12. By making the current source output proportional to $v_m(t)$, the frequency also becomes proportional to $v_m(t)$. The reader is reminded, should this be necessary, that a current source produces a current that is unaffected by changes in its load. Circuits functioning in the manner described here are often referred to as serrasoid (sawtooth) modulators.

4.7.2 Phase Modulators and Indirect Frequency Modulators

We saw in section 4.3 that an angle-modulated wave could be obtained by means of a product modulator, provided that the maximum phase-excursion was small.

From equations 4.6 and 4.8

$$v(t) = A_c \cos(2\pi f_c t) - A_c k_1 v_m(t)\sin(2\pi f_c t)$$

This equation shows that we may generate a phase-modulated wave as the sum of a carrier component and a small product-modulated wave. A system block-diagram for a modulator based upon this principle is shown in figure 4.13. This system, known as the 'Armstrong phase modulator' after its inventor, may be used to establish a frequency-modulated carrier if the

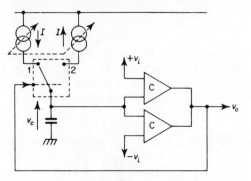

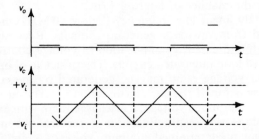

Switch Position	
v_o	position
O	1
$+V$	2

Figure 4.12 The serrasoid frequency modulator. Note that the current sources produce an output proportional in magnitude to the modulating signal, v_m. (See figure 6.9 for a definition of the operation of the comparator modules)

modulating signal is first integrated before it is multiplied by the phase-shifted carrier.

4.7.3 Wide Deviation Modulation

With the exception of the serrasoid modulator, all the systems that have so far been described in section 4.7 suffer from the distinct disadvantage that swings of instantaneous frequency must be kept to a small fraction of the modulator nominal centre-frequency. Wide excursions of instantaneous frequency would result in a non-linear modulation characteristic. Furthermore, many of the modulators described in the previous sections are inoperable at very high frequencies, so that some form of frequency translation is necessary. An increase in deviation can be obtained by applying the modulated carrier to a severe non-linearity. This generates harmonics of the carrier frequency, any one of which may be isolated by

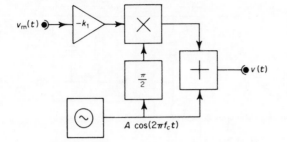

Figure 4.13 The Armstrong phase modulator

means of a bandpass filter. If the nth harmonic is extracted in this manner, the modulated carrier will become

$$v'(t) = A'_c \cos\{2\pi nf_c + n\phi(t)\}$$

Thus frequency translation and increased phase and instantaneous frequency-deviation may be obtained. Further spectral relocation may, of course, be performed by means of a mixer circuit (see section 3.7).

4.8 System Implementation: Demodulators

The operation of a frequency-modulation detector may be defined in terms of the modulated carrier

$$v(t) = A_c \cos\{2\pi f_c t + \phi(t)\}$$

as the extraction and differentiation of the phase term $\phi(t)$. Phase-modulation detectors may be realised by integrating the output of an FM detector. Alternatively, a product modulator may serve to provide phase detection if a locally generated and phase- and frequency-locked version of the quadrature carrier

$$A'_c \sin(2\pi f_c t)$$

is available. In this context, a low index phase-modulated wave would yield the required carrier component most readily.

In this section, we shall confine our interest to the two most commonly encountered frequency demodulators: the FM discriminator and the phase-locked loop.

4.8.1 FM to AM Conversion: The Discriminator

Many different types of discriminator have been devised, most of which operate on the principle of converting frequency fluctuations to amplitude fluctuations by means of some frequency-sensitive network and following this conversion by envelope detection.

The simplest such discriminator is illustrated in figure 4.14. Its operation may be analysed very easily. The FET small signal drain current is given in

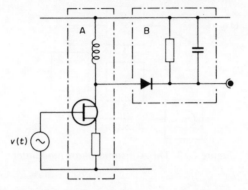

Figure 4.14 FM *detection: the use of an inductance as an* FM *to* AM *converter (block* A) *followed by envelope detection (block* B)

terms of the input voltage $v(t)$ (the frequency-modulated carrier) as

$$i(t) = g_m v(t)$$

It follows that

$$i(t) = g_m A_c \cos\{2\pi f_c t + \phi(t)\}$$

The a.c. voltage developed across the inductor is

$$v_L(t) = -L \frac{\mathrm{d}i(t)}{\mathrm{d}t}$$
$$= g_m A_c L \{2\pi f_c + \dot\phi(t)\}\sin\{2\pi f_c t + \phi(t)\}$$
$$= \{m\dot\phi(t) + c\}\sin\{2\pi f_c t + \phi(t)\}$$

This is an envelope and frequency-modulated wave and the envelope fluctuations occur in direct proportion to $\dot\phi(t)$. Since, for a frequency-modulated wave

$$\dot\phi(t) = k_2 v_m(t)$$

it follows that

$$v_L(t) = \{k_2 m v_m(t) + c\}\sin\{2\pi f_c t + \phi(t)\}$$

The envelope detector, as was remarked in section 3.10, is insensitive to phase or frequency fluctuations of the carrier. Consequently, its output will be proportional to $v_m(t)$.

This very simple form of discriminator is not widely used because, although it is highly linear its frequency-to-voltage conversion factor is small: 6 dB octave^{-1} of frequency swing.

The discriminator conversion factor may be substantially improved by employing an off-resonance tuned circuit as the frequency-sensitive element. Figure 4.15 illustrates such a circuit and compares its frequency-to-voltage conversion characteristic with that of the simpler, single-inductor circuit. Interpretation of the conversion characteristic may be aided by thinking of the modulated carrier from a quasi-static viewpoint, as a moving finger in the frequency domain. Providing sweeps of the carrier are restricted to a suitably small range about the nominal carrier frequency f_c, operation of the frequency-to-voltage converter is close to linear and the distortion will be low. As a rule of thumb, good linearity can be achieved by operating the discriminator with the carrier at the point of inflexion of the conversion characteristic.

While this circuit has a high sensitivity, the carrier deviation must necessarily be restricted if distortion is to be avoided. To overcome this difficulty, we may form a frequency-to-voltage conversion characteristic which is much wider, is linear and has a high sensitivity, by combining two off-resonance tuned circuits as shown in figure 4.16. This type of detector is known as a 'Travis discriminator' and is not dissimilar in its cost and complexity to those other circuits, the Foster–Seeley discriminator and the ratio detector which have, in the past, found extensive application in FM detection equipment.

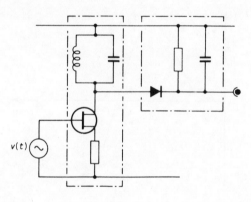

(a)

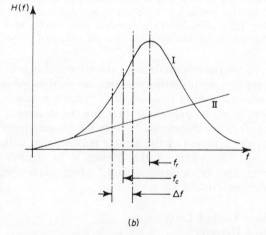

(b)

Figure 4.15 FM detection: (a) the use of a tuned circuit to enhance the sensitivity of the FM to AM conversion, and (b) the resulting frequency response of the detector. Curve I: tuned-circuit converter; curve II: inductance converter

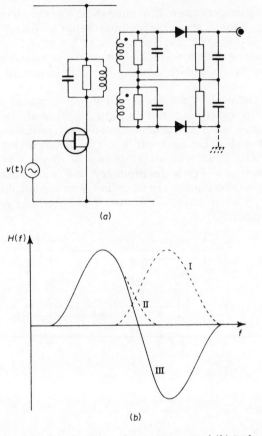

Figure 4.16 FM *detection: (a), the Travis discriminator, and (b) its frequency response. Curves* I *and* II *are the frequency responses of the upper and lower tuned-circuits respectively. Curve* III *is the difference between these curves and is the result of connecting the two tuned circuits together in the sense indicated on the circuit diagram*

One feature of all the discriminators described above is their inherent sensitivity to carrier amplitude-fluctuations, as well as phase fluctuations. Carrier amplitude-fluctuation may occur for many reasons and is quite a common phenomenon. To prevent it affecting the detection operation it is customary to precede the discriminator with a high-gain amplifier known as a limiter. Often the function of the limiter is combined with pre-detection bandpass filtering. The effect of the limiter is to remove all amplitude fluctuations from the modulated carrier, while preserving the relative positions of the zero crossings.

4.8.2 The Phase Locked Loop as a Frequency Detector[6,22,35]

All the circuits mentioned in the previous section suffer from the disadvantage that they require inductors or transformers. These components are both

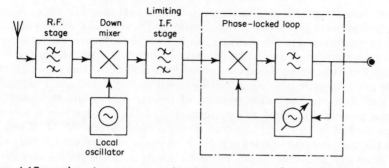

Figure 4.17 FM *detection: an* FM *receiver incorporating a phase locked loop demod-ulator*

bulky and costly and the more complicated of the discriminator circuits are difficult to align in such a way as to produce a linear frequency-to-voltage conversion characteristic. None are suitable for integrated-circuit fabrication.

An economical and convenient solution to the problem of frequency detection is found in a subsystem known as the *phase locked loop*,[22] (PLL). An FM detector incorporating a PLL demodulator is shown in figure 4.17 and functions in the following way. The incoming modulated carrier

$$v(t) = A_c \cos\{2\pi f_c t + \phi(t)\}$$

is multiplied by the voltage-controlled oscillator (VCO) output

$$v_1(t) = A_1 \sin\{2\pi f_c t + \phi_1(t)\}$$

to yield sum- and difference-frequency terms. The difference-frequency term is proportional to

$$\sin\{\phi(t) - \phi_1(t)\}$$

and for small phase differences, this quantity may be expressed as

$$\phi(t) - \phi_1(t)$$

This difference, or error signal, is applied to the VCO in such a sense as to drive its frequency towards 'lock'.

When in lock

$$\phi_1(t) \approx \phi(t)$$

so that the input to the VCO, which is a frequency modulator, will be proportional to $\dot{\phi}(t)$ and hence to $v_m(t)$. It follows that the loop output is a close approximation to the modulating signal when lock has been attained.

As it happens, not only is the phase locked loop preferable to the FM discriminator for reasons of economy, its noise performance is substantially better than that of the discriminator at low values of carrier-to-noise ratio. We shall discuss this property at greater length in section 4.11.

4.9 Noise Analysis: Frequency Modulation

In this section, we shall study the performance of a simple FM detector when the carrier is immersed in white, gaussian channel noise. We shall derive results which present the detector output signal-to-noise ratio, s, as a function of the input carrier-to-noise ratio, p. These results will be compared with those obtained in the previous chapter which pertain to the detection of envelope-modulated waves. In the next section we shall discuss the noise analysis of phase-modulated carriers and we shall show that, if we suitably scale the amplitude of the modulating signal so that the channel bandwidth requirements are the same as those of the FM system and the noise and carrier powers are equal, the performance of the two systems is identical when judged on the basis of signal-to-noise ratio curves. We shall also see that the output-noise spectra are different in shape, even though they yield the same signal-to-noise ratio. The noise spectrum at the FM detector output is coloured, having predominantly high-frequency components whereas that at the PM detector output is white. This difference makes PM more attractive for some applications. We shall extend this argument to systems which are part way between FM and PM. These systems employ a frequency modulation in which the modulating signal is passed through a pre-modulation filter which serves to distort the signal spectrum, enhancing high-frequency components to obtain a substantial improvement in the detected signal quality.

Our model of the FM detector consists of a system block, the 'discriminator', which extracts from the modulated carrier

$$v(t) = A_c \cos\{2\pi f_c t + \phi(t)\}$$

the differential $\dot{\phi}(t)$. We shall find it convenient to think of the discriminator as a phase detector followed by a differentiator, although in practice these operations are not usually separable.

The modulated carrier is immersed in white noise. To minimise the noise-power corruption of the carrier, it is customary to precede the discriminator with a bandpass filter of width B, determined by Carson's rule

$$B = 2f_m(m + 1)$$

In the following work, we shall assume a reasonably large value of modulation index (greater than unity, certainly) because this is a common condition of operation. We may then approximate the bandwidth as

$$B = 2mf_m = 2\,\Delta f \tag{4.32}$$

During transmission, long-term fluctuations of the received signal amplitude may occur. This type of effect, which may come about for a variety of reasons, is known as 'fading'. Since many discriminators are amplitude sensitive as well as phase sensitive it is common practice to include, either within the discriminator or within the bandpass-filter circuitry, a high-gain saturating amplifier—or limiter—which removes all amplitude fluctuations before detection.

As we shall see, the discriminator output-noisewave has spectral components outside the frequency range of the baseband information signal. Consequently, it is usual to follow the discriminator by a rapid-cut-off lowpass filter. The complete system model is then as shown in figure 4.18.

We shall assume that both the pre-detection and post-detection filters have an ideal rectangular characteristic. As we saw in section 3.9, this is a

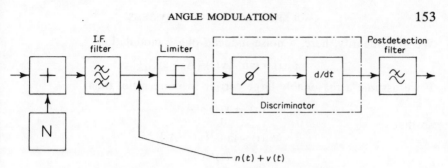

Figure 4.18 The FM *discriminator: noise analysis*

very reasonable assumption to make for the pre-detection filter. However, it is not entirely a necessary assumption. A fairly poor pre-detection filter could be used—a gaussian characteristic for example—without unduly degrading the system performance. In contrast, a sharp-cut-off post-detection filter most certainly is necessary to realise the full effectiveness of the system. We shall return, very briefly, to discuss the requirements of the lowpass post-detection filter at the end of this section.

At the output of the pre-detection bandpass filter we have a wave which is the sum of the modulated carrier $v(t)$ and the band-limited noise process $n(t)$. We discussed the nature of the noise process at some length in section 3.9. Briefly to summarise our conclusions, we may think of $n(t)$, of power p_n and bandwidth B as the sum of an in-phase and a quadrature component

$$n(t) = x(t)\cos(2\pi f_c t) + y(t)\sin(2\pi f_c t)$$

where $x(t)$ and $y(t)$ are white, baseband gaussian-noisewaves of power p_n and bandwidth $B/2$.

As a first step in our analysis, we shall assume an unmodulated carrier. This is not as severe a restriction as it might at first sight appear. It can be shown[31] that, when a quasi-static spectral analysis of the modulated carrier waveform is valid (that is, for reasonably large values of modulation index) modulation does not affect the noise performance of the detector.

We let

$$v(t) = A_c \cos\{2\pi f_c t + \phi(t)\}$$

and set $\phi(t)$ to zero, so that

$$v(t) = A_c \cos(2\pi f_c t)$$

The process at the output of the bandpass filter is a waveform

$$v(t) + n(t) = A_c \cos(2\pi f_c t) + x(t)\cos(2\pi f_c t) + y(t)\sin(2\pi f_c t)$$
$$= [\{A_c + x(t)\}^2 + y^2(t)]^{\frac{1}{2}} \cos(2\pi f_c t - \tan^{-1}[y(t)/\{A_c + x(t)\}])$$

This is a rather formidable expression, and indeed further analysis of the detection process would be very difficult without additional simplification. First, we note that the limiter removes amplitude fluctuations so that the detector has only to determine the instantaneous frequency of the wave

$$\cos(2\pi f_c t - \tan^{-1}[y(t)/\{A_c + x(t)\}])$$

We may identify, here, a noise-induced phase modulation

$$\phi_n(t) = \tan^{-1}[y(t)/\{A_c + x(t)\}]$$

If we assume a reasonably large carrier-to-noise ratio, then

$$A_c + x(t) \approx A_c$$

so that

$$\phi_n(t) \approx \tan^{-1}\{y(t)/A_c\}$$
$$\approx y(t)/A_c$$

Thus the input to the discriminator is essentially the wave

$$\cos\{2\pi f_c t - y(t)/A_c\}$$

With a phase detector constant of one volt per radian, the wave at the output of the detector will simply be $y(t)/A_c$ and since $y(t)$ has a mean square value p_n (see section 3.9) the mean square value of the output-noise wave will be p_n/A_c^2. Recall also that $y(t)$ is white and gaussian. We may define, as a consequence, the noise power spectrum at the detector output as

$$P_1(f) = p_n/A_c^2 B \quad \text{volt}^2 \text{ Hz}^{-1} \tag{4.33}$$

for the range of frequencies $-B/2 \le f \le +B/2$. This spectrum is sketched in figure 4.19. The noise process at the differentiator output will have a power spectrum $P_2(f)$, given in terms of the differentiator transfer-function $H(f)$ as

$$P_2(f) = |H(f)|^2 P_1(f)$$

Since, from table 1.2, for a differentiator, we have that

$$H(f) = 2\pi jf$$

it follows that

$$\left.\begin{aligned} P_2(f) &= 4\pi^2 f^2 p_n/A_c^2 B \quad -B/2 \le f \le +B/2 \\ &= 0 \quad \text{elsewhere} \end{aligned}\right\} \tag{4.34}$$

As figure 4.19 shows, the output-noise power spectral density produced by an FM discriminator is parabolic. (Contrast this with the output-noise power spectral density produced by the phase detector, under nominally the same conditions, which is uniform.)

The next step in analysis is simply to estimate the total output-noise power emerging from the post-detection filter. Assuming, as we stated above, a sharp-cut-off filter, this power is

$$\int_{-f_m}^{+f_m} P_2(f) \, \mathrm{d}f = \frac{8\pi^2 f_m^3 p_n}{3A_c^2 B} = p_n' \tag{4.35}$$

In order to determine the signal power at the detector output, we must specify the nature of the signal waveform. It is customary to assume a sinusoidal modulation, so that with a phase detector constant of 1 volt rad^{-1} and a differentiator giving an output of 1 volt per volt s^{-1}, the discriminator constant is 2π volt Hz^{-1}. Thus with a modulating signal

$$v_m(t) = A_m \cos(2\pi f_m t)$$

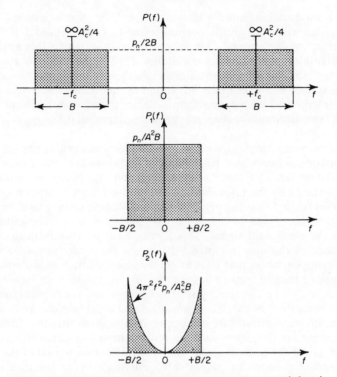

Figure 4.19 Noise spectra in FM *detection: carrier unmodulated*

a maximum frequency deviation of Δf will result, yielding a detected signal amplitude of $2\pi\,\Delta f$ volts. Hence the signal power will be

$$\frac{4\pi^2\,\Delta f^2}{2}\quad \text{volt}^2 \tag{4.36}$$

Combining equations 4.35 and 4.36, we may calculate the signal-to-noise ratio at the detector output as

$$s = 3\,\frac{\Delta f^3}{f_m^3}\frac{(A_c^2/2)}{N}$$

$$= 3m^3p \tag{4.37}$$

Equation 4.37 may be expressed thus

$$s(\text{dB}) = p(\text{dB}) + 30\log_{10}(1.44m) \tag{4.38}$$

where m is the modulation index and the modulating signal is a sinusoid. Recall the condition specified above that the modulation index should be reasonably large and we see that the performance of the FM system is substantially better than that of the AM system, which, as we saw in section 3.10 yields a result

$$s(\text{dB}) = p(\text{dB}) + 3 \tag{4.39}$$

At low modulation-index values, the performance equations derived above predict that the output signal-to-noise ratio should fall to zero. However, we have assumed that m was large in pursuing this analysis. In fact, the results presented in equations 4.37 and 4.38 are reasonably accurate for modulation-index values as low as $m \approx 3$. For small values of m, when the system becomes quasi-linear and the modulator and demodulator can be implemented with product modulators, the best we can hope to do is approach the optimum curve for product demodulation quoted above, equation 4.39.

It is worth comparing equation 4.38 with the result that is obtained when the modulation is noise-like. Both types of signal are presumed to produce a peak deviation Δf. The mean square deviation and thus the output signal power generated by the noise-like modulation on the assumption quoted in the previous section that the peak-to-r.m.s. deviation ratio should be three is $\Delta f^2/9$. Thus the power in the noise-like signal, is only two-ninths of the power in the sinusoidal signal. This corresponds to a uniform decrease in performance of the detector of 6.5 dB below the figure quoted above.

It would appear then, that FM is as good as, and for high modulation-index much superior to, all forms of linear envelope modulation. In fact this is not necessarily so. When the noise power becomes comparable with the carrier power (at low values of carrier-to-noise ratio) a condition can arise whereby a very serious corruption state can occur. If it happens that the carrier has a low instantaneous frequency and the noise a high instantaneous frequency and the phase of the noise is momentarily in opposition to that of the carrier, it is possible for an extra pair of zero crossings to be inserted into the detected carrier. This sudden doubling of frequency produces a pulse at the discriminator output. Viewed on the same time scale as baseband events, this pulse has the appearance of an impulse of area 2π radians (one extra cycle having been slipped in). A similar effect occurs when the carrier has a high instantaneous frequency and the noise has a low instantaneous frequency, except that in this case a cycle is dropped out rather than inserted, producing a negative impulse of area 2π radians. As the carrier-to-noise ratio falls, the expected number of noise impulses per second increases. The actual value of this impulse rate is[42]

$$E \approx \frac{\exp(-p)}{2} \, v_m(t) \quad \text{impulses s}^{-1}$$

The spectrum of such an impulse train is uniform for all frequencies and of a power spectral density which increases with decreasing p. The result is a substantial worsening of the output signal-to-noise ratio when $\exp(-p)$ becomes significantly large. This occurs at about 10 dB carrier-to-noise ratio. As with the envelope detector described in section 3.11 a severe *threshold effect* is produced, resulting in the set of curves shown in figure 4.20.

One final point with respect to the above-threshold performance of the FM discriminator is worth mentioning. We have assumed in the preceding analysis that the post-detection filter has a sharp cut-off. This is, in fact, necessary if the full noise-improvement capability of the FM system is to be realised. For example, a first-order filter, with an asymptotic roll-off of

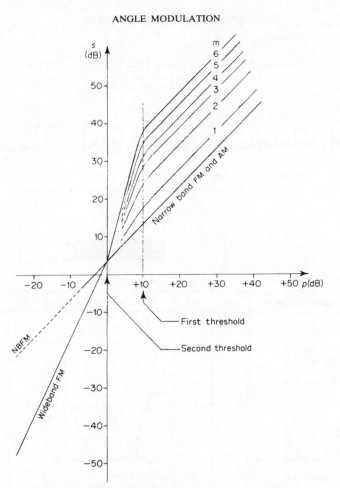

Figure 4.20 Noise performance of the FM *discriminator*

-6 dB octave^{-1} will only attenuate the out-of-baseband noise to the extent of flattening the parabolic spectrum in this region. Thus a considerable block of unwanted noise is admitted together with the received signal. The careful design of a post-detection filter is of greatest importance when the modulation index is large. For small modulation indexes, a post-detection filter of any sort is largely redundant. If $m = 1$, then $f_m = B/2$ and all the baseband noise will be admitted by the post-detection filter anyway.

Another way of looking at this phenomenon is to regard the pre-detection filter as performing all the necessary filtering at low values of modulation index. This observation is of some importance when we come to discuss digital-data transmission which, for reasons of economy of bandwidth is customarily operated at low values of modulation index.

4.10 Noise Analysis: Phase and Pre-emphasised Frequency Modulation

In this section, we wish to demonstrate that the noise performance of a phase-modulation system is identical to that of a frequency-modulation

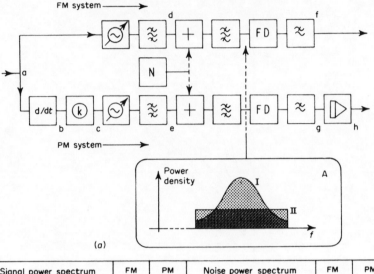

(a)

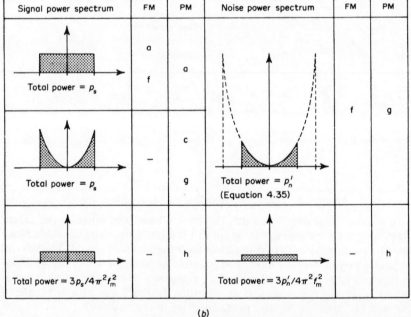

(b)

Figure 4.21 Comparative performance of PM and FM detectors in the presence of noise. The PM system is realised by differentiating the modulating signal and applying it to an FM generator. Integration follows the frequency-detection operation to yield the original modulating signal

system operating under equivalent conditions. We shall assume that the carrier amplitude and the noise-power spectral density for both modulations shall be the same. In order that both systems operate at identical carrier-to-noise ratios, the bandwidth in both systems must be identical. We shall assume a noise-like, band-limited modulating signal. The two systems are illustrated in figure 4.21, the phase modulator being regarded as a frequency modulator preceded by a differentiator. This is simply to afford an easy comparison of the operations being performed on the modulating signal throughout the system.

The signal power at point a, figure 4.21, common to both phase- and frequency-modulation systems is p_s. At point b the spectrum is modified by differentiation

$$P_2(f) = P_s(f) \, |H(f)|^2$$

$$= \frac{p_s}{2f_m} \, 4\pi^2 f^2$$

By suitably scaling the amplitude of the signal, a parabolic spectrum containing a total power p_s is obtained at point c. It follows that both frequency modulators will have at their inputs signals of the same power and with gaussian distributions. (A linear filter, such as the differentiator, does not alter the amplitude distribution of a zero-mean gaussian-noisewave, save in changing the mean square value of that distribution.) Admittedly, the power spectra of the two signals are different but the spectrum of the frequency-modulated carrier at reasonably high values of modulation index, where the quasi-static analysis may be said to apply, is independent of this property. It follows that the carrier deviations and transmission bandwidths at points d and e are the same.

At points f and g the parabolic FM noise spectrum is the same for both detectors. Likewise, the signal power is the same, although, again, the spectra differ. It follows that the signal-to-noise ratios at this point must be identical. Since the integrator operating on the signal and noise at point g is a linear device and both power spectra have the same shape, being square-law, and the same bandwidth, f_m, the signal-to-noise ratio as measured at point h is identical to that at point g. It follows that the noise performance graph for the FM discriminator, figure 4.20, applies equally well to the phase detector, provided that the phase-modulated carrier is operated with the same modulated carrier bandwidth. To operate the phase-modulated carrier in this way does, however, mean scaling the input signal amplitude by a factor $2\pi f_m/\sqrt{3}$.

Although the performance graphs for both systems are identical, the noise performance as such does differ, in that the noise spectrum at the output of the discriminator post-detection filter is parabolic, whereas that at the output of the phase detector is uniform. Depending on the nature of the analogue transmission this difference may determine our choice of modulation method. For example, suppose that we employ an angle modulation to transmit a bank of AM multiplexed telephony channels. If we specify a 'worst case' or maximum value of noise spectral density to which any 'subcarrier' is to be subjected, this value will only be encountered by the channel with the highest subcarrier frequency if FM is employed. All other channels will be operating under conditions far less noisy. The reader may, at first, feel that this is a good thing to have achieved, but in fact it is not. All the subcarriers at the output of a PM system are immersed in noise of the same (worst case) value, but since the spectrum is uniform the total noise output is much larger, corresponding to a greater input-noise power and in turn a lower carrier-to-noise ratio. In fact the carrier-to-noise ratio for the phase-modulation main carrier system need only be one-third of that of the frequency-modulation system to guarantee the same worst case subcarrier-noise spectral density. Thus, under these conditions of operation, the phase-modulation system has a very significant 4.8 dB advantage.

Unfortunately, other properties of PM systems give rise to detection problems. For the multichannel telephony system outlined in the previous paragraph, the 4.8 dB advantage will be realised if the lowest frequency subcarrier is not too close to d.c. This is because the signal spectra, as seen at points b and g are of low absolute spectral density in the vicinity of the ordinate (when $f = 0$). Thus any ambient system-noise (other than the channel noise) will swamp the signal components in this region. For just this reason, a normal, single-channel baseband modulation, extending to a low frequency, will also be adversely affected by low-frequency system-noise. To alleviate this problem, we can effect a compromise, by designing angle-modulation systems which behave like FM systems towards low-frequency signal components and like PM systems towards high-frequency components.

Another way of looking at this problem is suggested by the conclusion reached in section 2.1, that for given noise and signal powers, and a white signal spectrum, the signal would be least adversely affected if the noise were also white. If we assume a white signal spectrum, the high-frequency signal components are badly contaminated by the large high-frequency components in the parabolic FM noise spectrum.

The PM noise spectrum would be a much better background to work against, but for the objections stated above. Indeed, with typical audio-signal spectra of the form shown in figure 2.1, the position is even worse. Such spectra possess most of their power at low frequencies. Consequently a severe degradation of the high-frequency signal-to-noise ratio takes place with FM transmission. Unfortunately, the human ear is more sensitive to high frequencies than it is to low frequencies, and this further compounds the issue.

To reduce the cumulative effect of all these phenomena, we 'pre-colour' the modulating-signal spectrum, amplifying the high-frequency components preferentially. At the detector, a complementary network removes the spectral distortion, restoring the original modulating signal. In the process it also serves to reduce the high-frequency noise power. The process of signal pre-colouring is known as *pre-emphasis* or, in some television picture transmission systems, *pre-distortion* and the restoration process is known as *de-emphasis*. A typical pre-emphasis characteristic is shown in figure 4.22 and corresponds to a transfer function of the form

$$H_1(f) = k(1 + 2\pi jfCR)$$

The constant k is chosen so that the signal power applied to the modulator remains constant, ensuring the same quasi-static spectrum for a noise-like modulation and hence the same band occupancy and carrier-to-noise ratio. The general angle-modulation could, in fact, be written as

$$v(t) = A_c \cos\left(2\pi f_c t + k_2 \int_0^t v'_m(\tau)\, d\tau\right)$$

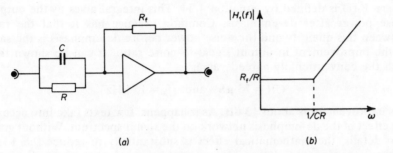

(a)   (b)

Figure 4.22 (a) Pre-emphasis circuit and (b) its transfer function plotted on logarithmic frequency and amplitude scales

where
$$v'_m(t) = v_m(t) \otimes h_1(t)$$
and
$$h_1(t) \leftrightarrow H_1(f)$$

and where our three linear angle-modulation subclasses are given by

$$
\begin{aligned}
H_1(f) &= 1 && \text{(frequency modulation)} \\
&= 1 + 2\pi jfCR && \text{(FM with pre-emphasis)} \\
&= 2\pi jfCR && \text{(phase modulation)}
\end{aligned}
$$

The de-emphasis circuit, located after the FM discriminator, is typified by the transfer function

$$H_2(f) = \frac{1}{(1 + 2\pi jfCR)}$$

which is illustrated in figure 4.23. The reader will find that many texts apply this transfer function to the normal parabolic noise-spectrum at the output of the FM discriminator, and calculate the decrease in total noise power which this produces. The calculation is simple in principle and necessitates evaluation of the integral

$$\int_{-f_m}^{+f_m} P_2(f) |H_2(f)|^2 \, df$$

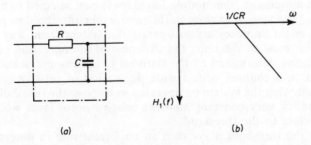

(a)   (b)

Figure 4.23 (a) De-emphasis circuit, and (b) its transfer function

where $P_2(f)$ is defined by equation 4.34. This integral gives us the output-noise power after de-emphasis. Common practice has it that the ratio between this quantity and the noise power before de-emphasis is the same as the improvement in output signal-to-noise ratio. It can be shown that, with the conventionally agreed values

$$CR = 75 \ \mu S \quad \text{and} \quad f_m = 15 \ kHz$$

this improvement is about 13 dB. As it happens, few texts take into account the effect of the de-emphasis network on the *signal* spectrum. Without going into details, the mathematical effect is substantially to reduce the 13 dB improvement quoted above. The extent of the reduction depends on the nature of the transmitted-signal spectral shape, and is therefore difficult to quantify. However, the subjective improvement, together with the reduction of system (as opposed to channel) noise is sufficient to make the use of some form of pre-emphasis virtually mandatory for analogue-signal transmission by means of angle modulation.

Because the noise at the output of envelope-modulation systems is uniform and of relatively small bandwidth (usually 3 to 4 kHz) the effect of pre-emphasis on such systems is small. As a consequence, the use of pre-emphasis is restricted to angle modulation.

4.11   The Threshold and its Importance in System Design

In many applications the power available at a transmitter is limited. If the channel noise level rises, the system performance will deteriorate. One possible strategy when this situation is encountered is to increase the carrier deviation. This results in an increase of the modulation index and since

$$s = 3m^3 p$$

brings about an increase in the output signal-to-noise ratio, s. Thus a doubling of the carrier deviation causes m to double and p to halve (assuming no change in the transmitter power). Consequently a fourfold increase in s will occur.

Unfortunately, when the system is at, or close to, the threshold, increasing the carrier deviation and consequently decreasing p will take the system over the threshold and s will decrease. Figure 4.24 illustrates this phenomenon.

An important corollary to these observations is that, when transmitter power is at a premium, the modulation index is best selected to bring about operation of the system as close to (but above) the threshold as possible. In practice it might be necessary to operate the system some way above the threshold for most of the time, the closeness of the operating point to the threshold being determined by the statistics of the communication channel itself. That is, a channel with a wide fluctuation of relative noise power would require that the system be operated well above the threshold for most of the time. A very constant ambient relative noise level would permit operation close to the threshold.

Because the threshold plays such an important role in determining the performance of angle-modulation systems, many techniques have been

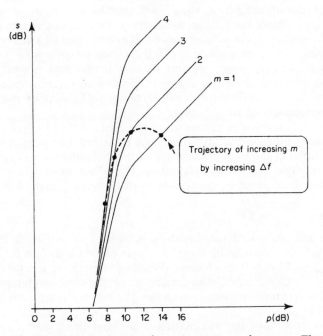

Figure 4.24 The threshold as a limiting factor in system performance. The illustrated trajectory has as its initial values, m = 1 and p = 14 dB

devised to reduce its value, thereby extending the geographical range or permitting a reduction in output power from the transmitter. The most widely used threshold-extension detector is the phase locked loop[22,35] which we have discussed in section 4.8.2.

The reader should recall, from section 4.9, that the FM discriminator exhibits at its output a noise waveform that consists of a parabolic spectrum quasi-gaussian component plus an impulse component. The quasi-gaussian component occurs because the zero crossings of the modulated carrier 'jitter' as the result of the impressed channel noise. The impulse component, which only begins to appear at values of carrier-to-noise ratio below about 10 dB, is caused by the skipping or insertion of cycles of carrier before detection. This causes an impulsive halving or doubling of instantaneous frequency. The result of the relatively rapid onset of impulse generation when the carrier-to-noise ratio falls below 10 dB is a sudden deterioration in detection performance. It is this rapid deterioration which is referred to as the FM threshold and which places the limit on the utility of angle-modulation systems.

In part, the early onset of impulse formation may be ascribed to the rapid dynamic response of the discriminator. Under the common condition of narrow-band operation ($B \ll f_c$, not low modulation-index operation) changes of instantaneous frequency take place over many thousands of cycles of operation. It is quite unnecessary for the detector to be able to respond to sudden doublings or halvings of instantaneous frequency. The phase locked loop exhibits a much lower impulse rate than a conventional discriminator simply because of its inherent 'inertia' to changes in instantaneous frequency. Its operation may be likened to that of a heavy flywheel, being slowly run up to a given speed by a long succession of 'pushes', of slowly increasing frequency, against its rim. If one push is omitted or an extra push included, the effect on the instantaneous rotation speed will not be noticeable. The rotation speed will certainly not halve or double and then return immediately to its old value.

The above-threshold performance of the phase locked loop is exactly the same as that of the FM discriminator, since its action is to yield at its output, the differential of the total phase angle of the incoming wave. Typically, the reduced impulse rate at the output of the phase locked loop causes a corresponding decrease in the threshold of between 5 and 10 dB.

Problems

4.1   It is quite easy to determine the spectrum of an amplitude-modulated carrier when the modulating signal is a pair of sinusoids (see for example, question 3.5). Why is it much more difficult to determine the spectrum of a frequency- or phase-modulated carrier, given the same modulating signal? Under what circumstance can such an analysis become reasonably tractable?

4.2   Show that both the modulation index and the nominal carrier frequency of a frequency-modulated wave may be increased in integer multiples by applying it to a severe non-linearity and filtering the output.

4.3   What would be the result of applying a low modulation-index frequency-modulated wave to a hard limiter, in spectral terms? Assume a white, band-limited noise-like modulating signal and sketch spectra of both the input and output signals.

If the input-signal carrier frequency is 100 kHz and its bandwidth is 40 kHz, what is the maximum frequency multiplication which can be achieved without serious spectral overlap?
(*Answer* 3)

4.4   Which of the following frequency modulators are inherently capable of producing wideband frequency-modulation without further processing

   (a) Integrator plus Armstrong phase modulator
   (b) Serrasoid modulator
   (c) Reactance-device modulator
   (d) Varactor diode or capacitor microphone modulator?

4.5   What advantages does narrow-band frequency modulation have over conventional amplitude modulation? What disadvantages does it exhibit? (*Hint* Compare noise performance, efficiency, channel capacity, effect of channel non-linearity.)

4.6   If broadband frequency-modulation is to be obtained from a reactance-device modulator by following a narrow-band frequency modulation with a fairly large frequency multiplication, what will be the effect on the stability of centre frequency of the final frequency modulation?

Which type of modulator would offer the best stability under these circumstances, and why?

4.7 A frequency-modulated wave is generated by an Armstrong phase modulator preceded by an integrator. The modulation index is 0.2. If the modulating-signal bandwidth is nominally 15 kHz, what is the maximum carrier deviation and, by Carson's rule, what is the required signal bandwidth?
(*Answer* 3 and 36 kHz)

4.8 Given that you wished to verify experimentally that the conditions imposed in question 4.7 were met, how would you achieve this, using a sinusoidal test signal and the method of Bessel zeros?

4.9 Suppose, for the modulator specified in question 4.7, that pre-emphasis was required. Sketch the basic modulator block-diagram and show, by means of sketches of the overall transfer-function of the networks placed before the phase modulator, that pre-emphasis results in the frequency modulation of low-frequency signal components and phase modulation of high-frequency signal components.

4.10 A modulating signal has a bandwidth of 4 kHz and is used to frequency modulate a carrier of 100 kHz. The modulation technique establishes a narrow-band frequency-modulated signal. It is required to obtain a broad-band frequency-modulated signal with a modulation index of 3 at a carrier frequency of 120 MHz. Describe a system which could be used to achieve this, specifying the values of any frequency multipliers and mixer local-oscillator frequencies, required.

What channel bandwidth will be required for the signal? Does your proposed system place any unduly stringent demands on the system modules you specify?
(*Answer* 32 kHz)

4.11 The use of quasi-static spectral analysis is required when slow sweeps of frequency occur in the modulated carrier. A random binary-digit sequence is used to frequency modulate a carrier of amplitude 10 volts and frequency 2×10^3 Hz. The amplitude of the digit sequence is adjusted to make the maximum frequency deviation ± 200 Hz. The digit duration is 50 ms and the digits are presumed equiprobable. The waveshapes corresponding to the binary digits 0 and 1 are $s_0(t)$ and $s_1(t)$ respectively, with

$$s_1(t) = -s_0(t)$$

Two types of modulating digit waveshape are proposed

(a) Isosceles triangular
(b) Rectangular

Show that the power spectra associated with these pulse shapes are

(a) $P(f) = 0.06025 \text{ volt}^2 \text{ Hz}^{-1} \quad 1.8 \times 10^3 \le |f| \le 2.2 \times 10^3$

(b) $P(f) = 12.5\{\delta(f + 1.8 \times 10^3) + \delta(f - 1.8 \times 10^3)$
$$+ \delta(f + 2.2 \times 10^3) - \delta(f - 2.2 \times 10^3)\}$$

4.12 Sketch the spectra derived in question 4.11 and comment on the extent to which you feel they may be representative of the real spectra of such waveforms.

If the digits are not equiprobable, what will happen to the power spectrum of the modulated carrier? If, for the triangular pulse shape, the occurrence probability of the binary 1 is 0.8 and that of the binary 0 is 0.2, re-evaluate the power spectrum.

4.13 Given a frequency-modulated sinusoid, modulated by a sinusoidal test signal at a sufficiently large modulation index for quasi-static analysis to be meaningful, what will be the effect of applying this wave to a simple RCL bandpass filter which is sufficiently narrow to invalidate Carson's rule (that is, it is too narrow to accommodate sweeps of the carrier)? How may the effect you deduce affect the detection performance of the frequency detector?

4.14 Draw phasor diagrams illustrating the processes of amplitude and frequency modulation, given the defining equations

$$v(t) = A_c\{1 + m \cos(2\pi f_m t)\}\cos(2\pi f_c t) \quad \text{(AM)}$$
$$v(t) = A_c \cos\{2\pi f_c t + m \cos(2\pi f_m t)\} \quad \text{(FM)}$$

Assume m to be small so that a quasi-linear expansion of the second equation is possible.

5　Composite Modulation

In the previous two chapters we have discussed those specialisations of the general sinusoidal modulated carrier

$$v(t) = A(t)\cos\{2\pi f_c t + \phi(t)\}$$

in which either $A(t)$ or $\phi(t)$, but not both, was varied as a linear function of a modulating signal $v_m(t)$.

We saw that envelope modulation, for which $A(t)$ is a linear function of $v_m(t)$ and $\phi(t)$ is a constant, was characterised by a carrier bandwidth which extended over twice the frequency range of the modulating signal. Envelope-modulation systems use this excess bandwidth effectively to duplicate the transmitted information. This redundancy, inherent in the modulation operation, results in a +3 dB improvement in detected signal-to-noise ratio over the carrier-to-noise ratio.

Angle modulation, for which $A(t)$ is a constant and $\phi(t)$ a linear function of $v_m(t)$ exhibits an even greater tradeoff of bandwidth for signal-to-noise ratio improvement. Although there are many situations in which transmission power is at a premium and the bandwidth exchange phenomenon provides a useful way of improving the detected signal quality, it is equally true that, on occasion, it is the bandwidth which is the more costly commodity. In this chapter we shall examine some analogue modulation systems in which the use of bandwidth is minimised. The most important such system is known as 'single-sideband AM', or SSB. This name stems from the generation process, which results in the elimination of one of the sidebands from a product-modulation carrier. The wave itself is not 'amplitude modulated' in the sense used in chapter 3, but is a combined amplitude and phase modulation. It is a *composite modulation* for which

$$A(t) = g_1\{v_m(t)\}$$
$$\phi(t) = g_2\{v_m(t)\}$$

As it happens, the functional relationships g_1 and g_2 are complex and non-linear. However, if we express the carrier in the alternative form

$$v(t) = x(t)\cos(2\pi f_c t) + y(t)\sin(2\pi f_c t) \tag{5.1}$$

we shall be able to go a long way towards formally defining the various composite modulations which are used in practice, without encountering any very difficult mathematics.

5.1 Quadrature Amplitude Modulation

Quadrature amplitude modulation, QAM, is a scheme whereby two baseband channels may occupy the same carrier-frequency band; it is a development of product modulation. Suppose we have two baseband signals $v_{m_1}(t)$ and $v_{m_2}(t)$. If we use product modulation to form modulated carriers

$$v_1(t) = v_{m_1}(t)\cos(2\pi f_c t)$$

and

$$v_2(t) = v_{m_2}(t)\sin(2\pi f_c t)$$

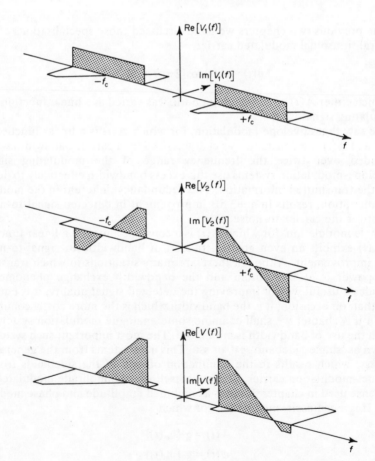

Figure 5.1 Spectral asymmetry of a quadrature amplitude-modulated carrier

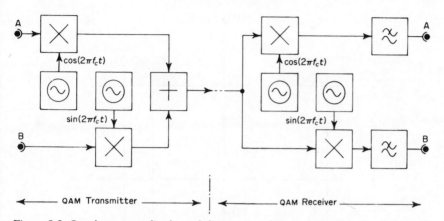

Figure 5.2 Quadrature amplitude modulation. A and B are the two baseband channels

then each of the waves $v_1(t)$ and $v_2(t)$ will exhibit complex conjugate spectral symmetry about the carrier frequency. The sum

$$v(t) = v_1(t) + v_2(t)$$
$$= v_{m_1}(t)\cos(2\pi f_c t) + v_{m_2}(t)\sin(2\pi f_c t) \tag{5.2}$$

is a composite modulated carrier which does not necessarily exhibit complex conjugate symmetry about the carrier frequency and as a consequence is non-redundant, figure 5.1. The extraction of the modulating signals is an easy matter. In-phase and quadrature-locked local oscillators are employed at the receiver to permit product demodulation to take place, figure 5.2.

Quadrature AM systems find their greatest application in digital-data transmission, especially at high data rates when the band occupancy of the digital-data waveform is considerable. Any opportunity to improve the information rate of digital-data systems is eagerly sought by the system designer.

The disadvantage inherent in this kind of non-redundant composite modulation is the need to transmit a pilot tone for carrier reconstruction. Although a notch filter may be employed to achieve this, problems may occur in situations where rapid changes of phase take place. If phase lock is lost then, unlike the simple attenuation which would occur were product modulation to be used instead, the quadrature AM system will also exhibit severe cross-talk between the two modulating signals.

5.2 Single-sideband Modulation[23]

The most obvious method of generating a single-sideband signal is to select either the upper or the lower sideband of a product-modulated carrier with a suitable bandpass filter, figure 5.3. The only problem that this method presents is the choice of the method of achieving the filtering. If the product modulation takes place at a relatively low frequency, in the range 10 to 100 kHz for example, the sideband filter may be designed according to well-established filter synthesis principles by using lumped inductance and

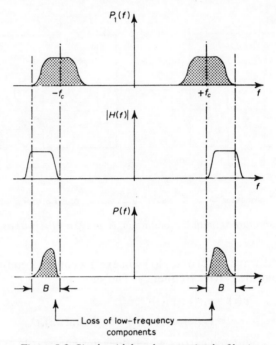

Figure 5.3 *Single-sideband generation by filtering*

capacitance. Of course, such a generation process produces a single-sideband wave at a frequency that is too low for electromagnetic propagation, so that a further upmixing and filtering will be necessary to establish the required sideband at its propagation frequency.

Often, it is desirable to produce the single-sideband wave at the propagation frequency, which may be well in excess of the frequency range within which a lumped-constant filter can be used. Then it is necessary to have recourse to distributed-parameter filters, such as monolithic quartz or mechanical filters or filters in which quartz elements and lumped inductance and capacitance are all used to achieve a sufficiently rapid cut-off in the region between the upper and lower sidebands of the product-modulated wave.

For applications involving speech transmission, the lowest significant frequencies are about 30 Hz above d.c. However, to relax the filtering problems, a lowest usable frequency of 300 Hz is taken to be the norm. This means that a band of width 600 Hz is available within which to attenuate the unwanted sideband to a suitable level.

A method of generating a single-sideband wave does exist, however, which eliminates the need for highly selective filtering. It is far less commonly encountered than the filtering methods, because, as we shall see, it introduces problems of its own. None the less, it provides us with an elegant formal bridge between the mathematical statement of product modulation and the mathematical statement of single sideband, which we have not yet attempted.

The spectra illustrated in figure 5.1 provide a clue as to the nature of the single-sideband modulation. Consider, for example, the spectrum $V_2(f)$. The real part of this spectrum exhibits odd symmetry about the carrier frequency, f_c. In contrast, the real part of $V_1(f)$ exhibits even symmetry. Likewise, the imaginary part of $V_1(f)$ exhibits odd symmetry, and the imaginary part of $V_2(f)$, even symmetry. If we could so form $v_{m_2}(t)$ from $v_{m_1}(t)$ that the spectra $V_1(f)$ and $V_2(f)$ cancelled on either the upper or the lower sideband, we should have established a single-sideband wave.

In principle, we can achieve precisely this if we form $v_{m_2}(t)$ from $v_{m_1}(t)$ by phase shifting all components by 90°. The diagrams in figure 5.4 illustrate the formation of a single-sideband wave in this way.

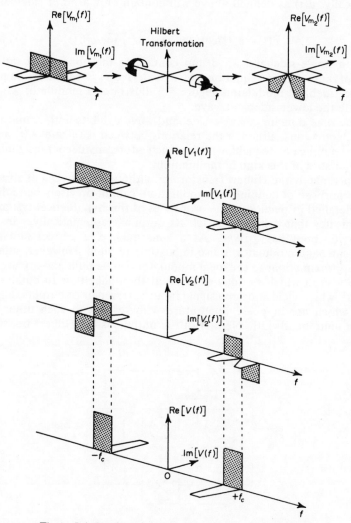

Figure 5.4 Single-sideband generation by phase shifting

The 90° phase shifter is known as a 'Hilbert transformer' because its output is the Hilbert transform[1,6] of its input. We need not enter into a discussion of the mathematics of the Hilbert transform; suffice it to say that we denote the Hilbert transform of any function $v_m(t)$ by the symbol $\widehat{v_m(t)}$. Thus if we let

$$v_{m_1}(t) = v_m(t)$$

then

$$v_{m_2}(t) = \widehat{v_m(t)}$$

and, from equation 5.2

$$v(t) = v_m(t)\cos(2\pi f_c t) + \widehat{v_m(t)}\sin(2\pi f_c t)$$

Specifically, $v(t)$ as defined above will contain only a lower sideband. The wave

$$v(t) = v_m(t)\cos(2\pi f_c t) - \widehat{v_m(t)}\sin(2\pi f_c t)$$

is also a single-sideband wave, but containing the upper sideband. From either of these defining equations, we may derive a system block-diagram for a single-sideband modulator. Figure 5.5 illustrates a modulator which will generate the lower-sideband wave.

In the time domain, a single-sideband wave exhibits both amplitude and phase fluctuations, although the relations between $v_m(t)$ and $A(t)$ and $\phi(t)$ are too complicated to yield, without much effort, any deeper insight into the characteristics of this kind of modulation.

Unfortunately the Hilbert transformer, although a convenient abstraction for the purpose of defining the modulation, cannot precisely be realised. A more detailed inspection of the properties of this hypothetical system module indicates that it is non-causal. Its output, mathematically, can appear before its input has arrived. As a consequence, a perfect and general single-sideband modulator is also impossible to build. However, sufficiently good approximations to the ideal modulator can be built and are used.

One way in which we may circumvent the difficulty is to build a causal network which yields, for one signal input $v_m(t)$ a pair of outputs, $v_{m_1}(t)$ and $v_{m_2}(t)$ which are in phase quadrature with respect to each other over a certain finite bandwidth. Neither of the outputs is the Hilbert transform of

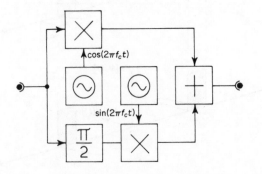

Figure 5.5 Phase shift SSB modulator: theoretical system block-diagram

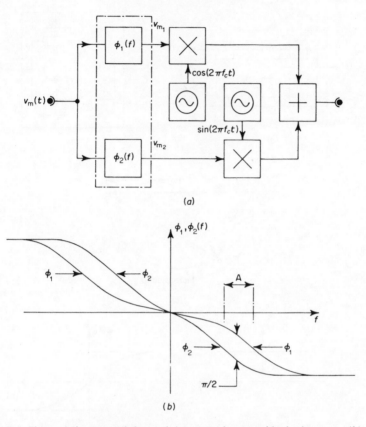

(a)

(b)

Figure 5.6 Phase shift SSB *modulator: (a) practical system block-diagram; (b) phase characteristic, region* A: *operating range within which modulating signal components will receive a phase shift of* $\pi/2$ *radians*

the input. Indeed, both are delayed and phase-distorted versions of $v_m(t)$. The phase distortion is of no importance in voice communication since the human ear is not phase sensitive. Because phase distortion is inherent in this type of modulator, it is unsuitable for digital-data transmission where it is important that the pulse shape be preserved during detection.

The block diagram of a phase shift modulator is shown in figure 5.6. As the phase characteristics sketched on this diagram indicate, the 90° relative phase shift can only be achieved for signals which do not have appreciable low-frequency content. Since speech signals fall into this class, this method of synthesising a single-sideband wave finds application primarily in the transmission of such waveforms.

The phase shift network, figure 5.7*a* is formed from all-pass sections, figure 5.7*b*. The precise nature of the realisation of the all-pass circuit depends on the design criteria imposed upon the system as a whole. The circuit operation may be understood by an examination of figure 5.7*c*. The phase splitter yields antiphase signals v_3 and v_4 which drive a common

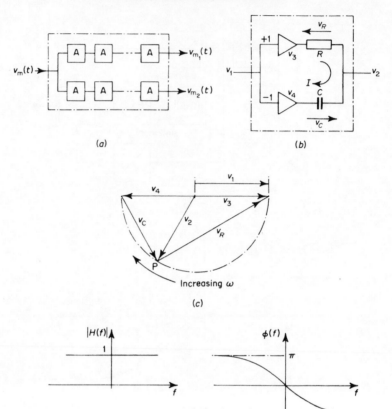

Figure 5.7 (a) *The all-pass phase shift network, derived from* (b) *the basic all-pass circuit. From a phasor diagram,* (c), *it is seen that because the locus of the point* P *is a semicircle, the amplitude and phase characteristics are as shown at* (d)

current through R and C. Consequently the voltages across these elements will be in phase quadrature. As the frequency of the input signal increases, the reactance of the capacitance decreases. So also does the voltage across it. Since the right-angle between the phasors v_C and v_R must be maintained, their point of junction, P, will move in the indicated direction with increasing frequency, along the periphery of a semicircle. Thus, the phasor v_2, defining the output voltage, will be of constant length whatever the frequency, although its phase will change with respect to the input phasor v_1. As a result we have a circuit with a transfer characteristic of the form shown in figure 5.7d. Typically up to ten networks might be included in each leg of the phase shifter. The values of R and C in the networks in either leg would differ, being selected to give as wide as possible a range of frequency over which the relative phase shift would be 90°. Again typically, an individual all-pass network phase-shift of the order of 10° at the lower edge of the signal band would be chosen as the basis for design.

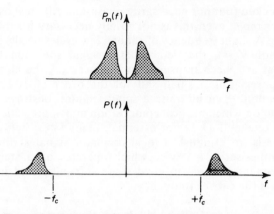

Figure 5.8 Spectrum of a speech-modulated SSB *carrier*

5.3 The Detection of Single-sideband Modulation

We shall restrict our attention to the type of SSB modulation in which the modulating signal, like a speech waveform, contains no very-low-frequency components or a d.c. level. The power spectra of a typical modulating signal and the modulated carrier are illustrated in figure 5.8. Demodulation is very simply obtained by multiplication of the modulated carrier with a sinusoid at the nominal carrier frequency. If, as is the case with speech transmission, the detected waveform-shape is not important, phase coherence is not necessary. This is not the case when digital data is to be transmitted. Then, either a pilot tone must be transmitted as a phase reference or a modified modulation process must be employed which yields a carrier spectrum from which the required phase information may be extracted by suitable signal processing.

We see, from the detector block-diagrams shown in figure 5.9 that the demodulator simply produces a frequency shift to baseband. A post-detection filter may be needed in some applications to eliminate the sum-frequency terms generated after product demodulation. Although the use of

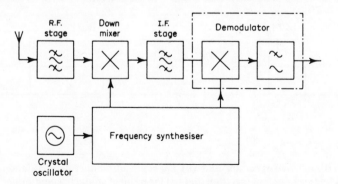

Figure 5.9 SSB *receiver employing frequency synthesis*

a frequency-locked (but not necessarily phase-locked) local oscillator might be thought desirable, even this is not strictly necessary for the detection of speech signals. A slight frequency offset of a few cycles results in a frequency transposition of $V_m(f)$, the demodulated-signal spectrum, by the same amount. As far as speech transmission is concerned, the human ear is not capable of appreciating a small shift of the order of 10 Hz. For music, spectral relocation, even by quite a small amount, destroys the harmonic relationships upon which musical composition and appreciation is based.

Because frequency lock is not essential, many SSB systems employ 'frequency synthesis' to establish a local oscillator signal at the detector. A frequency synthesiser is a device which operates on a standard crystal-controlled frequency source to yield some submultiple of its natural frequency which is the carrier frequency.

5.4   Asymmetric- and Vestigial-sideband Modulation

If the modulating signal which is to be transmitted contains important low-frequency terms, and perhaps, also, a d.c. level, the SSB modulation technique described in the previous two sections is obviously unsuitable. One way of obtaining much of the economy of bandwidth of SSB while still transmitting the low-frequency information is to employ a sideband filter which admits part of the unwanted sideband in the region adjacent to the carrier, figure 5.10a. The remnant of the unwanted sideband is wasteful of bandwidth and carrier power, but the wastage need only be slight. This type of signal spectrum defines asymmetric-sideband (ASB) modulation.

Since the object of using ASB is to retain the low-frequency components and d.c. level, and hence also the signal shape, the demodulation technique used for SSB is unsuitable. Coherent product demodulation, such as would be required to demodulate a product-modulated wave is necessary. The demodulated-signal spectrum, figure 5.10b, will then exhibit the 'foldover'

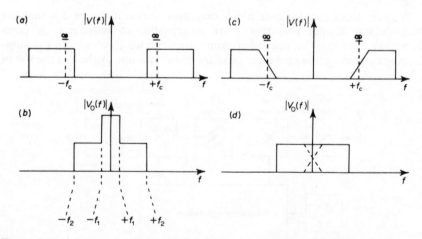

Figure 5.10 (a) ASB spectrum and (b) the result of product demodulation, showing sideband foldover. (c) VSB spectrum and (d) the result of product demodulation, showing that the correct baseband signal is restored

caused by product demodulation in the region zero to f_1 Hz, and the frequency translation effect caused by demodulating that part of the carrier spectrum which is purely SSB, in the region f_1 to f_2 Hz. As a consequence, some form of spectral shaping is necessary to restore the correct baseband-signal spectrum. This may be achieved by filtering to yield a spectrum of the general form shown in figure 5.10c either before or after transmission. Product demodulation now automatically restores the correct baseband-signal spectrum, figure 5.10d, provided that the spectral shape shown in figure 5.10c is defined in the region $(f_c - f_1) \leqslant |f| \leqslant (f_c + f_1)$ such that

$$|V(f_c + f)| = |V(f_c + f_1)| - |V(f_c - f)|$$

The spectrum shown in figure 5.10c is taken to define a vestigial-sideband (VSB) signal.

5.5 Independent-sideband Modulation

Independent-sideband modulation, ISB, is widely used as a means of obtaining economical use of bandwidth on high frequency (HF: 3–30 MHz) point-to-point radio links. Single-sideband modulators are used, forming upper and lower sidebands for a single carrier frequency. A pilot tone, providing a carrier phase-reference is usually also incorporated. Figure 5.11 shows a block diagram of a complete ISB system, including carrier recovery at the receiver.

5.6 Noise in Single-sideband Detection

The reader will recall the result, pertinent to product demodulation and envelope detection above the threshold relating the detector output signal-to-noise ratio s to the input-modulated carrier-to-noise ratio, p

$$s = 2p$$

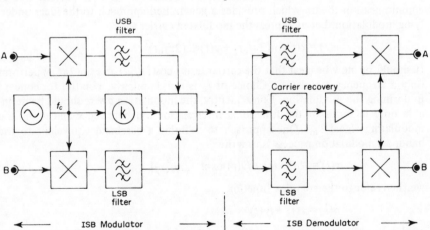

Figure 5.11 Independent sideband transmission. A and B are the two baseband channels; k determines the pilot-tone amplitude and is small

The 3 dB improvement which this equation predicts comes about in the following way. On demodulation, the upper and lower sidebands add, doubling in amplitude and consequently quadrupling in power. The noise components in the upper and lower sidebands are not coherently related. That is, the noise spectrum, unlike the modulated-carrier spectrum, does not exhibit complex conjugate symmetry about the carrier frequency. On demodulation, noise components add in power, so that the noise power emerging from the detector doubles. Thus the signal has gained a 3 dB advantage over the noise as the result of the spectral redundancy.

If we employ any of the SSB techniques discussed in the foregoing sections we lose the advantage of coherency between the sidebands, with the result that the demodulated-signal power decreases by a factor of four. However, the noise power at the detector input halves because, with a given channel noise-power spectral density, the bandwidth is halved by SSB operation. Thus

$$s = p$$

This result does not mean that SSB performs only half as well as product modulation (DSB) or conventional AM above the threshold. Given that a fixed amount of transmitter power is available at the transmitter, this may all be inserted into the single transmitted sideband with the result that

$$p_{SSB} = 2p_{DSB}$$

Viewed from this standpoint, it is apparent that

$$s_{SSB} = s_{DSB}$$

5.7 Baseband-equivalent Modulation Processes

In section 5.2, when we introduced the concept of the Hilbert transform and the phase-shifting single-sideband modulator, we touched upon an important area of communication theory which provides a generalised approach to the ideas underlying modulation. Let us express the modulated carrier as

$$v(t) = x(t)\cos(2\pi f_c t) + y(t)\sin(2\pi f_c t)$$

It should by now be clear that the carrier terms $\cos(2\pi f_c t)$ and $\sin(2\pi f_c t)$ perform only a frequency translation. Choice of f_c is not, implicitly, a matter for concern in defining the modulation. Consequently, the modulation *per se* should be definable only in terms of the functional interrelationship between x and y and the modulating signal v_m. One approach to defining a baseband equivalent to the bandpass modulation process is to write

$$v(t) = Re\left[(x(t) + jy(t))\exp(-2\pi jf_c t)\right]$$

we then refer to the complex function

$$u(t) = x(t) + jy(t)$$

as the *complex pre-envelope* of the modulated carrier $v(t)$. Like x and y, $u(t)$ is a baseband function. However, whereas x and y (being *real*, which is to say having zero-valued *imaginary* parts) exhibit complex conjugate spectral symmetry, the 'non-realisable' $u(t)$ does not possess this property. In this respect it mirrors, about zero-frequency, the property possessed by bandpass functions, namely that they may be spectrally asymmetric about the carrier frequency. In fact, the spectrum $U(f)$ may be formed by deleting the negative frequencies part of the spectrum of $v(t)$ and downshifting the positive frequencies part by an amount equal to the carrier frequency value. (In this respect, the reader should note the distinction between this operation and normal product demodulation, in which both positive and negative frequency lobes are downshifted and possibly overlap at zero frequency.)

Baseband equivalent signals, their spectra, processing and properties are of considerable importance in radar waveform design. In particular, they form the basis for the development of a complex time–frequency correlation function, known as the *ambiguity function*, which indicates the relative merits of rival signal designs in the presence of range-delay and Doppler-shift.

For single-sideband communication studies, the complex pre-envelope is further formalised in the concept of the *analytic signal*, which is similarly defined, but is subject to the additional constraint that x and y be a Hilbert transform pair

$$x(t) = \pm \widehat{y(t)}$$

This constraint has the effect of ensuring that the spectrum is single-sided about zero frequency, thereby mirroring the bandpass phasing single-sideband modulation process at baseband. The analytic signal has been used in many formal studies of asymmetric-spectrum modulation processes. Of these, perhaps the best known is *compatible single sideband*, CSSB. This form of modulation purports to create a single-sided spectrum of width $B = f_m$, such that the *envelope* of the modulated carrier is a faithful replica of the modulating signal. In this way, economy of bandwidth is combined with simplicity of detection and compatibility with existing receiver equipment used for the detection of conventional broadcast AM. It should perhaps be mentioned that, at the present time, CSSB has not found extensive use as a broadcast modulation.

A final area of extreme significance in which complex baseband considerations are encountered is in the processing and analysis of communication and other waveforms by means of digital computers. In particular, digital computer algorithms for efficiently computing Fourier series and hence power spectra commence by processing a complex 'time function' to yield an asymmetric spectrum.

5.8 Applications of Composite Modulation

5.8.1 Frequency Division Multiplex Telephony

Possibly the single most important application of composite modulation is to be found in the use of single-sideband modulation in frequency-division multiplex trunk telephony. This topic is considered in more detail in section 9.2.

5.8.2 The Use of Vestigial-sideband Modulation in Digital-data Transmission

High data-rate digital signals present a problem when electromagnetic propagation becomes necessary, since they are wideband processes with signal components extending down to zero frequency. It is common practice to form a VSB signal before transmission and employ coherent product detection at the receiver. A variety of quite complex local-oscillator reference-signal extraction methods have been devised for this purpose. This topic is considered in greater detail in section 8.6.

5.8.3 The Use of Asymmetric-sideband Modulation in Television Transmission

Like digital-data signals, television video signals are wideband and contain important components down to zero frequency. Because the signal powers handled at the transmitter are relatively high, no attempt is made rigidly to control the shape of the transmitted signal spectrum, other than to establish a wave of basic ASB form. A VSB filter, that is, a filter with a characteristic

$$|H(f + f_c)| = 1 - |H(f - f_c)|$$
$$|H(f_c)| = \frac{1}{2}$$

is then used to establish, at the receiver, prior to detection, a VSB spectrum. Envelope detection, rather than product demodulation, is used to extract the baseband signal. Provided the rate of fall in the region $(f_c - f_1)$ to $(f_c + f_1)$ is not too rapid, the envelope of a VSB wave approximates to the baseband modulation, although the distortion level is quite high, and would be unacceptable for most speech transmissions. The form of distortion, however, is such that it is not perceptible when translated into a visual image on the television picture tube.

Problems

5.1 Show that if the summing module in figure 5.5 is replaced by a differencing circuit, then an upper-sideband signal will be formed instead of a lower-sideband signal.

5.2 It is required to design an experimental SSB system in which the method of filtering is used to eliminate the unwanted sideband. Assume the required transmission to be a speech signal occupying the normal telephony band from 300 Hz to 3.4 kHz. If a passive filter falling asymptotically at $6n$ dB per octave, where n is the order of the filter, is to be used for upper-sideband elimination, estimate the order of the filter required to attenuate the low-frequency components of the upper sideband by at least 6 dB. Assume that the nominal cut-off frequency of the lowpass filter is located at the frequency $f_c = 300$ Hz (that is, the highest significant information frequency) and perform the estimation for $f_c = 4$ kHz (as might be the case in a simple bench experiment) and for $f_c = 100$ kHz (that is, within the normal line-telephony band). Comment on the suitability of passive lumped filters for the intended application.

5.3 For the system described in question 5.2, if it is assumed that the speech-power spectral density is of triangular law over the band 300 Hz to

3.4 kHz with predominantly low-frequency components, plot graphs showing the power spectral density of the upper and lower sidebands before and after filtering and estimate the relative powers in the two sidebands. Consider only the bench experiment in which $f_c = 4$ kHz.

5.4 The same system is employed for the demodulation of SSB as would be used for the demodulation of product modulation (see section 3.1). Because of problems of phase and frequency synchronisation, product modulation is not used in practice for radio communication. Why is SSB not rejected on the same grounds and what other advantages does it exhibit?

5.5 Compatible SSB is a form of single-sideband modulation in which the wave is so formed as to be capable of demodulation with an envelope detector. Show that ordinary SSB is not capable of detection in this way by considering the case where the modulation is a simple test sinusoid.

5.6 A digital test-signal consisting of alternate marks and spaces of duration 20 ms is premodulation filtered by a filter which closely approximates an ideal rectangular characteristic with a cut-off at 30 Hz. The resulting waveform is then used to SSB modulate a sinusoidal carrier. Detection is accomplished by mixing with a local oscillator at a frequency which, by chance, is displaced by 10 Hz from the nominal carrier frequency. Deduce a mathematical expression for the output signal and carefully sketch the demodulate. Why is SSB unsuitable for the transmission of digital information?

5.7 Contrast the suitability of the following composite modulations for the transmission of digital data: (a) SSB; (b) ISB; (c) ASB; (d) VSB; (e) QAM. (Hint What are the important relevant properties of digital data and what are the requirements for its undistorted transmission?) Would a pilot tone yielding a carrier-phase reference be necessary in any of the systems you consider to be suited to the transmission of digital data?

6 Sampling and Pulse Code Modulation

In the previous three chapters, we have discussed the modulation of a sinusoidal carrier of a suitably high frequency by means of an analogue baseband-signal such as a speech or music waveform. The object of modulation was primarily to achieve a relocation of baseband information at a carrier frequency that was suitable for electromagnetic propagation.

We turn next to consider the use of pulse waveforms as methods of conveying information. Unlike the continuous-wave modulation systems which we have been considering, pulse systems produce from a baseband signal a waveform which is still, itself, baseband in nature. For electromagnetic propagation to be possible, this signal would have to be subjected to some subsequent continuous-wave modulation.

Pulse techniques fall into two broad categories

(1) The amplitude, rate (frequency) or duration modulation of a rectangular-pulse waveform, or the amplitude or rate modulation of an impulse train.
(2) The generation of a sequence of fixed-length binary codewords sometimes representing a 'sampled' version of an analogue waveform and sometimes existing as a data or telegraphy signal in its own right.

The first of these classes is, with one important exception, not of great importance within communication systems. The exception is the amplitude modulation of a periodic-impulse train

$$\sum_{k=-\infty}^{+\infty} \delta(t - kT)$$

which, as we shall see in section 6.1, defines the operation of 'sampling', referred to above. Sampling permits us to represent continuous-in-time signals as a sequence of amplitude values. In section 6.1 we shall also show that the discrete-in-time sample values may be processed to yield the original continuous-in-time waveform, provided certain rules are obeyed.

The sampling principle is important because, since the samples are discrete-in-time, samples from several different signal sources may be interleaved, transmitted through a common medium and separated into individual sample sequences at the receiver. This technique is known as time division multiplexing (TDM). A basic TDM system is shown in figure 6.1. The system consists of a pair of synchronised 'sampling switches'. The first switch extracts and interleaves the sample values from N continuous-in-time information sources and the second separates them after transmission. It then passes each sample sequence to the circuitry which performs the reconstruction of the original continuous-in-time signal.

The 'transmission medium' shown in figure 6.1 usually contains a considerable body of shared electronic equipment, as well as the communication channel itself. This feature of the TDM system makes it attractive from an economic standpoint as an alternative to the system of frequency division multiplexing which was introduced in section 5.8.1.

The second of the two classes of pulse modulation listed above requires that we convert each sample value into a suitable *codeword* and transmit this, instead of the sample value itself. Usually, we convert the sample value into a fixed-length equivalent-binary number. All codewords then consist of a certain number of binary digits which are transmitted in the interval between consecutive sampling instants. Typically, seven- or eight-digit codewords are sufficient to represent most analogue waveforms with adequate accuracy.

Thus far, we have assumed that our digital codeword has been derived by means of an impulse amplitude-modulation followed by some electronic coding operation. We refer to this entire process as *pulse code modulation*, PCM. However PCM is not the only source of digital signals. The earliest electrical communication systems involved the use of telegraphy in which a crude form of digital signalling was employed. Modern telegraph communication systems employ electrical teletypewriters which generate five- or seven-binary-digit codewords to represent the various alphanumeric and punctuation characters which they are required to transmit.

A sector of the communication industry which is of rapidly increasing importance is that which is concerned with the transfer of digital data. An example of a digital-data communication system is provided by the communication link found between computers and remote job-handling terminals.

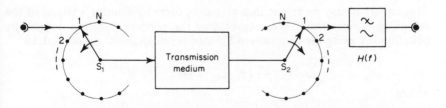

Figure 6.1 The principle of time division multiplexing sampled-data channels. S_1: *multiplexing switch*; S_2: *de-multiplexing switch*; $H(f)$: *reconstruction filter*

The great advantages of using digital processing techniques in communication systems are

(1) The convenience of handling binary waveforms within an electronic system.

(2) The ease of design and economy of implementation of digital systems when using integrated-circuit techniques.

(3) The possibility of regenerating a sharp-edged, noise-free version of the digit sequence by 'slicing' at intermediate relay 'stations', known as regenerative repeaters, within a long communication link.

(4) When intermediate regeneration is not possible: the requirement at the receiver of having to decide between only two well-defined signal states corresponding to the binary symbols 0 and 1.

6.1 The Sampling Principle

When we draw the graph of a mathematical function from a sequence of calculated values of ordinates, we apply, albeit unconsciously, the twin principles of waveform sampling and waveform reconstruction. We imagine that, given sufficiently frequent points along the curve (the 'samples') we should be able to obtain an adequate free-hand sketch of the function itself. Normally, we should calculate values of our function at equally spaced points along the abscissa. The same is usually true of an electronic sampling system—samples are extracted at equal intervals of time.

In section 1.13, when we first discussed the impulse function $\delta(x)$, we saw that the operation of sampling at a single point $x = a$ was defined by the 'sifting integral'

$$\int_{-\infty}^{+\infty} f(x)\, \delta(x-a)\, \mathrm{d}x = f(a)$$

Here, the function $\delta(x-a)$ is the *sampling impulse*. The periodic sampling of a waveform is performed mathematically by means of a *sampling-impulse train*

$$\sum_{k=-\infty}^{+\infty} \delta(t - kT) \tag{6.1}$$

so that the sampled waveform $v_s(t)$ is given by the relationship

$$v_s(t) = v_m(t) \sum_{k=-\infty}^{+\infty} \delta(t - kT) \tag{6.2}$$

This equation may be recast in a revealing form by Fourier analysis of the sampling-impulse train. We may expand the periodic function defined by equation 6.1 using the generalised Fourier series analysis, equation 1.18

$$\sum_{k=-\infty}^{+\infty} \delta(t - kT) = \sum_{n=-\infty}^{\infty} V_n \exp(+2\pi \mathrm{j}nt/T)$$

where

$$V_n = (1/T) \int_{-T/2}^{+T/2} \delta(t)\exp(-2\pi \mathrm{j}nt/T)\, \mathrm{d}t$$

$$= 1/T \quad \text{all } n$$

so that

$$v_s(t) = v_m(t)(1/T) \sum_{n=-\infty}^{\infty} \exp(+2\pi jnt/T) \qquad (6.3)$$

We may identify a general term in this summation, namely $v_m(t)\exp(+2\pi jnt/T)$ which describes a frequency translation, yielding a spectrum $V_m(f - n/T)$. Consequently, the spectrum of the sampled wave is given by the result

$$V_s(f) = (1/T) \sum_{n=-\infty}^{+\infty} V_m(f - n/T) \qquad (6.4)$$

If we assume that $V_m(f)$ is band-limited

$$|V_m(f)| = 0 \quad |f| > f_0$$

then, provided

$$1/T \geqslant 2f_0 \qquad (6.5)$$

the spectrum $V_s(f)$ will have the general form illustrated in figure 6.2a.

Notice that the spectral lobes depicted in figure 6.2a do not overlap. This provides us with a criterion whereby we may select the sampling rate. Reconstruction is a necessary adjunct to the sampling operation and can be achieved by lowpass filtering of the spectrum $V_s(f)$ by a filter with the characteristic

$$H(f) = 1 \quad |f| < f_0$$
$$= 0 \quad \text{elsewhere}$$

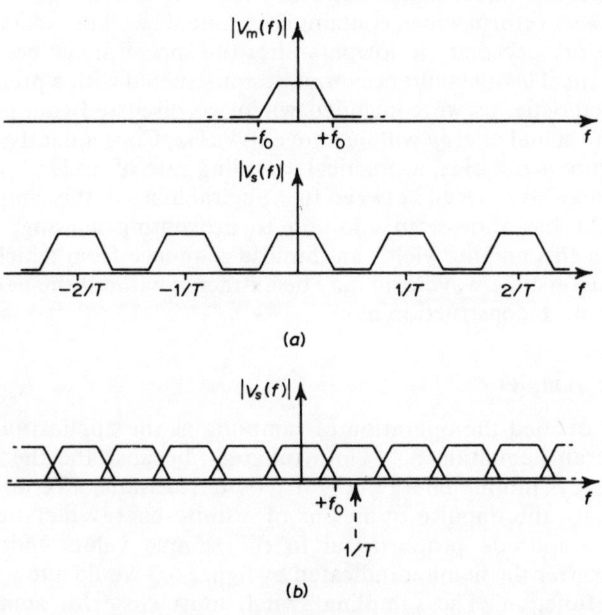

(a)

(b)

Figure 6.2 (a) A correctly sampled baseband signal. (b) The effect of sampling at a rate such that $1/T < 2f_0$ is to introduce aliasing which prevents correct reconstruction since the output of such a filter is a baseband spectrum which is identical with that of the sampled signal $v_m(t)$. If we assume such a reconstruction-filter characteristic, then provided the inequality of equation 6.5 is adhered to in establishing the sampling rate, reconstruction must, in theory, be possible.

We often refer to the lower bound to the sampling rate, $2f_0$, as the 'Nyquist rate'. Nyquist was one of the earlier investigators of the properties of waveforms and sampling systems.

Equation 6.5 embodies the principle of the *sampling theorem* which may be stated in its simplest form thus

'Given a waveform $v_m(t)$ with a baseband spectrum $V_m(f)$ such that

$$|V_m(f)| = 0 \quad |f| > f_0$$

then the waveform may be completely reconstructed from samples extracted at a rate greater than or equal to $2f_0$'.

If the sampling theorem is not obeyed, the situation depicted in figure 6.2b will occur. The spectral lobes will overlap and perfect reconstruction will not be possible. The spectral overlap is sometimes referred to as 'aliasing'.

The Nyquist rate, then, places a lower bound upon the sampling rate. Since sampling is followed by a digital coding, we might suppose that the slowest possible sampling rate was an advantageous choice in that it allows us the greatest time in which to complete all subsequent signal processing. This is indeed the case. However, there are often circumstances under which the Nyquist rate must be exceeded. For example, in PCM telephony systems, the nominal maximum signal-frequency is 3.4 kHz. The signal to be sampled is a speech waveform which contains components well in excess of this value. It is therefore necessary to lowpass-filter the speech signal before sampling. Since practical lowpass filters cannot be constructed with a precise rectangular characteristic, as we concluded when we discussed causality in section 1.17, some signal energy will lie above 3.4 kHz. Consequently, although the Nyquist rate is 6.8 kHz, a practical sampling rate of 8 kHz is chosen. Then 'guard spaces' are placed between the spectral lobes of the sampled signal, as figure 6.2a has shown. In addition to preventing aliasing, pre-sampling filtering in this manner yields an impulse sequence from which the original continuous-in-time waveform may be extracted without the need for a very-sharp-cut-off reconstruction filter.

6.2 The Sampler

We have defined the operation of sampling as the application of a sifting-impulse train, equation 6.1. Unfortunately, because the the sampling impulse conveys infinite energy, it is strictly unrealisable. We might choose to approximate the impulse by means of a finite-energy rectangular voltage-pulse of amplitude proportional to the sample value. Indeed, a switch operating after the manner indicated by figure 6.3 would allow us to perform just this function. The sampling switch must close for some small time interval τ every T seconds. As τ tends to zero, the sampler 'resolution' approaches that of the ideal. Unfortunately, the energy in the sampled signal

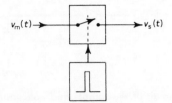

Figure 6.3 The sampler: $v_m(t)$ is the input signal and $v_s(t)$ the sampled sequence

also approaches zero. This is undesirable, since noise within the sampling system would then cause an unacceptably large perturbation to the extracted sample value.

One obvious way in which this difficulty might be avoided would be to amplify the input signal in direct proportion to the decrease in τ. However, correct system design would normally ensure that the sampler input signal was 'full range'. Then an increase in signal amplitude would only result in unacceptably frequent clipping by the power-supply line voltages.

In practice, we usually avoid the problem of requiring narrow, large voltage pulses (approaching impulses) by using a pulse-stretching technique. Instead of extracting a narrow voltage sample, we store on a capacitor the sample value of the waveform for the duration of the sampling interval. This has two advantages

(1) It provides a reference voltage level equal to the sample value during any subsequent digital-coding operation.

(2) The voltage 'impulse' is replaced by a current 'impulse' which charges the capacitor.

The amplitude restriction on the current impulse is usually less severe than that on a hypothetical voltage impulse. We shall discuss this topic in greater detail in the next section when we investigate the practical implementation of such pulse-stretching circuits. The entire process of extracting and storing the sample value is referred to as a 'sample and hold' operation.

6.3 The Sample and Hold Operation

Figure 6.4 shows the block diagram representation of a basic sample and hold circuit. The circuit consists of a capacitor, acting as an analogue 'sample

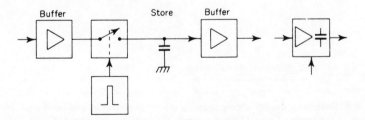

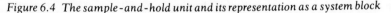

Figure 6.4 The sample-and-hold unit and its representation as a system block

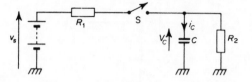

Figure 6.5 The equivalent circuit of the sample and hold unit. R_1 is the source and switch-closed resistance and is small. R_2 is the amplifier-input resistance and is large

store' which is rapidly charged to the sample value by a low output-impedance buffer amplifier when the sampling switch closes. The duration of closure of the sampling switch is short in comparison with the holding period, so that, on opening, the capacitor is isolated from subsequent fluctuations of the input waveform. A high input-impedance buffer amplifier following the capacitor ensures that the 'droop' of the held-sample value, caused by leakage of charge during the 'hold' period, is small.

Figure 6.5 illustrates a simple equivalent circuit for the sampler. The appropriate system waveforms, figure 6.6, show both the 'store' phase and the effect of leakage during the 'hold' phase. The capacitor charging-current waveforms during the 'store' phase illustrate the way in which, as the output impedance of the input buffer is decreased, the output current from the buffer tends to form an impulse.

The most difficult part of the sampling system to implement is the analogue sampling switch. Two commonly used techniques are[39]

(1) The switching diode bridge
(2) The FET analogue gate

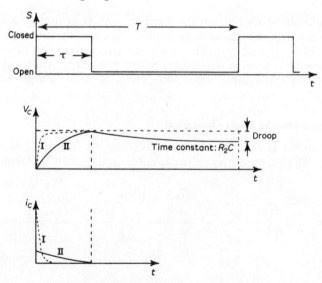

Figure 6.6 Switching and charging waveforms for the sample and hold unit. Note that the areas under curves I and II on the graph of i_c versus t are equal. Curve I shows R_1 smaller in value than in curve II

The speed of operation of the bridge is generally greater than that of the FET gate, but its ratio of 'on' to 'off' impedance is smaller and the circuitry is more involved and critical of component matching.

6.4 Quantisation and Coding

We have seen how a waveform $v_m(t)$ may be sampled to give a set of impulses $v_s(t)$ which can, under the conditions specified by the sampling theorem, convey exactly the same information as was present in $v_m(t)$. The magnitude of the impulses in $v_s(t)$ we have regarded as being continuously variable in sympathy with $v_m(t)$.

Initially, we think of the sample magnitudes as decimal numbers, capable of expression to a degree of accuracy determined by our measuring equipment. For the reasons presented at the conclusion of the introduction to this chapter, we prefer to handle binary, rather than decimal numbers in electronic systems. Thus we wish to express each sample value in the form of a finite-length binary number. This we may achieve if we regard the voltage range which encompasses all possible sample magnitudes as divided into a suitably large number of levels, with one binary number corresponding to each level. For example, suppose we wish to express the sample magnitudes by means of five-digit binary numbers. Then, since there are $2^5 = 32$ such numbers, each of these numbers may correspond to one of 32 voltage levels within the voltage range allowed to the sample values.

The process of breaking the voltage range of the sample magnitudes into a finite number of levels is known as *quantising*. The operation of forming the binary number corresponding to the nearest quantising level to the input-sample magnitude is known as *coding*. The binary number is referred to as a *codeword*. The binary codeword may be transmitted exactly as it is generated or it may be subjected to some further processing. We shall consider a number of reasons for manipulating the codeword in some manner in chapter 7.

After transmission, the reconstruction of the analogue samples from the received codeword is referred to as decoding. Because quantisation results in the quantised-sample magnitudes only approximating the original-sample magnitudes, the decoded binary words produce a waveform which does not exactly match the original informational waveform. However, provided a sufficiently large number of quantisation levels is employed, the approximation is adequate.

It is sometimes helpful to think of quantisation being performed by a system module: a 'quantiser'. The quantiser yields an output voltage v_o for an input voltage v_i according to a law

$$v_o = v_k$$

when $v_k - \Delta v_k/2 \leqslant v_i \leqslant v_k + \Delta v_k/2$. Here v_k is the kth voltage threshold and Δv_k the voltage step about the kth voltage threshold. A *uniform* quantiser, for which

$$\Delta v_k = \Delta v \quad \text{all } k$$

is depicted in figure 6.7.

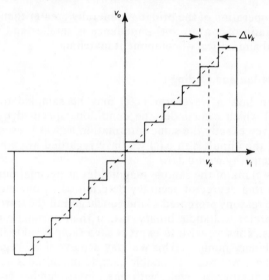

Figure 6.7 A uniform quantisation law

6.5 Quantisation Noise

In the previous section we defined and illustrated the process of quantisation and it was mentioned that a large number of quantising levels are required if the decoded signal is to be a faithful reproduction of the original. Typically, the encoding of a speech waveform would involve the use of several hundreds of quantising levels. Naturally, we should like to establish, as a design aid, some criterion of quality associated with the quantisation operation and, in particular, with the effect of quantisation on the *decoded* signal.

In general, the output-sample magnitude will differ from that of the input sample. The difference can be no greater than a single quantising step and may be regarded as equivalent to a small noisewave superimposed upon the output signal after decoding. Consequently this form of signal corruption is known as *quantising noise*. The coarser the quantisation (that is, the fewer the quantising levels) the more severe will the effect become.

It is not very difficult to obtain a rough estimate of the severity of the quantising noise as a function of the number of quantising levels. Let us assume a quantisation step of Δv, and m quantising levels, so that a full-range noise-like signal will have an amplitude of $m \, \Delta v$. The quantising noisewave can only have a total range of Δv. The signal, then, will be m times as large as the quantising noisewave and will therefore contain m^2 times its power. Consequently the signal-to-quantising noise power ratio will be given approximately by m^2, or $20 \log_{10}(m)$ dB. Despite the brevity of this assessment, the result is a good indication of practical operating behaviour. For example, although only eight quantising levels will permit a speech signal to remain intelligible, a common criterion for acceptability for any communication system is a signal-to-noise ratio of about 40 dB. This corresponds to a quantiser with at least one hundred levels. As we shall see, many telephone services utilising pulse code modulation, and therefore involving the process of quantisation, are designed to accommodate 128 quantising levels.

If we assume equal-sized quantising steps, the quantisation noise affects the signal most adversely when the latter is of small amplitude. If the signal distribution were typically gaussian, this would frequently be the situation encountered at the quantiser input. Large signal excursions would be relatively rare. To alleviate this problem, non-uniform quantisation may be employed. This has the effect of causing the spacing, Δv_k, to increase as v_k increases. Non-uniform quantisation may be achieved in two important ways

(1) Non-linear amplification of the signal at the quantiser input. The non-linearity is chosen to force the gaussian signal distribution towards a uniform distribution. A complementary non-linear amplification to remove the signal distortion so imposed upon the input waveform takes place after transmission, decoding and signal reconstruction.

(2) Special coding to obtain a non-linear relation between the codewords and the input-sample values.

We shall discuss these two techniques in greater detail in section 6.11, using as examples the methods applied to obtain non-uniform quantisation in PCM telephony systems.

6.6 Coding for Technological Convenience

The generation of binary codewords rather than, perhaps, decimal codewords to represent sample values in pulse communication systems is a matter of technological convenience. Binary signals are relatively easy to generate and handle in electronic systems and offer the important advantage to the communication engineer that a decision between only two signal states need be made. It is true that some special communication systems employ transmission by means of ternary, quaternary or still higher-order codes. However, even these would normally be generated from a primary binary signal by means of suitable logic circuitry.

It is worth examining three further points with respect to coding for technological convenience—points which may help to place the overall problem of coding in perspective.

The first point concerns the structure of the natural binary code. Notice that when we change the decimal number 0 to the decimal number 1, the corresponding binary number, . . . 000 changes by one digit only, to the binary number . . . 001. Contrast this with the change in the binary number corresponding to the decimal number 7 when its value is increased to 8, namely . . . 0111 to . . . 1000. Now all four binary digits must be changed.

The need to alter large numbers of binary digits for small changes in the corresponding decimal numbers can be something of a disadvantage in many applications. For example, certain digital control-systems accept a coded input which is obtained by an electro-optical system. The changeover from decimal 7 to decimal 8 may cause the photodetectors to register the entire range of intermediate values as well

$$...0111$$
$$...0110$$
$$...0100$$
$$...0000$$
$$...1000$$

so that a succession of spurious samples may be generated

$$...\quad 7\quad 6\quad 4\quad 0\quad 8\quad ...$$

instead of, perhaps

$$...\quad 7\quad 7\quad 7\quad 8\quad 8\quad ...$$

To eliminate this problem, a special binary code, the 'Gray', or 'reflected' binary code, has been developed. In this code, successive decimal numbers correspond to binary numbers differing from each other in only one symbol, table 6.1.

Although the Gray code is primarily used in instrumentation and control, rather than communication engineering, it does allow us to introduce a term quite widely used to describe codes in general. This is the term *Hamming distance*, which is the number of symbols by which successive codewords differ. Thus the natural binary code has a Hamming distance which is variable. The Gray code has a Hamming distance of one and is consequently referred to as a 'unit distance' code.

The Gray code was devised in the late nineteenth century by E. Gray for use on telegraph systems. It was resurrected in 1947 by F. Gray for use in electron-beam coding tubes. The term 'Hamming distance' is named after R. W. Hamming, one of the pioneer workers in the field of error detecting and correcting codes.

As we shall see in section 6.10, some coders lend themselves to the generation of *symmetrical* binary codes. A symmetrical code is depicted in table 6.1 and can be seen to consist of two half-length natural binary codes placed 'back-to-back' about the midline of the code table. The most significant digit indicates *sense* and the code is usually encountered in situations where the midline corresponds to a d.c. level.

Finally, we often need to process decimal quantities. This is frequently the case when computing peripherals and measuring instruments are being devised. If this is the case, then a natural binary code may be applied in a rather different manner to that which we have envisaged, namely with each decimal number corresponding to one natural binary number. Instead, we may use a four-digit binary number to represent each digit of a decimal number. For example, the decimal number 982.3 would appear as 1001100000100011. The use of the binary system in this way is, from the point of view of the communication engineer, very inefficient. Sixteen possible symbols could, in principle, be represented by all the possible combinations of four binary digits, where we represent only ten. In addition, the implied redundancy is not incorporated in such a way as to provide any inherent error-reducing property in the coded signal. However, the convenience of the decimal notation makes this method of coding, which is known as 'binary coded decimal', BCD, particularly attractive for the applications mentioned above.

TABLE 6.1 COMPARISON OF DECIMAL AND BINARY NUMBERS

Decimal	Natural Binary	Gray or Reflected Binary	Symmetrical Binary
0	0000	0000	0111
1	0001	0001	0110
2	0010	0011	0101
3	0011	0010	0100
4	0100	0110	0011
5	0101	0111	0010
6	0110	0101	0001
7	0111	0100	0000
8	1000	1100	1000
9	1001	1101	1001
10	1010	1111	1010
11	1011	1110	1011
12	1100	1010	1100
13	1101	1011	1101
14	1110	1001	1110
15	1111	1000	1111

6.7 Pulse Code Modulation[24,25]

A block diagram of the simplest pulse code modulation system is shown in figure 6.8. An analogue signal is first converted to digital form in the coder, known as an *analogue-to-digital converter*, or ADC. It is then passed through the communication channel and is reconverted to analogue form by the decoder, the *digital-to-analogue converter* or DAC.

A wide variety of coding techniques have been devised during the development of PCM as a viable communication process. In the main, only three categories are frequently used and these are

(1) Parallel encoding
(2) Feedback encoding
(3) Hybrid encoding

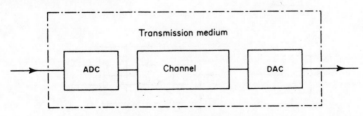

Figure 6.8 *The basic pulse code modulation system*

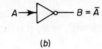

(b)

Inputs	A
$v_i > v_r$	1
$v_i < v_r$	0

(a)

A	B	I	&	⊕	Ī	&̄
0	0	0	0	0	1	1
0	1	1	0	1	0	1
1	0	1	0	1	0	1
1	1	1	1	0	0	0

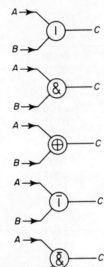

(c)

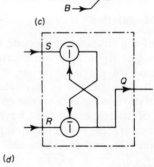

(d)

(e)

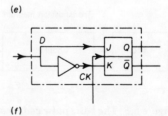

(f)

Before we proceed with a discussion of these various forms of coder, it is necessary for us to introduce and define some system functional blocks frequently employed in the synthesis of coders. These functional blocks are the comparator, a variety of logic gates and three bistable circuits, figure 6.9.

The general format of a parallel analogue-to-digital converter is shown in figure 6.10. The coder is formed from a string of comparators which perform an interface function between the analogue and digital parts of the system. Inspection of figure 6.10 indicates that, for any input in the range $-m \Delta v/2 \leqslant v_i \leqslant +m \Delta v/2$ all comparators with reference voltages taken from points on the potential divider at values less than v_i will exhibit a binary 1 at their output. The rest will exhibit a binary 0.

By applying the outputs from the comparators to a suitable logic matrix, it is possible to generate the binary equivalent of the input-sample magnitude. If a large number of quantising levels are required, the design of the logic matrix may prove difficult and its implementation costly. However, parallel encoders have the advantage that they operate virtually instantaneously and, by varying the resistance values in the potential divider, they can be arranged to provide non-uniform quantisation.

Because the parallel encoder is expensive to implement, it is most frequently employed to yield the first few most-significant digits of a codeword at high speed, the least-significant digits being obtained by a slower, but more economical feedback-encoder. This mode of usage results in an encoder of the type referred to at the start of this section as 'hybrid'. Figure 6.11 illustrates the parallel analogue-to-digital converter capable of providing the first two most-significant digits of a codeword. In this instance the logic matrix required to generate these digits from the comparator outputs is not too complex.

The feedback encoder may be regarded as a feedback control system incorporating a digital-to-analogue converter in the feedback loop. Viewed in this manner, the analogue-to-digital converter may be depicted in block-diagram form after the manner of figure 6.12. Both the analogue signal and

---

Figure 6.9 Logic and interface blocks. (a) The comparator, (b) the logical inverter, (c) logic gates 'OR', 'AND', 'EXCLUSIVE OR', 'NOR' and 'NAND', (d) Set–reset latch

$$R = 1 \text{ sets } Q \text{ to } 0$$

$$S = 1 \text{ sets } Q \text{ to } 1 \text{ from reset state } Q = 0$$

(e) JK flip–flop or bistable

$$\left. \begin{array}{l} J = 0 \text{ and } K = 0 \text{ then } Q_{n+1} = Q_n \\ J = 0 \text{ and } K = 1 \text{ then } Q_{n+1} = 0 \\ J = 1 \text{ and } K = 0 \text{ then } Q_{n+1} = 1 \\ J = 1 \text{ and } K = 1 \text{ then } Q_{n+1} = \bar{Q}_n \end{array} \right\} \begin{array}{l} \textit{for each trigger pulse} \\ \textit{applied at } T \end{array}$$

(f) D-type flip–flop or bistable, showing also its synthesis from a JK flip–flop

$$Q_{n+1} = D_n \text{ (digital delay)}$$

for each system clock-pulse applied at CK

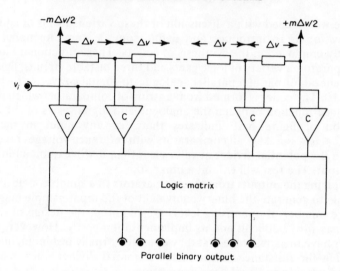

Figure 6.10 The general parallel analogue-to-digital converter

a decoded digital 'first guess' supplied by the logic circuitry are applied to the comparator, which acts as an interface between the analogue and digital parts of the system. The comparator provides a logical TRUE at its output if the analogue input is greater than the decoded digital guess and serves to increase the guess until the converse situation is encountered. There are many ways of implementing the logic circuitry. In the following sections we

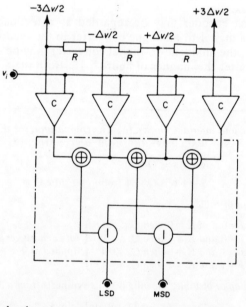

Figure 6.11 A three-level coarse quantiser. MSD: most-significant digit LSD: least-significant digit in the two-digit binary codeword

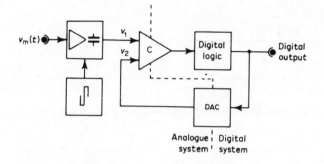

Figure 6.12 The feedback analogue-to-digital converter

shall discuss three of the more important ones. However, since the digital-to-analogue converter is a fundamental functional block in all feedback converters, it is to this item we next turn our attention.

6.8 Digital-to-analogue Conversion

Digital-to-analogue conversion is very conveniently described in terms of the conversion of a binary number into a decimal one. Suppose the binary codeword contains N digits, and let the word be represented by the sequence of digits

$$I_{N-1}I_{N-2} \ldots I_3I_2I_1I_0$$

where the binary digits $I_0, I_1, \ldots$ can take on the values 0 and 1 only. The decimal equivalent, D, of this binary number is given by the relation

$$D = I_{N-1}2^{N-1} + I_{N-2}2^{N-2} + \ldots + I_12^1 + I_02^0$$

Consider, for example, the six-digit binary word 100110. This corresponds to the decimal number

$$D = 1 \times 2^5 + 0 \times 2^4 + 0 \times 2^3 + 1 \times 2^2 + 1 \times 2^1 + 0 \times 2^0$$
$$= 1 \times 32 + 0 \times 16 + 0 \times 8 + 1 \times 4 + 1 \times 2 + 0 \times 1$$
$$= 38$$

Hence this binary number would be converted to a quantised analogue sample of value

$$v_0 = 38 \, \Delta v$$

where Δv is the voltage corresponding to the difference between quantising levels as seen at the digital-to-analogue converter output.

A block diagram illustrating the parallel-input digital-to-analogue converter is shown in figure 6.13a. If, as is often the case, the binary digits are only available in time-serial form, then the parallel-input converter is interfaced with the rest of the decoding system by a logical subsystem known as a *shift register*.

An N-stage shift register is shown diagrammatically in figure 6.13b and functions in the following manner. On receiving a clock pulse, the contents

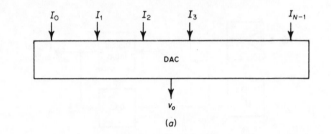

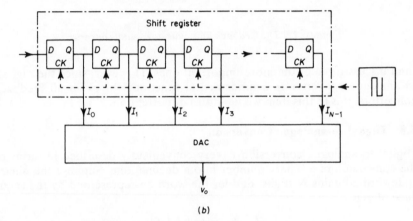

Figure 6.13 (a) Parallel digital-to-analogue conversion

$$v_o = \Delta v (I_{N-1} \times 2^{N-1} + \ldots + I_0 \times 2^0)$$

(b) The serial digital-to-analogue converter

of each cell are transferred to the cell immediately to its right. The final-cell content is lost and the vacant initial-cell is reloaded with a new input. Thus in N clock pulses, one N-digit binary word can be removed and replaced with another. In this way the shift register acts as a digital delay-line and storage medium.

The register may be examined at any or all of its cells. The output from the final cell is a replica of the input delayed by N clock-pulse intervals.

In practical terms, the shift register may be constructed from bistable, or 'flip–flop' logical elements, of which a variety of different forms exist. A considerable body of literature is available to guide the reader in the use of these components, both in textbooks and manufacturers' 'application notes'.

Having defined the operation of the shift register, it is relatively easy to form a serial-input analogue-to-digital converter, figure 6.13b. Normally, some form of gating, either analogue or digital, is incorporated so that the decoded sample is only made available at the end of the interval during which data read-in takes place.

We turn next to consider the basic parallel-input converter in greater detail. One method of achieving conversion relies on current summation at the input to an operational amplifier. The operational amplifier and the basic

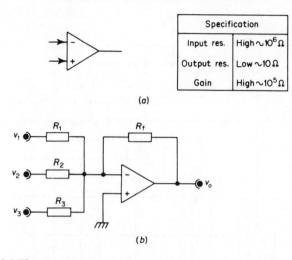

Specification	
Input res.	High $\sim 10^6\,\Omega$
Output res.	Low $\sim 10\,\Omega$
Gain	High $\sim 10^5\,\Omega$

(a)

(b)

Figure 6.14 (a) The operational amplifier and (b) its use in a summing configuration for which

$$v_o = -(v_1/R_1 + \ldots + v_k/R_k)R_f$$

summing circuit are shown in figure 6.14. A suitable choice of input voltage (as a reference) and input resistors, together with the provision of current routeing switches controlled by the binary digits being converted, leads to the circuit configuration shown in figure 6.15. This circuit, as it stands, would perform its required function quite adequately and is well suited to integration. It suffers from the drawback that its range is restricted to only sixteen quantising levels. As we saw in section 6.5, for most purposes we should need very much better resolution than this. As a consequence, the digital-to-analogue converter would need to be able to handle binary words containing more than four digits. Merely increasing the number of weighting resistors and current routeing switches is unsatisfactory because the range of resistance values increases rapidly with increasing word-size. Obtaining high individual-component precision over a wide range of values is an undesirable requirement in both mass-production situations and integrated-circuit technology as a whole.

One way of getting round this problem is to cascade several identical four-digit digital-to-analogue converters, passing the current outputs from the weighting resistors of each into successive 'divide-by-sixteen' circuits before final summation by the operational amplifier. An eight-digit converter based on this principle is illustrated in figure 6.16.

Another system that has been employed in the formation of integrated digital-to-analogue converters relies on the use of a simple ladder-network to provide a means of generating and summing voltage, rather than current increments.

Figure 6.17a shows that we may obtain the smallest quantising step Δv from the next step value to its left, $2\,\Delta v$, by means of a simple potential divider. Each resistance in this divider has the value R. Viewed from the left,

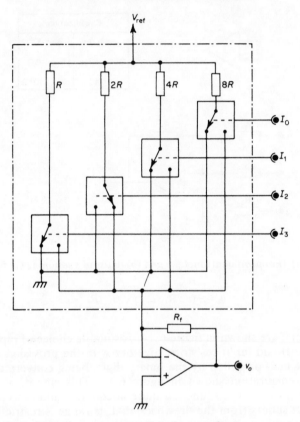

Figure 6.15 *Four-digit current summing digital-to-analogue converter*

$$v_o = \Delta v(I_3 \times 2^3 + I_2 \times 2^2 + I_1 \times 2^1 + I_0 \times 2^0)$$

$$\Delta v = v_{ref}(R_f/8R) = quantising\ step\ size$$

as shown in figure 6.17*b*, its total resistance is 2*R*. A resistance of value 2*R* taken from the input to earth will reduce the total resistance viewed from the left to *R*, figure 6.17*c*. Then another stage of division may be added, to yield the step 2 Δv from its neighbour, of value 4 Δv, figure 6.17*d*. We see then, that the ladder network depicted in figure 6.17*e* has the property of providing potential division by integer powers of two, of voltages appearing at its nodes. It has, in addition, another important property. The impedance measured at any node is 2*R*/3.

To see why this is so, consider figure 6.18*a*. The impedance looking to the right at any of the intersection lines a–a' is 2*R* and looking to the left, *R*. Any node equivalent-circuit is then as shown in figure 6.18*b*, so that a current generator of constant d.c. value *I* feeding that node will generate *at the node* a voltage

$$V = \frac{2IR}{3}$$

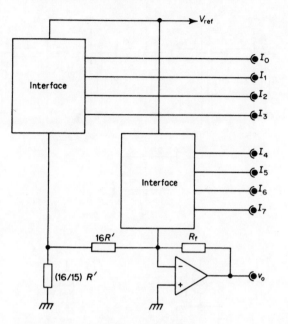

Figure 6.16 Eight-digit current summing digital-to-analogue converter. Each interface consists of a four-digit current summing DAC *(figure 6.15)*

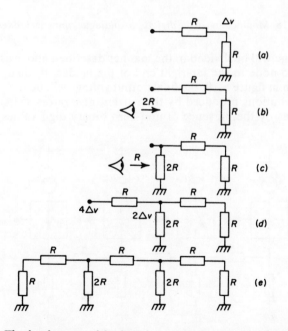

Figure 6.17 The development of the digital-to-analogue converter ladder-network

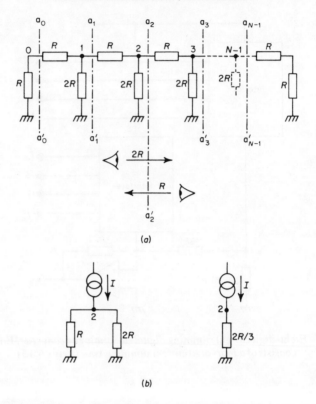

(a)

(b)

Figure 6.18 Modification of the digital-to-analogue converter ladder-network

This voltage will be divided in the manner described above as we progress from node to node to the far-right end of the ladder. If, then, we form the circuit shown in figure 6.19, the final output voltage will be the superposition of the contributions produced by the current generators switched in at the various nodes by the presence of non-zero binary digit values in the input word.

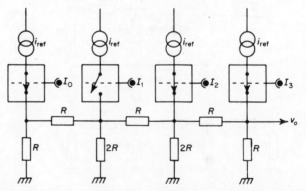

Figure 6.19 Four-digit voltage summing digital-to-analogue converter

The far-right node adds the largest individual contribution, corresponding to the most significant binary digit

$$v_o = \Delta v 2^{N-1} = \frac{2RI}{3}$$

so that the current-generator values may be determined as

$$I = \frac{3 \Delta v 2^{N-2}}{R}$$

6.9 Feedback Analogue-to-digital Conversion

6.9.1 Time-interval Conversion Coding

The simplest feedback analogue-to-digital converter operates on the principle of time-interval conversion coding. A ramp waveform sometimes continuous, often quantised—a 'staircase', is initiated at the start of the 'hold' period and is terminated when it exceeds the sample value. The time interval during which the ramp is rising is then proportional to the sample value. By allowing the clock to increment a binary counter at some fixed rate, a binary number may be generated which is also proportional to the sample value.

Figure 6.20 illustrates a simple 4-digit time-interval conversion-coding system. At the beginning of the 'hold' interval, the binary 'up-counter' is started. The binary count it generates is converted to a staircase waveform by the digital-to-analogue converter. The comparator detects the transition of the held-sample level by the staircase waveform and operates the logic gate to isolate the counter from the clock and terminate the count. The counter value is then the required digitised-sample size.

The binary up-counter may be fabricated from bistable elements and details of the methods involved are readily available in the technical literature on digital systems. Modern practice would, however, suggest the use of an up-counter fabricated as a single integrated circuit.

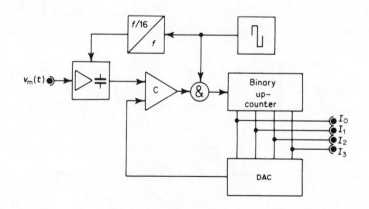

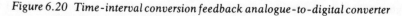

Figure 6.20 Time-interval conversion feedback analogue-to-digital converter

6.9.2   The Tracking Coder

Time-interval conversion coding suffers from the disadvantage that its operation is relatively slow. The 'hold' interval must have a duration equal to the
time required for a full N-digit count, requiring 2^N clock-pulse intervals in
all. A modification of the time-interval conversion system allows us to create
a converter with a potentially faster response. We first define a new system
block, the binary 'up–down' counter. This subsystem counts from its current
value towards either the binary number 1111 or the binary number 0000
depending on the binary state (0 or 1) at the 'mode control' input. Like the
binary up-counter introduced in the previous section, this unit would normally be incorporated as a single integrated circuit, for reasons of simplicity
and economy.

The tracking converter may now be formed by replacing the binary
up-counter used in the time-interval conversion coder with the up–down
counter, employing the comparator output to provide mode control. The
resulting block diagram is shown in figure 6.21a. The waveform v_2 will track
towards the input v_1 and, on reaching it, will 'hunt' about this value, as
shown in figure 6.21b. It is worth noting that a sample and hold circuit may
not be necessary with this type of converter, providing that the input signal
v_1 does not vary too rapidly for the tracking waveform to keep pace with it.
The sampling theorem must still be obeyed, of course, so that the input
signal must be band-limited and the digital clock maintained at a suitably
high pulse-rate.

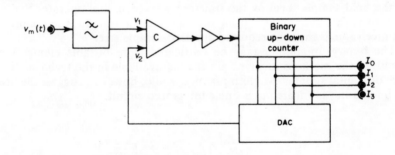

(a)

(b)

Figure 6.21 (a) The tracking feedback analogue-to-digital converter, and (b) the
converter response to an input waveform

6.9.3 The Successive-approximation Encoder

The successive-approximation encoder is the fastest and most commonly encountered method of feedback analogue-to-digital conversion. It also offers the advantage of providing a direct serial-readout of the binary word, as we shall see. The penalties we pay for these advantages are system complexity and cost.

A simplified block diagram of a four-digit encoder is shown in figure 6.22. The system consists, as usual, of a comparator, establishing at its output a logical TRUE or FALSE depending on whether the output of the digital-to-analogue converter, v_2, is less than, or greater than the current held sample value, v_1.

We first outline the operation of the entire system. The logic circuitry tests the input sample to determine whether it lies above, or below the converter half-range voltage level. If it does lie above this level, a binary '1' is registered for the most-significant digit and the half-range voltage value is, effectively, subtracted from the input-sample value. The modified sample-value is then tested in the same way against the quarter-range voltage level. By repeating this set of operations, all the binary digits in the code may be evaluated by a set of 'successive approximations'.

In detail, the operation of the four-digit encoder may be understood thus. The eight-stage sequencer shift register shifts a binary '1' along its entire length, from left to right during one sample 'hold' period. While in the first (far-left) cell, it activates the first bistable in the memory register, setting its

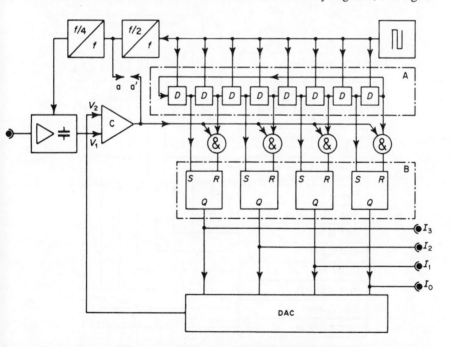

Figure 6.22 The successive-approximation analogue-to-digital converter. The sequencer, A, is a shift register circulating the binary number 1 0 0 0 0 0 0 0 at the clock rate. Its purpose is to set and interrogate each of the memory register, B, stages in turn

output to '1'. The reset input to the first bistable, and all the other bistables in the memory, are not activated at this point in the cycle, because all other shift-register cells are at binary '0'. The digital-to-analogue converter generates a half-range voltage at its output which is compared with the input-sample value. During the next clock-pulse, the sequencing digit shifts into the second cell of the sequencing register, leaving the first cell empty. The furthest left input-gate of the memory register examines the contents of the second cell of the sequencing register and the comparator output. If both are a logical '1', then the input sample lies below the half-range voltage level. The gate then applies a logical '1' to the bistable *reset* input, causing its output to switch back to '0'. If the comparator output is a '0', on the other hand, no reset pulse is passed to the bistable and the half-range voltage remains applied to the comparator. The third clock-pulse shifts the '1' in the sequencer shift-register to the third cell. This activates the second bistable, adding in a quarter-range voltage component to the output of the digital-to-analogue converter. It is in this operation that the 'subtraction' of the half-range voltage, alluded to in the previous paragraph, actually takes place. The cycle continues in this manner to establish the values of the remaining binary digits in the codeword.

A serial output, with the most-significant digit delivered first may be obtained by the additional circuitry shown in figure 6.23. The serial digits

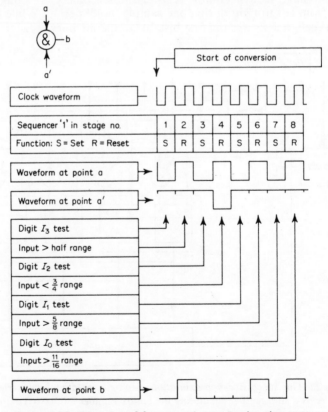

Figure 6.23 Operation of the successive-approximation ADC

become available at the comparator output during the second, fourth, sixth and eighth clock-pulse intervals. Conversion to a suitable binary format, such as 'full-length' binary pulses, is then simply a matter of adding the appropriate logic circuitry.

6.10 Generating a Symmetrical Binary Code

The feedback PCM systems described in the previous sections produce a natural N-digit binary code

$$I_{N-1}I_{N-2} \ldots I_1I_0$$

for which the state $0\,0 \ldots 0\,0$ corresponds to an input-sample voltage of zero and the state $1\,1 \ldots 1\,1$ corresponds to the maximum possible positive quantised-sample value. Thus the coder inherently operates over a positive-voltage range. Although both positive and negative signal values could be handled by adding a fixed offset-voltage, it is often considered preferable to provide additional circuitry to determine the *sense* of the input-sample value and then to determine its *modulus* by some form of conventional feedback PCM system. Then the most-significant digit, I_{N-1}, of an N-digit codeword has a value 0 if the input sample is positive, and 1 if the input sample is negative. Since digits I_{N-2} to I_0 determine modulus, the code is symmetrical having the same general form as that of the four-digit symmetrical code illustrated in table 6.1.

A system capable of generating a symmetrical binary code is illustrated in figure 6.24. The held input-sample value, $+v_1$, is applied to a phase splitter, to yield two outputs, $+v_1$ and $-v_1$. These outputs are applied to a pair of comparators feeding a toggle switch. In practice, the toggle would be implemented with suitable logic circuitry. The toggle is set as shown in the illustration, at the start of the coding interval. The successive approximation logic provides, as a 'first attempt' an output codeword $0\,0 \ldots 0\,0$. The output of the DAC, determined by the digits I_{N-2} to I_0, will then be zero.

If the input-sample value is positive, the output from the upper comparator will be a logical TRUE and that from the lower comparator a logical FALSE. The input to the successive-approximation logic will thus be a logical TRUE, because of the initial toggle setting. Such an input instructs the logic to

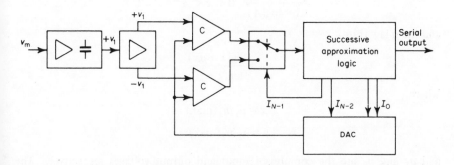

Figure 6.24 Generation of a symmetrical binary code

leave the switch unaltered. This sequence of operations confirms that the value of the most-significant digit is, indeed, 0.

If the input-sample value is *negative*, the output states of the two comparators are reversed. The upper comparator presents a logical FALSE to the successive-approximation logic. The logic therefore alters the most-significant digit to the value 1 and this sets the toggle to the output of the lower comparator, presenting a satisfactory logical TRUE to the input of the successive-approximation logic.

Once the most-significant digit has been determined, the toggle is left in the position set by this first sequence of operations. The remaining digits are determined by a straightforward feedback conversion as described in the previous section, using the upper comparator as the analogue-to-digital interface if v_1 is positive and the lower comparator if v_1 is negative.

6.11 Generating a Symmetrical Code Corresponding to a Non-uniform Quantiser Law

The most extensive application of PCM as a communication process lies in speech telephony. Speech signals exhibit a wide dynamic range and differ considerably in mean power level prior to coding. The difference in mean power level, sometimes as much as 40 dB, is caused both by variations in the characteristics of the line system connecting each user's handset to the coding equipment at the local exchange and by variations from person to person in speech loudness level. If uniform quantising were employed, small-amplitude signals would, after decoding, exhibit an unacceptably low signal-to-quantising noise ratio. To combat this effect, a logarithmic quantising law is employed. This produces an amplitude compression of the signal to be coded, reducing its dynamic range. The distortion so imposed upon the signal must be removed after decoding, and this is achieved by means of a complementary expansion operation. The entire process of signal compression and expansion is referred to as *companding*.

Two empirical rules defining signal compression have been widely used in practice. These are the '*A*-law' adhered to in Europe and the 'μ-law' employed in the United States. The *A*-law may be expressed thus

$$y = \frac{1 + \log(Ax)}{1 + \log(A)} \quad A^{-1} \leqslant x \leqslant 1$$

$$= \frac{Ax}{1 + \log(A)} \quad 0 \leqslant x < A^{-1}$$

and the μ-law thus

$$y = \frac{\log(1 + \mu x)}{\log(1 + \mu)}$$

where

$$x = v_1/v_1(\max)$$

$$y = v_2/v_2(\max)$$

and v_1 and v_2 are the compressor input and output voltages respectively. The constants A and μ determine the severity of the compression characteristic.

Typical values of these parameters which have been used in practical PCM systems are quoted in table 6.2.

TABLE 6.2 TYPICAL COMPRESSION SYSTEMS

System	Number of Quantising Levels	Companding	Word Structure $I_7I_6I_5I_4I_3I_2I_1I_0$	Other Features
U.K. 24 Channel	128	Digital 13 Segment $A = 87.6$	$W \pm SSSLLL$	24 channels per frame. W alternating between binary states on successive words
CEPT 32 (Europe)	256	Digital 13 Segment $A = 87.6$	$\pm SSSLLLL$	30 channels plus one 8-bit slot for signalling and one 8-bit slot for frame synchronisation per frame
D1 (U.S.A.)	128	Diode $\mu = 100$	$\pm WI_5I_4I_3I_2I_1I_0$	24 channels per frame plus one extra frame synchronising digit per frame
D2 (U.S.A.)	256	Digital 15 Segment $\mu = 255$	$\pm SSSLLLL$	As D1 but with I_0 used for signalling in every sixth word of each frame

W: Word synchronisation digit S: Segment (or 'chord') specification L: Location within segment (or 'chord')

The '$\mu = 100$' law, figure 6.25a, curve I, can be reasonably closely approximated by means of biassed-diode analogue function generators. In practice, the simplest such function generators, consisting of padded diode-pairs, figure 6.26, have been found to be adequate for this purpose. Although extensively used in the first American PCM telephony system, the biassed-diode approach does introduce problems. In particular, the diodes require careful matching and the circuit has to be trimmed after installation.

In order to eliminate these problems, the first United Kingdom PCM system, and all subsequent systems developed both in Europe and the United States have employed a digital compression technique, yielding a piecewise linear approximation to the logarithmic non-linearity, figure 6.25a, curve II. The following features of this curve are of importance

(1) As a result of the geometry of the construction of the curve joining points $A'B$ . . . I, all these points lie on a logarithmic curve. That is, for equal spacing of ordinate levels, the line segments, or chords as they are alternatively known, exhibit abscissa spacings which successively double as we proceed to the right-hand side of the graph. This is an undesirable compression characteristic, since the region AA' is then a 'dead zone' within which any input signal is completely suppressed.

(2) The curve passing through the points AB . . . I is logarithmic, except in the vicinity of the point A. The straight-line interpolation between the points AB . . . I approximates well to the A-law.

(3) The entire compression characteristic, for both positive and negative inputs is shown in figure 6.27. As can be seen, thirteen distinct linear segments occur, the central segment being formed from the five co-linear points $C'B'ABC$. The $\mu = 255$ law is similarly approximated but with fifteen, rather than thirteen segments.

(4) Each segment of the characteristic has ascribed to it either eight or sixteen quantising levels, the former corresponding to the implementation of the United Kingdom 24-channel system, the latter to the CEPT 32 system.

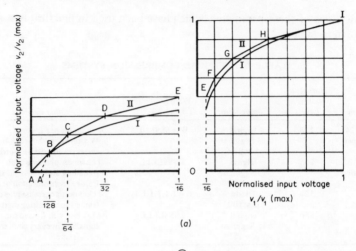

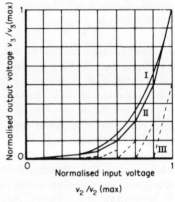

(a)

(b)

Figure 6.25 (a) PCM *compressor characteristics and* (b) *expander characteristics. Curve* I: $\mu = 100$ *law* (D1 *system—U.S.A.); curve* II: *piecewise linear approximation to the* 'A-law' (13 *segments—U.K. and Europe); curve* III: *see text*

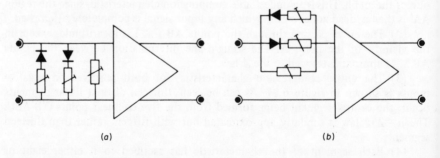

(a)   (b)

Figure 6.26 Companding in the D1 *system (U.S.A.)* (a) *compression and* (b) *expansion circuits*

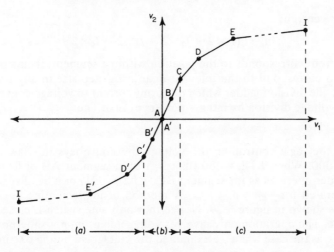

Figure 6.27 Thirteen-segment piecewise linear approximation to the PCM *compression law (U.K. and Europe). (a) and (c) six negative and six positive segments; (b) one central segment*

Since CEPT 32 is now being installed generally in Europe we shall use it as the basis for our further discussions in this section. In this system, the digits in each binary word have the following significance

I_7	$I_6 I_5 I_4$	$I_3 I_2 I_1 I_0$
Sign	Segment (or 'chord') selection	Position within segment (or 'chord')

The piecewise linear approximation to the logarithmic compression law may be obtained in two basic ways. The first involves the use of a non-linear DAC in a feedback encoder of the type described in the previous section. A codeword yielding the correct number of information digits (eight in the case of CEPT 32) is automatically generated. The non-linear DAC has a conversion characteristic which follows the complementary piecewise linear-expansion law, figure 6.25b, curve II. Its operation may be understood by considering figure 6.28. A four-digit current-summing DAC generates a

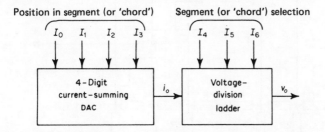

Figure 6.28 Implementation of the non-linear seven-digit DAC *used in the CEPT 32 system. The U.K. 24-channel system is organised similarly, but uses a three-digit current-summing* DAC

reference current

$$i_o \propto (I_3 \times 2^3 + I_2 \times 2^2 + I_1 \times 2^1 + I_0 \times 2^0)$$

This current corresponds to the position within a segment; its magnitude is scaled to correspond to the relevant quantising-step size in any given segment by the division ladder which performs current to voltage conversion as well as voltage division by integer powers of two. Thus

$$v_o \propto i_o \times 2^{(I_6 \times 2^2 + I_5 \times 2^1 + I_4 \times 2^0)}$$

Strictly the logic controlling the voltage division obeys this law only for $I_6 I_5 I_4 \neq 000$. When $I_6 I_5 I_4 = 000$ (that is, within segment AB of figure 6.27) the divider operates as for segment BC ($I_6 I_5 I_4 = 001$) or a dead zone would be generated for $-\frac{1}{256} < v_1 < +\frac{1}{256}$. A method of implementing the division circuit is shown in figure 6.29. Notice that only one switch is closed at any one time. The operation only involves voltage division, not superposition as well, as was the case when we examined the voltage-summing DAC in section 6.8.

The entire conversion operation depicted in figure 6.28 generates the curve III in figure 6.25. This, of course, is not quite what is required, each segment of curve III except for the first, which starts at the origin, must be elevated upon a pedestal of amplitude equal to its maximum value. To achieve this we modify the four-digit current-summing DAC so that

$$i_o \propto (J \times 2^4 + I_3 \times 2^3 + I_2 \times 2^2 + I_1 \times 2^1 + I_0 \times 2^0)$$

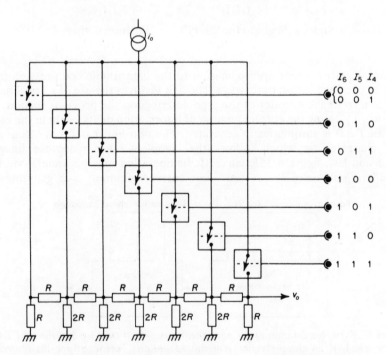

Figure 6.29 Voltage-division ladder-network used in the CEPT 32 system

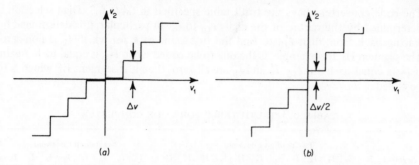

Figure 6.30 (a) Quantiser law corresponding to figure 6.28; (b) corrected quantiser law derived from the modified linear current-summing ADC shown in figure 6.31

where

$$J = 0 \quad \text{if} \quad I_6 I_5 I_4 = 000$$
$$= 1 \quad \text{if} \quad I_6 I_5 I_4 \neq 000$$

A further small modification is required to generate the correct symmetrical non-linear quantisation graph. As it stands, the converter generates a curve with the first quantising step of the first segment of zero value: figure 6.30a. This is incorrect, and a current contribution to produce a fixed offset of one half-quantising step must be included to produce the correct conversion characteristic at the origin: figure 6.30b. Consequently, the entire linear DAC law is defined by the relation

$$i_o \propto (J \times 2^4 + I_3 \times 2^3 + I_2 \times 2^2 + I_1 \times 2^1 + I_0 \times 2^0 + 2^{-1})$$

The current-summing DAC then has the basic form shown in figure 6.31.

The second method[43] of achieving non-linear coding is to employ purely digital methods. First a twelve-digit linear ADC is employed to generate a redundant codeword. Then a digital code converter is used to select digits, forming the required eight-digit codeword specified as above. Let the twelve-digit codeword be

$$I'_{11} I'_{10} \dots I'_1 I'_0$$

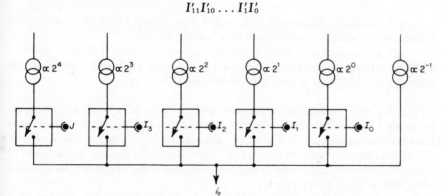

Figure 6.31 The four-digit current-summing DAC used in the CEPT 32 system

The code converter obeys the truth table specified in table 6.3. Digit selection is determined by the nature of the digits I'_{10} to I'_4. In particular, it is determined by tracing back from digit I'_{10} to find the first value of k for which I'_k is non-zero. The segment HI, for example, is the one to be coded when I'_{10} is equal to 1. Again, if I'_7 is equal to 1 but I'_{10}, I'_9 and I'_8 are all zero, then it is segment EF which is to be coded.

TABLE 6.3 TRUTH TABLE FOR CODE CONVERTER

Segment	Twelve-digit Codeword												Eight-digit Codeword							
	I'_{11}	I'_{10}	I'_9	I'_8	I'_7	I'_6	I'_5	I'_4	I'_3	I'_2	I'_1	I'_0	I_7	I_6	I_5	I_4	I_3	I_2	I_1	I_0
HI	1	1	K	L	M	N	—	—	—	—	—	—	1	1	1	1	K	L	M	N
GH	1	0	1	K	L	M	N	—	—	—	—	—	1	1	1	0	K	L	M	N
FG	1	0	0	1	K	L	M	N	—	—	—	—	1	1	0	1	K	L	M	N
EF	1	0	0	0	1	K	L	M	N	—	—	—	1	1	0	0	K	L	M	N
DE	1	0	0	0	0	1	K	L	M	N	—	—	1	0	1	1	K	L	M	N
CD	1	0	0	0	0	0	1	K	L	M	N	—	1	0	1	0	K	L	M	N
BC	1	0	0	0	0	0	0	1	K	L	M	N	1	0	0	1	K	L	M	N
AB	1	0	0	0	0	0	0	0	K	L	M	N	1	0	0	0	K	L	M	N
B'A	0	0	0	0	0	0	0	0	K	L	M	N	0	0	0	0	K	L	M	N
.	.	.	.	.	.	.	.	.	.	.	.	.	.	.	.	.	.	.	.	.
.	.	.	.	.	.	.	.	.	.	.	.	.	.	.	.	.	.	.	.	.

Recoding for expansion is performed in a complementary manner using entirely digital logic following by a twelve-digit linear digital-to-analogue conversion.

The digital system has the merit of ease of implementation using large-scale integrated circuits but suffers from the disadvantage that it requires an expensive twelve-digit ADC.

6.12 Differential PCM and Predictive Encoding

Differential PCM establishes quantisation and coding of *rate-of-charge* (rather than amplitude) of an analogue signal. The method is of importance as the basis of

(1) *predictive* differential PCM coders which effect a desirable reduction of redundancy in wideband television 'video' waveforms, and

(2) a 'one-digit-codeword' encoding technique known as *delta-modulation* which is used, as we shall see in section 6.13, in some kinds of integrated-circuit coder-decoders (CODECs) used in voice-telephony systems.

Starting with the tracking coder illustrated in figure 6.21, it would be possible to create a differential pulse code modulator (DPCM) by placing a differentiator circuit at the signal input. This strategy, although obvious, is not favoured because the differentiator transfer function, with 'gain' magnitude directly proportional to frequency, exhibits substantial high-frequency noise which degrades the signal-to-noise ratio at the converter input.

To avoid this problem, the configuration shown in figure 6.32 is adopted. Here differentiation at the input (outside the converter feedback loop) is replaced by

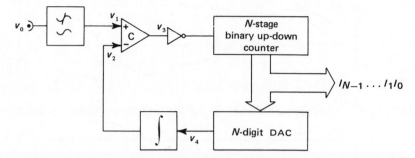

Figure 6.32   Development of a primitive differential PCM system from the tracking coder illustrated in figure 6.21

integration within the feedback loop. Exactly the same *overall* response is obtained, and the integrator now serves to smooth the step transitions at the loop DAC output. Noting that $v_3 = A(v_1 - v_2)$ with A the comparator 'gain' large, it follows that closure of the feedback loop must establish an equilibrium condition in which

$$v_1 \cong v_2 = \int v_4 \, dt$$

It therefore follows that v_4 is expressible as the derivative of v_1. Consequently, the equivalent digital codeword $I_{N-1} \ldots I_1 I_0$ is, itself, proportional to dv_1/dt, as required.

It is possible to gain an appreciation of the advantages conferred by DPCM by considering its effect on channel bandwidth. We know that

(1) signal-to-quantising noise ratio (the single most significant gauge of PCM system efficacy) increases with increasing codeword size, *but*

(2) the required transmission bandwidth (per channel, and assuming a fixed sampling frequency determined by signal spectral content) also increases with increasing codeword size.

We shall see that DPCM allows a decrease in transmission channel bandwidth without a concomitant degradation of signal-to-quantising noise ratio *for signals which contain a (usually considerable) measure of redundancy*.

Let us assume an input signal v_1, bandlimited and correctly sampled at intervals T, so that we may discuss the effect of differentially encoding sample amplitudes $v_1(kT)$, figure 6.33. A new waveform for encoding, proportional to the sample sequence slope (or approximate differential) may be obtained by writing

$$v(kT) = v_1(kT) - v_1\{(k-1)T\} \tag{6.6}$$

This expression describes a *finite difference* differentiation. We should note that if (to establish DPCM encoding) $v(kT)$ rather than $v_1(kT)$ is to be quantised, then a complementary finite difference integration at the decoder output will be necessary to recover v_1 from v. Manipulating equation 6.6 we obtain the 'recursive' (or 'feedback') finite difference equation for a simple numerical *integrator*

$$v_1(kT) = v(kT) + v_1\{(k-1)T\} \tag{6.7}$$

We may then illustrate the PCM and DPCM encode/decode operations as figure

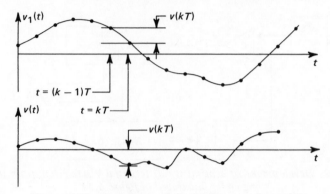

Figure 6.33   Derivation of the DPCM *waveform* v(t)

6.34 indicates. In both cases we apply an input signal v_1 and hope to obtain at points A and B output signals v_1' that are identical to each other, and approximate closely to v_1. That the processes v_1 and v_1' are not exactly the same is a consequence of quantising error on decoding and is of secondary importance in the present context. The interesting aspect of these two encode/decode operations is the comparative 'utilisation' of quantising levels at the coder input by v as compared with v_1.

We assume that v_1 is a zero-mean random process and that the PCM coders exhibit quantisation laws which operate symmetrically about zero (as, for example, in figure 6.7). We can show that the 'spread about the mean' (the mean being zero for both v_1 and v) can be substantially smaller for v than for v_1. Consequently, and assuming identical encoder quantising step size, Δv, for the two comparison systems shown in figure 6.34 excursions in signal amplitude v span far fewer quantising levels than do those in v_1. It follows that N_2, the codeword size for the DPCM system encoder, need not be as large as N_1 for the PCM system encoder. Consequently, with fixed sampling rate, the channel bandwidth may be smaller for DPCM. The argument proceeds as follows.

The mean square sample amplitude in v_1 (the 'variance' or 'spread about the

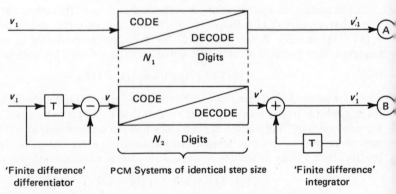

Figure 6.34   Performance comparison between PCM *and* DPCM

mean', according to common statistical usage) is

$$\sigma_1^2 = 1/N \sum_k v_1^2(kT)$$

where the sum over k is taken over a large number, N, of contiguous sample points. The mean square sample amplitude in v is

$$\sigma^2 = 1/N \sum_k v^2(kT)$$

$$= 1/N \sum_k [v_1(kT) - v_1\{(k-1)T\}]^2$$

$$= 1/N \sum_k v_1^2(kT) + 1/N \sum_k v_1^2\{(k-1)T\}$$

$$- 2/N \sum_k v_1(kT)v_1\{(k-1)T\}$$

The first two terms are, for large N, both equal to σ_1. The whole expression may be recast as

$$\sigma^2 = 2\sigma_1^2(1-R)$$

where

$$R \equiv \frac{\sum v_1(kT)v_1\{(k-1)T\}}{\sum v_1^2(kT)}$$

We see that R is a *correlation coefficient* (by analogy, for example, with equation 1.58). In its more general form, and omitting the perhaps redundant inclusion of sampling time, we might write

$$R(n) = \frac{\sum v_1(k)v_1(k+n)}{\sum v_1^2(k)}$$

and we should interpret $R(n)$ as indicating the averaged degree of 'alikeness' between samples of v_1 separated by a time interval nT. Figure 6.35 shows typical correlation functions for speech and video waveforms. In both cases, $R(1)$ is high.

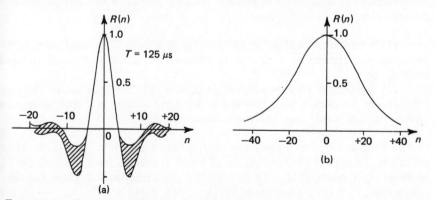

Figure 6.35 Sample amplitude correlation functions for (a) speech sampled at the normal 8 kHz rate and (b) a sampled horizontal video raster (one line of a TV picture)

Considering first the speech waveform correlation function, we see that $R(1) = 0.85$, so that

$$\sigma^2 = 0.3\sigma_1^2$$

The immediate implication is that we might expect to occupy $\sqrt{0.3} \cong 0.5$ of the quantising levels at the coder input, for identical overall performance, by utilising differential encoding rather than conventional PCM. The corollary is that the code-length might be decreased by one digit, so that $N_2 = N_1 - 1$, thus bringing about a reduction of required transmission bandwidth in the ratio $(N_1 - 1)/N_1$. Taking conventional eight-digit PCM by way of example, this would correspond to a reduction in required bandwidth of 12.5%, a figure too small to warrant the use of DPCM in a standard telephony context. However, in some more specialised speech-coding situations and often in the encoding of bandwidth-costly video waveforms where, as figure 6.35b has shown, $R(1)$ is very close to unity, DPCM has much merit.

It is interesting to note that DPCM is the simplest example of *predictive* encoding. In more general form, predictive encoding finds its major area of application in television picture processing because of the high level of redundancy in the video waveform. Particular areas of interest are digital video-recording, cable-television relay-systems (as potential competition for satellite relay in the coverage of major international events), tele-conferencing, satellite imaging and video-telephone development ('Viewphone' and 'Videophone' systems). The primary objective in invoking the use of predictive encoders is the reduction of required channel bandwidth; the trade-off is picture quality assessed by means of subjective tests. By way of example, commercial 625-line television requires (about) 5 MHz of video bandwidth and encodes well with (about) 32 levels of grey, corresponding to five-digit PCM words taken at a minimum rate of 10 million per second. The digit rate is thus at least 50 million per second and the required channel bandwidth of the order of 25 MHz. By contrast, reduced resolution (about) 300-line video-telephone signals can be encoded and transmitted using predictive PCM over a bandwidth of, perhaps, 1–2 MHz, and still remain subjectively acceptable, at least so far as the requirements of this particular application are concerned.

Considered in the context of picture encoding, predictive methods fall broadly into two classes

(1) intra-frame (within-frame) prediction, in which sample-to-sample or line-to-line redundancy is exploited to obtain a reduction in required channel capacity, or
(2) inter-frame (frame-to-frame) prediction, which makes use of the fact that, except for picture areas involved in depicting *motion*, very little change in picture element 'value' occurs between consecutive frames.

The basic structure of a predictive PCM system is shown in figure 6.36a. Here $v_2(kT)$ is the current *predicted* value of input as derived from a knowledge of previous input values. That is, we infer $v_2(kT)$, this being our best 'guess' as to the actual value of $v_1(kT)$, from values $v_1\{(k-1)T\}$, $v_1\{(k-2)T\}$, . . . , by means of some suitably chosen prediction algorithm

$$v_2(kT) = F[v_1\{(k-1)T\}, v_1\{(k-2)T\}, v_1\{(k-3)T\} \dots]$$

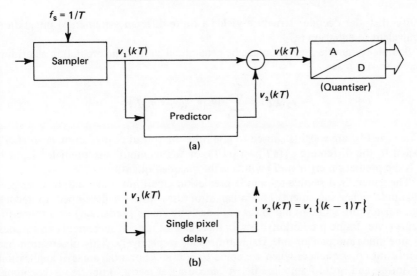

(a)

(b)

Figure 6.36 (a) Predictive encoding, realising in its simplest form differential
PCM *when the predictor is (b) a single-pixel (single picture-element) delay*

If, as figure 6.36b suggests, we choose to make the prediction algorithm $F[\ ]$ a
simple single-pixel (picture element) delay, then prediction occurs on a sample-to-
sample intra-frame basis, with the algorithm predicting, essentially, that the current
sample will equal the previous sample. It is the 'error' in this 'guess' which is
encoded. We have that

$$v_2(kT) = v_1\{(k-1)T\}$$

for the single-pixel delay. The encoder input is

$$v(kT) = v_1(kT) - v_2(kT)$$

which may be rewritten as

$$v(kT) = v_1(kT) - v_1\{(k-1)T\}$$

which, being merely a restatement of equation 6.6, defines the operation of
DPCM.

The generalised decoder for predictive PCM is shown in figure 6.37. Here, for
the specific case of the single-pixel delay prediction element, the reader may readily

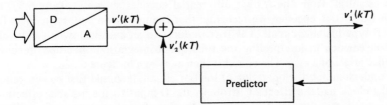

Figure 6.37 Decoder for the predictive encoder illustrated in figure 6.36a

verify that the decoder structure yields a finite difference numerical integration equivalent to equation 6.7.

Sample-to-sample prediction can be generalised so that the prediction algorithm may be written as

$$v_2(kT) = \sum_{m=1}^{M} W_m v_1 \{(k - m)T\}$$

where the W_m are weights chosen to minimise the spread of prediction error $v(kT)$ (equal to the difference $v_1(kT) - v_2(kT)$, or 'actual input' less 'predicted input'). It is the prediction error $v(kT)$ which is the encoded quantity.

The generalised sample-to-sample prediction algorithm is based upon a sample-to-sample delay increment T. Similar structures may be developed to reduce redundancy on a line-to-line basis (still an intra-frame prediction) or a frame-to-frame (inter-frame prediction) basis. In these cases, the delay increment corresponds to one line-timespan or one frame-timespan, respectively. This observation has significant consequences when we come to consider potential areas of application of intra- and inter-frame predictive encoding. Clearly, inter-frame encoding, involving as it does a substantial delay—memory requirement, represents a considerably more costly investment in capital equipment than intra-frame encoding. In the context of the line telephone system, it is thus considered that the less costly (albeit also less effective) intra-frame approach would be best suited to applications on relatively lightly loaded junction-cable systems. Set against this, complex inter-frame encoding would find application on high-toll, heavily loaded, trunk circuits where transmission bandwidth would be at a premium.

6.13 Delta Modulation Systems

6.13.1 Fixed Slope Delta Modulation

As was noted at the start of section 6.12, delta modulation (DM) is a sub-class of differential PCM (DPCM) in which the generated codeword is only one binary digit in length. Delta modulators have the advantage over more conventional PCM systems of a particularly simple architecture, which has caused some manufacturers to favour them as the basis for 'single-chip' coder—decoder (CODEC) integrated circuits. Because delta modulation is a 1-digit code, sampling rate and output digit rate are identical. In order for DM to achieve performance comparable to that which can be obtained from a conventional N-digit PCM system, the sampling rate for the DM system must be increased substantially over that required for PCM, as we shall see.

To establish, from the N-digit differential encoder shown in figure 6.32, the simple 1-digit DM encoder, we recognise that the up—down counter reduces to a single D-type bistable circuit. The DAC reduces to an analogue switch addressing (for convenience in interpreting the subsequent integration operation) precision reference levels of $\pm V_{ref}$. The circuit is then as shown in figure 6.38a.

In understanding the operation of the DM circuit, it should first be appreciated that the clock has the effect of 'strobing' the D-input to the bistable, effecting a synchronised sampling of the status of the interface comparator. An arbitrary initial status of $v_3 = 0$ (logical FALSE) at time $t = 0$ is assumed. Thus Q sets to 0

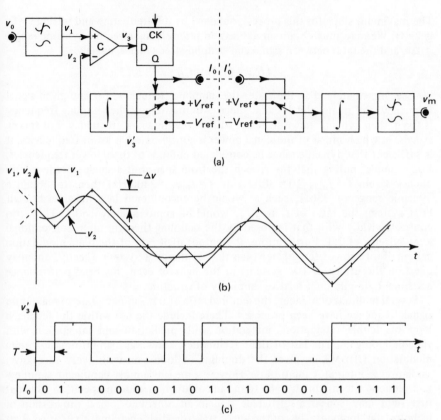

*Figure 6.38   Operation of the basic delta modulator as derived from the differen-
tial PCM system illustrated in figure 6.32*

and $v'_3 = -V_{ref}$ for the interval $t = 0$ to $t = T$. During this interval, the integrator
output ramps down from its initial level as shown in figure 6.38*b* (the value of
which depends upon the past history of the conversion process). By chance, in
ramping down, v_2 crosses v_1, so that at $t = T$ the comparator output has been
established as $v_3 = 1$ (logical TRUE). Consequently, Q sets to 1 and v'_3 to $+V_{ref}$
for the interval $t = T$ to $t = 2T$. The integrator ramps upward, following the input
signal, until the input signal rise slows down and v_2 again crosses v_1.

Although the delta modulator shown in figure 6.38 has an attractively simple
structure, it suffers from several shortcomings. Firstly, the system is unsuitable for
the transmission of waveforms (such as television picture signals) in which a d.c.
level must be maintained and within which important low-frequency components
may exist. This is because of its differentiating action. As its modulus of transfer
function is directly proportional to frequency, any differentiator is inherently a.c.
coupled.

A second problem is that the simple delta modulator is slew-rate limited. If
the quantising step size is σ and the sampling frequency is $f_s = 1/T$, then the
maximum rate of change of the loop integrator output voltage is $\Delta v f_s$ v s^{-1}. To
see how this affects conversion, assume a sinusoidal modulating signal $A\sin(2\pi ft)$.

The maximum slope for this process, obtained by differentiating and setting $t = 0$, is $2\pi Af$. We may thus obtain an expression interrelating effective dynamic range, $A/\Delta v$, and the ratio between signal and sampling frequencies, namely

$$A/\Delta v = (1/2\pi)(f_s/f)$$

We see immediately that the faster the sampling frequency, for any given signal frequency, the greater the dynamic range. Alternatively, if the sampling frequency is fixed, then dynamic range decreases with increasing signal frequency. For speech signals, in which much of the signal power is concentrated at lower frequencies, it is sufficient that dynamic range be considered in terms of these lower frequencies. For example, noting that the speech spectrum spans but a single decade of frequency (from $f \cong f_{max}/10 = 300$ Hz to $f = f_{max} = 3400$ Hz) then, to obtain a dynamic range of 256:1, such as would be encountered in a linear eight-digit PCM system, the ratio of f_s to f_{max} would be approximately 160:1. This ratio contrasts vividly with that imposed by the sampling theorem upon conventional PCM systems of 2:1. Furthermore, the output digit rate of the delta modulation system is a factor of ten greater than that of the PCM system. Clearly, one may question the utility of DM systems in the light of even this brief performance assessment, despite their relative simplicity of structure.

Several methods of reducing the required ratio of DM sampling-rate to maximum signal frequency have been proposed. These include the use within the feedback loop of double integration, integration with prediction and integration with variable loop gain. The last of these techniques, known as high-information delta modulation (HIDM), involves the doubling of loop gain with every successive, similar-sense integrator input pulse. However, the single most significant sampling-rate reduction technique is to be found in conjunction with an operation which at first sight may appear a retrograde step in an otherwise logical progression of technical development: the conversion of DM (one-digit encoding) to PCM (N-digit encoding).

The rationale behind such a move stems from the desire to accommodate in integrated-circuit form, companding by all-digital conversion from (say) a 12- or 13-digit linearly encoded (uncompressed) word. We have seen how this may be accomplished, in section 6.11. The code conversion is straightforward. The problem of acquiring 12- or 13-digit words at multiplexed rates is, however, by no means trivial if the use of one of our standard PCM architectures (section 6.9) is contemplated.

The simplest DM to PCM converter is realised by applying the DM output to the input of an N-digit binary up-down counter, figure 6.39. The up—down counter, acting as a digital integrator, establishes an N-digit binary word incrementing or decrementing by one least-significant digit, for each input pulse. The count value

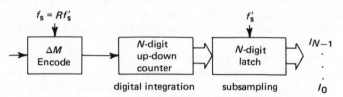

Figure 6.39   Conversion of delta modulation to PCM

thus changes by an amount equivalent to a quantising step, at the delta modulation sampling rate, f_s. At a lower sampling rate f_s' (every Rth delta modulator clock pulse) a binary latch digitally 'samples' the up–down counter output, establishing parallel N-digit PCM words

$$I_{N-1} I_{N-2} \ldots I_1 I_0$$

For speech telephony applications, the (sub) sampling rate f_s' would be chosen as 8000 per second per channel. The delta modulation sampling rate, $f_s = R f_s'$, is chosen to ensure an adequate signal-to-quantisation noise ratio. The higher f_s, the better will be the system fidelity. By means of subjective trials, it has been found that $R \sim 100$–200. For an M-channel multiplexed system, the delta modulation clock rate will then be $f_s = MR f_s'$. Considering a worst-case situation, in which $R = 200$ and $M = 32$ (corresponding to the C.C.I.T.T. CEPT 32 standard for European PCM) with $f_s' = 8000 \text{ s}^{-1}$, we find that $f_s \cong 50 \times 10^6 \text{ s}^{-1}$. Such a figure is prohibitively high if, as has been suggested, integrated-circuit fabrication with reasonably low operating power requirements are desired objectives.

Although the simple DM to PCM converter illustrated in figure 6.39 is unsuitable as the basis of an integrated-circuit CODEC, a modified version utilising the principle of *interpolative* conversion (see section 6.13.4) has been successfully developed for commercial application.

6.13.2 Continuously Variable Slope Delta Modulation

More detailed consideration of system behaviour suggests that the relatively poor performance of the elementary delta modulator may be substantially enhanced by dynamically varying the loop gain in sympathy with the average power level of the input signal. By means of this stratagem, known as *continuously variable slope delta modulation*, CVSD, the delta modulator may actually be persuaded to perform better than the conventional PCM system, in respect of output digit rate.

The basic CVSD system is shown in figure 6.40. Its structure is identical to that of the simple delta modulator of figure 6.38 except that the integrator is provided with a capability for voltage-controlled gain. The signal used to establish integrator gain is provided by an additional module, the *syllabic estimator*. The

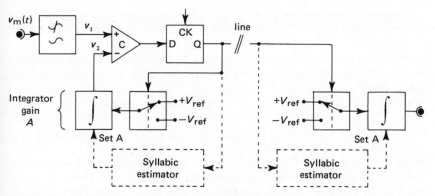

Figure 6.40 Syllabically companded continuously variable slope delta modulation (CVSD)

syllabic estimator establishes an overriding control loop of slower response than the 'inner' loop containing the integrator. Both the syllabic estimator and controlled-gain integrator can be realised using analogue circuit techniques. The estimator is then simply a rectifier followed by a 'syllabic filter'. The syllabic filter is a first-order lowpass filter with a response-time similar to the time-duration of power fluctuations in typical speech signals. Subjective tests have suggested that time-constants in the range 4—10 ms produce the most acceptable speech transmission. The voltage variable gain can then be achieved by driving the integrator from the analogue switch via an analogue multiplier. Although this approach is perfectly viable, a mixture of digital and analogue circuitry in integrated-circuit fabrication is generally considered undesirable, if it can readily be avoided. In this case, at least two manufacturers have elected to use all-digital realisations of the analogue items discussed above. Figure 6.41 shows how this may be achieved.

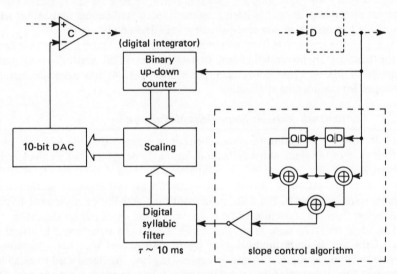

Figure 6.41   Digital syllabic companding and integration for the CVSD CODEC

Integrator conversion-slope control is achieved by monitoring the 'activity' at the loop bistable output. The 'slope-control algorithm' presents a logical TRUE at its output when (and only when) it identifies a string of contiguous 1s or 0s *of length three or more* at its input. This condition is indicative of a situation in which the integrator is sustainedly ramping up or down, while trying to follow a too rapidly rising or falling input. The objective is thus to increase loop gain for a reasonable period of time, in order to accommodate such large bipolar signal swings. The time duration during which increased loop gain should be maintained will be of syllabic duration, as we have seen, and will necessarily be *much longer than the sampling interval, T*. The appropriate smoothing is inserted by the syllabic digital filter, with (as stated above) a time constant in the range 4—10 ms. The denser the grouping of binary 1s during positive ramping (or the denser the grouping of binary 0s during negative ramping) the greater will be the implied request for 'gain-increase' by the faster-acting integrator loop. Also, the denser the grouping of 1s, the greater will be the digital output accumulated by the syllabic digital filter. This output may thus be used to effect a scaling of the output of the digital integrator. The digital integrator itself is simply a binary up–down counter. Up-counting is effected by (say) each binary 1 emerging from the loop bistable. Down-counting, by each binary 0. Finally, the output of the scaling logic is passed to a parallel-input DAC, to generate an appropriate analogue signal for comparison with the input signal.

At the detector, a syllabic estimator identical to that used in the transmitter is used to control the detector integrator gain, as figure 6.40 has shown. In those practical CODECs which have been developed from the CVSD, a common integrated circuit is used for both transmit and receive functions. Conversion of function from transmit-mode to receive-mode is effected by opening the feedback loop between the comparator output and the bistable D-input. The received signal is then addressed to the D-input and the demodulated output is taken from the loop integrator output.

The CVSD approach to CODEC design results in companding which obeys neither A-law nor μ-law. Despite this formal shortcoming, it none the less provides an entirely satisfactory method of encoding speech signals with similar dynamic range to those normally encountered in junction telephony situations. The compressing action of the encoder is such as to establish a conversion slope proportional to the r.m.s. value of the input signal, so that the delta corrections are larger for large input signal amplitudes.

The CVSD CODEC is considered to produce speech transmission at a line (output) digit rate of 32 Kbit s^{-1} per channel which is equal in quality to that which can be obtained using conventional 8-bit PCM with companding. The latter requires, of course, 64 Kbit s^{-1} per channel. It is further noted that perfectly intelligible, if somewhat degraded (the adjective 'fuzzy' is sometimes used) speech transmission can be achieved when the digit rate is as low as 9.6 Kbit s^{-1} per channel.

6.13.3 Delta–Sigma Modulation

We have seen that the limited slew-rate capability of the basic delta modulator can be overcome by means of syllabic companding. The resulting encoder is still, however, a one-bit differential pulse code modulator. Consequently, its overall transfer characteristic exhibits a.c. coupling and poor low-frequency response. This of course in no way diminishes its utility in the encoding of speech waveforms, which are considered to contain no significant frequency components below about 300 Hz. However, CVSD remains unsuitable as a processor for waveforms in which d.c. level and low-frequency content must be preserved during the encoding/decoding operation.

An alternative approach, known as *delta–sigma modulation*, effectively removes the shortcomings of the basic delta modulator in respect of d.c. coupling and low-frequency response. However, it does this by establishing a coder which is no longer *differential*. Figure 6.42 shows how the delta–sigma modulator may be developed from the delta modulator and ultimately the differential pulse code modulator, shown in figures 6.38 and 6.32, respectively. Recall first that the development of the differential pulse code modulator implied the placement of a differentiator at the input of a tracking converter. This differentiator physically transforms into the integrator within the feedback loop of the delta modulator.

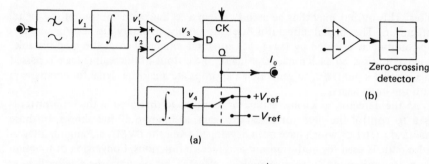

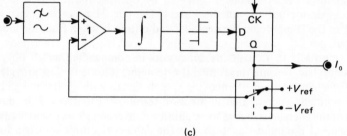

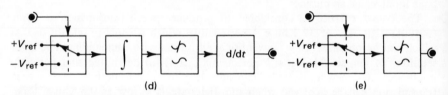

Figure 6.42 Development of the delta-sigma modulator and its detector. (a) Integration at the input to a conventional delta modulator to remove the differential mode of operation. (b) Alternative realisation of the comparator in terms of a difference amplifier and zero-crossing detector. (c) Translation of integration operation. (d) The modified detector with following differentiation to cancel modulator input integration. (e) Collapsed detector wherein integrator and differentiator themselves cancel in terms of overall transfer function.

Although not to be seen at the delta modulator *input* (in figure 6.38 for instance), its *effect* of creating an essentially differential encoder remains. If, as in figure 6.42, the basic delta modulator is preceded by an integrator, v_4, previously determined for the delta modulator as equal to dv_1/dt, may now be written as $v_4 = dv_1'/dt$ where v_1' is the integral of v_1. It follows that, for the modified encoder, $v_4 = v_1$. The coder thus responds in generating its output binary sequence, to v_1, not its derivative.

The realisation of the delta—sigma modulator presented in figure 6.42a is less than completely satisfactory. Firstly, it requires the use of two integrators and secondly, the input integrator must be capable of accommodating signals of wide dynamic range. Neither criterion is necessary, if a simple modification to the circuit is entertained. The comparator may be redrawn, as figure 6.42b shows, in terms of a unity-gain difference amplifier followed by a zero-crossing detector. While overall function is preserved, the difference amplifier (being a linear circuit element, unlike the comparator, which is highly non-linear) allows the two integration operations at its input to be translated to a single integration of a process of necessarily small dynamic range, at its output. In a sense, the combination of zero-crossing detector and D-type bistable circuit now act as a 'pulse modulator' on the analogue input provided by the displaced integrator, figure 6.42c.

The operation of detection performed on the output of a delta modulator must now be modified to accommodate the integration imposed on the modulating signal by the delta-sigma modulator. This may readily be achieved, as figure 6.42d shows, by adding a complementary differentiator at the detector output. Of course, once figure 6.42d is inspected it becomes obvious that the integrator- and differentiator-transfer functions, $(2\pi jf)^{-1}$ and $2\pi jf$, respectively, cancel, thereby establishing the extremely simple detector configuration shown in figure 6.42e.

6.13.4   Interpolative DM to PCM Conversion

In section 6.13.1 we considered the use of a binary up–down counter at the output of a delta modulator to effect the conversion of delta modulation code to PCM. We noted that, for multiplexed speech applications, a prohibitively high sampling rate at the delta modulator was required. However, the use of *interpolative* delta modulation permits a lower sampling rate to be used than would normally be the case and has thus provided the basis for the development of several practical integrated-circuit CODECs.

A restructured version of the DM to PCM converter illustrated in figure 6.39 is presented in figure 6.43. Here, a modified $(N - K)$-digit up–down counter is used to create digits

$$I_{N-1}I_{N-2}\ldots I_K$$

of an N-digit codeword.

Because this codeword is shorter and the equivalent quantising step-size coarser, it is now possible to reduce, substantially, the DM system sampling rate, $R'f_s'$. Of course, merely doing this will not yield an acceptable code converter, since the remaining, fine quantisation digits in the required N-digit codeword are missing. These digits, I_{K-1} to I_0, are found from the delta modulator output sequence, by a process known as *interpolation*.

Interpolation is mathematically equivalent to an averaging at the (oversampled) DM encode rate. The argument runs as follows: clearly if, in the original DM to

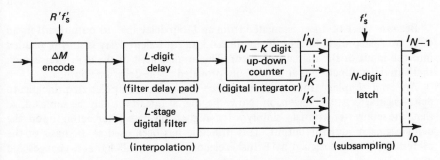

Figure 6.43   Interpolative DM *encoder*

PCM converter, figure 6.39, $R \sim 100\text{--}200$, then, by comparison with a normal PCM system, the DM encoder is vastly oversampled. If oversampling occurs, then massive guard spaces are inserted between lobes of the spectrum of the sampled signal (see for example, figure 6.2a). A digital averaging (equivalent in its effect upon the baseband lobe of the spectrum to low-pass filtering with a small cut-off frequency) then serves further to reduce the width of spectral lobes. A reduction in sampling rate pulls all the lobes towards the ordinate axis, decreasing the relative guard space. However, given even a substantial sample rate reduction, aliasing need not be expected because of the high initial value of R and, one may anticipate, the large 'time-constant' of the digital averager.

The digital averager takes a weighted sum of L consecutive digits from the delta modulator output. This it acts as a digital low-pass filter of the type known as a 'finite-impulse-response' (FIR) filter. The structure of such a filter is illustrated in figure 6.44. It consists of a tapped digital delay-line in which each stage delay corresponds to the sampling interval. This yields a particularly simple structure in the present case, since the delta modulator encoder operates to generate 'one-digit' PCM words. Each word is scaled by a digital weight W_k for $k = 0, 1 \ldots L - 1$. The weight 'resolution' is so chosen that the sum of all weights establishes the maximum-size fine-quantisation part of the generated N-digit codeword, namely

$$I_{K-1}I_{K-2} \ldots I_0 \equiv 1\,1\,1 \ldots 1$$

The weight 'values' are chosen to establish a *linear* interpolation between coarse PCM word states.

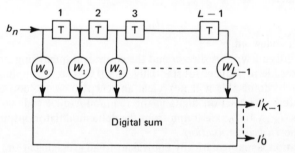

Figure 6.44   Interpolative finite impulse response (FIR) digital filter used to generate the K least significant digits of the N-digit codeword

Because the FIR filter is created from an L-tap delay line, its output suffers an effective L-step digital delay. In figure 6.43 an equivalent delay is shown, padded into the input of the digital integrator. The arrangement of the FIR filter is such that this delay function is automatically provided at the delay-line output.

An even simpler structure results if we apply the interpolation principle to delta–sigma to PCM conversion. Now the digital integrator may be omitted, so that the converter consists simply of a digital low-pass filter acting upon the delta–sigma modulator output. This principle has been used as the basis of the preferred CODEC designed by British Telecom for use in all-digital exchanges and PBXs.

6.13.5 *Quantisation Noise in* DM *Systems*

Careful consideration of figure 6.38*b* will indicate that the error signal, or *quantising noise*, encountered at the delta modulator decoder output will be the *difference* between waveforms v_1 and v_2. This difference waveform must, necessarily, have amplitude extremes of $\pm \Delta v$, where Δv is the magnitude of the quantising step. Δv is determined by the system parameter V_{ref}, by the integrator time constant, τ, and by the sampling interval, T, as $\Delta v = V_{ref}(T/\tau)$. Clearly, decreasing T (increasing the sampling rate) will have the effect of reducing the quantising noise power. The quantitative assessment of the effect of changes in sampling rate on both delta and delta–sigma modulation and a comparison with the performance of conventional PCM is the subject of this section.

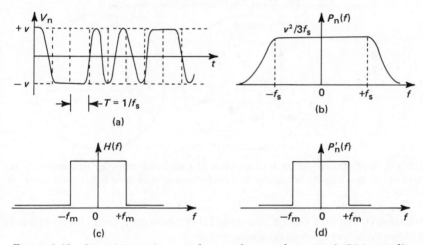

Figure 6.45   Quantising noise waveform and spectral content in DM *encoding*

The superficial appearance of the quantising noisewave is illustrated in figure 6.45*a*. During periods of high state transition activity at the integrator input (that is, when its input *frequently* moves between $+V_{ref}$ and $-V_{ref}$ because the slope of the input signal to the *encoder* is low), the waveform has the superficial appearance of a roughly sinusoidal wave of frequency approaching f_s. During such a phase of operation, the short-term averaged noise power may be estimated as for a sinusoid of peak amplitude Δv, yielding the result

$$N = \tfrac{1}{2} \Delta v^2$$

The reader may find this argument clarified by referring to inset B of figure 6.46.

When the slope of the input signal applied to the modulator is high (see, for example, figure 6.46, inset A), the integrator input state transition rate falls (the integrator then spends much of its time sustainedly ramping up or down). Under this circumstance, the quantising noisewave tends to hold to a peak value, $+\Delta v$ or $-\Delta v$. Then the noise power, averaged on a short-term basis may be expressed as

$$N = \Delta v^2$$

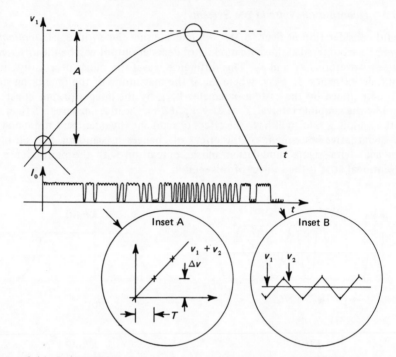

Figure 6.46 Delta modulation conversion of a sinuosid, showing slew-rate limiting (inset A) at the origin and conversion performance with zero input slope (inset B)

On overall (long-term) average, one should therefore expect the noise waveform to lie between the extremes states above, so that

$$\tfrac{1}{2}\Delta v^2 \leqslant N \leqslant \Delta v^2$$

A good compromise, generally accepted as representative of practical delta modulator decoder performance, is found to be given by the result

$$N = \tfrac{2}{3}\Delta v^2$$

Because the maximum transition rate of the (random) quantising noisewave approaches f_s, we are at liberty to make the assumption that the noise power spectral density extends to (about) that frequency, and then quite rapidly diminishes. We presume further that, below f_s, the power spectrum is uniform, figure 6.45b. We may estimate the power spectral density of the noisewave as

$$\eta = \Delta v^2 /3f_s \qquad -f_s < f < +f_s$$

We may thus consider the use of a post-detection filter bandlimiting the decoder output to f_m (which is much less than f_s) to be mandatory. Figure 6.45c illustrates the transfer characteristic of an appropriate post-detection filter. The decoder output noise process may now be defined, spectrally, as figure 6.45d shows. The noisewave exhibits a noise power

$$N' = \tfrac{2}{3}\Delta v^2 (f_m/f_s) \tag{6.8}$$

In order to estimate the signal-to-quantising noise power ratio, we require to be able to estimate the output signal power. We assume first that the output process is a sinusoid of amplitude A and frequency f. The limiting factor determining 'maximum signal swing' is slope overload (see inset A, figure 6.46). We know that the maximum slope of signal input that the encoder can sustain is is $\Delta v/T$, or $\Delta v f_s$. Furthermore for a process

$$v_1 = A\sin(2\pi ft)$$

dv_1/dt is a maximum when $t = 0$, and has a value $2\pi Af$. At the onset of slope overload (slew-rate limiting) we then find that

$$2\pi Af = \Delta v f_s$$

Using this result, we may easily estimate the maximum signal power capable of being handled by the modulator as

$$A^2/2 = (\Delta v^2/8\pi^2)(f_s/f)^2 \tag{6.9}$$

We may then immediately derive an expression for the signal-to-quantising noise power ratio, s, from equations 6.8 and 6.9 as

$$s = k(f_s^3/f_m f^2) \tag{6.10}$$

where

$$k = (3/16\pi^2) \cong 0.02$$

This result pertains specifically to DM decoding. Before discussing its significance, let us complement the analysis presented above by considering briefly the derivation of s for delta–sigma decoding.

Figure 6.47 illustrates the development of a delta–sigma system from a DM system. We assume, again, an input signal

$$v_1 = A\sin(2\pi ft)$$

The integrator at the input of the coder, which effectively converts the delta modulator to a delta–sigma modulator, has the effect of causing the amplitude of

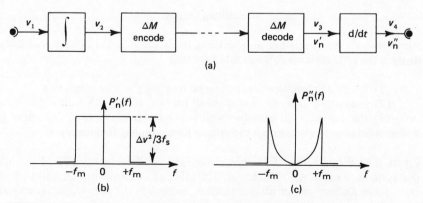

Figure 6.47   Quantising noise analysis for delta-sigma modulation decoding

v_2 to fall with rising frequency.

$$v_2 = (A/2\pi f)\cos(2\pi ft)$$

The slew-rate limiting problem now becomes one of equating the slope of v_2 to maximum slope at the loop integrator output (since it is the delta modulator within the delta–sigma modulator structure which is actually going to bring about the slew-rate limiting effect). We have, simply, $dv_2/dt = A$ when $t = 0$ and thus $A = \Delta v f_s$ defines the onset of overload for the delta–sigma modulator. Consequently we may calculate the signal power as

$$A^2/2 = \Delta v^2 f_s^2 /2 \qquad (6.11)$$

Turning finally to consider the effect on output quantising noise of the restructuring of the delta modulator in forming the delta–sigma modulator, note that v_n' has spectral and statistical properties as deduced before. These are modified by the output differentiator, which has a transfer function $H(f) = 2\pi jf$. We evaluate

$$N'' = \int_{-f_m}^{+f_m} P'(f) \mid H(f) \mid^2 df$$

and this readily yields the result

$$N'' = (8\pi^2/9)\Delta v^2 (f_m^3/f_s) \qquad (6.12)$$

It is then a simple matter to establish, from equations 6.11 and 6.12, the result

$$s = k(f_s/f_m)^3 \qquad (6.13)$$

where

$$k = (9/16\pi^2) \cong 0.06$$

We are now in a position to compare the expressions for signal to quantising noise power ratio, s, for delta and delta–sigma modulation. However, it is convenient at this stage to recall from section 6.5 the comparable result for PCM

$$s = m^2$$

$$= 20\log_{10}(m) \text{ dB}$$

where $m = 2^N$ is the number of quantising levels and N is the number of binary digits in the PCM codeword. We should note that

(1) for PCM, s is independent of signal frequency and sampling rate
(2) the output digit rate (per channel) for PCM is $Nf_s = 8N$ Kbit s^{-1}
(3) the output digit rate for both DM systems is simply f_s (but now f_s will be substantially greater than the PCM system sampling frequency).

Figure 6.48 shows a plot of s versus normalised signal frequency f/f_m. For both DM systems, a sampling frequency of 120 kHz and consequently an output digit rate of 120 Kbit s^{-1} per channel is assumed, since then the ratio (f_s/f_m) is such as to establish similar signal-to-quantising noise power ratios as for linear seven- or

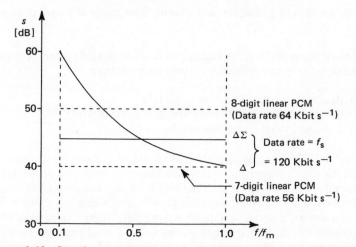

Figure 6.48   Signal-to-quantising noise comparison between PCM *and* DM

eight-digit PCM. The most striking features displayed in the curves presented in figure 6.48 are

(1) The signal-to-quantising noise power ratio for delta modulation degrades with increasing signal frequency.

(2) By contrast, and in common with PCM, the signal-to-quantising noise power ratio for delta–sigma modulation remains constant with increasing signal frequency, thereby providing a superior operating background for signals with uniform or low-frequency biased power spectral densities.

(3) In both DM systems, signal-to-quantising noise power ratio improves rapidly (as the third power) with increasing sampling rate.

(4) Again for both delta modulators, to attain performance roughly comparable with practical PCM systems, significantly greater (by a factor of about two) output digit rates are required.

6.14   The CODEC

6.14.1   *Integrated Circuit Technologies*

The term CODEC (COder/DECoder) has been adopted to describe any of a range of integrated circuits devised primarily for voice telephony applications and preferably available as one- or two-chip processors. As is usually the case when circuit integration is envisaged, volume production and low device-cost are immediate goals for the manufacturer. Choice of process (fabrication) technology and choice of CODEC architecture then become critical factors in attaining these targets. Consequently, the CODEC designer will seek an implementation capable of providing

(1) a quantising step-size reference of suitable precision and stability, and
(2) combined analogue and digital circuitry, preferable with the ability to

implement, on chip, the complex anti-aliasing filter required before coding takes place.

Three of the many available integrated circuit technologies have emerged as particularly suitable, when constraints such as these are postulated.

(1) Bipolar/Integrated Injection Logic (I^2L)
(2) Complementary Metal Oxide Semiconductor (CMOS)
(3) n-channel Metal Oxide Semiconductor (NMOS)

Bipolar technology is employed in the fabrication of analogue integrated circuits. Individual transistors require physical separation on the integrated-circuit substrate to ensure isolation. This results in a relatively large chip-size for a given density of active elements. Since the essentially analogue elements within any CODEC involve the use of a relatively small number of active elements, by comparison with the number required in the digital circuitry, this is but a small penalty to pay for the enhanced speed capability available as a consequence of the use of bipolar technology. However, the corollary to such a statement must be that the bipolar approach is quite unsuitable, as it stands, for compatible and compact digital circuitry to be fabricated on the same substrate. This is indeed the case. To solve the problem, 'integrated-injection logic' is used. I^2L involves the use of 'inverted' bipolar transistors and thereby eliminates the need for physical isolation, producing a consequent improvement in active-device packing density while remaining process-compatible with the analogue bipolar circuitry.

An alternative, much-favoured solution to the packing-density problem is the use of complementary metal oxide semiconductor technology. Although at one time substantially slower than the bipolar approach, which relies for speed on thinness of base layer (a parameter readily controlled by diffusion during manufacture), improvements in photo-optic masking have now resulted in CMOS devices competitive in speed and packing density and considerably more economical in power-handling. This last advantage results from the use of both n- and p-channel field-effect transistors on the same substrate. Quiescent currents are contrived to be negligible and dissipation occurs only during logic-state changes. In the conventional CMOS process, analogue circuitry is difficult to incorporate in the manner suggested by the bipolar precedent. However, in this respect, a suitable choice of CODEC architecture can come to the rescue. The CMOS approach is particularly well suited to the fabrication of analogue switches. Consequently, as we shall see later in this section, the use of CODEC structures that take advantage of this feature are not uncommon.

The n-channel MOS carries with it speed advantages over CMOS, because the latter requires the use of both p- and n-channel devices. This is a consequence of the inferior mobility of the carriers (holes) in a p-channel device, by comparison with those (electrons) in an n-channel device. Further advantages accrue once more if particularly appropriate CODEC architectures are selected. In this context, it is interesting to note that NMOS appears particularly well suited to the fabrication of charge-coupled delay lines (CCD). Such structures can be used to establish high-order filtering of input signals, to achieve anti-aliasing. They are also readily fabricated upon the same substrate as the CODEC itself, making for a compact device realisation.

6.14.2 CODEC *Architecture*

Some insight into the range of architecture encompassed in production CODECs will be gained by consulting table 6.4. A broad subdivision of coder type is seen to be

(1) Continuously variable slope delta modulation (CVSD).
(2) Delta–sigma-based CODECs using interpolation or digital filtering to achieve sample-rate reduction.
(3) PCM using successive approximation logic.

The CVSD coder is intended for single-channel, specialised voice-telephony applications. Since it provides neither A- nor μ-law companding, it must be considered an unlikely candidate for inclusion within major national telephone networks. It might well find application, however, as a compact, economical interface of wide dynamic range in digital speech-processing systems. Because the companding is syllabic, and thus linked to the peculiar structural nature of speech, the use of this type of coder in more general instrumentation applications may well be limited.

The delta–sigma-based CODECs are A- and μ-law compatible. They have been developed in a range of process technologies. Choice of technology is often determined by the previous in-house experience and the available fabrication facilities within a given manufacturing organisation. All the listed CODECs of this type are primarily intended for line-telephony applications, mainly but not exclusively on a dedicated (single-channel) basis. A discussion of the implications behind and impact upon network architecture and growth, of single- versus multi-channel operation is presented in section 9.4.

The range of successive approximation PCM CODECs adopt conventional feedback encoder structures. However, novel approaches to the creation of fully integrated DACs (the precision element in any encoder) allow the designer to exploit the advantages of a given process technology. Historically, PCM encoder architecture was developed on the assumption that fabrication would involve the use of discrete component and (relatively) small-scale integrated-circuit mixes. Taken in the more recent context of fully integrated CODEC design, two particularly interesting approaches to the fabrication of an on-chip DAC have emerged. These are

(1) the resistor-string development of the $R-2R$ ladder network and
(2) the switched-capacitor, or charge redistribution ADC.

The resistor-string DAC is illustrated in figure 6.49. A conventional $R-2R$ ladder is used to obtain node-to-node voltage spans of $V_{ref}/2$, $V_{ref}/4$, ... across resistors of value R. Each such resistor is formed, during fabrication, as a string of sixteen smaller $(R/16)$ resistors. Thus voltage levels corresponding to steps within any given chord can be obtained by suitably addressing digits $I_0 I_1 I_2 I_3$ to the four-digit switch-tree logic block. Digits $I_4 I_5 I_6$ then allow selection of voltage level within a particular segment or 'chord'.

The switched-capacitor ADC was developed to provide a fast, precision CODEC architecture suited to MOS process technology, in which the fabrication of tightly toleranced resistor strings and ladders presents quality-control difficulties and

TABLE 6.4

Manufacturer	Coder type	Internal DAC	Process technology	mW Power dissipation On	mW Power dissipation Stand-by	General comments
Harris (Motorola)	CVSD	10-digit R–2R ladder	CMOS	10	10	Harris HC55516: Neither A- nor μ-law. 3-digit slope control algorithm (SCA). Single-channel. Intended for clock rates below 24 Kbits s^{-1}. HC 55532 for higher rates. Similar CVSD CODEC's with 3- and 4-digit SCA (MC3417/8) intended for military and civilian telephony applications, respectively, produced by Motorola.
British Telecom GI Microsystem AY-3-9900	Delta Sigma to PCM		NMOS			British Telecom CODEC intended for use in all-digital local exchanges and PABXs. LSI chip provides delta-sigma to linear 12-digit PCM conversion and digital-side parallel-to-serial conversion (and vice versa).
British Telecom Ferranti ZNPCM1 ZNPCM2	Delta Sigma to PCM	–	Bipolar	400	–	External assemblies provide analogue-side delta-sigma modulation. CCITT G712 standard. Companding is A-law, based upon 12- to 8-digit code conversion by interpolation. AY-3-9900 and ZNPCM1/2 are pin-compatible despite different process technologies. Single channel.
Bell System	Delta Sigma to PCM	R–2R ladder	Bipolar/I^{2}L	200	–	A single-chip, single-channel interpolative coder based upon a delta-sigma modulator encorporating a bi-directional shift-register clocked by the one-bit coder output and feeding, via a binary-weighted DAC, the delta-sigma loop difference amplifier input.
Hitachi	Delta Sigma to PCM	R–2R ladder	Bipolar/I^{2}L and NMOS	–	–	4-channel interpolative coder based upon modified delta-sigma modulator (see general comments on Bell System CODEC). Oversamples and codes input to linear 16-digit PCM at 32 kwords s^{-1}, then uses digital filter to establish compressed 8-digit word at 8 kwords s^{-1}.

Device	Method	DAC type	Technology			Description
Intel (Texas) 2910A, 2911A 2912	SAR PCM	8-digit resistor string	NMOS	230	30	NMOS voltage reference. 2910A and 2911A are μ- and A-law devices, respectively. 2912 family provides single-chip transmit and receive filtering to D3/D4 or CCITT G712 specification using the switched-capacitor method.
AMI S3501 encoder S3502 decoder	SAR PCM	modified charge redistribution	CMOS	125	35	Encoder and decoder on separate chips to improve isolation. On-chip filtering using switched-capacitor method. Transmit chip: 5th order elliptic LP cutting at 3.4 kHz (anti-alias) plus 3rd order Chebyshev HP cutting at 300 Hz (power-line component rejection). Receive chip: 6th order elliptic LP cutting at 3.4 kHz (smoothing and gain-equalisation after decode S/H operation. Single-channel.
National MM58150 LF3700	SAR PCM	8-digit resistor string	CMOS Bipolar	250	10	Two-chip, single-channel CODEC providing transmit/receive functions. Bipolar (analogue) chip contains comparator, input and output S/H amplifiers, voltage regulation and reference. Digital (CMOS) chip contains input and output PCM buffers, non-linear DAC, SAR and control logic.
Mostek MK5150 Fairchild 5150	SAR PCM	13-digit charge redistribution	CMOS	30	–	Single channel CODEC; charge redistribution method also used by Siliconix (DF341/2) in same process technology.
Plessey	SAR PCM	R–2R ladder	Bipolar/I²L and NMOS	500	NO	8-channel, five-chip C.C.I.T.T. specification CODEC using high-speed circuitry. Of the five chips per block, one performs the basic CODEC function. The remaining four provide transmit and receive side filtering at two channels per chip. Expandable in five-chip blocks to suit CEPT-32 requirements. Filtering used CCD method. Comprehensive compatible Plessey product range of PCM communication circuits.
PMI	SAR PCM	Current Summing	Bipolar	110	–	Multiple-channel, multichip- CODEC, based upon PMI companding DAC chip. Expandable in 8-channel blocks. Compatible with PMI product range of multiplexers and PCM carrier repeaters. μ or A-law companding; junction PCM application.

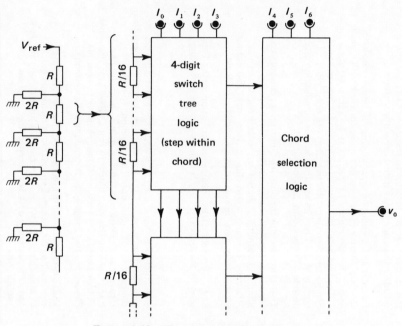

Figure 6.49   The resistor-string DAC

would result in a complex, mixed-process approach. The basic principle behind the charge-redistribution method may be understood by considering the operation of the simplified, positive-sense, four-digit, linear encoder illustrated in figure 6.50. The circuit establishes a conversion by sequencing through three operational modes.

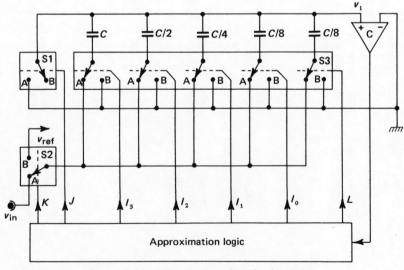

Figure 6.50   The charge-redistribution DAC

(1) *The Sample Mode*: (S1, S2, S3 — all five switch elements — set to pole A). This combination of switch settings establishes the upper plates of the banked capacitors at zero volts (earth potential) and all the lower plates at the sampled input voltage, V_{in}.

(2) *The Hold Mode*: (S1, S2, S3 — all five switch elements — set to pole B.) On entering the hold mode, the lower capacitor plates are clamped to zero, while the upper plates are disconnected from earth potential. They thus float to a value $V_1 = -V_{in}$, this value being 'stored' until the final 'charge-redistribution' mode commences.

(3) *Redistribution Mode*: (S1, S2 remain set to B, S3 poles tested in a 'successive approximation' sequence, with the exception of the rightmost, which is set permanently to A. The rightmost capacitor still plays a part in the conversion, in the sense that it is required to balance out the capacitor ratios correctly.) With S1 remaining set to B, V_1 is free to float. The most significant digit, corresponding to the extreme left-hand switch in S3, is tested first, thereby connecting the lower end of the leftmost capacitor to V_{ref} (since S2 is set to B). The effect of applying this test may be clarified by referring to figure 6.51. Immediately before the test is applied, the switched capacitor bank has the equivalent circuit shown in figure 6.51a. Here we see that the capacitor bank has been represented as a series connection of two equal-valued capacitors, C. These share applied charge and exhibit equal stored voltages. Relative to earth, the upper plate of the lower capacitor exhibits a voltage $-V_{in}$. When the switch (S3) operates to 'test' for status of the most significant digit, current flows to charge the series pair of capacitors so that the earth-point to upper-plate potential of the upper capacitor is V_{ref}. The charging current is common to both capacitors because they are in series connection. It must, in effect, raise the upper plate potential of an *equivalent* single capacitor, of value $C/2$, to V_{ref}. It therefore follows that the effect of the common charging current is to establish voltage drops of $(V_{in} + \frac{1}{2}V_{ref})$ and $(-V_{in} + \frac{1}{2}V_{ref})$ across the upper and lower capacitors, respectively. Consequently, the comparator input voltage is

$$V_1 = -V_{in} + \tfrac{1}{2}V_{ref}$$

The comparator now establishes the sense of the most significant digit and the approximation logic either confirms or restores, as appropriate, the test-switch

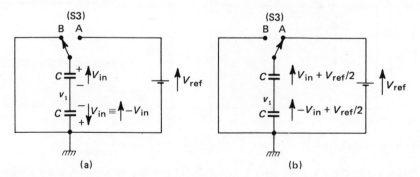

Figure 6.51 *Obtaining the most significant digit in charge-redistribution conversion*

setting, thus

$$I_3 = 0 \text{ if } V_1 > 0; \quad \text{test-switch reset to B}$$

$$I_3 = 1 \text{ if } V_1 < 0; \quad \text{test-switch left set at A}$$

Analogous operations are then used to determine the sense of the remaining digits, I_2, I_1 and I_0, in that order.

The charge redistribution method has the advantage over competing techniques of providing an inherent sample-and-hold function, an advantage somewhat offset by the difficulties it introduces in effecting timesharing between transmit and receive modes with a single CODEC.

6.14.3   CODEC *Evaluation Criteria*

Intended as they are for application within large, geographically distributed communication networks, CODECs must conform to globally acceptable specifications. C.C.I.T.T. Recommendation G712 establishes detailed criteria governing CODEC performance targets. In order to appreciate the implications behind these criteria, it is necessary that certain technical conventions and terminology are introduced and explained.

System measurements, if they are to bear comparison and offer repeatable and independent checking, require the careful specification of any test input. Both sinusoidal and random or pseudo-random noise inputs are used as test signals. Figure 6.52*a*, for example, illustrates an obvious and important bound for CODEC operation which governs allowable signal-to-quantising noise ratio. This quantity is measured in decibels (dB) because it is a *ratio of attributes* (namely, output signal power and quantising noise power). It is plotted against sinusoidal input signal level, *referenced to 1 mW*. Since the reference is so specified, and a ratio of attributes is not implied, the notation 'dBm' is applied. In this case, and typically, a test-tone frequency of 1004 Hz is dictated.

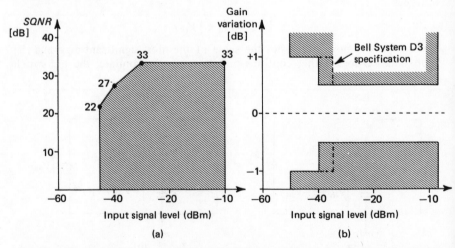

Figure 6.52   C.C.I.T.T. (μ-law) G712/Bell D3 specification of required CODEC *performance bounds: (a) signal-to-quantising noise ratio and (b) gain variation versus input signal level (test signal: 1004 Hz sinusoid)*

If a noise test waveform were used, some suitable spectral shaping to constrain frequency components within the normal limits for speech telephony (300–3400 Hz) would be required. The input signal power would be measured relative to a reference noise power of −90 dBm and would be denoted 'dBrn'.

Figure 6.52*b* illustrates a second important evaluation criterion: allowable *gain-tracking error*. This quantity measures the ratio, in decibels, of decoder analogue output to encoder analogue input. It is thus an estimate of overall system departure from linearity, consequent upon inadequacies of compression and expansion functions.

A third criterion is the *idle-channel noise*, which is a measure of the 'jitter' seen at the decoder analogue output when no signal is being transmitted. It is customary to filter this noise component prior to measurement, in order to give it a spectral weighting representative of the response of the human ear and telephone handset combination. Two weighting transfer functions are commonly used. In North America, 'C-message' weighting is used and the idle-channel noise is measured in 'dBrnC'. Elsewhere, the C.C.I.T.T. 'psophometric response' is favoured and the measurement is made in 'dBrnP'. Both transfer functions are *superficially* similar, being bandpass in nature, with the passband extending from (about) 1 kHz to (about) 3 kHz. The C.C.I.T.T. limits of acceptability for idle channel noise are 23 dBrnC or 25 dBrnP.

The decibel terminology introduced above will frequently be encountered written in slightly different form. Often 'dBm' will be seen written as 'dBmO', or 'dBrnC' as 'dBrnCO'. The additional zero signifies that the decibel ratio is referenced to 'zero transmission level point' (0 TLP), an arbitrary reference point within the network.

6.14.4 CODEC *Filters*

All the telephony CODECs described in the preceding sections require input (pre-encoding) and output (post-decoding) filters. The input filter is required to eliminate aliasing and also to suppress 50 Hz power-line interference. The first of these functions is achieved by lowpass filtering. Because signals may pass through several CODECs during transmission, the passband ripple specification is severe: ripple magnitude should be less than 0.1 dB. To satisfy this requirement, while maintaining adequate stopband attenuation and a suitably narrow transition region between pass- and stopbands, a fifth-order elliptic lowpass characteristic, cutting at 3.4 kHz, is usually taken as the design target.

The elimination of line interference may be achieved by means of a third-order, highpass Chebycheff characteristic, cutting at 200 Hz.

Before describing the output filter, we note that, as a consequence of the application of latched binary words to a DAC during the decode operation, an implicit 'hold' function is present at the decoder output. It is as though sample values were applied to a 'first-order hold' circuit which has a square-pulse impulse response of duration T, equal to the sampling interval. Such a 'hold' operation has two consequences, both of which must be compensated for by the output filter. These consequences are

(1) Spurious high-frequency components are generated by the output transition steps. These must be smoothed by lowpass filtering with a suitably chosen time constant.

(2) The square-pulse impulse response transforms to correspond to a frequency weighting $W(f) = \text{sinc}(fT)$. The output filter must provide equalisation to eliminate this weighting.

The overall output filter transfer function is usually derived by computer-aided design and is of similar order to that required for the input filter.

Both filters present a significant problem in terms of the economics of their realisation, if conventional active or passive filter structures are contemplated. Consequently, efforts have been made to develop process-compatible, single-chip or on-chip filters using either

(1) charge-coupled devices (as analogue delay lines) in FIR transversal digital filters, or

(2) switched-capacitor realisations of complex reactances in developments of conventional passive filter structures.

The first of these techniques results in a filter structure superficially similar to that illustrated in figure 6.44. The differences are matters of detail, in that the input (b_n in figure 6.44) becomes a sample amplitude and summation an analogue operation. Standard digital filter design techniques, well reported in the literature, allow selection of the tap weights W_k to produce an appropriate frequency-domain response. The CCD approach, requiring as it does a precise charge-transfer operation, is particularly well suited to NMOS process technology.

The switched capacitor method makes use of the notion that a circuit such as is shown in figure 6.53a behaves as a resistor. Since this circuit is actually synthesised from an analogue switch and a capacitor, it is (by contrast with the precision resistor it purports to replace) particularly readily implemented in CMOS process technology. The operation is as follows. Assume first that v_1 and v_2 are slowly

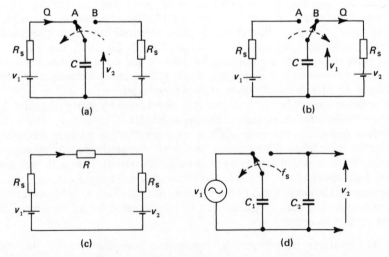

Figure 6.53   *The switched capacitor realisation of an equivalent resistor and its use in electronic wave filtering*

fluctuating functions of time, by comparison with the switch-throw frequency, f_s. Assume also, the dwell of the switch on poles A and B to be equal and thus of duration $1/2f_s$ seconds. Finally, assume that the time constant $R_s C$ is short by comparison with the dwell time, so that the capacitor charge or discharge cycle between voltage levels v_1 and v_2 may be considered complete at the end of each dwell.

As the switch throws from B to A, figure 6.53a, a charge transfer $Q = C(v_1 - v_2)$ flows to raise the capacitor voltage from v_2 to v_1. When the switch throws back to B, figure 6.53b, the capacitor voltage (now v_1) discharges to v_2 with exactly the same charge transfer magnitude but this time, of opposite sense. Over one complete cycle (dwell on A, dwell on B) a mean current flow from v_1 to v_2 takes place, which is of magnitude $Cf(v_1 - v_2)$. The switched capacitor thus functions as an effective resistance of value $R = 1/Cf_s$, figure 6.53c. (Note that our third assumption listed above carries with it the implication that $R \gg R_s$.)

To illustrate, in a filtering context, the application of the resistor 'simulated' by the switched capacitor, consider figure 6.53d. Here, the simulated resistor of value $R = 1/C_1 f$ feeds a shunt capacitor C_2, from a source $v_1(t)$ which, again, is presumed to vary slowly by comparison with the switch-throw frequency, f_s. The component configuration is thus that of a lowpass filter with time constant RC_2. Eliminating R and manipulating, the cut-off frequency of this filter is found to be $f_0 = 2\pi f_s (C_1/C_2)$. The output voltage $v_2(t)$ will thus exhibit all the characteristics (with respect to attenuation and phase-shift as functions of frequency) of the signal seen at the output of a first-order RC lowpass filter of identical cut-off frequency.

Extensions of this technique have successfully been used to achieve on-chip synthesis of complex CODEC transmit and receive filters. Usually, these filters are derived from active ladder-network equivalents to conventional passive filter structures. The active 'element' in such ladders is an integrator configuration in which the input resistor is replaced by its switched-capacitor alternative.

Problems

6.1 Compare and contrast continuous wave and pulse modulations as methods of conveying information.

6.2 To what extent may pulse code be regarded as a modulation, and to what extent may it be considered to be a primary data source?

6.3 A waveform is sampled strictly in accordance with the sampling theorem, at the Nyquist rate. Reconstruction is effected by passing the sampled wave through an ideal lowpass filter with a cut-off frequency equal to one-half of the sampling frequency. Show that the reconstructed wave, $v(t)$ is given in terms of the sample values by the relation

$$v(t) = \sum_{k=-\infty}^{+\infty} v_s(kT)\operatorname{sinc}\{(t/T - k)\}$$

6.4 Sketch and explain the reconstruction operation when it is stated in the manner of question 6.3. What is the effect of a slight error in sampling rate? How is reconstruction affected if a substantially higher sampling rate is used and the reconstruction filter has a gradual, rather than an abrupt cut-off?

6.5   It is intended to employ PCM without signal compression to convey a television picture signal. The signal bandwidth extends from zero to 1 MHz. How many binary digits are required to ensure that the noise level is at least 30 dB below the signal level. What transmission bandwidth will be required to convey the PCM wave? (*Hint* The worst case PCM digit sequence, from the standpoint of band occupancy, consists of alternating 1s and 0s, thus: . . . 101010 . . . . Such a signal, filtered at half the digit frequency, would yield a sinewave from which the original sharp-edged digital signal could be regained by slicing. A fuller discussion of this topic is presented in chapter 8.)

6.6   Contrast the various forms of pulse code modulator listed below with respect to speed and economy of implementation: parallel, time interval conversion, tracking, successive approximation.

6.7   For the predictive PCM decoder illustrated in figure 6.37 show that

$$v'_1(kT) = v'(kT) + v'_1\{(k-1)T\}$$

and explain why this equation corresponds to a finite difference integration and hence is equivalent to the decoder for DPCM.

7 Coding for Error Protection and Security

In chapter 6, we studied the methods used to generate binary codewords from an analogue signal. A measure of system performance that is of great importance in such a context is the signal-to-quantising noise ratio. This quantity is a function only of the number of quantising levels used in the modulation system, not of the channel noise level. The channel noise is of concern to us in so far as it may cause errors in interpretation of the received binary digits. However, in most PCM systems, the error rate can be reduced to a low level by using repeater amplifiers in the transmission path at sufficiently frequent intervals that regeneration of a sharp-edged, noise-free version of the original signal is possible. The correspondingly rare noise components that occur in the decoded signal are unobjectionable.

When a digital data link is to be implemented, the problem of noise-induced digit errors becomes more serious. If digital data is received with errors it is simply incorrect. Much effort has therefore been devoted to devising techniques whereby the purely informational digits are coded into a longer binary word which contains built-in 'redundancy'. This redundancy permits us to detect and even, under some circumstances, to correct noise-induced errors at the receiver, greatly improving the communication system reliability. In this chapter we shall investigate the nature and properties of coding systems designed to afford error protection.

It is worth mentioning that many other reasons exist for performing digital coding. We have spoken of coding to increase the redundancy of a purely informational (non-redundant) data signal. We have also noted that the redundancy contained in a speech signal makes it so robust that when it is conveyed by PCM telephony, no further increase in redundancy is required. In fact, some analogue signals are sufficiently redundant that it may be worth while to consider redundancy-reducing coding schemes. This may allow a substantial reduction in the required channel bandwidth. For example, consideration has been given to the application of this form of coding to PCM television signals because television line-scan waveforms often exhibit long periods of low activity—typically when the scan is passing over a low-definition area of picture background. In particular, it has been suggested that 'run-length encoding' be adopted for this application. Run-length encoding involves transmitting 'start' and 'duration' information for segments of each line-scan in which the picture brightness does not change.

Another method of economising on bandwidth without redundancy reduction being implied is to code a binary message into a multilevel message. Consider, for example, the conversion of a binary to a quaternary message, with pairs of binary digits corresponding to each quaternary digit, thus

$$00 \equiv 0$$
$$01 \equiv 1$$
$$10 \equiv 2$$
$$11 \equiv 3$$

Each quaternary digit is generated at one-half of the binary-digit rate (the 'bit rate') and the resulting message therefore requires one-half of the channel bandwidth of the original binary process. This type of encoding is of particular importance in the transmission of data at high bit rates over voice-grade telephone lines, which are strictly band-limited to the range 300 Hz to 3.4 kHz. We shall consider this topic at greater length in chapter 8. The cost of the reduction in required channel bandwidth, or the possible increase in data rate, is a reduced immunity to channel noise for a given maximum-permitted transmitted power.

Coding may also be used to establish a message which is difficult to decode. This kind of code conversion is known as *encrypting* and is of considerable concern at the present time because much confidential information is handled by data-processing computer systems.

Yet other forms of coding have been proposed to yield a digital signal with some preferred spectral properties. Codes which aid in obtaining digit synchronisation are a case in point. The spectrum of the digital signal, after coding, is arranged to contain a discrete line-component, corresponding to a single-frequency sinewave, at some multiple of the bit rate. This component can be extracted by filtering at the decoder and, after suitable frequency division, yields a phase and frequency-locked reference wave.

Some codes have been devised to reduce *disparity*. Disparity is the difference between the number of 1s and the number of 0s in each codeword. A high disparity may be undesirable, since a predominance of 1s or 0s may lead to a large low-frequency component, or even a d.c. offset in the binary sequence, which will make propagation difficult through a medium with no d.c. coupling. Coding for disparity reduction may therefore be considered as performing some form of spectral shaping on the digital signal, removing low-frequency components.

7.1 The Principles of Error Protection[27]

The most extensive use of error-protection coding is concerned with safeguarding digital data and telegraphy (teletypewriter and TELEX) links. The coding procedures used in telegraphy links are usually fairly simple, partly for reasons of economy and partly because the messages conveyed, being written in the text of some human language incorporate, like speech, a considerable measure of redundancy. For example, a sqntenve wish slelling miktakes in it can usually still be read. It is in digital data transmission that the real problem lies since the codewords to be transmitted contain no inherent redundancy.

Two distinct kinds of error condition arise in digital data transmission. The first kind, *random* errors, involve no correlation between the digits in error. The second kind involves *burst* errors: a number of consecutive digits, rather than individual and probably widely-spaced digits are corrupted. Certain kinds of error-protecting codes are best suited to one or other of these two error conditions.

As a gross generalisation, burst errors are typical of data transmission through the switched telephone-network, in which impulsive, rather than gaussian noise predominates. Random errors characterise channels corrupted with gaussian noise.

The transmission system itself can play an important part in determining the kind of coding chosen. For example, if we are operating a two-way link and can therefore request re-transmission when necessary, we may restrict our attention to *error-detecting* codes. If the link is one-way, and re-transmission cannot be called for, then codes which *detect and correct* errors must be investigated.

All methods of obtaining error protection require the addition of extra digits to the basic binary codeword. These digits are used in some way to check the validity of the received informational digits and are referred to as *parity* digits. They are generated from the information digits by some suitable logical manipulation.

The simplest parity check involves a count of the number of 1s in the informational part of the codeword. If this count is even, a 1 is inserted as the parity-check digit. If it is odd, then a 0 is inserted instead. Examples of this method of parity-digit generation are shown in table 7.1, on the basis of which, the sequence

$$\ldots 19\ 27\ 20 \ldots$$

would be transmitted as

$$\ldots 100110110111101001 \ldots$$

Every sixth digit in this sequence is a parity digit. Denoting an error by means of bold-face type, suppose that the first word is received as

$$\ldots 101110$$

a second parity-digit generator physically located at the receiver would count an even number of 1s, would generate a 1 as the parity digit and, since the received and locally generated parity-digits were not identical, an error would be registered.

This particular kind of parity check is so constructed that it can detect the presence of an odd number of errors. An even number of errors produces a self-cancelling parity-check situation. Hence a code based on this principle is

TABLE 7.1 EXAMPLES OF PARITY-DIGIT GENERATION

| | Binary Word | |
Decimal Equivalent	Information Digits	Parity-check Digit
19	10011	0
27	11011	1
20	10100	1

suitable only for independent and rather rare errors. Furthermore, since the code is only capable of error detection and has no built-in error correction, it can only be employed on two-way links.

Many codes have been invented to cope with the various situations described above, all of which are generically derived from the simple parity-check technique. A large number of them bear a stamp of individuality which makes further categorisation difficult. However, the discipline of coding seems to be dividing into two areas

(1) Block coding
(2) Convolution coding

We shall restrict our attention to simple examples of these two classes of code. Block codes are so-called because the final codeword is of fixed, finite length. Convolution codes, in contrast, generate a digit sequence from the informational digits in which no finite group of informational digits can be ascribed to one informational codeword.

7.2 Modulo-2 Arithmetic

In the following sections of this chapter we shall frequently have recourse to the use of modulo-2 arithmetical operations. Operations 'modulo-2' are readily performed with simple logic circuits involving exclusive-OR gates and serial shift-registers.

The two input exclusive-OR gate has already been defined by the truth table specified in figure 6.9. The logical function performed by the exclusive-OR gate is equivalent to the arithmetical operation of *modulo-2 addition* if we regard the logical states TRUE and FALSE as equivalent to the binary numbers 1 and 0 respectively. Calculations performed using modulo-2 arithmetic are the same as those performed using ordinary arithmetic with the following restrictions

(1) Only the digits 0 and 1 are used
(2) $1 \oplus 1 = 0$

The symbol $\oplus$ stands for 'addition modulo-2'. Notice that the second condition implies that no 'carry' operation is necessary in modulo-2 addition. The various arithmetic operations are best described by example.

Addition of two numbers proceeds as follows

$$10110 \oplus 11010 = 01100$$

the calculation being carried out thus

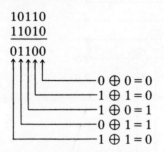

$$10110$$
$$\underline{11010}$$
$$01100$$

$$0 \oplus 0 = 0$$
$$1 \oplus 1 = 0$$
$$1 \oplus 0 = 1$$
$$0 \oplus 1 = 1$$
$$1 \oplus 1 = 0$$

Subtraction is performed as a modulo-2 addition since because

$$0 = 1 \oplus 1$$

it follows that

$$0 \ominus 1 = 1$$

Note that the number -1 is not permitted as a symbol: restriction 1.

Multiplication is as in ordinary arithmetic, but with modulo-2 addition and therefore no carry.

$$1101$$
$$\underline{110}$$
$$0000$$
$$11010$$
$$\underline{110100}$$
$$101110$$

Division is the same as in ordinary arithmetic, with modulo-2 addition taking on the role of successive subtraction

$$\begin{array}{r} 1101 \\ 110\overline{)101110} \\ \underline{110} \\ 111 \\ \underline{110} \\ 011 \\ \underline{000} \\ 110 \\ \underline{110} \\ 000 \end{array}$$

Although modulo-2 arithmetic does not produce the same result as the normal arithmetical manipulation of binary numbers, the operations themselves obey a defined set of laws which facilitate an algebraic approach to the solution of problems and they are easily mechanised. Figure 7.1 illustrates the mechanisation of addition, multiplication and division by means of shift registers involving the use of 'D-type' bistables (or 'delay stages') and exclusive-OR gates.

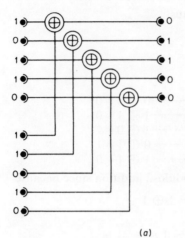

(a)

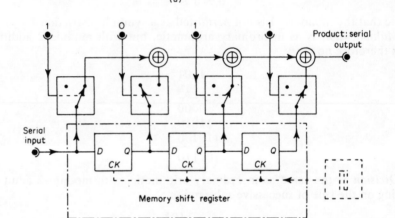

(b)

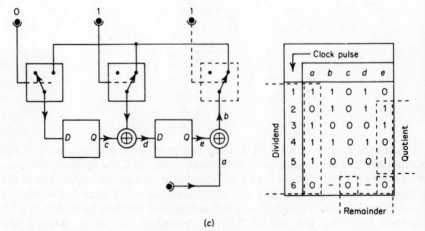

(c)

Figure 7.1 Operations modulo-2: (a) addition, (b) multiplication and (c) division

7.3   Elementary Block Coding and Decoding

In section 7.1, we introduced the concept of the 'parity check' which, when added to an otherwise non-redundant codeword, provides a measure of controlled redundancy. This added redundancy allows error detection and, in some circumstances, error correction to be performed when one or more of the information digits in the codeword becomes corrupted during transmission. We shall adopt the following notation to allow us to distinguish between the information and parity-check digits in a code

$C_0 C_1 \ldots C_{J-1}$ the J parity-check digits in, or associated with the codeword

$I_0 I_1 \ldots I_{K-1}$ the K information digits in the codeword

Thus an L-digit block code will consist of K information digits and $J = L - K$ parity-check digits. A convolution code cannot be specified in quite these terms, since the codeword is, as we shall see in section 7.6, a rather indistinct entity.

All the codes we shall investigate will be of the type known as *systematic*. A systematic code is one in which the information digits appear unchanged within the codeword, although they may not necessarily occur in natural order. Thus

$$I_0 I_1 I_2 I_3 C_0 C_1 C_2$$

is a systematic block code.

The parity check in the codeword may be formed in one of four ways. A check digit required to provide a parity check on any given set of information digits may be chosen so that the number of

$$\begin{Bmatrix} \text{binary 1s} \\ \text{binary 0s} \end{Bmatrix} \text{ in the information-digit sequence is } \begin{Bmatrix} \text{even} \\ \text{odd} \end{Bmatrix}$$

The simplest parity check for a succession of three-digit codewords, an odd check on 1s, would be obtained thus

$$C_0 = I_0 \oplus I_1 \oplus I_2$$

yielding a codeword

$$I_0 I_1 I_2 C_0$$

We shall adopt the use of an even check on 1s throughout this chapter since the formation of the check digits is a straightforward modulo-2 addition.

As we observed in section 7.1, such a simple strategy allows any even number of errors to go undetected and does not provide for error correction. A more powerful error-protection scheme, known as *iterated coding* allows us to extend the simple parity-check technique. We form an array containing a given number of successive codewords. Consider, for example the array of three three-digit codewords

I_0	I_1	I_2
0	1	0
1	1	1
1	0	1

We then perform parity checks on both rows and columns (horizontal and vertical parity checks). With an odd check on the binary 1s we obtain the array

$$
\begin{array}{ccc|c}
0 & 1 & 0 & 1 \\
1 & 1 & 1 & 1 \\
1 & 0 & 1 & 0 \\
\hline
0 & 0 & 0 & 0
\end{array}
$$

$\left.\begin{array}{l}\\ \\ \\ \end{array}\right\}$ horizontal checks

$\leftarrow$ check on checks

$\underbrace{\qquad\qquad}$
vertical
checks

and we transmit, instead of the sequence

$$\ldots 010111101 \ldots$$

the sequence

$$\ldots 0101111110100000 \ldots$$

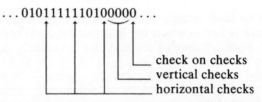

check on checks
vertical checks
horizontal checks

An error in any codeword in the array can not only be detected, its position within the codeword can also be found and hence it can be corrected. Consider, for example, an error in the first codeword. Recall that we use the convention that the digit in bold-face type is the one in error.

$$\ldots 0 1 \mathbf{1} 1 \ldots$$

The recomputed parity checks are

$$
\begin{array}{ccc|c}
0 & 1 & \mathbf{1} & ⓪ \\
1 & 1 & 1 & 1 \\
1 & 0 & 1 & 0 \\
\hline
0 & 0 & ① & ①
\end{array}
$$

The encircled checks do not agree with those received and they provide co-ordinates which pinpoint the incorrect digit. The fact that two digits are in error can still be deduced, but the errors cannot be corrected. Again, in the first codeword, suppose the errors to be

$$\ldots 0 0 \mathbf{1} 0 \ldots$$

This word yields recomputed parity checks which indicate that two errors must have occurred

$$
\begin{array}{ccc|c}
0 & \mathbf{0} & \mathbf{1} & 1 \\
1 & 1 & 1 & 1 \\
1 & 0 & 1 & 0 \\
\hline
0 & ① & ① & 0
\end{array}
$$

This sort of checking scheme could, of course, be further extended but still more powerful methods exist.

One of the early formal coding procedures was devised by R. W. Hamming[34] and is named after him. The general format of a typical Hamming code is shown below. Digits $I_0 I_1 \ldots$ are the information digits and $C_0 C_1 \ldots$ are the parity-check digits as usual. The codeword structure for four information digits is

$$C_0 C_1 I_0 C_2 I_1 I_2 I_3$$

This rather strange arrangement of information and check digits has some purpose, as we shall see shortly. The check digits for this seven-digit Hamming code are determined from the four information digits thus

$$C_0 = I_0 \oplus I_1 \oplus I_3$$
$$C_1 = I_0 \oplus I_2 \oplus I_3$$
$$C_2 = I_1 \oplus I_2 \oplus I_3$$

For example, if

$$I_0 = 1 \quad I_1 = 1 \quad I_2 = 0 \quad I_3 = 1$$

then

$$C_0 = 1 \quad C_1 = 0 \quad C_2 = 0$$

The transmitted codeword is then

$$1010101$$

Suppose, now, that the codeword was received with an error in information digit I_1

$$1010001$$

If we strip the information digits from the codeword and recompute the parity digits we find that

$$C_0 = 0 \quad C_1 = 0 \quad C_2 = 1$$

The ingenuity of the Hamming code lies in its ability to locate which of the digits in the codeword is in error. A comparison indicates the following differences between the received and recomputed parity-check digits

$$C_0\text{---change}$$
$$C_1\text{---no change}$$
$$C_2\text{---change}$$

If we regard 'change' and 'no change' as being equivalent to the binary numbers 1 and 0 respectively, we may determine the position of the error within the codeword by means of a binary-to-decimal conversion.

$$A = 1 \times 2^2 + 0 \times 2^1 + 1 \times 2^0 = 5$$

The error is therefore in digit five, or I_1 (as we should hope) and this digit need only be reversed to be corrected. The other digit positions are similarly covered by unique parity-difference patterns, as table 7.2 shows.

MODERN COMMUNICATION SYSTEMS

TABLE 7.2 HAMMING CODE CHECK METHOD

Check C_0	Digit C_1	Change C_2	Digit in Error
0	0	0	NONE
0	0	1	C_0
0	1	0	C_1
0	1	1	I_0
1	0	0	C_2
1	0	1	I_1
1	1	0	I_2
1	1	1	I_3

We might now examine the problem of code creation from a rather different viewpoint. Instead of merely allowing intuition or ingenuity to lead us towards a coding scheme of presumably unquantified merit, let us ask a more fundamental question. How many information digits, in principle, can we protect with a given number of parity digits? Let us also make the proviso that, if the parity digits must check information digits, they must also be capable of checking themselves. After all, an incorrect parity digit might cause us to attempt to correct an information digit which was not, in fact, in error. Remember that the communication channel, in introducing errors into a transmitted digit stream, will make no distinction between parity and information digits.

We assume again a block code of length L, with $J = L - K$ parity digits. Clearly, J parity digits may be combined in 2^J ways. Each such combination may be used to identify an 'error state' in the received codeword. If we restrict our attention to single error correcting codes, the L error states must be uniquely identifiable. Assuming that one of the 2^J combinations of the J parity digits (000 . . . 0 possibly) is used to identify a 'no-error' condition, then

$$L \geqslant 2^J - 1$$

If, as in our example, $J = 3$, then our value of L of 7 suggests that a code is performing as well as any single-error correcting code can be expected to. The fact that L actually equals (rather than exceeds) $2^J - 1$, leads us to refer to the Hamming single-error correcting code as a *perfect* code (of which there are but few).

While we may be able to calculate a lower bound to code *redundancy* (the ratio, J/L, of parity to transmitted digits, per block) actually arriving at some prescription whereby parity digits may be established from information digits in such a way that error correction may be effected, remains a matter for the ingenuity of the code designer. In synthesising the Hamming code structure, we accept that, for a seven-digit codeword containing four information digits protected by three parity digits, the seven non-zero combinations of parity digits may be used to pinpoint a single erroneous digit location. If, in comparing recomputed and received parity digits, a *single* point of difference is established

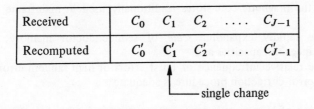

Received	C_0	C_1	C_2	....	C_{J-1}
Recomputed	C_0'	$\mathbf{C_1'}$	C_2'	....	C_{J-1}'

single change

then only a parity digit error can have occurred. To establish the one-for-one position correspondence of the parity digits in the codeword, therefore, note that $C_0 \equiv 2^0$, $C_1 \equiv 2^1$, $C_2 \equiv 2^2 \ldots C_{J-1} \equiv 2^{J-1}$. Thus we locate the first parity digit in position 1 within the codeword, the second in position 2, the third in position 4 and so on (the $\smile$ symbol denotes a space, later to be filled by an information digit).

Parity digit C_0 C_1 $\smile$ C_2 $\smile$ $\smile$ $\smile$ C_3 $\smile$ $\smile$ $\smile$ $\smile$ $\smile$ $\smile$ $\smile$ C_4

Position   1   2   3   4   5   6   7   8   9   10   11   12   13   14   15   16 ...

The sequencing of the information digits is then a natural ordering from position 3, to fill available spaces contiguously. Identification of error location follows automatically

$$C_0' = I_0 \oplus I_1 \oplus \quad\;\; I_3$$
$$C_1' = I_0 \oplus \quad\;\; I_2 \oplus I_3$$
$$C_2' = \quad\;\; I_1 \oplus I_2 \oplus I_3$$
$$\begin{array}{cccc} . & . & . & . \\ . & . & . & . \\ . & . & . & . \end{array}$$

Thus, recalling that this is a *single*-error correcting code, an error in I_0 will cause C_0' and C_1' to change by comparison with the received and necessarily presumed unaltered parity digits thereby, according to our previously noted convention, allowing us to compute the error location within the codeword as $11_2 = 3$.

Extension of the single error correcting Hamming code to protect more than four information digits is a straightforward task. For most communication purposes, the low level of protection afforded by the Hamming code has inspired the design of more powerful (albeit less 'perfect') codes. However, for error correction in microprocessor-based memory systems, three factors do militate in favour of the use of the relatively easily implemented and well-understood Hamming code. These are

(1) the favoured use of semiconductor memory, more compact and more conveniently written to or read from but more prone to generation of stored-bit

errors than the magnetic core-stores traditionally used in mainframe computer systems,

(2) the rapidly expanding *scale* of semiconductor memory, currently approaching megabit capacities and

(3) the relative infrequence of burst errors or high random error rates, so that a single error correction procedure is adequate.

The application of Hamming codes to microprocessor-based memories recognises that most microprocessors utilise 8- or 16-bit architecture. The word structure and required correction logic are presented in table 7.3 for these two cases. Note that truncation after information digit I_7 allows computation of the code for an 8-bit machine.

TABLE 7.3 ERROR LOCATION LOGIC FOR 8- OR 16-BIT PROTECTION USING HAMMING SINGLE ERROR CORRECTING CODE

A	1	2	3	4	5	6	7	8	9	10	11	12	13	14	15	16	17	18	19	20
B	C_0	C_1	I_0	C_2	I_1	I_2	I_3	C_3	I_4	I_5	I_6	I_7	I_8	I_9	I_{10}	C_5	I_{11}	I_{12}	I_{13}	I_{14}

A = single error position-in-codeword indicator

$$= P_4.2^4 + P_3.2^3 + P_2.2^2 + P_1.2^1 + P_0.2^0$$

8-bit processor $\longrightarrow$ 16-bit processor $\longrightarrow$

$$P_0 = C_0 \oplus I_0 \oplus I_1 \oplus I_3 \oplus I_4 \oplus I_6 \quad \oplus I_8 \oplus I_{10} \oplus I_{11} \oplus I_{13} \oplus I_{15}$$
$$P_1 = C_1 \oplus I_0 \oplus I_2 \oplus I_3 \oplus I_5 \oplus I_6 \quad \oplus I_9 \oplus I_{10} \oplus I_{12} \oplus I_{13}$$
$$P_2 = C_2 \oplus I_1 \oplus I_2 \oplus I_3 \oplus I_7 \quad \oplus I_8 \oplus I_9 \oplus I_{10} \oplus I_{14} \oplus I_{15}$$
$$P_3 = C_3 \oplus I_4 \oplus I_5 \oplus I_6 \oplus I_7 \quad \oplus I_8 \oplus I_9 \oplus I_{10}$$
$$P_4 = C_4 \oplus I_{11} \oplus I_{12} \oplus I_{13} \oplus I_{14} \oplus I_{15}$$

One problem which is evident when many error detecting and correcting codes are devised is the difficulty of implementing them. A widely used practical tele-printer code which will guarantee the correction of single errors and the detection of double errors is known as AUTOSPEC.[37] This acronym stands for 'automatic single-path error correction'. It is a ten-digit block code, of which five digits are informational. These digits are, in fact, the digits of the international five-unit ('Baudot') teleprinter code.[4] Thus AUTOSPEC is designed around an existing but non-redundant alphanumeric coding scheme. That its redundancy is high, so that its possible information rate is only one-half that which might be achieved with the unmodified teleprinter code is of no great consequence since the ultimate operator of the teleprinter is a slow, inefficient human being. In this respect, AUTOSPEC differs markedly in the looseness of the constraints placed upon it when compared with those codes devised to protect, say, digital data being relayed between computing installations.

The AUTOSPEC code block is created thus

$$I_0 I_1 I_2 I_3 I_4 C_0 C_1 C_2 C_3 C_4$$

The parity checks, again, may be even or odd. We shall assume, as usual, an odd parity check on binary 1s. The check digits are formed according to the following rules

$$C_0 = I_1 \oplus I_2 \oplus I_3 \oplus I_4$$
$$C_1 = I_0 \oplus I_2 \oplus I_3 \oplus I_4$$
$$C_2 = I_0 \oplus I_1 \oplus I_3 \oplus I_4$$
$$C_3 = I_0 \oplus I_1 \oplus I_2 \oplus I_4$$
$$C_4 = I_0 \oplus I_1 \oplus I_2 \oplus I_3$$

These rules have the effect of causing the parity digits to *repeat* the information digits if the number of 1s in the codeword is even, and to *complement* the information digits if the number of 1s in the codeword is odd. For example

$$I_0 I_1 I_2 I_3 I_4 C_0 C_1 C_2 C_3 C_4$$

1 0 1 1 1 1 0 1 1 1

1 1 0 1 0 0 0 1 0 1

Error correction may therefore proceed along the following lines. Assume a single error in the information sequence. This will result in an odd number of 1s being turned into an even number, or vice versa. Consequently, a single informational error will switch the formation of the parity sequence to repetition from complementing, or vice versa. Modulo-2 summation of the received and reconstituted parity-check digits will therefore consist entirely of 1s, except at the position of the error. Consider for example, the codeword

1011110111

Suppose that an error occurs on the fourth digit, so that the received codeword is

1010110111

Recalculation of the parity digits from the received information-digits yields the binary sequence

01010

Modulo-2 summation with the received parity sequence takes place thus

01010
10110
___
11101

We see that the error is pinpointed as lying in position four in the information-digit sequence, because the zero lies within a sequence of all 1s and is in position four.

If the single error occurs in the parity sequence, then reconstituting this sequence at the receiver and subjecting received and reconstituted sequences to modulo-2 addition will result in a pattern of zeros, except for a single 1 at the position in the parity sequence which is in error.

AUTOSPEC guarantees the detection of two errors within a codeword. In practice, however, it is unlikely that a situation in which more than two errors occur will elude the detector, because the code is highly redundant. There are $2^5 = 32$ possible combinations of 1 and 0 to make the information words, and hence 32 valid codewords in all. However, there are $2^{10} = 1024$ possible combinations of ten binary digits. Thus the probability that random errors form another valid codeword is exceedingly small. Instrumentation of the decoder is such that a detected, but uncorrectable error is registered by causing the teleprinter to type a special character. If the text being conveyed is a human language, its own inherent redundancy will further aid the correct interpretation of the message. Thus AUTOSPEC is a robust code, relatively easy to implement, and, as such, finds wide use, particularly in marine radio teleprinter circuits.

We turn next to consider a class of block codes in which the level of redundancy is more readily controllable, and for which simple error-detection decoders are available. These are the 'cyclic block codes'.

7.4 Cyclic Block Codes

Cyclic block codes are codes in which the combination of information and parity digits in any one codeword forms another valid codeword if given an end-about shift of one digit. Thus the seven-digit codeword

$$I_0 I_1 I_2 C_0 C_1 C_2 C_3$$
$$1\ 0\ 0\ 1\ 0\ 1\ 1$$

taken from a set of codewords we shall study shortly, forms another valid codeword from the set generated by the same coder when given such a shift, so that the digit sequence

$$0010111$$

corresponds to that codeword generated by the information digits 001.

Cyclic codes are of importance because the coder may be implemented very simply by means of a modulo-2 division circuit such as was described in section 7.2.

A codeword of length L with K information digits is referred to as an (L, K) cyclic code. The words of the (L, K) code, when formed by modulo-2 division, are the result of the following simple calculation. A binary number of length L, consisting of K information digits followed by $(L - K)$ padding zeros, is divided by a binary number of length $(L - K + 1)$

$$D_0 D_1 \ldots D_{L-K}$$

ensuring that, after division, the remainder, which must be of length $(L - K)$, will 'fit into' the space left by the $(L - K)$ padding zeros, forming the check digits. As an example, the divisor required to establish the members of the code set quoted above is

$$D_0 D_1 D_2 D_3 D_4$$
$$1\ 0\ 1\ 1\ 1$$

Division takes place thus (we are not interested in the quotient, only the remainder)

$$D_0 D_1 D_2 D_3 D_4 \overline{) I_0 I_1 I_2\ 0\ 0\ 0\ 0}$$

$$. \quad . \quad . \quad . \quad . \quad .$$
$$. \quad . \quad . \quad . \quad . \quad .$$
$$. \quad . \quad . \quad . \quad . \quad .$$
$$\overline{C_0 C_1 C_2 C_3}$$

The codeword is, then, the sum of dividend and remainder. Since addition and subtraction are identical in modulo-2 arithmetic, this codeword must be a perfect multiple of the divisor. This property is of great value in that it makes such a code ideally suited to error detection. It is simply necessary to divide the received codeword by the same divisor as was used in the initial code-generation operation. If the remainder is zero, the codeword is at least a valid member of the transmitted code set. With careful selection of the divisor and hence the code structure, it will also most probably be the correct transmitted codeword. We shall investigate the decoding of cyclic codes in the next section. However, it is worth mentioning at this stage that, although both error detection and error correction are possible, correction is considerably more difficult and costly to achieve.

As an example of the formation of a code, let us consider the generation of the word used above We presume the information digits to be

$$I_0 I_1 I_2$$
$$1\ 0\ 0$$

Division yields the result

$$
\begin{array}{r}
10111 \overline{) 1000000} \\
\underline{10111} \\
11100 \\
\underline{10111} \\
1011
\end{array}
$$

so that the remainder is

$$C_0 C_1 C_2 C_3$$
$$1\ 0\ 1\ 1$$

and the entire codeword

$$I_0 I_1 I_2 C_0 C_1 C_2 C_3$$
$$1\ 0\ 0\ 1\ 0\ 1\ 1$$

This coding procedure may be applied to generate seven codewords in the set corresponding to information digits

$$I_0 I_1 I_2 = 001, 010 \ldots 111$$

The codeword corresponding to information digits 000 is an all-zero word and is therefore not a member of the cyclic set of codewords. The complete code set is listed in table 7.4.

TABLE 7.4 COMPLETE
CYCLIC CODE SET

Cyclic Block Code	
Inf. Digits	Parity Digits
001	0111
010	1110
011	1001
100	1011
101	1100
110	0101
111	0010

The division required in forming a codeword may be performed by means of a linear sequential-switching circuit such as was introduced in section 7.2. Applying the method described therein, we arrive at the configuration illustrated in figure 7.2a. The basic binary number $I_0 I_1 I_2$ is entered serially, followed by four padding zeros. During the first three clock-pulses, division is accomplished. A serial output from the divider during this phase of operation could be taken, yielding the quotient. However the quotient is not of interest to us in forming the codeword. At the end of the fourth clock-pulse the remainder is available at the outputs of each of the register memory-elements. By opening the feedback loop around the register, the latter becomes a shift register which will feed the remainder digits into the communication channel. A simple method of instrumenting the entire coding operation so that the serial remainder digits are fitted into the space provided by the four trailing padding-zeros on the input information-digits is shown in figure 7.2b.

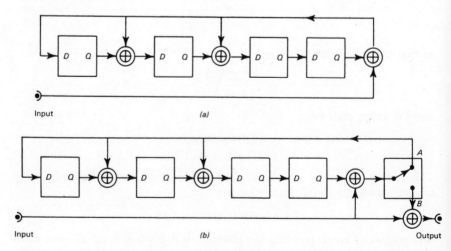

Figure 7.2 (a) Modulo-2 division circuit used for forming the parity-check digits of the (7, 3) cyclic code; (b) the complete coder

This description of the cyclic coding procedure raises one important question. How do we select the divisor which determines the properties of the code? Unfortunately no simple answer to this question can be given. A number of different classes of cyclic codes are known and some have been extensively investigated. The strategy of choice of class of code and code structure within a given class is a problem that is beyond the scope of this text. None the less, some useful pointers can be provided to indicate the general nature of the codes that are available.

The code described above is a member of the class of 'maximal length' codes. Codes in this class are usually applied in a slightly modified form, since any basic (L, K) maximal length code is of length

$$L = 2^K - 1$$

For values of K of a reasonable size to be useful, the code exhibits high redundancy. For example, a code operating upon only five information digits would be unusual. Yet even with this small number of information digits the length of the code is 31 digits and the information digits only form about 20 per cent of the total codeword.

A well-known and intensively investigated class of codes is known as the BCH set. BCH stands for Bose Chaudhuri Hocqenghem, the names of the three innovators of the class. A short BCH $(15, 5)$ code which is reasonably easy to instrument, in so far as error-correction circuitry is concerned, may be generated by the divisor

$$10100110111$$

Again, this code exhibits a considerable measure of redundancy, although it is an improvement upon the $(31, 5)$ maximal length code. It is capable of correcting all patterns of three or fewer errors within each code block.

The selection of the proportion of redundancy within a code block depends very much upon the nature of the application of the code. For example, if the code is only required to provide error detection (such as might be the case in the transmission of digital data over switched or leased telephone-circuits) correction may be most economically achieved by requesting a repeat of invalid received codewords. This system of operation, which implies the existence of a return channel from receiver to transmitter is known as ARQ, which stands for 'automatic request repeat'. ARQ is the C.C.I.T.T. recommended mode of operation for teleprinter links, as well as finding frequent application in data links. When the ARQ mode is used, the proportion of parity to information digits will be small. As examples of practical cyclic codes which have been developed specifically for this application, we have the $(240, 228)$ code generated by the thirteen-digit divisor

$$1000010000101$$

and the C.C.I.T.T. V41 code, a $(256, 240)$ code generated by the seventeen-digit divisor

$$10001000000100001$$

These codes are designed for operation in a general signalling equipment such that each very long informational-digit sequence may be fabricated at will by the user from successions of smaller informational words. The intention is to place no restriction on the manner in which the user's data is packed into the informational sequence. Such codes are referred to as 'transparent' for this reason.

To demonstrate the level of performance which may be expected of such codes, the second specified above has been found to fail to detect only sixteen erroneous 256 digit blocks in a total of 222 034 erroneous received blocks. The greatest probability of failure to detect errors within blocks occurs when the number of errors in the block is small. A large number of errors is very likely to be detected. In contrast, if this code were considered for error correction, the presence of a large number of errors would lead to an uncorrectable situation. Only relatively small numbers of errors could be corrected. Thus the philosophy that use be made of cyclic codes for their error-detecting, rather than error-correcting properties, when this is possible, seems a reasonable one.

Furthermore, since the problem of devising simple and economical error-correcting circuits for cyclic codes is a difficult one, the general trend has been to consider, for automatic error-correction either

(1) Less sophisticated non-cyclic codes, such as AUTOSPEC, discussed in the previous section, or

(2) Non-block codes: the 'recurrent' or 'convolutional' codes typified by those developed by D. W. Hagelbarger.[33] We shall discuss these codes, which have relatively simple error-correction circuits, in section 7.6.

The exceptions to these basic trends have involved the use of cyclic codes in an error-correcting mode and with high redundancy in extremely adverse single-path operating conditions. The classical example must be the instrumentation of telemetry and PCM television links from deep-space probes.[40] Here, the high capital expenditure required for the decoder implementation is mitigated by the inordinate cost of acquiring the data in the first place.

One final point worth noting is that it is the choice of divisor (that is, the code structure) which enables us to devise codes to combat either of the two basic situations in which errors tend to occur: namely burst or random errors.

7.5 Decoding Cyclic Codes

In this section we shall discuss the methods which may be used to decode cyclic codes, using as our example the maximal-length (7, 3) code described in the previous section. The same techniques may be taken to apply to other cyclic codes. The methods we shall investigate are

(1) Decoding for error detection alone
(2) Decoding to yield error detection and correction

In some circumstances, the use of error detection and correction is mandatory, if no return channel is available to request a message repeat. More commonly, a choice of strategy is possible in implementing a system. Although automatic error-correction appears attractive, some correction systems are sensitive to phenomena other than noise-induced errors. For example, slipped synchronisation may cause disastrous apparently correctable errors. Indeed, with our simple (7, 3) code, slipped synchronisation would simply yield another set of valid codewords so that no error could be registered. Total system failure in this way indicates a situation in which more reliance should be placed upon the use of code redundancy to detect, rather than correct errors. In general, any decoder can detect more errors than it can correct.

In section 6.6, we encountered the term 'Hamming distance'—the number of places in which two successive code words differ. If we examine the set of codewords in table 7.3, we find that the (7, 3) code has a Hamming distance of four. Consider, for example the differences between the two codewords

$$0 \begin{array}{|ccc|cc|c|} \hline 0 & 1 & 0 & 1 & 1 & 1 \\ 1 & 0 & 1 & 1 & 1 & 0 \\ \hline \end{array}$$

Both error detection and error correction are ultimately based upon the 'distance' properties of the code. In any (L, K) cyclic code there are K information digits and, at most, 2^K distinct combinations of these digits. Rejecting the all-zeros combination since it does not form a valid codeword in the cyclic set, there can only be $2^K - 1$ valid L-digit codewords. However, there are 2^L possible combinations of 1s and 0s in blocks of L. It follows that not all of the possible combinations of L binary digits will be valid codewords. In our (7, 3) maximal-length cyclic code, there are seven valid codewords out of a possible 128 different combinations of seven binary digits. Any transmission errors which do not generate another valid codeword must, therefore, indicate the presence of an error simply because the received codeword is invalid.

A single error results in a received codeword which is 'nearest' in the table of all codewords (in the Hamming-distance sense) to the valid transmitted codeword. It is therefore both detectable and correctable.

If two errors occur, the result will be equidistant between words. Thus 0010111 received as 1010011 could be interpreted as corresponding to the information digits 001 (correctly) or 100 or 111 (both incorrectly). Two errors in the (7, 3) codeword lead to a detectable, but uncorrectable errorpattern.

If three errors occur, the 'nearest' codeword will not be the one which was transmitted. Any attempt at error correction will result in an error of fact, although the decoder will not realise this.

If four errors occur in our (7, 3) code, then because the Hamming distance is four, they may (but will not necessarily) result in the formation of another valid codeword. Thus 0010111 received with four errors: 1011100 is the valid codeword corresponding to the information digits 101. We are obliged, at the receiver, to accept it as such! This is an undetectable error.

As far as the instrumentation of the decoder is concerned, let us turn first to the detection of errors. We see that provided fewer than three errors occur, detection of the presence of these errors must be possible. In fact, any cyclic code of minimum Hamming distance H will guarantee the detection of $H-1$ errors. Notice that the term minimum Hamming distance is used. Although the (7, 3) code has a constant Hamming distance, this is by no means a general attribute of cyclic codes. For example, the C.C.I.T.T. V41 error-detecting code described in the previous section exhibits a variable Hamming distance, as the reader may easily verify by deriving the first few codewords and comparing them.

Even given a constant Hamming distance, the detection of more than $H - 1$ errors may well be possible. In our example, it is only those (relatively rare) situations in which more than three errors occur in such a pattern as to generate another valid member of the code set that an undetected error will occur. Herein lies the relative strength of the cyclic code as an error detector as opposed to an error corrector.

One way in which the operation of error detection can be achieved is to employ the division circuit used to generate the code. We saw in the previous section that the division of the received codeword by the generating binary number 10111 will result in a non-zero remainder only if the codeword is not a valid member of the set listed in table 7.3. Thus the error detector is simply a division circuit of the same configuration as that used in coding. This results in an economy of plant in instrumenting two-way links, since the same hardware may be used for both coding and decoding. During decoding, the outputs from the stages of the shift register which holds the remainder after division are taken to a binary comparator which generates a logical FALSE when the register stages hold any other final result than zero. Figure 7.3a illustrates such a decoder. The binary-comparator output provides an 'error detected' signal which, given two-way working, can be used to initiate a 'request repeat' signal to the transmitter.

The error-correction decoders we shall consider are

(1) Threshold decoding

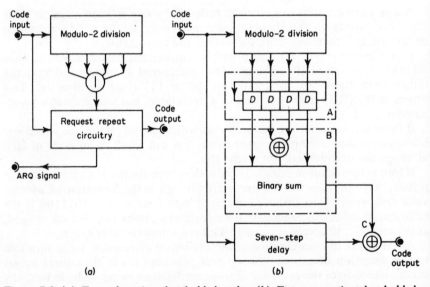

(a)   (b)

Figure 7.3 (a) Error-detecting threshold decoder. (b) Error-correcting threshold decoder, with the error syndrome held in the cycling register A and identified by the threshold logic, B, when the binary sum is greater than $10_2 (= 2)$ at which time the input C to the correction gate is set from 1 to 0

(2) Permutation decoding

(3) Maximum-likelihood decoding

These various decoders have slightly different properties and performance levels. The maximum-likelihood detector is the best, but is costly to implement and not technologically feasible for long cyclic codes.

Notice that the ability of a system to combat either of the two common error patterns, burst or random, is determined not by the decoder which can be any one of the three specified above, but by the coder which must generate a code suitable for the environment in which it is to operate. In any decoding operation, one of three error conditions may be brought into being by the presence of errors within a codeword

(1) Correctable errors

(2) Detectable, but not correctable errors

(3) Undetectable and therefore uncorrectable errors

Just as the detection of $H - 1$ errors is guaranteed by a cyclic code of minimum Hamming distance H, so the correction, in principle at least, of (the integer part of) $(H - 1)/2$ errors should be possible.

Let us investigate the technique known as *threshold* decoding first. In order to aid our discussion, let us suppose that the transmitted codeword be represented as

$$T \equiv I_0 I_1 \ldots I_{K-1} C_0 C_1 \ldots C_{J-1}$$

We shall further assume that the received codeword be denoted R and that the divisor employed to generate the code be denoted

$$D \equiv D_0 D_1 \ldots D_{L-K}$$

The presence of errors in the received codeword may be considered as being the result of adding (modulo-2) an error word

$$E \equiv E_0 E_1 \ldots E_{L-1}$$

to the transmitted codeword. Any E_k which is non-zero may be thought of as contributing an error. At the receiver, we have to extract, as far as is possible, the errors from the codeword

$$R = T \oplus E$$

Now, because T is, itself, an exact integer multiple of the divisor D, it follows that the *remainder* after dividing R by D will equal the remainder after dividing E by D. This conclusion may be interpreted as follows. Either division

$$\frac{R}{D} \quad \text{or} \quad \frac{E}{D}$$

will yield the same remainder which thus uniquely determines the error pattern of a correctable number of errors in the received codeword. We refer to the remainder corresponding to any given error-pattern as a *syndrome*. From the syndrome, we hope to be able to determine

(1) The nature of the error; that is, whether it is correctable, and

(2) The precise location of the error if it is correctable.

These aims imply the existence, at the decoder, of either a 'look-up' table or memory recording all possible correctable-error patterns and the corresponding syndromes by means of which they may be identified, or some logical circuitry capable of immediately establishing any of the entries in the look-up table. The first technique would appear to require an overwhelming amount of computing machinery and for that reason and in view of the superior performance of the maximum-likelihood decoder, which we have yet to discuss and which is of similar complexity, could well be considered unsuitable.

The second technique appears much more attractive. We can certainly devise such a system for our (7, 3) code. Table 7.5 lists the error patterns and corresponding syndromes for single, double and triple errors on the information digits. The method we shall investigate could, in principle, be extended to provide for correction of errors within the parity digits as well. Notice that the number of binary digits in each syndrome indicates the nature of the error. If the sum is zero, no errors have occurred. If the sum is one, three errors have occurred; two, and two errors have occurred. Neither of these last two cases is correctable. If the number of binary 1s is three, a single correctable error has occurred. Now, it is possible in the case of this particular code to devise a combinational-logic circuit which generates a binary sum at its output in such a way as to pinpoint the error in the received codeword, if it is correctable. Consider the decoder illustrated in figure 7.3b. The received codeword enters both the division circuit, which has the same structure as the divider used for encoding, and a buffer register. When division has been completed, the remainder is available and is transferred into the cycling-syndrome register. The first information digit is ready to emerge from the buffer register. The combinational logic is such as to obtain an indication of the binary sum of three 1s in the syndrome corresponding to an error in the first digit. The output of the combinational logic will therefore be a binary 1 and will serve to correct the incorrect first digit by modulo-2 addition at the exclusive-OR gate at the output of the buffer. If the syndrome does not correspond to the first digit being in error, but to the second, a binary zero will be present at the output of the combinational logic and the first information digit will emerge from the decoder unchanged.

If it is the second digit which is in error, the syndrome will be that corresponding to an error word

$$0100000$$

TABLE 7.5 ERROR PATTERNS AND SYNDROMES

Error Pattern $E_0E_1E_2$	$E_3E_4E_5E_6$	Syndrome $S_0S_1S_2S_3$	Binary Sum	Comment
1 0 0	0 0 0 0	1 0 1 1		
0 1 0	0 0 0 0	1 1 1 0	$11_2 = 3$	Correctable
0 0 1	0 0 0 0	0 1 1 1		
1 1 0	0 0 0 0	0 1 0 1		Uncorrectable
1 0 1	0 0 0 0	1 1 0 0	$10_2 = 2$	but
0 1 1	0 0 0 0	1 0 0 1		Detectable
1 1 1	0 0 0 0	0 0 1 0	$01_2 = 1$	
0 0 0	0 0 0 0	0 0 0 0	$00_2 = 0$	No Error

That is 1110. The syndrome register will step this syndrome around by one place to create the number 1101 and this will be recognised by the combinational logic. Thus on the second clock-pulse after division has been completed, the conditions will have been fulfilled which will obtain correction of the second digit. The same argument can, of course, be applied to the possibility of a single error in the third informational digit. By extending the logic, the binary sums zero, one and two could also be detected, leading to a comprehensive analysis of the errors detectable in the codeword.

The threshold detector, as described here, appears to be the essence of simplicity and economy. Unfortunately, no general rules exist for the specification of the contents of the combinational logic. For practical codes, the technique is of limited usefulness because the logic circuitry becomes very complex, when it can be deduced.

A somewhat simpler system to implement is known as *permutation* decoding. The information digits of the received codeword are used to regenerate the parity digits at the decoder. These are compared with the received parity-digits. If they are identical, no errors were incurred during transmission. In fact, if the received and reconstructed parity-digits differ in only one place, the received information-digits must be presumed correct, since the recomputed codeword lies within unit distance of the received codeword. This condition would enable correction of the single correctable error when it occurred within the parity-check digits, rather than the information digits. The correction of incorrect parity-digits might be of interest if, for example, it was desired to clean up the codewords at a repeater station in a communication link.

If, in the case of the (7, 3) code, more than one difference exists between the received and re-computed parity-check digits, an error has been detected. It may be corrected in the following way. The digits $I_1I_2C_0$, $I_2C_0C_1$, $C_0C_1C_2$, ... are used successively as information digits. New parity-check digits are formed until one set is found which agrees with the received parity-check digits exactly. For example, suppose that the codeword 1001011 is received as 1011011. The sequence of operations performed during decoding is that listed in table 7.6. The information digits taken from the received codeword, and used to generate the parity digits in each shift are enclosed in boxes. Notice that the first digit(s) preceding the digits used

TABLE 7.6 SEQUENCE OF OPERATIONS FOR (7, 3) CODE

Shift Number	Permutation Decoding Received Codeword							
	1	0	**1**	1	0	1	1	← Third information-digit depicted in error
0	[1	0	1]	1	1	0	0	
1	1	[0	1	1]	1	0	0	
2	0	1	[1	1	0]	0	1	
3	1	0	0	[1	0	1]	1	← Received and regenerated parity sequences agree
4					[0	1	1]	Information digits have been
5	[1]					1	1	corrected and shifting may cease
6	[1	0]					[1]	

Note: Only the boxed digits are abstracted from the received codeword. The rest are regenerated as information digits are the tail-end of the regenerated parity-check sequence, for the shifts after that at 'zero'. For example, on the first shift, the first received digit is 1 because the last reconstituted parity-check digit corresponding to the digits 011 used as information digits is a 1, not because the first received digit is a 1.

The third method of decoding is known as *maximum-likelihood, minimum-distance* or *correlation* decoding.[40] We have seen, in section 1.24, that cross-correlation is a method of determining how 'alike' two signals $v_m(t)$ and $v_n(t)$ are, by establishing a correlation coefficient

$$\rho_{mn} = R_{mn}(0)\{R_{mm}(0)R_{nn}(0)\}^{-\frac{1}{2}}$$

If the two signals are of the same finite energy, then $R_{mm}(0)$ and $R_{nn}(0)$ will be the same, and the comparison need only be made on the basis of examining $R_{mn}(0)$, where

$$R_{mn}(\tau) = \int_{-\infty}^{+\infty} v_m(t)v_n(t+\tau)\,\mathrm{d}t$$

The correlation decoder operates on the principle of determining the cross-correlation between the received (and possibly corrupt) codeword and each member of a set of template codewords identical to the set of valid codewords for the coder in question. Since the codeword digit sequences are 'discrete' rather than continuous functions of time, we may replace the cross-correlation integral with a simple summation performing essentially the same task. In the case of our previous example, we have a template set, as defined by table 7.4, corresponding to the seven valid codewords

$$I_0 I_1 I_2 C_0 C_1 C_2 C_3$$

We may define a received digit sequence

$$I_0' I_1' I_2' C_0' C_1' C_2' C_3'$$

If no digit errors are encountered during transmission, then, for one of the templates in the set

$$I_a' = I_a \quad \text{for } a = 0 \text{ to } 2$$
$$C_a' = C_a \quad \text{for } a = 0 \text{ to } 3$$

The cross-correlation between the received codeword and members of the template set is given by the summation

$$R = I_0 I_0' + I_1 I_1' + \ldots + C_3 C_3'$$

and for each received data word, this summation must be performed seven times, once for each member of the template set. The template producing the largest value of R is then presumed to correspond to the correct codeword, even if the codeword, as received, contained errors.

To illustrate the principle of correlation decoding, suppose that we receive an uncorrupted codeword 0010111 corresponding to the information-digit sequence 001. We compare this, after the manner of table 7.7, with the templates corresponding to the seven possible valid codewords, computing the correlation summation for each. Clearly, the largest value of R, which is 4, corresponds to the transmitted codeword, as we should hope.

TABLE 7.7 CORRELATION DECODING

I_0'	I_1'	I_2'	C_0'	C_1'	C_2'	C_3'								
0	0	1	0	1	1	1				Error-free Transmission				
Template Set							Digit for Digit Products							Sum
I_0	I_1	I_2	C_0	C_1	C_2	C_3	I_0I_0'	I_1I_1'	I_2I_2'	C_0C_0'	C_1C_1'	C_2C_2'	C_3C_3'	R
0	0	1	0	1	1	1	0	0	1	0	1	1	1	4
0	1	0	1	1	1	0	0	0	0	0	1	1	0	2
0	1	1	1	0	0	1	0	0	1	0	0	0	1	2
1	0	0	1	0	1	1	0	0	0	0	0	1	1	2
1	0	1	1	1	0	0	0	0	1	0	1	0	0	2
1	1	0	0	1	0	1	0	0	0	0	1	0	1	2
1	1	1	0	0	1	0	0	0	1	0	0	1	0	2

Next we shall consider the effect of transmission errors on decoding. Suppose that the same transmitted codeword, 0010111, is received with just one error: 0110111. If we again perform the correlation operation, we list the results given in table 7.8. Again we can clearly identify the correct codeword, since the value of R corresponding to the information digits 001 is still larger than the values of R corresponding to the other six combinations of information digits. Notice that the values of R corresponding to the information digits 010, 011, 110, 111 have increased, however.

TABLE 7.8. EFFECT OF ONE
TRANSMISSION ERROR

	Received Codeword						
	I_0'	I_1'	I_2'	C_0'	C_1'	C_2'	C_3'
	0	1	1	0	1	1	1
	Template Set Inf. Digits						
	I_0	I_1	I_2	R			
	0	0	1	4			
	0	1	0	3			
	0	1	1	3			
	1	0	0	2			
	1	0	1	2			
	1	1	0	3			
	1	1	1	3			

If two errors are incurred, yielding a received codeword 0111111, the values of R change to those given in table 7.9. Now we are unable to correct the error we know must exist, because no single value of R predominates. Apart from registering an error *detection*, we can do nothing further to clean up the received codeword. In fact, on the evidence we are given by the correlator, the received codeword could equally well have been any one of three possible transmitted codewords, corresponding to the information digits 001, 010, 011. That this is indeed the case may be verified by considering first the corrupted, received codeword 0111111, and observing that this is equivalent to the codewords 0010111, 0101110 and 0111001 each with two errors.

TABLE 7.9 EFFECT OF TWO
TRANSMISSION ERRORS

Received Codeword						
I_0'	I_1'	I_3'	C_0'	C_1'	C_2'	C_3'
0	**1**	1	**1**	1	1	1

Template Set Inf. Digits			R
I_0	I_1	I_2	
0	0	1	4
0	1	0	4
0	1	1	4
1	0	0	3
1	0	1	3
1	1	0	3
1	1	1	3

To complete the picture, suppose that three errors occur: **0111101**. The corresponding values of R are listed in table 7.10 and it can be seen that in this case we are most likely to assume that the codeword corresponding to the information digits 011 is closest to the transmitted codeword: a completely false judgement!

TABLE 7.10 EFFECT OF THREE
TRANSMISSION ERRORS

Received Codeword						
I_0'	I_1'	I_3'	C_0'	C_1'	C_2'	C_3'
0	**1**	1	**1**	1	**0**	1

Template Set Inf. Digits			R
I_0	I_1	I_2	
0	0	1	3
0	1	0	3
0	1	1	4
1	0	0	2
1	0	1	3
1	1	0	3
1	1	1	2

The electronic implementation of such a decoding system is, at first sight, fairly straightforward. The system depicted in figure 7.4 would serve to achieve the required result. However, we have described only a very simple coding technique. In practice, much longer codes have to be used. The implementation of the decoder then becomes a very real problem. The method shown in figure 7.4 seems sensible but it is in fact inherently redundant of computing 'operations'. Specialised computer-techniques are used when the need for a minimum-distance decoding becomes necessary. The decoder then becomes, essentially, a digital computer

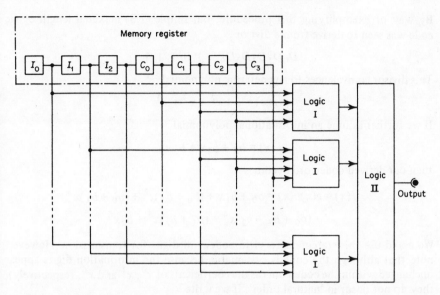

Figure 7.4 Minimum-distance or correlation decoding for the cyclic (7, 3) code. LOGIC I
performs binary addition to yield correlation coefficients R_k. LOGIC II *identifies the largest
R_k and presents the appropriate digital output corresponding to that value of k*

designed for just this purpose. One complex high-speed decoding system of this
kind was constructed and operated as a part of the Mariner Martian reconnaissance
spacecraft telemetry-system. This vehicle was launched during 1969.[40]

7.6 Polynomial Codes

The cyclic codes described in the previous section are members of a more general
class of block codes known as *polynomial codes*. Suppose we write any L-digit
codeword as a 'message polynomial' in x, the coefficients of which are determined
as the codeword binary digits

$$f(x) = a_0 + a_1 x + a_2 x^2 + \ldots \ldots + a_{L-1} x^{L-1}$$

where the a_k can take on only values 0 and 1 and addition is modulo-2. Here x is a
dummy variable; it is not assigned an actual *value*. Then the implication behind
error detection decoding is that some other polynomial $g(x)$ must exist, such that
the remainder, after polynomial division of $f(x)$ by $g(x)$, is zero. This therefore
requires that all $f(x)$ polynomials (one $f(x)$ for each codeword in a given set) must
be factorable, with $g(x)$ as a common factor. We may thus define the generation
of an (L, K) block code in terms of the multiplication of a K-digit *information
polynomial*

$$h(x) = b_0 + b_1 x + b_2 x^2 + \ldots \ldots + b_{K-1} x^{K-1}$$

with the characteristic *generating polynomial* $g(x)$ so that

$$f(x) = g(x) h(x)$$

By way of exemplifying this procedure, our simple $(7,3)$ maximal length cyclic code was seen to derive from a divisor

$$D_0 D_1 D_2 D_3 D_4 \quad 1\ 0\ 1\ 1\ 1$$

This divisor equivalences to a generating polynomial

$$g(x) = 1 + x^2 + x^3 + x^4$$

If we further assume an informational polynomial

$$h(x) = b_0 + b_1 x + b_2 x^2$$

then our derived codeword becomes

$$f(x) = g(x)h(x) = b_0 + b_1 x + (b_0 + b_2)x^2 + (b_0 + b_1)x^3$$
$$+ (b_0 + b_1 + b_2)x^4 + (b_1 + b_2)x^5 + b_2 x^6$$

We could use this statement to yield codeword digits for transmission. However, note that although the code is systematic, because the information digits appear unchanged within the codeword (as the coefficients of x^0, x^1 and x^6, respectively), they do not occur in 'natural order'. If we write

$$I_0 = b_0, \quad I_1 = b_1, \quad I_2 = (b_0 + b_2)$$

then we may force the code towards natural order. Solving the above equations, we find that

$$b_0 = I_0, \quad b_1 = I_1, \quad b_2 = (I_0 + I_2)$$

Substituting into $f(x)$, we have a generated codeword specified by the new polynomial

$$I_0 + I_1 x + I_2 x^2 + (I_0 + I_1)x^3 + (I_1 + I_2)x^4$$
$$+ (I_0 + I_1 + I_2)x^5 + (I_0 + I_2)x^6$$

This polynomial allows us to express parity digits directly and calculably in terms of information digits thus (note again: addition modulo-2)

$$C_0 = I_0 + I_1$$
$$C_1 = I_1 + I_2$$
$$C_2 = I_0 + I_1 + I_2$$
$$C_3 = I_0 + I_2$$

The reader may readily verify that the application of these rules leads to the code set for the $(7,3)$ cyclic code, defined in table 7.3. In using a polynomial approach to the generation of block codewords, we adopt a formalisation of the modulo-2 arithmetic used previously to assist in the description of coder operation. This formalisation has the useful consequence of permitting a more compact statement of code structure, in terms of the generating polynomial. Thus the C.C.I.T.T. V41 $(256,240)$ code may be derived using a generating polynomial

$$g(x) = 1 + x^4 + x^{11} + x^{16}$$

The reader will frequently encounter polynomial codes specified in this manner; an alternative is to present the defining binary number $D_0 D_1 \ldots D_{L-K}$ in octal form. Of course, the true value of the polynomial approach lies not in such utilitarian abbreviation but in the power it confers upon the coding theorist in the development of new code structures. While it is beyond the scope of a text of this nature to delve too deeply into coding theory, it is perhaps appropriate that some further areas of the map be sketched in, as a means of easing the interaction between theorist and practising engineer.

In order for the codeword polynomials to be factorable by generator polynomials, it is necessary that the coefficients be elements of a 'finite field'. This means that the coefficients a_k must be chosen from a set of digits which contain a finite number of members and which obey a specific set of rules regarding arithmetic manipulation. In our examples, this set has consisted simply of the binary digits 0 and 1. The set is finite, containing two members only. The finite field is very frequently referred to as a Galois field, being named after its discoverer. A Galois field containing q members is denoted GF(q). The binary set is thus written as GF(2). Manipulation rules in GF(q) parallel those employed in GF(2) which, essentially, embody the principles of modulo-2 arithmetic, as we have so far been using it. In GF(q) we may summarise the rules of manipulation thus

(1) Associative, distributive and commutative laws apply, as in ordinary arithmetic.

(2) Elements may be combined by means of additive or multiplicative operations the results of which must also be elements within GF(q) (whence $1 + 1 = 0$, in GF(2), for example).

(3) The field must contain additive and multiplicative elements 0 and 1 such that $a + 0 = a$ and $a.1 = a$

(4) In order that we may invoke the usual concepts of subtraction and division, we note the existence of the additive inverse element $-a$ (so that $a + (-a) = 0$) and the multiplicative inverse element a^{-1} (so that $a(a^{-1}) = 1$).

A consequence of the definition of a Galois field in this way is that q is not arbitrary. It may be prime (2, 3, 5, 7, 11 ...) or the power of a prime (4, 8, 9 ....). These restrictions result in there being a unique field for each valid q, in which the elements combine according to the manipulation rules, in one and only one set of ways. By way of example, addition and multiplication in GF(3) is performed after the manner indicated by table 7.11.

To illustrate the significance of Galois fields in the definition of code structures, consider the generator polynomial

$$g(x) = 1 + x^2 + x^3 + x^4$$

used to define the (7, 3) maximal length cyclic code. This polynomial is referred to as 'primitive in GF(2)'. This means that $g(x)$ is not, itself, factorable as a product of lesser order polynomials *also* derived in GF(2). The concept of a 'primitive polynomial' is analogous to that of a prime number in ordinary arithmetic. Primitive polynomials, like prime numbers, are found by trial and error and, also like prime numbers, are available, tabulated in standard reference works[27] and scientific papers.

TABLE 7.11 ADDITION AND MULTIPLICATION IN GF(3)

⊕	0	1	2
0	0	1	2
1	1	2	0
2	2	0	1

⊙	0	1	2
0	0	0	0
1	0	1	2
2	0	2	1

Stated formally, to *define* a maximal-length cyclic code for a q-state (q-symbol) transmission, it is *required* that its generating polynomial be a primitive polynomial in GF(q). The many other polynomial codes have formal definitions in terms of attributes of the mathematics of Galois fields. Although the majority of codes are based upon a two-state (binary) transmission format, it is possible to conceive of circumstances in which multistate transmission might suggest the use of non-binary codes. For example, high-speed data transmission involves the use of four- or eight-symbol sets, often using a multiphase phase-shift keying (see chapter 8) to achieve this.

7.7 Maximal Length Shift Register Sequences[27,51,53]

Our previous discussions of cyclic block coding and modulo-2 algebra lead us to the topic of *maximal length shift register sequences*. Such sequences are, in fact, periodic replications of possible maximal length cyclic block codewords. As we shall see in sections 7.9, 7.11 and 8.5 they are of importance in providing 'pseudo-random' scrambling and test functions for communication purposes. The striking advantage of maximal length sequences is the ease by which they may be generated and statistically characterised. The generator consists of a K-stage shift register with modulo-2 ('linear') feedback, figure 7.5. With appropriate feedback connections, such a generator creates a maximal-length pseudorandom sequence (output B) with a period of $L = 2^K - 1$ digits. That this is so can be appreciated by observing that a K-stage register is capable of assuming 2^K possible states (the 2^K possible combinations of K binary digits in the parallel output word A, figure 7.5). Of these states, one (the all zeros state) is 'prohibited' (or the generator would continually

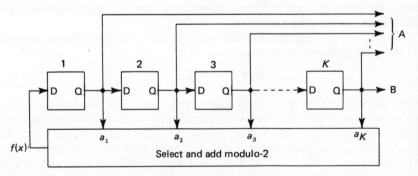

Figure 7.5 K-stage feedback shift-register. A: parallel K-tuple output word. B: serial pseudorandom sequence

cycle only zeros). Thus on each clock pulse, a state change to one of (at *most*) $2^K - 1$ states may take place. To ensure maximal length sequence generation, correct feedback connections must be established. A general statement of the feedback connections may be made by defining a polynomial feedback function

$$f(x) = 1 + a_1 x + a_2 x^2 + \ldots a_K x^K$$

addition being, as usual, over GF(2) (that is, 'modulo-2') with the tap weights $a_k = 0$ or 1. For this function to generate a maximum length sequence, it must satisfy certain criteria which, although beyond the scope of our consideration, are well-documented and are, for completeness, stated here. They require that $f(x)$ be

(1) irreducible, and
(2) of maximum exponent.

TABLE 7.12 MAXIMAL LENGTH REGISTER PROPERTIES

Register length	K	10	12	14	16	18	20	22	24
Sequence length	L	1023	4095	16 383	65 535	262 143	524 287	1 048 575	2 097 151
Number of sequences	N	60	144	756	2 048	8 064	24 000	120 032	276 480

The number, N, of such polynomials can be found from table 7.12. Even for quite short register lengths a considerable choice of possible sequences is available simply by selecting the correct tap weights. Thus for a ten-stage register, of more than a thousand allowable tap weights which effect the connection of at least two register outputs (one of which must be the last-stage output) to the input, *sixty* result in the generation of maximal length sequences. We note

(1) that the actual choice of these significant tap-settings may be achieved by reference to published tables,
(2) that individual maximal length sequences so generated are not merely end-about shifts of each other and that
(3) from these sequences, groupings may be determined with excellent orthogonality properties, particularly for large L.

We consider next the important properties of the maximal length sequence itself. Our interest lies in its elementary statistics, autocorrelation function and finally in its power spectrum, when realised as a two-state logic signal. We assume binary digits to be represented as bipolar non-return to zero signalling waveshapes (see section 8.1) with binary $1 \equiv +1$ V and binary $0 \equiv -1$ v. We further assume the digit duration to be T s so that the period is LT s. We expect, therefore, a line spectrum with fundamental frequency and line spacing equal to $(LT)^{-1}$ Hz. For the maximal length sequence

(1) The total number of 1s and the total number of 0s within a period differs by 1. The sequence thus exhibits a mean value of L^{-1} v and a d.c. power

spectral component $(L^{-2})\delta(f)$ which tends to zero for large values of L. Under this circumstance, the pseudorandom sequence is closely a zero-mean process.

(2) If one period of the pseudorandom sequence is compared against a (non-periodic) shifted version of itself, the number of terms that are the same differ from those that are different by one.

This second property allows us to compute first the autocorrelation function and then, by Fourier transformation, the power spectrum of the pseudorandom sequence. The approach parallels that used in section 1.27 to calculate the autocorrelation function of a truly random sequence. Let us assume a register clocked so that the digit duration is T and let us also assume that digit amplitudes of ± 1 are generated. We may write the autocorrelation function in normalised form as

$$R(\tau) = 1/LT \int_0^{LT} s(t)s(t + \tau)\mathrm{d}t$$

For shifts which are an integer multiple of the period LT it is clear that R takes on a value of unity. For all other shifts greater than $\pm T$ from an integer multiple period shift, it can be shown that

$$s(t)s(t + \tau) = s(t + \tau'); \quad \tau \neq \tau'$$

or, 'shift and multiply' results in the same sequence but with yet another shift. Since it is a fundamental property of maximal-length sequences that the number of zeros balances the number of ones, but for one digit (for example, for $K = 10$, $L = 1024$ and there will be 511 ones and 512 zeros) the value of R in this region will be simply $1/L$. In the remaining region, wherein τ is within $\pm T$ of an integer multiple period shift, the autocorrelation function will fall linearly from unity

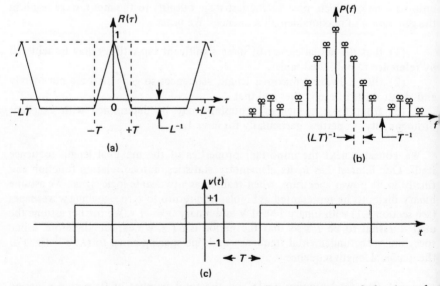

Figure 7.6 (a) Autocorrelation function and (b) power spectral density of a maximal-length pseudorandom sequence (c)

(at zero or integer multiple shift) to its minimum value of $1/L$. In this respect, the autocorrelation function resembles that of the purely random data sequence (for the same reasons, as described in section 1.27). The autocorrelation function is thus as sketched in figure 7.6a being, itself, periodic of period LT. Fourier transformation yields the power spectrum, which may be written as

$$P(f) = L^{-2}\delta(f) + (1 + 1/L)^2 \operatorname{sinc}^2(fT) \sum_{\substack{k=-\infty \\ k \neq 0}}^{+\infty} \delta(f - k/LT)$$

This spectrum is illustrated in figure 7.6b.

7.8 Convolution or Recurrent Codes[33]

The block code represents a non-redundant binary word by means of a fixed-length redundant binary word containing extra digits which provide a parity check. Decoding takes place on a word-for-word basis at the receiver. An alternative strategy is employed in convolution coding. Here, the non-redundant binary words are coded into a sequence which still contains information and parity bits but now no distinct coded-word block is available. Whereas the various block codes are classifiable according to precise mathematical definitions this has not proved to be possible with convolution codes. Furthermore, the specification of error-correcting decoders can be difficult for some convolution codes. None the less, convolution codes are easily implemented and offer performance which is at least comparable with block codes of similar redundancy.

Figure 7.7a illustrates the general form of a simple convolution encoder. This particular example builds in a considerable measure of redundancy—every other digit is a check digit. As the diagram indicates, the parity-check digits and information digits appear simultaneously and are interleaved for transmission through the channel by a multiplexing switch actuated at twice the digit rate. At the receiver, the information and parity digits are separated and the parity digits are compared with a regenerated parity-sequence derived from the received information digits. This comparison is used as a means of indicating the presence of errors in the received digit sequence.

As an example of the formation and detection of a convolution code, consider the coder illustrated in figure 7.7b. Here, the multiplexing switches are omitted to simplify the description of the operation of the system. The parity and information digits are presumed to be transmitted in exact synchronism by means of a pair of similar parallel channels.

Suppose, then, that the information source yields binary words

$$\leftarrow \text{WORD 1} \rightarrow \leftarrow \text{WORD 2} \rightarrow$$

$$I_0\,I_1\,I_2\,I_3 \qquad I_0\,I_1\,I_2\,I_3\,\ldots$$
$$0\ \ 0\ \ 0\ \ 1 \qquad 0\ \ 1\ \ 1\ \ 0\,\ldots$$

The first word is inserted, digit by digit, into the shift register which, for the sake of simplicity, we shall regard as having initially contained the digit sequence 0000.

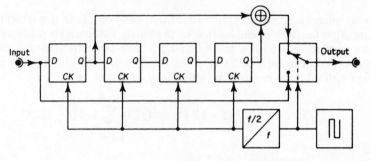

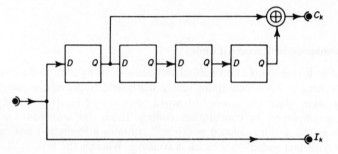

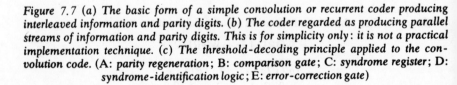

Figure 7.7 (a) The basic form of a simple convolution or recurrent coder producing interleaved information and parity digits. (b) The coder regarded as producing parallel streams of information and parity digits. This is for simplicity only: it is not a practical implementation technique. (c) The threshold-decoding principle applied to the convolution code. (A: parity regeneration; B: comparison gate; C: syndrome register; D: syndrome-identification logic; E: error-correction gate)

The parity sequence is generated thus

Initial
Contents $\leftarrow$ WORD 1 $\rightarrow$ $\leftarrow$ WORD 2 $\rightarrow$

$I_0 \; I_1 \; I_2 \; I_3 \; I_0 \; I_1 \; I_2 \; I_3 \; \ldots$

0 0 0 0 0   0 0 1 0 1 1 0 $\ldots$

$$\oplus$$

$C_0 C_1 C_2 C_3 C_4 C_5 C_6 C_7 \ldots$

0 0 0 1 0 1 0 0 $\ldots$

Given that the multiplexing switches were in operation, the output from the decoder would then be

$$I_0 C_0 I_1 C_1 I_2 C_2 I_3 C_3 I_0 C_4 I_1 C_5 I_2 C_6 I_3 C_7 \ldots$$

0 0 0 0 0 0 1 1 0 0 1 1 1 0 0 0 $\ldots$

Note that the parity-check digits can no longer be ascribed to a single informational codeword. This means that the code is not a block code, although it is still a systematic code, since the information digits are transmitted unchanged.

Error correction, although difficult to define mathematically, in comparison with correction in block codes, may be performed by two techniques

(1) Threshold decoding
(2) Sequential, or probabilistic decoding[47]

Threshold decoding follows the same general pattern described in the previous section when it was applied to block codes. Normally, the first task would consist of the demultiplexing of the information and parity digits at the decoder. However, this operation is unnecessary in the simplified schematic of figure 7.7c. If no errors exist in the received digit sequence, the reconstructed parity digits

$$C_0'' C_1'' C_2'' C_3'' C_4'' C_5'' C_6'' C_7'' \ldots$$

and the received parity digits

$$C_0' C_1' C_2' C_3' C_4' C_5' C_6' C_7' \ldots$$

will be identical. The syndrome generated by comparing these two sequences will be entirely zero

$$S_0 S_1 S_2 S_3 S_4 S_5 S_6 S_7 \ldots$$

0 0 0 0 0 0 0 0 $\ldots$

Consequently, the 'correction' output, from the AND gate, will be zero and the delayed information-digit sequence emerging from the output of the parity-digit regeneration register

$$I_0'' I_1'' I_2'' I_3'' I_0'' I_1'' I_2'' I_3'' \ldots$$

will remain unchanged.

Suppose that an error occurs in the information-digit sequence. For example, let I_3 of WORD 1 be in error

$$I_0 I_1 I_2 I_3 I_0 I_1 I_2 I_3 \ldots$$
$$0\ 0\ 0\ 1\ 0\ 1\ 1\ 0 \ldots$$
$$I_0' I_1' I_2' I_3' I_0' I_1' I_2' I_3' \ldots$$
$$0\ 0\ 0\ 0\ 0\ 1\ 1\ 0 \ldots$$

the recomputed parity digits will then be

$$C_0'' C_1'' C_2'' C_3'' C_4'' C_5'' C_6'' C_7'' \ldots$$
$$0\ 0\ 0\ 0\ 0\ 1\ 1\ 0 \ldots$$

which when compared with the received parity digits

$$C_0' C_1' C_2' C_3' C_4' C_5' C_6' C_7' \ldots$$

yield the syndrome sequence

$$S_0 S_1 S_2 S_3 S_4 S_5 S_6 S_7 \ldots$$
$$0\ 0\ 0\ 1\ 0\ 0\ 1\ 0 \ldots$$

and, because modulo-2 addition of the information digits to form the parity sequence takes place at points separated by two digits, it is the *pattern* ... 1001 ... which indicates an error. Not only does this pattern indicate the existence of an error, it also specifies its type and location: namely, an information-digit error on digit I_3 of WORD 1. The syndrome register logic is designed to detect this pattern, so that the AND gate will produce a 1 at its output when this condition arises. Delays within the decoder are so arranged that, at the time that this 1 appears at the output of the AND gate, the digit I_3 of WORD 1 is emerging from the parity regeneration shift register. The exclusive-OR gate at the decoder output then serves to correct the error, restoring I_3 to its pre-transmission value.

Because of the way in which the parity digits carry information concerning adjacent codewords, it is possible for this simple convolution-encoder to detect bursts of up to six digits in error, provided that at least nineteen correct digits separate the bursts. Naturally, the decoder logic has to be extended to cope with errors in the parity sequence as well as the information sequence. Even so, the decoder does not become excessively complicated.

In burst error situations, the threshold decoder performs well. Random errors, on the other hand, are more efficiently eliminated by means of sequential or probabilistic decoding. The sequential decoder does, however, require large amounts of buffer storage which have, in the past, made it unsuitable in all but specialised, capital-intensive applications. In the context of sequential decoding, it transpires that *systematic* convolution encoding results in significantly poorer *decoder* performance than non-systematic convolution encoding. This is because the inclusion of a second logic circuit, feeding the lower input of the multiplexing switch of the coder shown in figure 7.5a (rather than a direct feed of unmodified information

digits) can be shown to have the effect of increasing the Hamming distance properties of the code. For practical codes, utilising long shift registers, a systematic
coder will require approximately twice the register size of a non-systematic coder
of equivalent performance and decoder complexity.

The coder illustrated in figure 7.7 is systematic because it passes information
digits unchanged to the channel. A simple non-systematic encoder is shown in
figure 7.8. Its operation in encoding a digit sequence 0 1 1 0 1 0 ... (subject to
the presumption that the initial register states are zero) is presented in table 7.13.
Operation of such an encoder is deterministic, the output being uniquely established by the input digit I_i and the current register contents U_i and V_i, which
preserve a past history of relevent data input, with

$$U_i = I_{i-1} \quad \text{and} \quad V_i = U_{i-1} = I_{i-2}$$

The convolution encoder can usefully be regarded as a *finite state machine*. We
note that, when output digits are computed, it is as a unique function of (in this
example) I_i, U_i and V_i and that each pair of output digits (for a single input digit
I_i) is a consequence of a finite number of combinations of possible digit-pairs
(I_i, U_i) and (U_i, V_i). This is because the digit-pair (U_i, V_i) represents the previous
history (I_{i-1}, U_{i-1}) prior to which, because of the register length, data are discarded. We thus refer to (I_i, U_i) as the *current state* of the finite state machine
and to $(I_{i-1}, U_{i-1}) = (U_i, V_i)$ as its *previous state*. The machine output is dictated
not by (I_i, U_i) or (I_{i-1}, U_{i-1}) but by the *state transition* from previous to current
state

$$(I_{i-1}, U_{i-1}) \rightarrow (I_i, U_i)$$

There are, of course, four possible 'previous states' for the encoder we are examining, namely $(I_{i-1}, U_{i-1}) = (0, 0)$ or $(0, 1)$ or $(1, 0)$ or $(1, 1)$. Also, there are two
possible states for the input digit, I_i: 0 or 1. Tabulation of the possible state
transitions indicates therefore that there are eight, each yielding an output digit
combination (X_i, Y_i). The state-transition table for our encoder is shown in table
7.14. It will be noted that, for the eight possible state transitions, there are obviously only four possible output digit combinations. This does not mean that
ambiguous interpretation of similar digit pairs arising from different state transition
situations will occur during decoding. The sequence of output digit pairs, because
of the memory associated with the encoding process, is not arbitrary. For example,

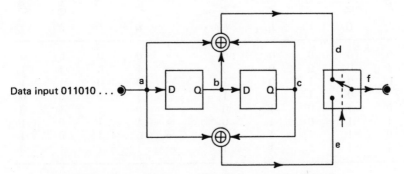

Figure 7.8   A simple non-systematic convolution encoder

TABLE 7.13   OPERATION OF NON-SYSTEMATIC CODES (FIGURES IN PARENTHENIS DENOTE PRESUMED INITIAL REGISTER STATES 0 0)

a	b	c	d	e	f
0	(0)	(0)	0	0	0 0
1	0	(0)	1	1	1 1
1	1	0	0	1	0 1
0	1	1	0	1	0 1
1	0	1	0	0	0 0
0	1	0	1	0	1 0
⋮	0 ⋮	1 0 ⋮	⋮	⋮	⋮

although $(X_i, Y_i) = (0, 0)$ may be *followed* by any of the four allowed combinations of (X_{i+1}, Y_{i+1}) the specific sequencing $(X_i, Y_i) = (0, 0)$ to $(X_{i+1}, Y_{i+1}) = (1, 1)$ can only occur if the *previous* state (X_{i-1}, Y_{i-1}) is one of the *restricted* subset of possible states, namely $(0, 0)$ or $(1, 1)$.

TABLE 7.14 STATE TRANSITION TABLE

Input I_i	Register U_i	Register V_i	Now at b I_{i-1}	Now at c U_{i-1}		Now at a I_i	Now at b U_i	Output X_i	Output Y_i
0	0	0	0	0	→	0	0	0	0
1	0	0	0	0	→	1	0	1	1
0	0	1	0	1	→	0	0	1	1
1	0	1	0	1	→	1	0	0	0
0	1	0	1	0	→	0	1	1	0
1	1	0	1	0	→	1	1	0	1
0	1	1	1	1	→	0	1	0	1
1	1	1	1	1	→	1	1	1	0

$U_i = I_{i-1}$ $V_i = U_{i-1} = I_{i-2}$

A useful aid in interpreting the code generation operation is the *state diagram*, figure 7.9*a*, which effectively embodies the information contained in table 7.14 in graph form. In the state diagram, a circular enclosure indicates (depending upon context) either previous or current state. The symbol adjacent to each arrowhead indicates output digits (X_i, Y_i). Thus a system previous state $(0, 0)$ translating to a current state $(1, 0)$ (bottom circle to right-hand circle) generates output digits $(1, 1)$.

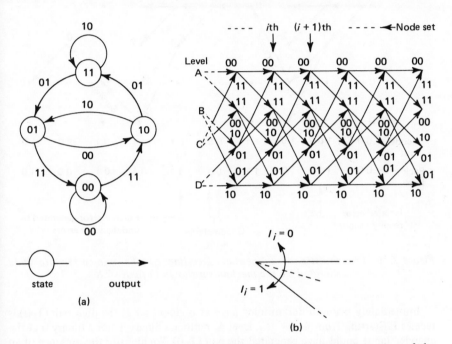

Figure 7.9 *(a) State diagram and (b) trellis diagram describing operation of the non-systematic convolution encoder shown in figure 7.8*

Applying the state diagram repeatedly allows us to develop another interpretive device, of particular value in appreciating the nature of the decoding operation: the *trellis diagram*, figure 7.9*b*. On the trellis diagram, output digit sequence is read by tracing from left to right on a node-to-node basis. Nodal decisions are taken thus: if the input digit I_i is 0, follow the upward-directed branch from the current node; if I_i is 1, follow the downward-directed branch, instead. By way of example, suppose that the initial register contents and data input sequence had all been zero. Then, starting along the horizontal upper limbs and assuming I_i (at the *i*th node-set) = 1, we are directed downwards to level B, node $i + 1$ and we read out output digits (1,1). A further input sequence $I_{i+1}, I_{i+2}, \ldots = 1\ 0\ 1 \ldots$ will thread node-sets $i + 2$, $i + 3$ and $i + 4$ at levels D, C and B, respectively, generating the output sequence $0\ 1\ 0\ 1\ 0\ 0 \ldots$.

It is now possible for us to examine, using the trellis diagram, the operation of sequential, or probabilistic decoding. Because output sequencing is *not* arbitrary, any received code deviating from the norm dictated by the state diagram will be indicative of the presence of transmission errors. Let us follow the consequence of attempting to decode an output sequence containing errors, as shown in figure 7.10. We start with the presumption that a protracted string of zeros had been presented to the decoder, determining a starting point at node-set i, level A.

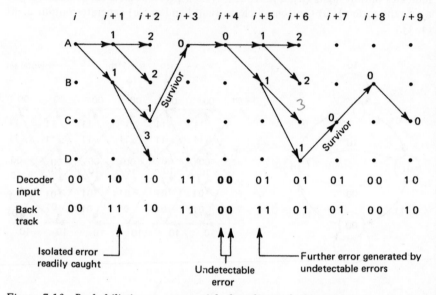

Figure 7.10 Probabilistic or sequential decoding of the non-systematic code generated by the mechanism shown in figure 7.8

Immediately prior to determining *level* at node-set $i + 1$, the digit pair $(1, 0)$ is received. Starting from node-set i, level A, neither a binary 1 nor a binary 0 at the encoder input could have generated the pair $(1, 0)$. We identify the presence of an error but can take no action to correct it, as yet. We are obliged to assume that it is equally likely that progress to node-set $i + 1$ *could* have ended at either level A or level B (indicating an error in the first digit, if level A were correct, or an error in the second digit, if level B were correct). To enable us to develop a measure of *probable error*, we compute, at node-set $i + 1$, the Hamming distance at each level (A and B in this case, at this stage) between the level code which the *coder* might be presumed to have generated (that is, $(0, 0)$ into A or $(1, 1)$ into B) and the binary digits under inspection (the received pair $(1, \mathbf{0})$). In both cases the Hamming distance is 1, a value we now inscribe above each appropriate node-level arrowhead. Clearly, no basis for preference between our hypotheses as to which sequence of digits really was transmitted is evident, using Hamming distance as our measure. We proceed to node-set $i + 2$, computing again the Hamming distances (this time at all four levels). The Hamming distance at level C is clearly the smallest and we must presume (for we have no other basis upon which to make a judgement) that *therefore*, the path threading nodes $\langle i,$ A$\rangle$, $\langle i + 1,$ B$\rangle$, and $\langle i + 2,$ C$\rangle$ was the correct one. Backtracking from node $\langle i + 2,$ C$\rangle$ and comparing with the definitive trellis in figure 7.9b, we find that the symbol pair $(1, \mathbf{0})$ should have been received as $(1, 1)$ and thus the first error has been corrected.

The next digit pair entered into the decoder (1, 1) prior to entering node-set $i+3$, can make a valid transition, as can its successor **(0, 0)**. The threading $\langle i+2, C \rangle$ to $\langle i+3, A \rangle$ to $\langle i+4, A \rangle$ occurs quite happily with Hamming distances of zero computed at each stage. Now our code input to the decoder was actually entered with two consecutive errors prior to node-set $i+4$. The decoder has been unable to detect and therefore cannot attempt to correct these errors. Furthermore, because the next received digits ((0, 1) prior to node-set $i+5$) *are* correct, the decoder becomes confused, recognising that **0 0** 0 1 is an invalid sequence. However, it now attempts to correct the last two of these digits having had no reason to suspect the undetectable error present in the first two. A further error is now propagated before the decoder settles and correctly re-establishes the original coded pattern.

The error correction procedure we have described is a sequential or probabilistic decoder, operating on 'hard decisions'. A hard-decision decoder involves the use of a measure (often referred to as a 'metric') which is immutable. In our example, the metric was Hamming distance; other criteria are available as alternatives. 'Soft-decision' decoding allows the metric to be modified as a consequence of some other relevant observation, such as signal-to-noise ratio at the decoder input. The presumption is thus that a best decoding strategy in a low error rate situation may not be the same as that required if error rate rises.

7.9 Encryption Systems

Encryption, the protection of sensitive information by means of suitably chosen codes, has long been of importance in military contexts. In recent years, it has also assumed a role of extreme significance in more general social situations. We identify data-base management and privacy of telephone voice communication as two particular areas in which secrecy may be of great importance.

Data-base management is concerned with the handling and storage of a wide range of potentially sensitive information. Obvious examples include secrecy of and security from interference to banking and commercial inventories, the protection of confidential industrial data and the security of personal information files maintained by state or other agencies, such as credit houses.

We shall treat cryptography primarily in the context of coding for data-base protection. The next section of this chapter has to do with the security of voice transmission by ciphering or scrambling. An encrypting coder is referred to as a *cipher system*. Its objective is to accept unprotected information code, often referred to as *plaintext* and denoted P, and translate it into a protected form known as *ciphertext*, denoted C. The coding or translation operation may be viewed as falling into one or both of two categories: *substitution*, whereby code symbols are replaced by others, according to some procedural law; or *transposition*, where rearrangement of code-symbol order takes place. An example of a binary *substitution coder* is to be found in a mechanisation referred to as the '*one-time pad*', figure 7.11a. Here, random binary digits are added modulo-2 to the plaintext to produce the ciphertext and the random digits are considered to provide the encryption/decryption *keystream*, denoted by K. Deciphering obviously requires a knowledge at the decoder of the random digit sequence used by the encoder and thus highlights an immediate disadvantage of the one-time pad: the need to supply, securely, a disproportionarely large decoding keystream. The coder does

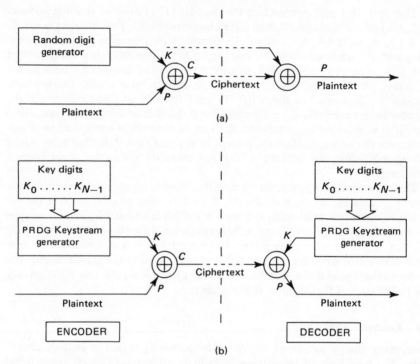

Figure 7.11   (a) The 'one-time pad' and (b) its development into a keyword cipher system

possess the attribute, however, of being unbreakable if the keystream can be kept secure and is unique among cipher systems in this single respect.

The modification to the one-time pad suggested by the structure illustrated in figure 7.11*b*, where an *N*-digit binary *keyword* is used to organise the logic of a pseudorandom digit generator (PRDG), removes the disadvantage of unmanageable key size. The cipher system is, unfortunately, no longer unbreakable. It is perhaps worth noting that the widely reported *linear* PRDGs, based upon the use of feedback shift registers with modulo-2 feedback, are unsuitable for this sort of application. If the cipher system is to withstand the efforts of a well-prepared cryptanalyst (code-breaker) *for adequate time*, the use of a *non-linear* PRDG would in terms of current technology, certainly be necessary.

The two methods of encryption discussed above share the attribute that no attempt is made to disguise machine structure. Confidentiality lies entirely in security of the key. This philosophy is also embodied in what is currently the single most widely used and important civil encryption scheme, the 'Data Encryption Standard' (DES) defined by the U.S. Bureau of Standards. Here, a 56-digit binary keyword is shared between users, serving thereby to effect both encryption and decryption. Since there are $2^{56} = 10^{17}$ possible keywords, the cryptanalyst is set a task which, given the confines of current technology, is to all intents and purposes impossible, certainly by straight search of keywords. Furthermore, even though the code *structure* is publically known, it is both complex and non-linear. Consequently, interference of keyword from ciphertext (and hence decipherment to yield plaintext) is exceedingly unlikely. It is true that additional security would accrue if code structure were not available. However, in a context where widespread commercial use in envisaged, with cipher systems produced by a plurality of manufacturers, structural secrecy would be difficult to achieve as would the evolution of standard procedures for establishing correct machine operation and uniformity of performance.

The DES utilises both transposition and substitution coding. An overall schematic illustrating operation is presented in figure 7.12. Coding takes place upon blocks of 64 binary input digits $I = I_0I_1I_2 \ldots I_{63}$ to yield equal length output blocks $I' = I_0'I_1'I_2' \ldots I_{63}'$. The coder keyword is 56 digits long but is input as a 64-digit word containing eight parity check digits so that its structure is of the form $K = K_0K_1K_2 \ldots K_{55}C_0 \ldots C_7$. The coding involves an initial transposition, defined by the standard algorithm and is matched by a complementary final transposition. Between these stages, sixteen complex and nonlinear substitution/transposition operations occur. Each of these stages is mechanistically identical but procedurally different, being dependent upon its own 48-digit subkey. The sixteen subkeys are derived from the 56-digit input keywrod by sequence transpositions.

Stage manipulations commence with a split of the transposed input data into two 32-digit registers, denoted 'left', L and 'right', R in figure 7.13 in which the Nth stage of manipulation is illustrated. Each stage of manipulation involves an

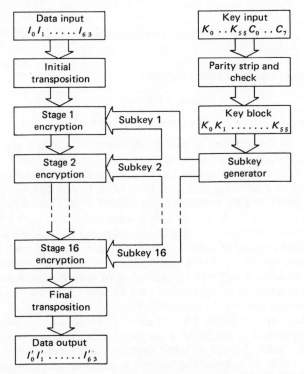

Figure 7.12   Structure of the U.S. Bureau of Standards 'Data Encryption Standard'
(DES)

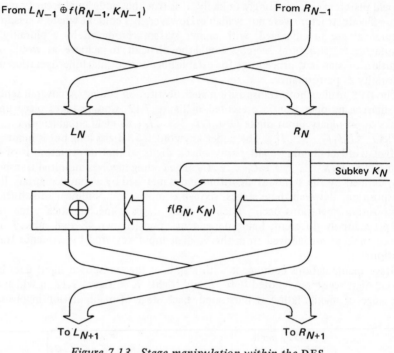

Figure 7.13 Stage manipulation within the DES

interchange of register contents such that

$$L_{N+1} = R_N$$

$$R_{N+1} = L_N \oplus f(R_N, K_N)$$

The power of the DES lies, in part, in the complexity of this sequence of operations and, also, in the non-linear nature of the functional operation $f(R_N, K_N)$. The function f involves accepting the 32-digit register contents R_N and expanding it by means of a spreading and scrambling table, to a 48-digit word R_N'. Addition modulo-2 of R_N' and K_N produces a new 48-digit word which is presented in eight six-digit words to a bank of eight cells known as *S-boxes*. Each S-box effects the non-linear data compression operation of collapsing the six-digit input to a four-digit output by means of entry to a look-up table. The entire S-box output now consists, once again, of an 8 by 4 = 32-digit word which, after one further permutation is summed modulo-2 with L_N, according to the prescription presented above.

All the methods of encryption we have discussed so far are of a type known as *key distribution systems*. In order that decoding may be effected, it is necessary that the keyword be supplied by means of a channel of high integrity. Key distribution procedure is, therefore, a matter of some concern to cryptographer and cryptanalyst alike. A quite different strategy, contextually extremely significant when the nature of information transfer in data-base management is taken into account, is provided by the suggested alternative *public key systems*.

The public key approach differs from key distribution (which requires a single key for both encryption and decryption) in that it utilises separate, but related code and decode keys. The task of establishing the secret decode key from the publically disclosed encode key is made impossibly difficult (in practical terms) by the design of the code. The strategic significance of the public key approach is that a non-secret 'encode-key' register facilitates the deposition of information to the advantage of a select recipient (a banking house, for example) by many external sources (the bank's clients, by analogy) who are individually ill-equipped to conform to the requirements of a necessarily high-security key distribution arrangement. The select recipient is then in a strong position to defend the security of the critical decode-key register of source assignations, to which only he should have access.

Many of the proposed public key systems are based upon the notion of 'one-way functions'. One-way functions are mathematical operations, used to generate ciphertext from plaintext which, although reversible, require such effort to effect the reversal that the operation becomes impractical, without prior knowledge of some decoding short-cut. To illustrate the concept of a one-way function, consider the problem of calculating and subsequently factoring an integer number N, which is the product of two primes K_1 and K_2. The operation $N = K_1 \cdot K_2$ of course presents no problems; this is the 'easy' way for the one-way function. Factoring, on the other hand, involves sorting through the list of all possible primes K_1, dividing N by K_1 and checking that the quotient is also prime, a formidable task if N is large and clearly the 'hard' way for the one-way function. We might thus observe that getting N from K_1 and K_2 is straightforward and parallels encryption of K_1 (as plaintext) by a key K_2. With the key withheld, K_1 from N (deciphering as viewed by the cryptanalyst) is extremely difficult. Provide the key (for the select recipient only) and deciphering is easy. Unfortunately, although the factoring problem illustrates the concept of a one-way function, we should prefer not to have to restrict all plaintext to the set of prime numbers. Also, the use of the one-way function as described above involves key distribution.

One proposed public key system, the RSA scheme (named after its authors: Rivest, Shamir and Adleman) illustrates a possible development of the method and, if adopted, would operate as follows. Ciphertext is formed from plaintext by the manipulation (expressing repeated division of P^{K_1} by N to leave remainder C; P and C representing plaintext and ciphertext, K_1 being the (public) encode-key and N defining code-class)

$$C = P^{K_1} \bmod(N)$$

Decryption is effected by the complementary manipulation

$$P = C^{K_2} \bmod(N)$$

where K_2 is the (secret) decode-key.

If the encryption and decryption manipulations *are* to be complementary, then a very specific choice of K_1, K_2 and N is required. By applying methods drawn from the Theory of Numbers, restrictions upon, and necessary interrelations between these quantities can be established.

The RSA scheme depends, in part, upon application of the factoring problem discussed above. N is restricted to be the product of two large primes. Typically, each prime would be about 100 digits in length. The cryptographer, having chosen these primes randomly, keeps them secret. He then chooses K_1 (with some minor restrictions) and, from K_1 and the factors of N (not N itself) can easily *calculate* K_2. So far, the cryptographer has N and K_1, with the latter quantity forming the *public* key for encoding. He retains K_2 as his secret decryption key and quietly 'destroys' the record of the two primes used to form N. The cryptanalyst, wishing to crack the code, has only N and K_1 to work on. His task is now incomparably harder than that of the cryptographer with his privileged knowledge of the two primes from which N was formed. It is estimated that the difficulty in finding K_2 from N and K_1 only is equal to that of factoring N and actually represents one of the hardest numerical tasks. To illustrate the significance of the task facing the cryptanalyst, it is further estimated that, assuming a 1 μS instruction time, calculating K_2 in this way would take about one million years, using the best known factoring algorithm. The RSA scheme may thus typify a public key approach to encryption which will supersede the DES key distribution system.

7.10 Protection of Voice Communication

It is perfectly possible and may in the future become preferable to view the problem of security of voice communication in terms of the classical cryptosystem (such as we have discussed in the preceding section) producing *speech ciphering*. For example, it is a simple matter, in system development terms, to accomplish the digitisation of speech by means of a low-cost PCM or adaptive delta-modulation CODEC. This can easily be followed either by

(1) *encryption* of the output code in 64-digit blocks, perhaps by using the DES implemented (also at low cost) as an LSI circuit, or by

(2) *masking*, whereby (and here compare with the 'one-time pad' and its related PRDG-based encryption system, figure 7.11) a pseudorandom binary sequence is added modulo-2, to the CODEC output code.

Either of these techniques has the valuable attribute that the ciphered speech waveform has noise-like properties. It is not even possible to tell when the speaker pauses. Furthermore, in this case, security (depending as it does upon the ciphering scheme being used) can be designed to be cryptographically sound.

The problem with speech ciphering, viewed from the standpoint of the telephone network, *as it is at present configured*, is that of bandwidth utilisation. If the ciphering unit is envisaged as being placed between handset and channel, and the latter has the normal voice signal constraint of being bandlimited between 300 Hz and 3.4 kHz, then a basic incompatibility with the ciphered code spectrum will be apparent. The ciphered code, producing (we may assume) eight-digit codewords at 8.10^3 words s^{-1}, requires a channel bandwidth of about 32 kHz (see chapter 8). Two approaches to solving this problem may be identified

(1) The use of complex, costly signal bandwidth compression techniques to effect massive redundancy reduction before encryption.

(2) The use of moderate redundancy reduction, followed by conversion of binary n-tuplets to M'ary symbols, thus obtaining a reduction in symbol rate inversely proportional to M (where $M = 2^n$). (This technique is described in chapter 8 in connection with the development of high-speed data modems.)

Since neither technique is particularly simple in application, the use of speech ciphering has, as yet, but limited use on voice-grade telephone systems. The use of some form of *speech scrambler* has thus been a commoner approach to voice security in this context.

Two basic scrambler structures (with several variants) may be envisaged. The first uses the method of *temporal permutation*. The waveform to be scrambled is first sampled. Sample values are then rearranged in a manner (agreed by both communicating parties) which destroys their natural order and renders the message unintelligible to a potential interceptor.

The second scrambler structure involves *spectral permutation*. Here, a bank of contiguous, bandpass filters spans the speech spectral range. They effect a frequency-domain waveform decomposition. This decomposition is followed by spectral rearrangement by frequency translation. Finally, summation of the translated components yields the disguised message.

Both methods can be implemented by using either analogue or digital technologies, although current practice, encouraged by the steadily decreasing cost of complex digital processing equipment, would favour the latter approach. Of the two scrambler structures described above, it must be admitted that spectral permutations eventually do little to reduce residual intelligibility, which may be quite high. Furthermore, the natural pauses which pattern speech are left unaltered, thereby further weakening the security of this scrambling method. The security of temporal permutation is substantially superior. However, complexity is *to an extent* limited by maximum acceptable subjective delay, when two speakers are attempting to hold a conversion. This delay, engendered by the coding process, is usually required to be rather less than one second in duration, if a reasonably 'natural' conversation is to be possible.

7.11   Spread Spectrum Communication Systems[52]

Radio communication systems are beset by the problem of excessive spectral crowding. In principle, transposition of services to higher frequency bands offers a possible solution to this dilemma. In many situations, however, further conflicts involving area of coverage and cost of service prohibit such a straightforward attack upon the problem. An alternative strategy, which presents a radically different approach to the problem of radio channel multiplexing, is to be found in the concept of *spread spectrum communications*. The coding procedures described in the earlier sections of this chapter are the generic precursors of the modulation techniques used in spread spectrum systems. They confer upon such systems benefits of quality of service and also of security against both eavesdropping and jamming. In essence, the spread spectrum approach seeks to create a modulated carrier spectrum which vastly exceeds the spectrum of the modulating signal. In this respect, it may be said to mirror the bandwidth-quality tradeoff which we have already identified as an important property of frequency modulation systems. However, with spread spectrum communication, a difference in *scale* of spreading factor (by some several orders of magnitude) is reflected in a difference in *kind* when we come to consider the modulation process in detail. For consistency, it should nevertheless be mentioned that the term 'spread spectrum' is applied to pulsed frequency modulation or 'chirp' signals, which are used in radar and other ranging systems. Although electronic distance-measuring is an extremely important

application of spread spectrum, it is considered inappropriate for detailed consideration in a text of this nature. For further information on this topic, the reader is
referred to modern texts on radar systems.

Spread spectrum communication systems fall into one of two broad categories

    (1) Direct (or Pseudorandom) Sequence Encoding
    (2) Frequency Hopping Encoding

Direct sequence encoding involves the spreading of a modulated carrier spectrum
by convolution in the frequency domain. This is achieved by multiplying the
modulated carrier with a suitably chosen spreading function, $s(t)$, as figure 7.14
illustrates. A first requirement placed upon the spreading function is that it should
possess wide bandwidth relative to the unspread modulated carrier bandwidth.
This ensures that the frequency domain convolution results in a transmitted signal
which exhibits an appropriately large spreading factor. A second requirement is
that $s(t)$ should be chosen from a mutually orthogonal set of possible spreading
functions.[51]

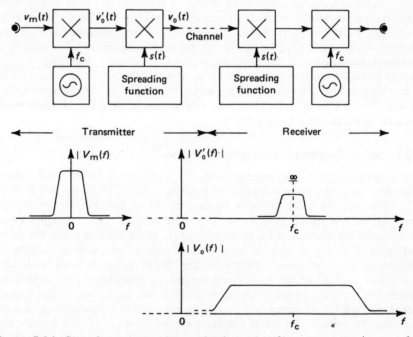

*Figure 7.14 Spread spectrum communication using direct sequence (or pseudo-
random) encoding*

To illustrate both these requirements, consider the example of a spreading
function generated by a maximal-length feedback shift register. We have already
seen, in section 7.4, that a maximal-length sequence of length $L = 2^K - 1$ may be
generated by means of a feedback shift register with linear modulo-2 feedback. We
may estimate the spectral width of the pseudorandom sequence by inspection of

its power spectrum, figure 7.6. Notice that the faster the pseudorandom digit generator is clocked, the greater will be the spreading factor, yielding a spread bandwidth of $B \cong 2/T$, where T is the digit period.

Inspection of the autocorrelation function, figure 7.6a, shows that, for large L and non-periodic shifts, quasi-orthogonal ($R \cong 0$) set-members may be obtained by the simple expedient of performing repeated end-about shifts of the basic set-sequence of digits. For a synchronised multi-user system, this provides an easy method of setting up code-division multiplexing. Alternatively, for non-synchronised operation, use may be made of the fact that, by choosing different tap settings on the generator register, other mutually orthogonal length L spreading functions may be obtained. Although maximal-length codes have been used to generate spreading functions, other codes (most notably the Gold code[50]) can also be used. Operation of the spread spectrum in this way allows users to be subject to *code division mutliplexing* because, on detection of any one user by correlation against his particular spreading function, the signals of all other users average to zero as a consequence of the code orthogonality properties.

The structure of a *frequency-hopped* spread-spectrum system is shown in figure 7.15. The pseudorandom code generator in this case causes the second up-mixer in the transmitter to make deterministic but non-sequential steps over a bandwidth which is wide (by some orders of magnitude) relative to the information band. This has the effect of engendering a massive spectral spreading at the second mixer output.

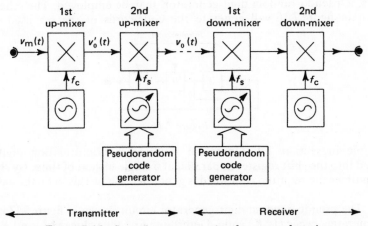

Figure 7.15 Spread spectrum using frequency hopping

Frequency hopping has been considered particularly attractive for satellite multiple access communication. Here, hopping rates are kept low and the spreading factor maintained by ensuring that the frequency synthesiser makes large frequency steps in response to input code changes. Many users participate in the use of a given satellite channel, each being assigned a unique 'key' for the generation of his orthogonal-code hopping-sequence. This form of channel access is referred to as *code division multiple access*.

Problems

7.1 (a) A hypothetical telegraph code transmits 26 alphabetic, 10 numeric and 28 punctuation and control characters. It uses five-digit codewords to achieve this, employing 'figure shift' and 'letter shift' codes as necessary. Is such a code redundant?

(b) Devise an iterated coding scheme which would check groups of five words from such a telegraph code.

(c) Compare your iterated coding scheme with the AUTOSPEC code described in section 7.3.

7.2 For the AUTOSPEC code described in section 7.3, the information-digit sequence

$$I_0 I_1 I_2 I_3 I_4$$
$$0\ 0\ 0\ 0\ 1$$

is to be transmitted. Form the complete codeword and show the effect of a single error in the information-digit sequence. Show also the effect of a single error in the parity-digit sequence. Repeat for all possible error conditions. Perform the same experiment for double errors in the information and parity sequences and a single error in each. Are double errors detectable? Are they guaranteed correctable?

7.3 Instead of using a modulo-2 division circuit for the generation of cyclic codes, a 'pseudo-random digit generator' may be employed. The schematic shown in figure 7.16 will generate the codewords of the set used as an

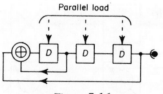

Figure 7.16

example in section 7.4. Operation requires that information digits are loaded into the shift register in parallel at a single instant of time. By shifting seven times the required codeword is generated. Show this to be the case.

7.4 The pseudo-random digit-generator circuit shown in figure 7.17 is used to generate a cyclic (L, K) code. Determine first the values of L and K, then

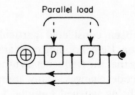

Figure 7.17

tabulate the allowed codewords in the set generated by the coder. Identify the parity and information digits. What is the Hamming distance of this code, and what is its significance?

7.5 For the coder illustrated in figure 7.17, deduce the structure of the alternative form of (modulo-2 division) coder which would establish the same code set. How many errors can this code detect and how many can it correct? Describe briefly how the decoder might be implemented.

7.6 (a) What are the essential differences between convolution and cyclic codes?
   (b) What is meant by 'burst-error correction'?
   (c) Explain the principle of threshold decoding.

8 The Transmission of Digital Signals

In chapters 6 and 7, we examined the generation of digital signals both from analogue waveforms and as the result of some form of digital coding. Very frequently, these baseband digital signals have to be transmitted through a channel to which they are poorly suited. As a consequence, special signalling formats are needed to 'match' the digital waveform to the channel.

At present, the majority of digital traffic is handled by means of the public telephone network which is often an *ad hoc* arrangement of existing system facilities. This is because the state authorities responsible for administering the various national and international communication networks have tended to release lines for digital signalling which were designed for voice-grade analogue signal transmission. As we have seen in chapter 2, such lines exhibit severe group-delay distortion as the result of having a highly non-linear phase characteristic. This does not seriously affect a voice signal, since the human ear is relatively insensitive to phase distortion, but it can cause unacceptable degradation to digital signals.

A problem that is caused not by the line, but by a variety of ancillary equipment is the lack of d.c. coupling between data source and sink within the switched telephone-network. This lack of coupling is detrimental to the preservation of pulse shape. In particular, a long 'run' of binary 1s and 0s will be characterised by a gradual 'sag' of the pulse tops towards zero. To prevent this happening, coding may be employed to generate a digital signal in which long runs of digits of one sense or the other cannot occur. This is known as coding for disparity reduction, disparity being the difference between the number of 1s and the number of 0s in a codeword.

More usually, both these problems are tackled by a suitable choice of format of the signal shapes used to represent the binary symbols 0 and 1 during transmission. As they are generated in the coding system, these symbols are represented by voltage levels $+A$ and 0, of duration T. Examples of the transmitted signal shape fall into two classes

(1) Formats typified by a ternary set of symbols represented by voltage

levels $+A$, 0 and $-A$, for a duration less than or equal to the binary-digit duration T.

(2) Formats typified by the modulation or *keying* of a sinusoidal carrier.

The first class is used predominantly in telegraphy and PCM telephony, and the second in digital data transmission systems. The reason for these distinct areas of demarcation is that data-transmission links have, in the past, been made over normal, lumped-loaded voice-transmission lines. Such lines are loaded to improve their voice-transmission characteristics and, because of the loading, have a sharp cut-off at about 4 kHz. Since they also exhibit a.c. coupling, they are essentially a bandpass channel and are best suited to some form of CW modulation. In contrast, PCM telephony systems use lines from which the lumped loading has been removed, re-establishing their inherently wideband nature. The lines are still a.c. coupled, however, because the 'd.c. path' is used to supply power to the line repeater-amplifiers.

Another unusual feature of line-communication links is the nature of the noise corrupting the digital signal. In the previous chapters, we have discussed system performance with respect to gaussian-noise corruption. Gaussian noise is certainly present on line links but, since the signal voltages can be kept fairly large (often above 1 volt in amplitude which is many orders of magnitude larger than the signal at the antenna of a radio receiver) the probability of error due to this phenomenon is usually negligible. Far more serious is the 'impulsive' noise generated by the switching systems associated with the line network. This impulsive noise is extremely difficult to quantify. Theoretical criteria of performance of the various possible data-transmission systems when corrupted by impulse noise have, to a great extent, eluded research workers. The difficulties of performance estimation 'in the field' are also considerable. To obtain statistically significant results, test durations of the order of months are often needed.

8.1 Band Occupancy of Random Digital Data

It is obviously desirable that we should have some appreciation of the frequency content of typical digital-signalling waveforms. We shall assume, in discussing this problem, that the binary symbols 0 and 1 are equiprobable and that the symbol sequence is random. We shall identify, for each binary symbol, an elementary signalling waveform, thus

$$0 \equiv s_0(t)$$
$$1 \equiv s_1(t)$$

We shall further assume that $s_0(t)$ and $s_1(t)$ are of finite duration T, so that the signalling, or symbol rate, is T^{-1} digits s^{-1}.

In our previous discussion of coding, we have spoken of the binary symbols as abstract digits, 0 and 1. As generated within an electronic coding system, however, they are voltage waveforms in their own right. Most frequently, they fall into the class of 'unipolar, non-return-to-zero (NRZ) waveforms' defined by the waveshapes

$$\left. \begin{array}{l} s_0(t) = 0 \\ s_1(t) = +A \end{array} \right\} \quad \text{Digit duration } T$$

'Non-return-to-zero' means that $s_1(t)$ does not fall to zero during the interval T. Reference to the signalling waveforms depicted in table 8.1 should make the distinction between non-return-to-zero and return-to-zero (RZ) signalling clear.

The reason why unipolar waveforms are encountered in the electronic coding system is because the value corresponding to $s_0(t)$ may be taken to be the system 'earth' level and that corresponding to $s_1(t)$ may be taken to be the supply-line voltage. Normally, the organisation of logic within coding systems is such as to preclude the need for a return-to-zero waveform.

Although the unipolar NRZ format is obviously convenient within the coder, it is unsuitable for transmission purposes. For example, if the channel is d.c. coupled, then it will sustain the large d.c. component of $+A/2$ volts and the power this conveys is non-informational. On the other hand, given an a.c.-coupled channel, pulse distortion (as described in the introduction to this chapter) will occur, leading to an unnecessarily high error rate. Table 8.1 provides several alternatives to the unipolar NRZ format which may be employed specifically to circumvent these and other signalling problems.

The most fundamental criterion employed in assessing the suitability of a given data format for a particular application is its *power spectrum*, $P(f)$. The power spectrum in general consists of two components: a continuous spectral density and, perhaps, a line spectrum with components at d.c. and integer multiples of the digit rate. The power spectrum is calculated by determining first the auto-correlation function of the random digit-sequence and Fourier transforming this quantity. An example of the principle involved has already been presented in section 1.27.3 and corresponds to the case of a bipolar NRZ format. A general equation, describing the power spectrum of a random digit-sequence with arbitrary signalling waveshapes and digit occurrence probability can be derived by extending the method.[28]

The relative band occupancy of the various signalling waveforms is a factor of considerable importance in selecting any pair of them for use in a given system. While the power spectrum provides all the detailed information we need to know about the band occupancy of each random process, we can obtain a very useful comparative assessment of channel usage in the following way. A 'worst case' transmitted signal would consist of that selection of signalling waveshapes which ensured the highest rate of state transitions. For example, given a unipolar NRZ waveform, the alternating sequence . . . 10101010 . . . would yield a rectangular-pulse train with the maximum possible number of state transitions per unit time. If ideal lowpass filtering were applied, then with a cut-off frequency just greater than $1/2T$, the filter output would consist of a sinusoidal wave from which the original signal could be reconstructed by 'slicing'. Thus the minimum essential signal bandwidth would be $1/2T$.

The same argument could be applied to the bipolar NRZ signal. In contrast, both the RZ (50 per cent duty cycle) and dipolar waveforms would exhibit worst-case pulse-trains with state transitions occurring twice as frequently as those observed for NRZ signalling at the same symbol rate. For example, the worst-case unipolar RZ signal would consist of the waveform generated by the symbol sequence . . . 111111 . . . . Such a waveform will require an essential signal bandwidth of $1/T$.

TABLE 8.1

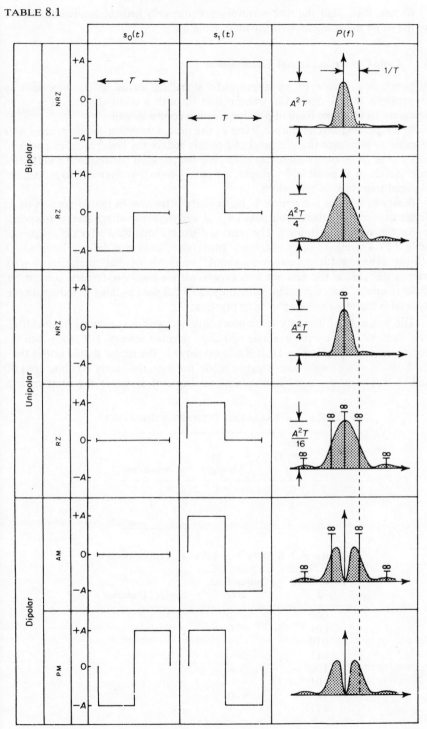

We see, then, that the NRZ waveforms require only half the bandwidth needed by the other signalling formats shown in table 8.1.

8.2 Code Conversion to Aid Transmission

Although the choice of an appropriate signalling waveshape is important in preparing a digital signal for transmission through a given channel, it is often necessary to use some form of pre-transmission coding as well.

By employing several output levels in the pre-transmission coding process, it is possible to eliminate the d.c. level and greatly reduce the low-frequency components in the coder output, without extending the required transmission bandwidth. In principle, it is possible, by employing binary-to-nary conversion, to reduce the required transmission bandwidth.

Binary-to-ternary conversion is particularly attractive in that it permits us to devise coders with balanced outputs $+A$, $-A$ and the zero voltage level corresponding to the system earth level. The ternary digits are identified after the manner of table 8.2. A straight binary-to-ternary conversion, such as is defined by table 8.3 affords a bandwidth reduction to about two-thirds of that of the input NRZ waveform. This is the best we can expect with a binary-to-ternary conversion. Unfortunately, the conversion defined by table 8.3 does nothing to reduce disparity, and is therefore not employed in practice.

The principle of disparity reduction combined with economy of bandwidth is best demonstrated by the example of *paired selected ternary*, PST, for which the coding scheme specified by table 8.4 is employed. The reader should notice that, for both 'positive mode' and 'negative mode' outputs, the binary combinations 00 and 11 lead to ternary combinations with no d.c. level. However, the combinations

TABLE 8.2 BALANCED TERNARY SYMBOL SET

Basic Ternary Set	Line Voltages	Convention
0	$-A$	$-$
1	0	0
2	$+A$	$+$

TABLE 8.3 BINARY TO TERNARY CONVERSION

Input Code T	Output Code 3T/2	← Symbol Duration
000	$-$ $-$	
001	$-$ 0	
010	$-$ $+$	
011	0 $-$	
100	0 $+$	
101	$+$ $-$	
110	$+$ 0	
111	$+$ $+$	

01 and 10 do produce d.c. levels of $+A/2$ and $-A/2$ depending on whether the output is in positive or negative mode. The coder operates to provide positive-mode output until either of the states 01 or 10 occurs at the input. Since the presence of either of these combinations introduces a bias of $+A/2$ to the output, the mode is changed to negative, so that the next time either of these combinations is encountered, the bias is removed.

TABLE 8.4 PAIRED SELECTED TERNARY

| | Output Code | |
| | Positive | Negative |
Input Code	Mode	Mode
00	− +	− +
01	0 +	0 −
10	+ 0	− 0
11	+ −	+ −

Inspection of table 8.4 indicates that this system operates in a bandwidth which is approximately equal to that required for the input NRZ wave.

Table 8.3 illustrated a 3B-2T code format and table 8.4 a 2B-2T PST format. Somewhat more representative of current practice is the 4B-3T PST conversion, table 8.5, wherein blocks of four binary digist convert to blocks of three ternary digits. This code structure builds up a maximum disparity (for binary input 0111) of ±3.

TABLE 8.5 4B-3T PST

| | Output Code | |
Input Code	Positive Mode	Negative Mode
0000	+ 0 −	+ 0 −
0001	− + 0	− + 0
0010	0 − +	0 − +
0011	+ − 0	+ − 0
0100	+ + 0	− − 0
0101	0 + +	0 − −
0110	+ 0 +	− 0 −
0111	+ + +	− − −
1000	+ + −	− − +
1001	− + +	+ − −
1010	+ − +	− + −
1011	+ 0 0	− 0 0
1100	0 + 0	0 − 0
1101	0 0 +	0 0 −
1110	0 + −	0 + −
1111	− 0 +	− 0 +

Another method of obtaining a ternary transmission signal is to employ the technique of *alternate mark inversion*, AMI. The coding law required for AMI is, in its general form, similar to that used for PST. In this case, however, mode change takes place each time the digit 1 is encountered. The circuitry required to instrument this code converter is much simpler than that which would be required for PST and is illustrated in figure 8.1*a*. For the converter to function it is necessary that each binary 1 starting edge should be available to trigger the bistable. It follows that a 100 per cent duty cycle NRZ format at the input to the converter is not operable. Common practice involves the use of a 50 per cent duty cycle, so that the input binary wave is applied in non-polar RZ format, yielding a ternary RZ output. Typical waveforms are shown in figure 8.1*b* and the spectra of the input and output waves are shown in figure 8.1*c*.

There are several reasons, apart from the technological one of triggering the bistable, which could be overcome, for using a 50 per cent duty cycle in the converter output waveform. These reasons are connected with aspects of noise immunity and equalisation and they indicate that 50 per cent is just preferable to 100 per cent duty cycle AMI for junction PCM systems. AMI has found favour both in American and European PCM telephony networks and is currently the standard method of preparing digital telephony-signals for line transmission.

The power spectrum of the AMI waveform shows that there is no d.c. level and that the low-frequency components in evidence in the original NRZ

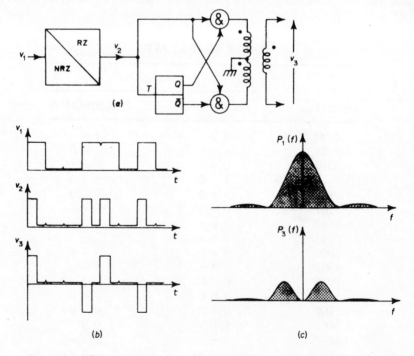

Figure 8.1 The generation of an alternate mark inversion (AMI) waveform

waveform are of greatly reduced amplitude. Consequently, the presence of a.c. coupling in the transmission path has little effect on the transmitted digits when this format is employed.

Since no discrete line-components are present in the AMI power spectrum, a digit-synchronising signal can only be obtained indirectly. The usual method of achieving this is to rectify the received AMI signal and pass the rectified wave into a notch filter to extract a component at twice the digit rate.

8.3 Pre-transmission and Pre-detection Filtering[28]

In the previous section, we have discussed the effect of signalling formats on spectral content and therefore band occupancy of a random pulse-sequence. Our interest lay predominantly with avoiding the problems caused by a.c. coupling within the transmission channel. One characteristic of the transmitted pulse-sequence which we did not vary was the actual pulse shape, all our examples involving the use of rectangular pulses. If we modify the pulse shape, we may alter the manner in which the digital waveform utilises the channel. This we may accomplish by means of a variety of filtering operations. Figure 8.2 shows a typical digital transmission link. Pre-transmission filtering, $H_1(f)$, is often employed to remove out-of-band signal components. This may be done to reduce cross-talk at high frequencies between adjacent conductors in multicore cable, or to conserve the amount of power inserted into the transmission medium. Pre-detection filtering, $H_3(f)$, is employed both to afford some pulse shaping and to reduce the noise level presented to the decision circuitry by eliminating those noise components which lie beyond the essential signal bandwidth. The transmission medium, itself, may impose some frequency-dependent distortion, $H_2(f)$, upon the signal. We have seen in chapter 2 that the 'ideal' channel would have a characteristic

$$H_2(f) = A_2(f)\exp\{\phi_2(f)\}$$

with

$$\left.\begin{array}{l} A_2(f) = 1 \\ \phi_2(f) = -2\pi f\tau \end{array}\right\} \text{ over the signal bandwidth}$$

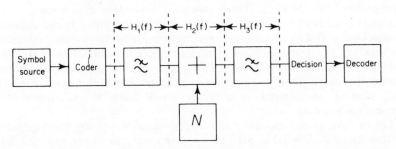

Figure 8.2 Sources of frequency-dependent distortion in pulse transmission. $H_1(f)$: pre-transmission filter; $H_2(f)$: channel transfer-function; $H_3(f)$: pre-detection filter; N: white gaussian channel-noise

Such a channel introduces only a signal delay equal to the slope of the phase characteristic. Two kinds of frequency-dependent (linear) distortion are encountered in practical transmission media. These are

(1) Attenuation distortion: $A_2(f)$ non-uniform, or
(2) Phase distortion: $\phi_2(f)$ non-linear over the signal bandwidth

The effect of both attenuation and phase distortion is to introduce 'echoes' of the transmitted signal into that which is observed at the receiver input (see problem 2.3). Both kinds of frequency-dependent distortion can be troublesome, but phase distortion usually causes the greatest problems. This is because, as the degree of distortion increases, each echo produces further echo pairs introducing, in the process, severe signal corruption.

At the expense of increased delay, both attenuation and phase distortion can be compensated for by equalisation (see section 8.9) either before or after transmission, by forming $H_1(f)$ and $H_3(f)$ so that the product $H_1(f)H_2(f)H_3(f)$ is equal to $\exp(-2\pi jf\tau)$, over the signal bandwidth.

We also saw in chapter 2 that the channel might introduce non-linear distortion, so that its output was no longer directly proportional to its input. This kind of distortion is not usually a problem when digital signals are being transmitted, since amplitude fluctuations of a continuously varying nature are not used to convey information.

Not only does the channel introduce distortion, it also contributes a noise component to the signal. As we have seen, this contribution may be impulsive in nature, a phenomenon typical of line systems, or it may have gaussian statistics. Some benefit may accrue from the selection of $H_3(f)$ so that the signal-to-noise ratio at its output is maximised. Then the design of $H_3(f)$ depends on the nature of signal shaping and the spectral distribution of power in the noisewave.

Possibly the single most important aspect of the combined effect of the transmission medium and the filtering at its input and output is the extent to which inter-symbol interference is produced. Let us suppose that the digit duration is T. Our investigations in section 8.1 have led us to the conclusion that the essential signal bandwidth is $1/2T$. In so far as any digital signal of a random nature occupies infinite bandwidth, the effect of band limiting must be to introduce attenuation distortion, and therefore echoes. These echoes spread energy from one pulse into adjacent digits and this effect is precisely inter-symbol interference. Thus, inserting a random digital-signal into a channel of bandwidth $1/2T$ will result in a corrupted output. In the absence of channel noise and given accurate synchronisation at the decision circuitry in the receiver, the degree of inter-symbol interference will not be so great as to introduce actual digit errors. It is in the presence of noise, cross-talk, channel attenuation and other signal-corrupting influences that inter-symbol interference assumes importance as a factor which limits the efficiency of the transmission system.

Let us take as our model of the digital-signal waveform the bipolar NRZ format illustrated in table 8.1. The power spectrum of the random digital waveform is given by the relation

$$P(f) = T^{-1} |S(f)|^2$$

This result presumes equiprobable binary symbols 0 and 1 and signal waveshapes such that

$$s(t) = s_0(t) = -s_1(t)$$

Since we assume a rectangular digit shape, $S(f)$ is readily evaluated as

$$S(f) = AT \, \text{sinc}(fT)$$

yielding a power spectrum

$$P(f) = A^2 T \text{sinc}^2(fT) \quad \text{all } f$$

If such a signal is sharply band-limited so that

$$P'(f) = A^2 T \, \text{sinc}^2(fT) \quad |f| < 1/2T$$

the corresponding signalling-pulse spectrum must be

$$S'(f) = AT \, \text{sinc}(fT) \quad |f| < 1/2T$$

Fourier transformation to obtain $s'(t)$ yields the signalling-pulse shape shown in figure 8.3a. This pulse exhibits undesirable inter-symbol interference

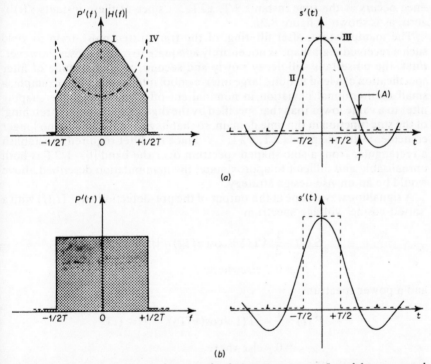

Figure 8.3 (a) Power spectrum of rectangular digit sequence, curve I, and the corresponding signalling-pulse shape, curve II, after band limiting by the channel. Curve III shows the pre-transmission pulse shape and indicates the extent of intersymbol interference (A). A uniform spectrum can be realised from P'(f) by ensuring an overall transfer characteristic H(f), curve IV, by suitably choosing H₁(f) and/or H₂(f). (b) The uniform power-spectrum and the corresponding signalling-pulse shape

properties because, at time instants $\pm T, \pm 2T, \ldots$, its amplitude is still significantly large. It is at these time instants that sampling of the received, filtered digital waveform would be carried out to determine the nature of the transmitted symbols. Furthermore, the pulse tails decay slowly, so that interference extends over many adjacent symbols.

If, instead of merely band limiting the digital waveform, we had devised $H(f)$ such that the received-pulse voltage spectrum was rectangular

$$S'(f) = AT \quad |f| \leq 1/2T$$
$$= 0 \quad \text{elsewhere}$$

then the signalling-pulse shape would be

$$s'(t) = A \, \text{sinc}(t/T)$$

and the corresponding random digital power-spectrum would be

$$P'(f) = A^2 T \quad |f| \leq 1/2T$$
$$= 0 \quad \text{elsewhere}$$

Inspection of the received digit shape indicates that no inter-symbol interference occurs at the time instants $\pm T, \pm 2T, \ldots$ since at these instants $s'(t)$ is zero, as is shown in figure 8.3b.

The manipulation, after filtering, of the transmitted pulse-train to yield such a received digit shape is not entirely adequate to our purposes, however. First, the pulse tails still decay slowly and second, an inexactitude of filter specification can lead to quite large inter-symbol interference. For example, a small unintentional deviation in nominal cut-off frequency of the shaping filter to a value lower than that specified by the digit rate leads to a 'stretching' of the sinc function in the time domain, so that its zero crossings are no longer coincident with the points $\pm T, \pm 2T, \ldots$. Since the filter required to establish a rectangular from a sinc-shaped spectrum over the band $|f| \leq 1/2T$ is both unrealisable and difficult to approximate, the manipulation described above would be an unwise design strategy.

A signalling waveshape at the output of the pre-detection filter $H_3(f)$ with a 'raised-cosine' voltage spectrum

$$S'(f) = \frac{1}{2} AT(1 + \cos(\pi fT)) \quad |f| \leq 1/T$$
$$= 0 \quad \text{elsewhere}$$

and a power spectrum

$$P'(f) = \frac{1}{4} A^2 T(1 + \cos(\pi fT))^2 \quad |f| \leq 1/T$$
$$= 0 \quad \text{elsewhere}$$

is frequently advocated as a design target. This spectrum is illustrated in figure 8.4 and corresponds to a signalling pulse shape given by the transform

$$s'(t) = A \, \text{sinc}(t/T)\cos(\pi t/T)\{1 - (2t/T)^2\}^{-1}$$

The raised-cosine law results in a signalling pulse which exhibits ringing of a small amplitude which rapidly dies down to zero. Furthermore, no inter-symbol interference occurs at time intervals $\pm T, \pm 3T/2, \pm 2T, \ldots$. Of course, as the spectrum illustrated in figure 8.4 shows, such a pulse can only be achieved at the expense of extended transmission bandwidth.

A complete system design, then, requires attention to the following points

(1) The selection of $H_1(f)$ and/or $H_3(f)$ to obtain equalisation with respect to the transmission-medium characteristics, should this be necessary.

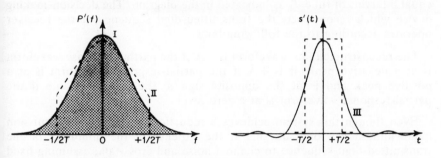

Figure 8.4 The raised-cosine voltage-spectrum: a design target, Curve I. Curve II shows the band-limited power spectrum corresponding to a rectangular digit sequence and curve III shows the digit shape corresponding to curve I

(2) The selection of $H_1(f)$ and $H_3(f)$ so that the overall-channel transfer-function

$$H(f) = H_1(f)H_2(f)H_3(f)$$

presents a raised-cosine spectrum at the receiver decision-circuitry input.

(3) The selection of $H_3(f)$ to ensure an adequate or optimised signal-to-noise ratio at the decision-circuitry input, depending on the channel-noise spectrum.

It does not follow that all these considerations may be mutually satisfied. Some compromise in system design would usually be necessary.

8.4 Partial Response Signalling

One problem introduced by suggesting a raised-cosine spectrum as the target for the design of a received digital signalling-pulse is the relatively large bandwidth (equal to the digit rate $1/T$) that this implies. A signalling method exists and is, indeed, quite widely used, whereby the target is a raised-cosine spectrum extending only to a frequency $1/2T$. That is

$$S'(f) = \frac{1}{2} AT\{1 + \cos(2\pi fT)\} \quad |f| \leqslant 1/2T$$

$$= 0 \quad \text{elsewhere}$$

Such a spectrum will obviously introduce gross inter-symbol interference. However, the nature of this interference may be accurately predicted and can be used to reveal the sequence of symbols in the original transmitted signal. Figure 8.5a illustrates the response of the overall transfer function $H(f)$ designed to achieve such a pulse spectrum. Clearly, only a pair of digits occurring together will exhibit the normal response depicted previously in figure 8.4. A single rectangular digit will only just intersect the zero voltage level—the direction of intersection depending on the sign of the previous digit. It provides only a 'partial' response.

The response of the entire transmission system to a typical bipolar NRZ waveform is shown in figure 8.5b. The reconstruction of the original waveform from the partial-response waveform is obtained by sampling at equal intervals of time T, as indicated in the diagram. The decision-making device which reconstructs the transmitted-digit sequence at the receiver operates according to the following laws.

The reconstructed NRZ waveform is $-A$ if the partial-response waveform is at a negative peak, it is $+A$ if the partial-response waveform is at a positive peak and is of the opposite sign to the previous value if the partial-response waveform is at a zero level.

Even though this system achieves a reduction of required transmission bandwidth, it can only do this at the expense of the immunity of the transmitted-digit sequence to channel noise and cross-talk, assuming fixed maximum-transmission voltage levels. This is because the separation between the three levels of decision, $+A$, 0 and $-A$ is one-half of that which would occur if straight binary signalling were used, employing only the levels $+A$ and $-A$.

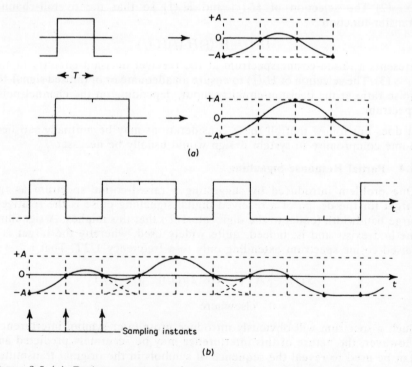

Figure 8.5 (a) Basic response waveforms for partial-response signalling. (b) The partial-response technique applied to a random sequence of binary digits

8.5 Eye Patterns

The 'eye pattern' test allows us to present a visual display, usually on an oscilloscope, of the effects of signal processing and the transmission path on a digital waveform. The heart of the test system, which is illustrated in figure 8.6, is a pseudo-random digit generator.[38] This sub-system is a shift register with modulo-2 feedback taken from suitably selected stages and returned to the input. The general properties of such mechanisations are well covered in the literature and have been discussed in section 7.7.

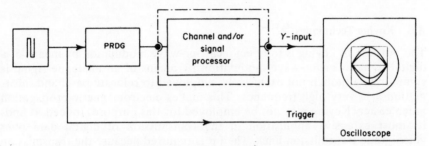

Figure 8.6 The eye pattern test system

The test system operates in the following manner. The clock generator increments the pseudo-random digit-generator output and also provides a trigger pulse to initiate the sweep of the oscilloscope trace. The oscilloscope sweep duration corresponds to the clock period and therefore to the length of one binary digit. The Y-input of the oscilloscope is obtained from the signal processor or channel output.

Each scan of the oscilloscope records the superposition of the response of the communication system to the voltage pulse currently presented to it by the pseudo-random digit generator and the sum of the tails of all previous pulses. Persistence of vision creates a pattern of responses which typically forms an 'eye'. Figure 8.7 shows an example of such an eye pattern, which

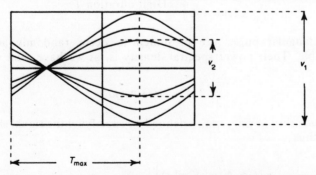

Figure 8.7 The eye pattern: T_{max} is the time from the start of the transmitted digit to the maximum eye-aperture

exhibits the combined effects of all possible digit sequences available at the generator output.

The upper and lower bounds to the 'lid' of the eye, v_1 and v_2, define the best and worst received-pulse amplitudes. The eye opening provides us with a method of measuring the practical worst-case operating condition. It tells us that we must not rely upon a separation of the received 1 and 0 digit amplitudes equal to the pre-transmission separation in assessing error rate. In addition, the location of the maximum eye opening, T_{max}, allows us to specify the optimum sampling instant in the decision circuit at the receiver.

8.6   Keying Techniques[36,41,46]

The purpose of keying is to effect a carrier-wave modulation by means of a digital signal. Carrier-wave modulation by means of an analogue signal is commonly, although not exclusively, employed to relocate baseband information at a very high frequency. This makes electromagnetic propagation much easier. Keying may not be employed for this purpose. Indeed, it finds its most extensive application in the transmission of digital data over voice-grade transmission lines. Then it is required because the transmission path is bandpass in nature, having a bandwidth extending nominally from 300 Hz to 3.4 kHz. Thus the carrier frequencies employed with land-line data transmission are typically of the same order of magnitude as the spectral width of the modulated wave itself. The system is broad-band and as a consequence waveforms may differ in spectral structure from the narrow-band processes which result when a high-frequency carrier is modulated with an analogue waveform. The differences stem from spectral overlap at zero frequency.

Before defining the basic keying techniques employed in modern communication practice, let us specify an appropriate digital-data modulating waveform, $v_m(t)$. In section 8.1, we denoted the signal shapes corresponding to the binary symbols 0 and 1 as $s_0(t)$ and $s_1(t)$ respectively. We shall presume that keying is effected by the modulation of a sinusoidal carrier with a bipolar NRZ waveform, for which

$$\left. \begin{array}{l} s_0(t) = -A \\ s_1(t) = +A \end{array} \right\} \quad \text{Digit duration } T$$

These rectangular pulses are presumed to occur randomly and to be equiprobable. Their power spectral density is, as we have seen in section 1.27.3.

$$P_m(f) = A^2 T \text{sinc}(fT) \tag{8.1}$$

Amplitude shift keying, ASK, is defined by specifying the signal shapes $s_0(t)$ and $s_1(t)$ thus

$$\left. \begin{array}{l} s_0(t) = A_0 \cos(2\pi f_c t) \\ s_1(t) = A_1 \cos(2\pi f_c t) \end{array} \right\} \quad \text{Digit duration } T$$

Such a wave is equivalent to employing the baseband process $v_m(t)$, defined above, to provide 'conventional amplitude modulation'. Specifically, we may regard it as directly equivalent to modulating a carrier of amplitude

$$A_c = \frac{1}{2}(A_0 + A_1)$$

with a rectangular, bipolar pulse train, $v_m(t)$, of amplitude

$$A = \frac{1}{2}(A_0 - A_1)$$

The equation for a conventional amplitude modulation, equation 3.7, corresponds to a power spectrum, equation 3.10, in which $P_m(f)$ is given by equation 8.1 above

$$P(f) = \frac{1}{4}\{P_m(f - f_c) + P_m(f + f_c)\} + \frac{1}{4}A_c^2\{\delta(f-f_c) + \delta(f+f_c)\}$$

This power spectrum was derived in chapter 3 on the basis that the modulated carrier was a narrow-band process. In the present circumstances, since the carrier frequency is relatively low in comparison with the keying rate, the processes involved are not really 'narrow-band'. However, the tails of the 'sinc-squared' distribution of power in $v_m(t)$, equation 8.1, decay rapidly, so that in almost all cases of interest, we may still assume the validity of the narrow-band formulae. Indeed, for very low carrier frequencies, overlap of the spectral tails would be most serious in the region about zero frequency. Since d.c. and low frequencies are a 'forbidden region' for line transmission of data, we would normally ensure that little signal energy was wasted in this region, so that the signal amplitude was maximised. It follows that the power spectral density of the amplitude shift-keyed carrier may be approximated by the relation, derived by inserting equation 8.1 into equation 3.10, namely

$$P(f) = \left\{\frac{1}{4}(A_0 - A_1)\right\}^2 T[\text{sinc}^2\{(f - f_c)T\} + \text{sinc}^2\{(f + f_c)T\}]$$
$$+ \left\{\frac{1}{4}(A_0 + A_1)\right\}^2 \{\delta(f - f_c) + \delta(f + f_c)\} \quad (8.2)$$

This spectrum may, for very broad-band processes, be regarded as providing an upper bound to the possible actual signal spectrum, which would otherwise be difficult to estimate with precision. Figure 8.8 illustrates both the ASK wave and its power spectrum.

In fact, ASK is not a widely favoured keying technique. One special case which is sometimes encountered is known as *on–off keying*, OOK. Here the signal shapes are defined by setting $A_0 = 0$ and $A_1 = A$ so that

$$\left.\begin{array}{l} s_0(t) = 0 \\ s_1(t) = A\,\cos(2\pi f_c t) \end{array}\right\} \quad \text{Digit duration } T$$

A very important keying technique may be derived from the class of ASK waveforms by setting $A_0 = +A$ and $A_1 = -A$ so that

$$\left.\begin{array}{l} s_0(t) = +A\,\cos(2\pi f_c t) \\ s_1(t) = -A\,\cos(2\pi f_c t) \end{array}\right\} \quad \text{Digit duration } T$$

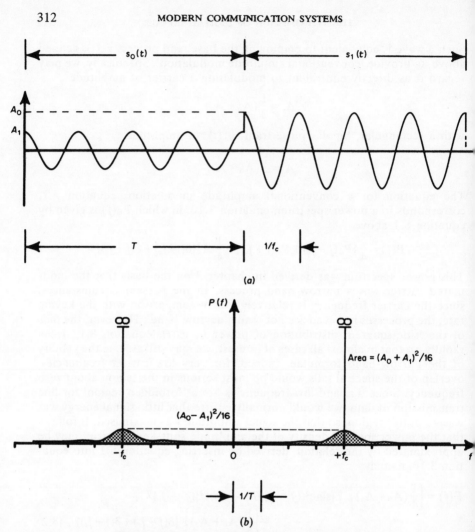

Figure 8.8 Keying waveforms and power spectra: ASK

The spectrum of such a signal is, from equation 8.2

$$P(f) = \frac{1}{4} A^2 T[\text{sinc}^2\{(f - f_c)T\} + \text{sinc}^2\{(f + f_c)T\}]$$

This wave, in contrast to the ASK and OOK waveforms, is a *suppressed carrier product modulation*. The defining equations given above may be rewritten as

$$\left.\begin{array}{l} s_0(t) = A \cos(2\pi f_c t) \\ s_1(t) = A \cos(2\pi f_c t + \pi) \end{array}\right\} \quad \text{Digit duration } T$$

Thus this envelope modulation may also be thought of as a phase modulation and is, indeed, commonly referred to as *phase shift keying*, PSK. A typical PSK waveform and its spectrum is shown in figure 8.9.

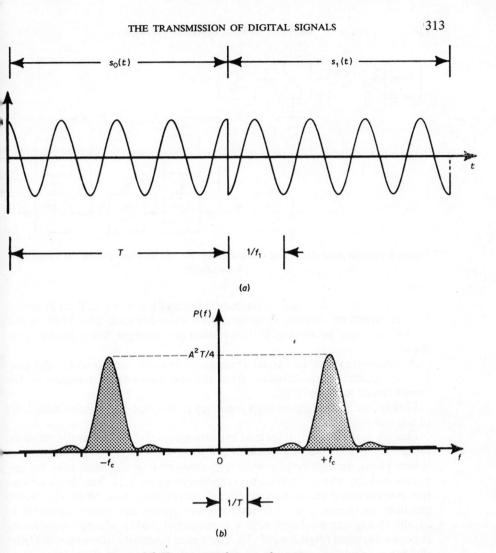

Figure 8.9 *Keying waveforms and power spectra*: PSK

A simple two-phase PSK system is illustrated in figure 8.10. The system shown employs a balanced modulator (see section 3.7.3) to change the phase of a tone generator by π radians according to the sense of the data-source output. (Assume v_1 in figure 8.10 to be a bipolar NRZ waveform. Some systems use digital techniques to yield a pair of square wavetrains in anti-phase, keying between these and subsequently filtering to remove harmonics.) Post-modulation bandpass filtering, $H_1(f)$, is used to band-limit the transmitted waveform. After transmission, pre-detection filtering, $H_2(f)$, minimises the channel noise admitted to the demodulator. Both $H_1(f)$ and $H_2(f)$, as well as the channel characteristic and the post-detection filter, $H_3(f)$, impose a spectral distortion on the demodulated waveform, v_5. H_1, H_2 and H_3 may, accordingly, be selected according to the general rules presented in section 8.3 to minimise

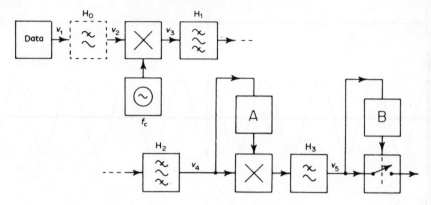

Figure 8.10 PSK *modulator and demodulator.* A: *carrier regeneration*; B: *digit synchronisation*

intersymbol interference and obtain channel equalisation. As we shall see in section 8.10, an 'optimum' detector structure, which minimises error probability in PSK transmission, may be obtained if H_3 is realised as a baseband 'integrate-and-dump' circuit.

A locally-regenerated carrier component is easily extracted for the purpose of product demodulation, from the PSK waveform, by means of the circuit shown in figure 8.11.

Finally, the demodulated digit sequence is sampled at the pulse midpoints of the waveform v_5.

One problem which this form of PSK introduces is the need, at the receiver, to identify the correct regenerated phase of the carrier for demodulation. When phase ambiguity is possible, a *differential* PSK system may be implemented, for which the detector is shown in figure 8.12. The detector uses two narrow-band resonators to 'store' successive tones. With the switch positions as shown, a tone is received and causes the lower resonator to exhibit (being narrow-band) a slow exponential growth of amplitude during the tone duration (digit length, T). The upper resonator, disconnected from the input, rings in response to the preceding tone. It provides a local oscillator signal for demodulation of the current tone, but with a phase which is that of the previous tone. If the current tone and the previous tone are of the same phase, the demodulator output will be of positive sense. If they are of opposite phase, the demodulator output will be of negative sense.

The problem of phase ambiguity may be resolved by employing this detector configuration in conjunction with 'differential' keying. Differential keying requires that the original baseband (unipolar or bipolar NRZ) waveform be recoded in the following way. A binary 1 is transmitted if a digit change from 0 to 1 or 1 to 0 takes place and a binary 0 is transmitted if no change takes place. This scheme is known as 'mark differential' encoding. Space-differential encoding results in the transmission of a binary 0 if a digit change occurs. The waveforms presented in figure 8.13 show that, given

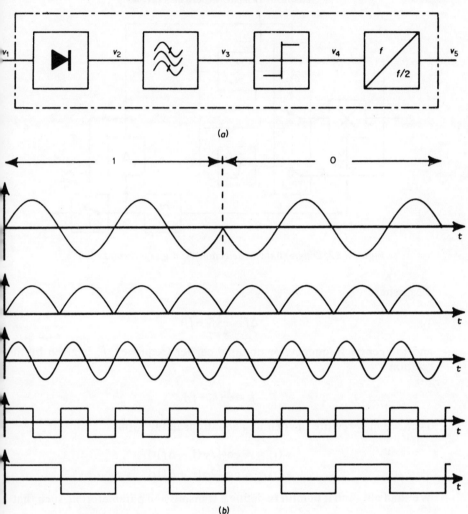

Figure 8.11 *Carrier regeneration for* PSK *demodulation*

differential encoding, the detector of figure 8.12 automatically restores the original baseband process.

Another widely used keying method is known as *frequency shift keying*, FSK, and is defined by the equations

$$\left.\begin{aligned} s_0(t) &= A \cos(2\pi f_0 t) \\ s_1(t) &= A \cos(2\pi f_1 t) \end{aligned}\right\} \text{ Digit duration } T$$

For the sake of argument, we shall assume that f_1 is greater than f_0. We shall find it convenient to rewrite these equations in terms of the 'tone spacing',

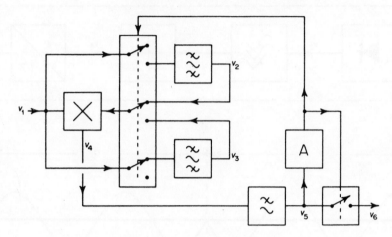

Figure 8.12 Differential PSK *detection.* A: *digit synchronisation*

2 Δf, where

$$\Delta f = \frac{1}{2}(f_0 - f_1)$$

and the centre frequency, or nominal carrier frequency, f_c, is given by the relation

$$f_c = \frac{1}{2}(f_0 + f_1)$$

Then we may rewrite the defining equations in the form

$$s_0(t) = A \cos\{2\pi(f_c - \Delta f)t\}$$
$$s_1(t) = A \cos\{2\pi(f_c + \Delta f)t\}$$

We shall also find it helpful to define a transmission parameter, m, such that

$$m = \text{tone spacing/digit rate}$$

This parameter is analogous to the 'modulation index' used in FM theory, as defined in chapter 4, since

$$m = 2 \Delta f T$$
$$= \Delta f/(1/2T)$$

and $1/2T = f_m$, the maximum modulation frequency. Indeed, if premodulation filtering to produce pulse shaping, as described in section 8.3, were employed on the random-digit sequence and this sequence were then used to modulate a voltage-controlled oscillator, the analogy would be a very close one.

The FSK wave may be thought of as the superposition of two OOK waves, one keyed with the data signal, and with a carrier frequency f_1; the other, of carrier frequency f_0 keyed with the complement of the data signal, so that

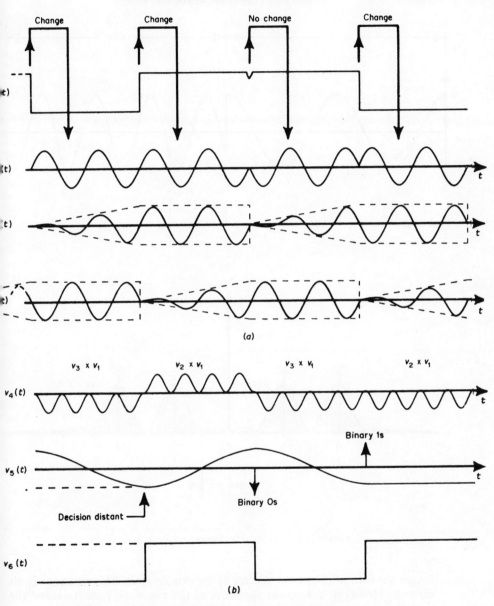

Figure 8.13 Mark differential signalling and DPSK detection waveforms

the binary digits 0 and 1 are interchanged. The power spectrum of such a wave is, for reasonably large tone-spacings, the sum of the power spectra of its constituent OOK signals, figure 8.14. As the OOK carriers are brought together by a decrease of tone spacing, the lobes surrounding each carrier overlap. Under this condition, cancellation of voltage spectral components may take place, with the result that the power spectrum of the FSK wave is no

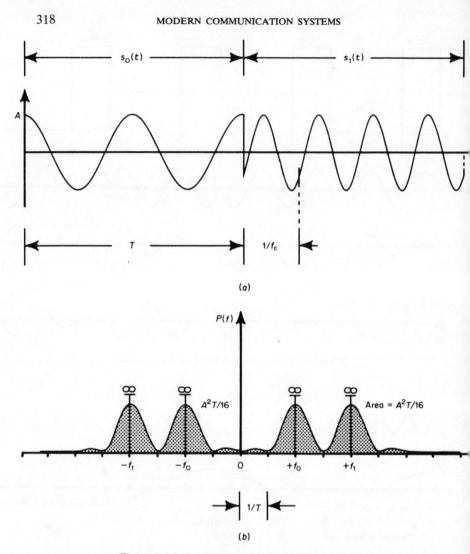

Figure 8.14 *Keying waveforms and power spectra*: FSK

longer the sum of the power spectra of the OOK carriers. This makes analysis difficult. However, the power spectrum of the FSK wave cannot exceed the sum of the power spectra of the two OOK carriers, so that we do at least have a convenient upper bound for all conditions of tone spacing and data rate. This upper bound is adequate for most purposes and may be derived from equation 8.2 quite easily.

Figure 8.15 illustrates the structure of an FSK system. The modulator consists of a pair of free-running oscillators, set to the signalling frequencies, f_0 and f_1. The keying switch selects the output of the appropriate oscillator, depending on the nature of the binary digit being transmitted. Bandpass filtering after keying would normally be employed to band-limit the trans-

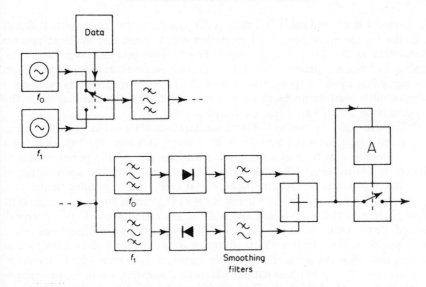

Figure 8.15 FSK *with discontinuous phase transitions.* A: *digit synchronisation*

mitted signalling-waveform. The demodulator is essentially a modified Travis discriminator (see section 4.8.1, figure 4.16). It consists of a pair of tuned circuits, tuned to the frequencies f_0 and f_1 respectively, each followed by an envelope detector. By differencing the outputs from the two envelope detectors, an output pulse which is positive-going for a transmitted 1 and negative-going for a transmitted 0 is obtained. At time-instants corresponding to the received pulse midpoints (that is, at the maximum amplitude of the received pulse) the received digit sequence, which will be distorted by the transmission channel and corrupted by channel noise, is sampled to determine the digit sense. Sample values greater than zero are taken to define a binary 1 and values less than zero are taken to define a binary 0. Thus the system earth level provides a 'decision threshold'. The sampling waveform is established by means of a 'digit synchronisation circuit'.

When we defined the FSK wave, we introduced a transmission parameter, m, analogous to the modulation index of an ordinary frequency modulation. Modern practice generally requires that the value chosen for m shall be 1. Then, the tone spacing equals the digit rate. Too low a value of m results in the tone frequencies being too close to be easily distinguishable and this leads to a high error rate in the presence of channel noise. It might be thought that a large value of m ($m \gg 1$) would permit the keying system to trade a reduced digit rate for an improved error-rate performance, much as an analogue FM system trades bandwidth for signal-to-noise ratio, increasing the modulation index in the process. However, the advantages accrued from such a strategy are insufficient to warrant the reduction in information throughput. This is because, although the FSK detector bears a close resemblance to the Travis discriminator, no lowpass filtering is included at the output prior to sampling and decision so that the FM improvement described in chapter 4 is not realised. Why, then, is the post-detection filter omitted? Recall that the FM threshold, described in section 4.9, is caused by an impulse-noise component at the discriminator output. If a lowpass post-detection filter is included, each noise impulse generates at the post-detection-filter output a waveform corresponding to the impulse response of the filter. This filtered impulse-noise component is much more damaging to the received digit sequence than either the gaussian noise component or the unfiltered impulse.

It is worth while comparing the transmission efficiencies of PSK and FSK waves. The mean power conveyed by both is $A^2/2$ volt^2. However, the PSK wave has a power spectral density containing no line components. All the power contained therein is informational. The FSK wave, being composed of the superposition of two OOK waves, has two spectral lines, one at each of the signalling frequencies. From equation 8.2, setting $A_0 = 0$ and $A_1 = A$, the carrier power in a single OOK wave is given by the second term, and is $A^2/8$. The carrier power in the superposition of the two OOK waves, the FSK wave, is $A^2/4$, leaving an informational power of $A^2/4$. Thus, PSK offers a +3 dB advantage over FSK, for a given amplitude of carrier, and this advantage is reflected in an increased noise immunity in detection.

Although FSK and bi-phase PSK are widely used signalling methods, an improvement in data-rate through a channel of fixed bandwidth can be obtained by resorting to multilevel keying, as we see in the next section.

8.7 Multilevel Keying Systems

We have seen that, when baseband signalling is used, a multilevel transmission can be used to increase binary digit rate, without requiring an increase in channel bandwidth. In like manner, presuming a fixed-bandwidth constraint, higher data rates can be obtained by multiphase keying. Instead of using only two phases, 0 and π radians, four or eight phases may be used. Each phase then represents pairs ('dibits') or triplets of binary digits. In effect, we are then using a binary to M'ary (M-symbol set) coding, where $M = 4$ or 8, respectively.

By doing this, we retain the same *symbol* rate (each symbol in this case corresponding to a transmission phase) and hence the same transmission bandwidth, but we increase the *binary* (coder input) data rate by factors of two and three respectively. Of course, if signal amplitude (transmitted power) is also constrained, the increased data rate can only be achieved at the expense of bit error-rate.

One way of achieving four-phase PSK is to employ a quadrature AM system such as was described in section 5.1. Such a keying is referred to as quadrature phase shift keying, QPSK. Carriers $A \cos(2\pi f_c t)$ and $A \sin(2\pi f_c t)$ are independently keyed by sub-sequences separated from the main digit sequence to be transmitted. The main digit-sequence rate may then be doubled, increasing the information throughput of the data link. The two keyed carriers are then summed, transmitted and separated after transmission by demodulation with a pair of local oscillator signals, one in phase, the other in phase-quadrature. In theory, the transmitted carriers are orthogonal. In practice, after transmission, some cross-talk between them will occur.

The phasor or 'signal-space' diagram for a four-phase PSK with natural binary coding of digits to 'phase-displacement from reference' is shown in figure 8.16a.

The reader should note that noise-induced digit errors can be introduced in two ways. Firstly, any phasor displacement greater than $\pi/4$ radians on either side of its ideal location will cause it to cross one of the broken-line phasor 'decision thresholds'. Secondly, an *inversion* of phase will cause diametrically opposite digit pairs to be interchanged. On average, because it involves a smaller phasor-perturbation, the first condition is more likely to arise. Of the twelve possible error-inducing perturbations ($00 \rightarrow 01, 00 \rightarrow 10, \ldots 11 \rightarrow 00$) only four involve phase inversion: $00 \rightarrow 10, 10 \rightarrow 00, 01 \rightarrow 11$ and $11 \rightarrow 01$. Of the remaining, more probable transitions, four involve digit-pair exchanges in which *all* digits alter. Thus the natural binary assignation of digits to phase results in a situation where the most detrimental digit-pair exchanges are also among the most probable.

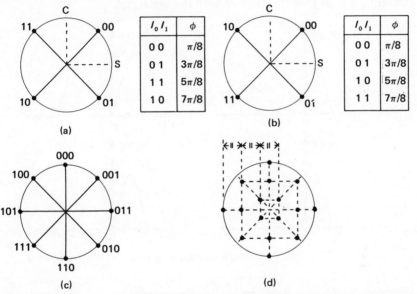

Figure 8.16 Signal space diagrams for multiphase PSK: (a) 4-PSK with natural binary assignation, (b) 4-PSK with Gray coding (C ≡ cosine carrier phase; S ≡ sine carrier phase), (c) 8-PSK with Gray coding, (d) 8-PSK with AM giving 16 state signalling to C.C.I.T.T. V29 specification

If instead the natural binary assignations were abandoned, and the four worst digit-pair exchanges were assigned to the *least* probable phase transitions in a noisy situation, one might hope to obtain some measure of improvement in overall bit-error rate. To do this, we place digit pairs 00 and 11 and digit pairs 01 and 10 at diametrically opposite points on the phasor diagram, figure 8.16b, and note that in so doing, we establish *Gray coding* of phase displacement from reference (see section 6.6).

To achieve (for fixed bandwidth) yet higher data rates, eight-phase PSK may be used, either alone or in conjunction with an amplitude keying which allows sixteen symbol-states to be used. The signal space diagrams corresponding to these formats are shown in figures 8.16c and d respectively. When the sixteen-state combined ASK/PSK system is used, it permits the transmission of four binary digits per symbol.

Another method of improving the use of the restricted channel-bandwidth available on voice-grade links is to derive a single-sideband waveform. Because the data signal contains important low-frequency components, a straightforward SSB modulation by filtering is not possible. Unrealisable networks would be required. Instead, VSB is employed. The basic system shown in figure 8.10 is used, but with the filters H_1 and H_2 adopting different roles and the filter H_0 introduced to provide pre-modulation pulse shaping, as described in section 8.3. The spectra illustrated in figure 8.17 show how the system generates the VSB signal. H_1 and H_2 each contribute half the spectral shaping necessary to yield the correct VSB spectrum. Equal shaping contributions from these filters can be shown to yield the best noise immunity, both practically and theoretically.[28] Carrier regeneration is obtained by extracting a pilot tone transmitted with the VSB signal.

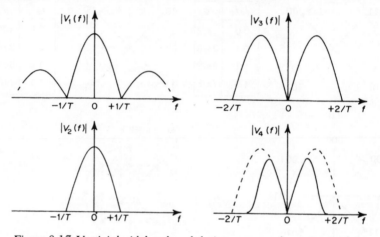

Figure 8.17 Vestigial-sideband modulation: spectra of system waveforms

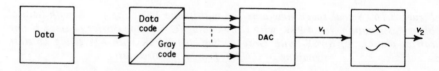

Figure 8.18 High-speed VSB pre-processing. Waveforms v_1 and v_2 replace the same waveforms in figure 8.10

If very high data rates are required, multilevel VSB transmission is employed. The same basic system as that depicted in figure 8.18 is used but with the data source generating an n-ary process, suitably band-limited to yield a waveform with the superficial appearance of an analogue, rather than a digital signal. A sub-system which performs this function is shown in figure 8.15. A Gray code (section 6.6) is established so that errors incurred in the channel, which are most likely to cause a given level to register as one of the two adjacent levels, will cause the binary equivalent of that level to change by only one digit.

A summary of telephone-channel modem alternatives is presented in table 8.6 and is discussed in terms of channel equalisation requirements in section 8.9 and error-rate performance in section 8.10.

8.8   Bandwidth Economical Keying Systems[55]

Satellite radio-frequency communication now provides an increasingly important vehicle for the transmission of digital data and places an important constraint upon the design of appropriate keying systems. First, notice that the various keying techniques we have so far discussed invariably introduce amplitude discontinuities at the digit transition instants (see figures 8.8, 8.9 and 8.14 for example). Necessarily, such waveforms require bandlimiting prior to transmission, to remove spectral spuria introduced by these discontinuities. This is particularly true of operation in multichannel frequency-multiplexed satellite systems where extraneous high-frequency components would cause serious adjacent-channel interference. Bandlimiting, however, invariably takes place at low power-levels (that is, before radio-frequency power amplification), because filter insertion-loss is then less significant in reducing the overall efficiency of an energy-constrained system.

It is a further consequence of the desire to effect economies of energy expenditure, that radio-frequency power amplification is operated close to, or at, active-device saturation. (Typically, power amplification for such applications involves the use of travelling-wave tubes or class-C solid-state circuits.)

The effect of bandlimiting upon our 'preferred' keying waveforms (FSK, PSK, DPSK, QPSK) is to introduce amplitude fluctuations into a waveform which was initially of constant amplitude. Indeed, we necessarily *equate* amplitude fluctuation with bandlimitedness, in the context of these modulations. The effect of subsequent hard-limiting amplification would be to eliminate amplitude fluctuation and the immediate effect of such an operation would be to restore the unwanted spectral spuria.

To overcome this problem, new classes of keying technique have been devised. We shall now consider two of the most significant representatives of these classes: Offset QPSK (OQPSK) and minimum (frequency) shift keying (MSK or MFSK). OQPSK, figure 8.19, merely involves realigning digit transitions to the inphase and quadrature inputs of the modulator so that one of the two demultiplexed digit-streams (each consisting of 'stretched' NRZ digits of duration $2T$ s) is subject to a stagger of T s. This apparently trivial manoeuvre has the effect of eliminating sudden phase transitions in excess of $\pi/2$ radians and consequently substantially reduces envelope fluctuations after bandlimiting. OQPSK may conveniently be expressed as

$$s(t) = A\{v_1(t)\cos(2\pi f_c t) + v_2(t)\sin(2\pi f_c t)\} \tag{8.3}$$

where v_1 and v_2 are *rectangular* bipolar NRZ pulse waveforms of unit amplitude derived by applying the demultiplexing defined above. For QPSK and OQPSK the power spectrum is the same, being given by the result

$$P(f) = \tfrac{1}{2}A^2 T[\text{sinc}^2\{2(f - f_c)T\} + \text{sinc}^2\{2(f + f_c)T\}]$$

MSK differs in definition from OQPSK (equation 8.3) only in the *shaping* of the bipolar NRZ pulse waveforms used to modulate the QPSK carriers. For this class

TABLE 8.6 TYPICAL DATA MODEM OPERATING SPECIFICATIONS

Input Data Rate (digits per second)	Output Data Rate (bauds or symbols per second)	Modulation Method	General Comments
200	200	FSK; $\Delta f = 100$ $f_c = 1080$ or 1750 $m = 1$	C.C.I.T.T. V21 Recommendation, asynchronous, full-duplex modem intended for the switched netowrk.
600	600	FSK; $\Delta f = 200$ $f_c = 1500$ $m = 0.67$	C.C.I.T.T. V23 Recommendation, asynchronous, half-duplex modem intended for the switched network. Incorporates a 75 digit per second backward channel for the transmission of supervisory signals or low-speed return data.
1200	1200	FSK; $\Delta f = 400$ $f_c = 1700$ $m = 0.67$	
1200	1200	2-PSK	C.C.I.T.T. V26 Recommendation, synchronous, asymmetrical duplex modem for use of the switched network. Fixed or preset equalisation.
2400	1200	4-PSK	

4800	VSB with 4-level Gray coding	Typical carrier frequency 2400 Hz. Typical passband 600–2000 Hz
7200	VSB with 8-level Gray coding	Requires preset equalisation at 4800 digits per second, adaptive equalisation at 7200 digits per second. Switched public network.
4800	Differential 8-PSK (figure 8.16c)	C.C.I.T.T. V27 Recommendation. Typical carrier frequency 1800 Hz. Typical passband 600–2000 Hz Requires adaptive equalisation; faster synchronisation than 4800 digits per second VSB modem referred to above. Error protection provided by cyclic error detection using generator polynomial $1 + x^{-6} + x^{-7}$; natural length 127.
9600	Differential 8-PSK with amplitude modulation (figure 8.16d)	C.C.I.T.T. V29 Recommendation, transmits 16 signal states. Requires adaptive equalisation. Error protection provided by cyclic error detection using generator polynomial $1 + x^{-18} + x^{-23}$; natural length 8×10^6. Leased circuit operation.

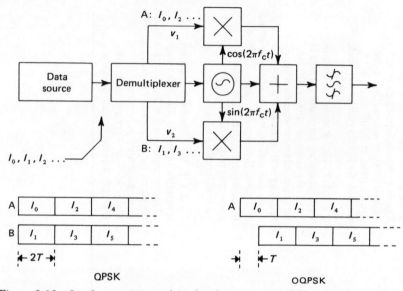

Figure 8.19   Quadrature PSK *and its development into Offset Quadrature* PSK

of keying we specify a *sinusoidal* digit-shape, so that

$$s(t) = A\{v_1(t)\cos(\pi t/2T)\cos(2\pi f_c t)$$
$$+ v_2(t)\sin(\pi t/2T)\sin(2\pi f_c t)\} \tag{8.4}$$

This modification can be shown to yield a power spectrum

$$P(f) = (4A^2 T/\pi^2)\left[\frac{\cos\{2\pi(f-f_c)T\}}{1 - 16(f-f_c)^2 T^2} + \frac{\cos\{2\pi(f+f_c)T\}}{1 - 16(f+f_c)^2 T^2}\right]$$

The MSK and QPSK spectra are compared, in normalised form, in figure 8.20. It should be noticed that, although MSK has a rather wider main spectral lobe, the skirt roll-off is faster, being displaced −12 dB per octave from centre frequency as opposed to −6 dB per octave for QPSK or OQPSK. Good skirt roll-off is often considered a desirable attribute if adjacent-channel interference in multichannel systems is to be minimised. Our objective in developing OQPSK and MSK was to ensure envelope constancy. By recasting equation 8.4 in polar form

$$s(t) = A(t)\cos(2\pi f_c t + \phi(t))$$

we see that this is, indeed, the case. Noting that $v_1^2(t) = v_2^2(t) = 1$ and writing

$$A(t) = A\{v_1^2(t)\cos^2(\pi t/2T) + v_2^2(t)\sin^2(\pi t/2T)\}^{1/2}$$

it follows that $A(t) = A$. The phase function is given by

$$\tan \phi(t) = v_2(t)/v_1(t) \tan(\pi t/2T)$$

In this case, because $|v_2(t)/v_1(t)|$ is always unity, we note that the instantaneous

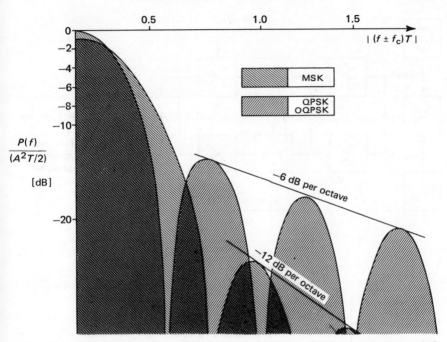

Figure 8.20 Normalised power spectra for quadrature PSK *and minimum shift keying (*MSK*)*

frequency displacement from centre frequency is

$$\mathrm{sgn}\{v_2(t)/v_1(t)\}/4T$$

where 'sgn' is the *signum function*

$$\mathrm{sgn}(x) = +1 \quad \text{for } x > 0$$

$$\mathrm{sgn}(x) = -1 \quad \text{for } x < 0$$

MSK is thus seen to be a special case of FSK with deviation of $\Delta f = 1/4T$ and modulation index $m = 0.5$.

The system illustrated in figure 8.21 may be used to generate and detect MSK. The modulator makes use of the identities

$$X = \cos(\alpha)\cos(\beta)$$

$$= \tfrac{1}{2}\{\cos(\alpha - \beta) + \cos(\alpha + \beta)\}$$

$$Y = \sin(\alpha)\sin(\beta)$$

$$= \tfrac{1}{2}\{\cos(\alpha - \beta) - \cos(\alpha + \beta)\}$$

where

$$\alpha = \pi t/2T \quad \text{and} \quad \beta = 2\pi f_c t$$

The detector shown in figure 8.21*b* employs synchronised integrate-and-dump

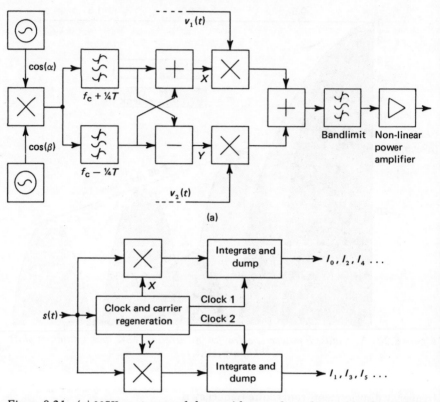

Figure 8.21   (a) MSK system modulator with v_1 and v_2 obtained by demultiplex-ing (see figure 8.19), (b) MSK detector (integrate-and-dump) circuit shown in detail in figure 8.29

detection. The integrate-and-dump circuit may be said to represent a close approxi-mation to the *optimum detector* for binary signalling waveshapes in the presence of gaussian channel noise. It is in fact, the optimum detector for *rectangular* bipolar signalling, as predicted by information theory. The fact that MSK uses sinusoidal digit-shaping means that a small (less than 1 dB) 'mismatch' loss would occur from using integrate-and-dump detection, rather than configuring the theoretically correct optimum detector. The optimum detector is *defined* to be a circuit which has an impulse response which is the *time-inverse* of the signal to which it is matched. Such a circuit is then referred to as a *matched filter*, being matched *not in the sense* of optimum power-transfer, but rather in the sense that it contains (in its impulse response) a built-in template against which all possible incoming signal shapes (corrupted by channel noise) may be matched. The time-reversal required by the matched filter definition has the effect of translating the filtering *convolution* integral (see section 1.16) into a *correlation* integral (see section 1.24). Thus the optimum detector effects the operation of determining the *correlation* between incoming signal and stored (transmitted) signal template.

Our previous discussion of multiple phase PSK signalling leads us to a generalisa-tion of MSK known as 'multi-*h* phase coded signalling'.[55] Recall first, the proposed use of Gray, as opposed to natural binary encoding of short binary words to phase displacement, in the four- and eight-phase PSK systems discussed in the previous section. Calculation of performance improvement shows that the former coding scheme offers only a modest benefit in improved error rate performance over the latter. However, once we appreciate that some effective improvement in bit error rate is to be obtained by proper choice of binary to M'ary coding scheme, then we may begin to investigate yet more favourable methods of establishing the keying format.

Consider, for example, the non-systematic convolution encoder described in section 7.8 and illustrated in figure 7.8. Here, an input binary digit sequence is coded into a double-rate output sequence with digit-pairs determined by coder 'state' and current information input. Since convolution coders purport to establish large 'distance' properties, then by so encoding, and subsequently assigning digit pairs to phase, a further improvement in coding gain may be achieved.

It is from this basis that the 'multi-h' format is developed. We presume

(1) a unit amplitude, NRZ rectangular bipolar modulating pulse sequence for which

$$\left. \begin{array}{l} s_0(t) = +1 \\ s_1(t) = -1 \end{array} \right\} \quad 0 \leqslant t \leqslant T$$

(2) a kth signalling pulse

$$s_i(t - kT); \quad kT \leqslant t \leqslant (k+1)T$$

with i chosen according to the 'sense' of the kth information digit and

(3) a frequency keying

$$s(t) = A \cos \{ 2\pi f_c t + \phi(t) \}$$

where instantaneous frequency, $\dot\phi$, is given by the relation

$$\dot\phi(t) = \frac{\pi}{T} \sum_{k=-\infty}^{+\infty} h_k s_i(t - kT)$$

Here h_k is a 'modulation index', variable on a pulse-to-pulse basis, according to some predetermined procedural law. In order that 'probabilistic' or 'sequential' decoding may be used, as was implied in the introductory paragraphs to this section, it is customary (and from a practical viewpoint necessary) to restrict the number of states which h_k may adopt. As a simple example, let us adopt one of four states and impose a cyclical rotation of state-value so that for all k, $h_{K+4} = h_k$. Choosing state-values in sequential order as $-\frac{1}{2}$, $-\frac{1}{4}$, $+\frac{1}{4}$, $+\frac{1}{2}$ has the effect of establishing sequential signalling tones in which the value of instantaneous frequency, $\dot\phi$, is given by $(f_c - \pi/4T)$, $(f_c - \pi/2T)$, $(f_c + \pi/2T)$ and $(f_c + \pi/4T)$. Figure 8.22a shows how a random digit sequence ... 1 0 0 1 0 0 0 0 1 1 ... codes into a multilevel ($M = 4$) instantaneous frequency waveform. Integrating this waveform, figure 8.22b, we obtain the 'phase code' waveform, ϕ, in which *slope* is proportional to *amplitude* of $\dot\phi$. If we next develop ϕ for all *possible* sequences of digits, a trellis diagram diagram emerges, figure 8.22c.

We see, then, that by applying within the modulator the keying rules outlined

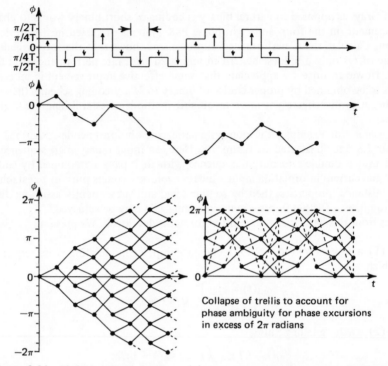

*Figure 8.22 Multi-h phase keying. (a) Instantaneous frequency displacement,
(b) phase excursions developed into a detection/decoding trellis (c)*

above, an angle-modulated, constant amplitude signal $s(t)$ is generated. During
transmission, channel noise may engender phase errors. The detector presents a
phase-state output sequence at each digit endpoint akin to status at each of the
nodal points of figure 8.22c. We recognise that, because of channel noise, the
phase-state output sequence may deviate from the transmitted or 'true' sequence.
Given a suitable 'metric' (see section 7.8) the methods of probabilistic decoding
may then be used to guide the phase-state output sequence back to a correct trellis
threading. This then allows us to provide partial error-correction or, equivalently,
establish significant 'coding gain' over such keying formats as the four-phase PSK
with which this discussion commenced. Choice of metric in realising the decoding
detector may now involve consideration of the effective 'geometrical distance'
between possible signal-state phasor endpoints (as illustrated in figure 8.16 for
example, for the simpler case of four-phase PSK). Thus, freedom to choose a
'best' metric neatly draws together the usually distinct requirements of detection
systems and decoders.

8.9 Line Equalisation Techniques

It was noted in section 8.3 that the transfer characteristic of a communication
channel may impose an unacceptable level of waveform distortion upon a transmitted digital signal. In order to reduce or eliminate such distortion, it is customary
to use correction ('line conditioning') circuits known as *equalisers*. Such circuits

effect, in particular, the correction of channel *attenuation* and *group delay* distortion. (Group delay distortion was introduced and defined in section 2.7.)

Decisions concerning the choice of equalisation technique are preceded by classification of the channel and assessment of its distortion characteristics. If the channel uses a fixed transmission path, as would be the case when operation entailed the use of a leased line, then distortion curves may be measured and the distortion virtually eliminated by the installation of computer-designed, passive conditioning networks. Such networks are referred to as *fixed equalisers*. Within the public, switched network, however, connection paths (and consequently distortion characteristics) vary on a call-to-call basis. In this situation, a fixed equalisation approach, referred to as *compromise equalisation* is used to compensate for average, rather than measured distortion curves. Average distortion characteristics for typical telephone connections are illustrated in figure 8.23. A *residual* distortion then remains. Normally, the residual distortion would not be a significant factor in degrading the performance of low-speed (< 600 digits s^{-1}) modems. For such systems, no further line conditioning would normally be envisaged.

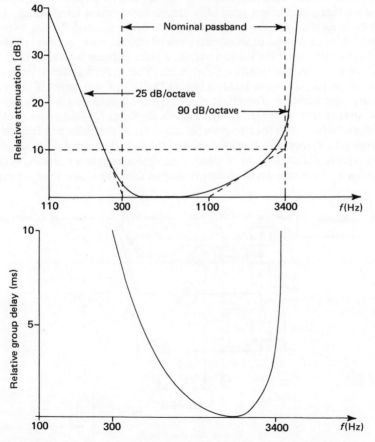

Figure 8.23 (a) Relative attenuation and (b) group delay as specified for a worst-case connection on a public switched network

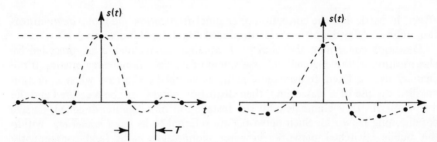

Figure 8.24 (a) Modem output pulse response exhibiting no intersymbol inter-ference, as judged by inspection at adjacent pulse decision instants. (b) Pulse response with gross intersymbol interference: s(kT) ≠ 0 for k ≠ 0 and s(0) of incorrect amplitude

By contrast, medium- and high-speed modems require further line conditioning. This is usually provided by 'transversal' equaliser circuits, which are digital filters operating upon the received bit-stream, sampled at the point of maximum eye-aperture (see section 8.5). Operation of the transversal equaliser relies on the observation that equalisation essentially cancels intersymbol interference. As we have seen in section 8.3, the combined effects of all spectral shaping (whether deliberate or, as in the case of an adverse channel characteristic, accidental) should be such as to produce, at the modem output, a pulse response with zero amplitude at adjacent pulse decision instants, figure 8.24a. That is, for a single isolated input the modem output, $s(t)$, must satisfy a law $s(kT) = 0$ for $k \neq 0$, where T is the output binary digit duration. The effect of intersymbol interference is to disrupt this orderly arrangement of zeros, as figure 8.24b illustrates. Arguably, we could re-establish a waveform with the *zero-crossing* attributes of that shown in figure 8.24a by choosing an appropriate weighted sum of the distorted signal decision-instant samples. This is, in fact, the way in which a transversal equaliser operates, as figure 8.25 indicates. Here, the decision-instant samples from the modem output pass to

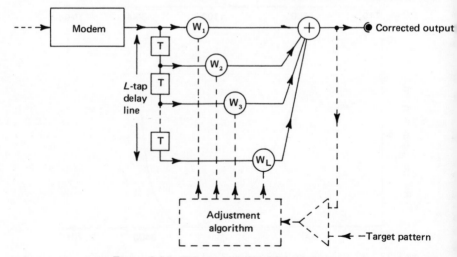

Figure 8.25   Transversal equaliser structure

an L-tap analogue delay-line, which effects a store-and-shift operation upon samples of arbitrary amplitude. The weighted sum is then, hopefully, the corrected modem output. Correction, however, depends upon the selection of appropriate tap-weights. This selection is effected by comparison of the 'corrected output' with a target pattern, according to some well-chosen 'adjustment algorithm'.

For medium-speed (1200, 2400 digits s^{-1}) modems, the target pattern is an initial binary 'training sequence' used each time a call-path is established. Operational experience with such modems indicates that no further equalisation is then necessary during data transmission. This approach establishes what is known as *preset equalisation*.

High-speed (4800, 9600 digits s^{-1}) modems exhibit such sensitivity to channel distortion that automatic and continuously variable, or *adaptive* equalisation is necessary.[54] In this case the target pattern is obtained directly from the 'corrected' modem output by passing the latter through a slicing or hard-limiting circuit. The sliced output is of fixed amplitude and, except for relatively rare digit errors, presents the appearance of the required, corrected sequence. Tap-weight adjustment then refines the variable-amplitude modem output, forcing the removal of the intersymbol interference and further reducing error probability.

In terms of modern practice, it would normally be considered desirable to replace the analogue delay-line shown in figure 8.25 with a digital shift register. This in turn implies analogue-to-digital conversion of decision-instant sample-amplitude at the modem output. The further, moderately complex processing demanded by the transversal filter and the adjustment algorithm, have made the use of microprocessor-based adaptive equalisers a particularly attractive and economical proposition.

8.10 Transmission Error Probability

The basic criterion used to establish the quality of a communication system carrying binary data is the *bit error rate*, often abbreviated in the technical literature to BER. Estimation of bit error rate usually presumes operation of the digital transmission system against a background of white, gaussian channel noise, $n(t)$, of spectral density η. This presumption, although unrepresentative of typical line noise (because signalling amplitudes are large by comparison with thermal or shot noise-source magnitudes, by contrast, for example, with received signal strength at the input of a radio receiver) is still valuable. It allows a mathematically tractable theoretical analysis of error rate, permits repeatable experimental assessment and establishes a rank-ordering of system performance. In this section, we shall derive theoretical expressions describing the bit error rate expected of a range of binary signalling and detection schemes. We note first the following assumptions

    (1) The binary data consists of equiprobable, random digits.
    (2) The transmitted signal is $s_0(t)$ or $s_1(t)$ depending upon whether a binary zero or a binary 1 is in the process of being transmitted.
    (3) The duration of each signalling pulse is T s, corresponding to a binary data rate of $(1/T)$ digit s^{-1}.
    (4) The energy in each signalling pulse is

$$E = \int_0^T s_0^2(t)\mathrm{d}t = \int_0^T s_1^2(t)\mathrm{d}t$$

(5) The energy *unique* to each signalling pulse, E_s, is the difference between E and the shared, or *cross-energy*. We may write

$$E_s = E(1 - R)$$

where R is the normalised cross-energy and is thus a cross-correlation function for $s_0(t)$ and $s_1(t)$ averaged over the signalling interval, being given by

$$R = \frac{1}{E} \int_0^T s_0(t)s_1(t)\mathrm{d}t \tag{8.5}$$

(5) The received signal is

$$y(t) = \left\{ \begin{matrix} s_0(t) \\ \text{or} \\ s_1(t) \end{matrix} \right\} + n(t)$$

Some general comments are now appropriate. The detection operation we are to consider is *optimum* in the sense that it minimises error rate subject to the stated constraint upon the nature of channel noise. Its development derives from considerations propounded within that branch of communication theory known as *statistical decision theory*. Such optimum detectors are often referred to as *coherent*, a term which implies the existence of ideal 'comparison templates' at the receiver, identical in shape to the signalling waveforms (in this case $s_0(t)$ and $s_1(t)$). Practical detection systems can be made which closely approximate the optimum detector in operation and performance, provided that the signalling waveshapes are not too complex.

In effecting an optimum decision, we ask whether $y(t)$ more closely resembles $s_0(t)$ than $s_1(t)$, within the signalling duration T. Mathematically, this test resolves to computing the minimum mean square distance between $y(t)$ and each of the possible transmitted waveshapes. Thus we seek to calculate

$$\int_0^T [y(t) - s_0(t)]^2 \,\mathrm{d}t \quad \text{and} \quad \int_0^T [y(t) - s_1(t)]^2 \,\mathrm{d}t$$

Expanding and simplifying, the decision operation reduces to establishing

$$\alpha_0 = \int_0^T s_0(t)y(t)\mathrm{d}t$$
$$\alpha_1 = \int_0^T s_1(t)y(t)\mathrm{d}t \tag{8.6}$$

Then if $\alpha_0 > \alpha_1$ we presume s_0 to have been transmitted and if $\alpha_1 > \alpha_0$ we presume s_1 to have been transmitted. These integrals calculate non-normalised cross-correlation coefficients between the received signal $y(t)$ and the possible transmitted signals $s_0(t)$ and $s_1(t)$. Receiver structures based directly upon these equations are therefore called *correlation detectors*. To simplify further mathematical formulation, we note that the decision operation embodied in equations 8.6 above is alternatively stated thus

$$\alpha = \int_0^T s(t)y(t)dt \qquad (8.7)$$

where $s(t) = s_0(t) - s_1(t)$, so that if $\alpha > 0$, s_0 is presumed to have been transmitted, whereas if $\alpha < 0$, s_1 is presumed to have been transmitted. The general form of a correlation detector is then as shown in figure 8.26.

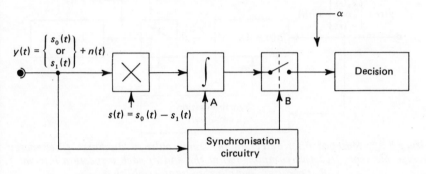

Figure 8.26 Correlation detection. A: Integrator 'dump' pulse to ensure integration only over the time duration T of each received signalling waveform $s_0(t)$ or $s_1(t)$. B: Pre-dump 'sampling' pulse to establish α

An alternative structure is obtained if we recall the similarity between the mathematical operations of correlation and convolution. Restating equation 1.36, which defines the operation of convolution, we write for the output of a hypothetical detection filter with transfer function $H(f)$

$$v_0(t) = \int_{-\infty}^{+\infty} h(\tau)y(t - \tau)d\tau$$

We express $h(\tau)$ as a time-reversal of $s(\tau)$ so that

$$h(\tau) = s(T - \tau)$$

thereby ensuring that it is also a causal impulse response defined over the signalling interval $0 \leqslant \tau \leqslant T$. $h(\tau)$ is zero-valued outside this interval. The filter impulse response now acts as an analogue 'store' of the transmitted signal template. We then calculate

$$v_0(T) = \int_{-\infty}^{+\infty} s(T - \tau)y(T - \tau)d\tau$$

as the filter output at the end of the signalling interval. Changing variables, for convenience in interpreting the result, we write $t = T - \tau$ and the integral is seen to calculate the cross-correlation

$$\int_0^T s(t)y(t)dt$$

This realisation of the optimum detector is referred to as a *matched filter*, because it involves storage of template information $s(t)$ in the impulse response of a linear wave filter, against which the received (noisy) signal is 'matched'. The matched filter detector is illustrated in figure 8.27. It should be clearly understood that the term 'matched' does not here connote matching of impedance for optimum power transfer.

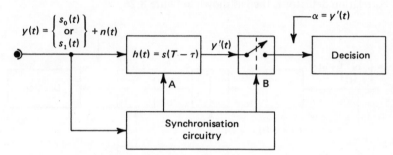

Figure 8.27 Matched filter detection. A: Dump pulse to 'discharge' filter energy-storage elements (reactive components) at the end of each inspection interval T. B: Pre-dump 'sampling' pulse to establish α

Irrespective of the choice of optimum detector structure (correlation or matched filter detector), we finally establish a decision based upon inspection of α at the end of the signalling interval. We must now determine the probability of incorrectly choosing $s_1(t)$ when $s_0(t)$ was in fact transmitted, consequent upon the effect of channel noise. This probability, at specified signal energy E, noise power spectral density η and cross-correlation R is the bit error rate for optimum detection.

For example, expanding equation 8.7 and assuming $s_0(t)$ to have been transmitted, we find that α (which should be greater than zero, according to our previously stated decision criterion) is given as

$$\alpha = \int_0^T \{s_0(t) - s_1(t)\}\{s_0(t) + n(t)\}\mathrm{d}t$$

$$= \int_0^T s_0^2(t)\mathrm{d}t - \int_0^T s_0(t)s_1(t)\mathrm{d}t + \int_0^T \{s_0(t) - s_1(t)\}n(t)\mathrm{d}t$$

The first two terms establish the unique signal energy, E_s, contained in the transmitted pulse. The third term describes an accumulated 'noise energy', E_n, perturbing the value of E_s registered at the end of the signalling interval. Clearly, although E_s must be greater than zero, E_n may well take on negative values. To determine the error probability, P_e, we seek to determine the probability that E_n exceeds E_s in magnitude, while exhibiting opposite *sense*, so that

$$\alpha = E_s + E_n$$

is negative, rather than positive, as it should be since $s_0(t)$ was presumed to be the transmitted signal. This probability is determined, as figure 8.28 indicates, by

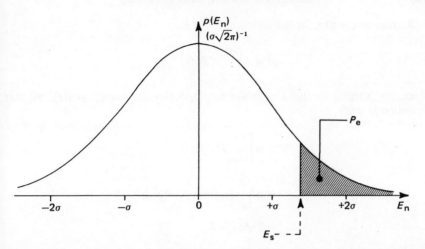

Figure 8.28 Integration of noise energy probability density distribution at the output of the matched filter to yield error probability P_e represented as the shaded area

integrating the probability distribution $p(E_n)$ thus

$$P_e = \int_{E_s}^{+\infty} p(E_n) \mathrm{d}E_n \qquad (8.8)$$

In order to specify $p(E_n)$ we consider operation of the matched filter in the absence of transmitted signal, so that its input is noise alone. By proceeding in this way we anticipate the use of superposition in interrelating noise-free signal energy and signal-free noise energy. This is permissible because the matched filter is a linear device. A further consequence of linearity is the fact that the zero-mean gaussian noise process at the matched filter input remains a zero-mean gaussian process at its output. We now calculate the standard deviation of this output noise process. First, however, a cautionary note must be sounded.

For a filter with transfer function $H(f)$ and input noise power spectral density $P_n(f) = \eta$, the output noise power, equal to the variance of the noise process, or the square of its standard deviation, is given by the integral

$$\int_{-\infty}^{+\infty} P_n(f) |H(f)|^2 \mathrm{d}f$$

Note carefully that the noise power is dimensionally a mean square voltage. In the case of the matched-filter equivalent to the correlation detector, because the integral defining the latter computes *energy*, not a voltage output, the filter transfer function $H(f)$ has dimensional significance. The effect of time reversal in establishing $h(t)$ from $s(t)$ is to cause $H(f)$ to equate to the complex conjugate of $S(f)$. The integral presented above may still be used to calculate the variance of the noise energy sample E_n. We note that $|H(f)|^2 = |S^*(f)|^2 = |S(f)|^2$ with $H(f)$ *necessarily* assuming dimensions of a voltage spectral density.

We may thus write, for the variance, σ^2, of E_n

$$\sigma^2 = \eta \int_{-\infty}^{+\infty} |S(f)|^2 \, df$$

Since the integral in this expression now specifies the energy in $s(t)$, we may equivalently write

$$\sigma^2 = \eta \int_{-\infty}^{+\infty} s^2(t) dt$$

$$= \eta \int_0^T \{s_0(t) - s_1(t)\}^2 dt$$

$$= 2\eta E(1 - R)$$

Not only does this statistic provide the 'spread' of the output noise process about zero, it *also provides the spread for samples* extracted from the output noise process. Furthermore, because the process is of zero-mean, even though an energy 'dump' operation takes place at the end of each signalling interval (immediately after the decision instant) the statistic as it applies to noise samples perturbing the detected signal remains unaltered.

We now return to the evaluation of the integral in equation 8.7 armed with the knowledge that $p(E_n)$ is a guassian distribution of zero mean and standard deviation $\sigma = \sqrt{\{2\eta E(1 - R)\}}$. This integral can only be evaluated numerically; an analytic solution does not exist. The integral is of such importance in statistics, however, that its values have been computed and tabulated in handbooks of mathematical functions as the *error function*

$$\text{erf}(z) = \frac{2}{\pi} \int_0^z \exp(-t^2) dt$$

Error function tables are used in much the same way as tables of logarithmic or trigonometric functions. The crucial relationship linking gaussian probability density distribution and the error function is

$$\frac{1}{\sigma\sqrt{2\pi}} \int_{-\infty}^{x} \exp(-(t - m)^2/2\sigma^2) dt = \tfrac{1}{2}[1 + \text{erf}\{(x - m)/\sigma\sqrt{2}\}]$$

It therefore follows that the error probability can be expressed as

$$P_e = \tfrac{1}{2}(1 - \text{erf}[\{E(1 - R)/4\eta\}^{1/2}]) \tag{8.9}$$

Inspection of this function indicates that P_e is minimised when $R = -1$. This condition, sometimes referred to as *antipodal* signalling, is established only if $s_0(t) = -s_1(t)$, as is the case with bipolar NRZ baseband signalling or two-phase PSK.

The practical realisation of the optimum detector for the first of these signalling formats is to be found in the *integrate-and-dump* circuit, which is illustrated in figure 8.29. By replacing filter H_3 in figure 8.10 the integrate-and-dump method

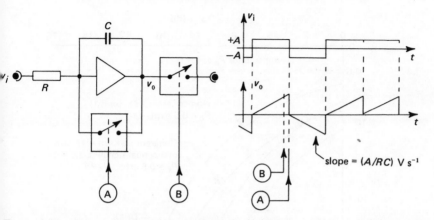

Figure 8.29 The integrate-and-dump detector. (a) Dump at digit end, (b) sample-before-dump. Both switches exhibit short dwell times by comparison with digit duration

may also be applied to yield optimum detection of PSK. Conventionally, equation 8.9 is often expressed in terms of a signal-to-noise energy ratio

$$s = E/2\eta$$

so that for both these signalling formats

$$P_e = 0.5 \text{ erfc}(s^{1/2})$$

where $\text{erfc}(x) = 1 - \text{erf}(x)$ is the *complementary error function*. The error probability curve for antipodal signalling with coherent detection is presented in figure 8.30. It is characterised by an error probability asymptote of 0.5 at extremely low values of signal-to-noise ratio. At high values of signal-to-noise ratio, the error rate falls dramatically. On leased (dedicated) lines, acceptable values of P_e would be of the order of 10^{-6} or better. For systems operating within the switched public network, a lower value of 10^{-4} or better would be regarded as satisfactory and would correspond to a signal-to-noise ratio of 8 dB or greater.

As might be expected, the error-rate performance of DPSK is inferior to that of PSK, because errors may propagate during the phase-reference storage operation. Assuming again coherent implementation of the detector, the performance of a DPSK system can be shown [48] to obey a law

$$P_e = 0.5 \exp(-s)$$

As figure 8.30 shows, DPSK (although strictly inferior to PSK) is competitive at higher values of signal-to-noise ratio. Thus, because of the ease of phase-synchronisation which it confers, the differential mode of operation is generally preferred.

Coherent detection of FSK implies product detection after the bandpass filterings used for tone isolation, rather than the envelope detectors illustrated in figure 8.15, which correspond to a *non-coherent detection*. The particular context in which coherent detection of FSK is especially significant is that subclass referred to as minimum shift keying (MSK) which we discussed in section 8.8. By applying equation 8.5 to our defining equations for FSK, we may show that the signalling

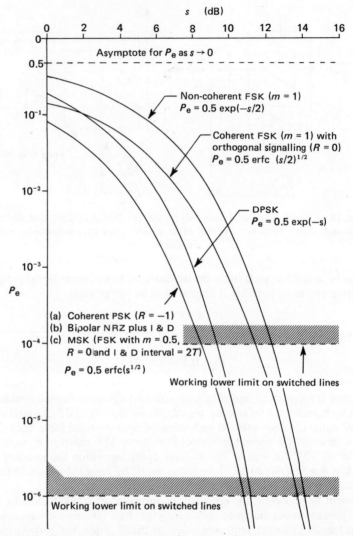

Figure 8.30 Error probability curves for binary data transmission systems

waveshape cross-correlation is given as $R = \text{sinc}(m)$ where m is the modulation index. This function is illustrated in figure 8.31. For both MSK ($m = 0.5$) and 'preferred' FSK ($m = 1$) we see that $R = 0$. Under this condition, the signalling is referred to as *orthogonal* and the error rate is expressible as

$$P_e = 0.5 \text{ erfc} \{(s/2)^{1/2}\}$$

However, MSK derives an effective 3 dB advantage in signal-to-noise ratio because the integration interval for the integrate-and-dump detector spans two signalling intervals. Consequently, MSK exhibits the same probability of error curve as the antipodal signalling schemes.

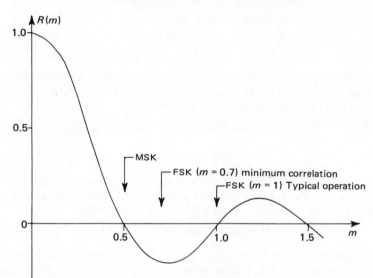

Figure 8.31   Cross-correlation function R for FSK signalling tones as a function of modulation index

For non-coherent detection of FSK and assuming orthogonal signalling ($m = 1$) it has been shown[49] that

$$P_e = 0.5 \exp(-s/2)$$

However, although non-coherent detection of orthogonal FSK is clearly the least attractive of the keying systems whose performance is illustrated in figure 8.30, it still forms the basis of modem design for low-speed operation. This is because such an approach yields a robust, simple implementation which does not require the careful phase synchronisation or phase continuity between signalling pulses which is demanded by coherent detection.

8.11   Block Error Probability

Although we have devoted some effort to deriving the individual digit error probability for a range of data transmission methods, this quantity may sometimes be of secondary importance in specifying the required capability of a data communication system. Often, evaluation of a *block error probability* before decoding or a *residual error probability* after decoding might be of greater significance. For example, let us suppose that, in a block of L digits

$$D_0 D_1 \ldots\ldots\ldots D_{L-1}$$

the first digit, D_0, is incorrect. That is, of the L possible single-error 'patterns' we presume a *specific* pattern $1\ 0\ 0 \ldots 0$. The probability of an error in any digit is P_e; the probability that a digit is error-free is $(1 - P_e)$. If we assume error generation to be inherently a random event (burst errors are unlikely) then the probability of occurrence of the error pattern specified above is the product of appropriate occurrence probabilities for each of its L digits, namely

$$P_e \qquad \times \qquad (1 - P_e)^{L-1}$$
for D_0 in error   for $D_1 \ldots D_{L-1}$ to be error-free

(The reader should note that in a practical situation the assumption that errors occur randomly rather than in bursts should be viewed with caution. Burst-error generation processes may frequently be identified.)

To cover all the L possible single-error patterns in an L-digit block, we determine a joint probability

$$LP_e(1 - P_e)^{L-1}$$

which is the probability that a single error occurs in any block of length L, subject to a bit error rate, P_e. This result may be generalised to allow determination of the probability that M errors occur in a block of length L, namely

$$[L!/\{M!(L - M)!\}]P_e^M(1 - P_e)^{L-M}$$

Practical operation of an N-error correcting code would presume that, for reasonably low redundancy, $N \ll L$. Furthermore, the bit error rate might well be expected to be subtantially below its maximum value of 0.5. Under such conditions, the probability that digit errors pass uncorrected from the decoder to the recipient is given approximately by

$$P_e' \cong \frac{(LP_e)^{N+1}}{N!}$$

For a single error correcting code

$$P_e' \cong L^2 P_e^2$$

yielding the improvement curves shown in figure 8.32. As can be seen, even modest coding power may yield substantial benefit in reducing the decoder output bit error probability. The shorter codes yield better performance in this respect, if the concomitant penalty of relatively high redundancy can be tolerated.

8.12   Data Channel Throughput

The philosophy expounded in chapter 7 with respect to choice of error-protection code suggests that, when possible, cyclic block codes should be used for error-detection on *long* code blocks, rather than error-correction on short blocks. If such a strategy can be adopted, an important criterion referred to as 'net data throughput' (often abbreviated to NDT) may be used to describe system performance and illustrate the significance of possible parameter tradeoffs. We write

$$\text{NDT} = \frac{(L - J)Q}{T}$$

Here, $(L - J)$ is the number of *informational* digits per block, being the difference between the block length L and the number of parity digits J. Actually, J may be further taken to include 'formatting' digits, such as those used in an asynchronous system to delimit a data block. Q is the probability that *no error* occurs in an L-digit transmitted block. It provides the probability that the $(L - J)$ informational

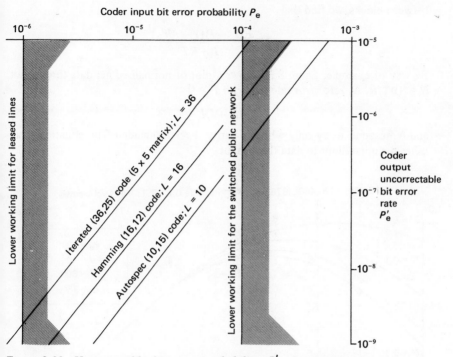

Figure 8.32 Uncorrectable bit error probability, P'_e, for single error correcting codes, as a function of input bit error probability, P_e

digits are, indeed, handed on to the intended recipient. Even a single error will, in an automatic request-repeat system, result in the entire L-digit block being discarded and retransmission demanded. With P_e as the individual digit error probability, $(1 - P_e)$ is the probability that no one digit is in error. The probability that neither the first, nor the second, nor any of the remaining L digits are in error is given by

$$Q = (1 - P_e)^L$$

This equation may be modified by the inclusion of a 'multiple-error discount factor', M, which acknowledges the fact that 'bursty' error situations at a modem output are rather more likely than random errors. This appears to be particularly true when the modem encorporates adaptive equalisation, since then the equalisation circuitry, responding to combat adverse channel conditions, tends temporarily to propagate errors. An observed error probability P_e may thus be *reduced* to a value MP_e on the grounds that retransmission will take place irrespective of the number of errors (*all* of which would be registered in assessing P_e) within a block.

Noting finally that the average block transmission time is given by

$$T = L/R + T'$$

where R is the modem data rate in digits per second and T' is the time interval between blocks, we find that

$$\text{NDT} = \frac{R(L - J)(1 - MP_e)^L}{L + RT'}$$

By way of example, figure 8.33 shows a plot of normalised net data throughput, $N = \text{NDT}/R$. At zero error rate and with $T' = 0$

$$N = 1 - J/L$$

and N becomes unity only when no parity check is included. This situation establishes the upper limit to data throughput.

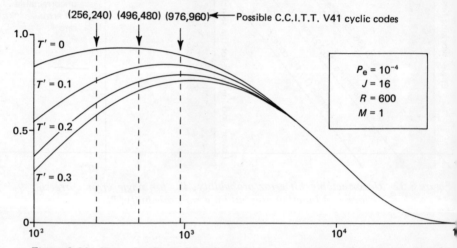

Figure 8.33   Normalised net data throughput as a measure of system quality for a switched-circuit, C.C.I.T.T. V23 recommended 600 digits s^{-1} FSK modem with block error detection

Figure 8.33 is plotted for a particular system, 600 digits s^{-1} FSK, operating at an error probability typical of an adverse switched line circuit. Cyclic error detection using 16 parity digits is also presumed. Large values of T' manifest their effect at shorter block lengths, since T' is then of disproportionate magnitude by comparison with the block transmission time LR. The normalised net data throughput reaches a maximum for $T' = 0$ at a block length value which would suggest the use of a (496, 480) C.C.I.T.T. V41 code. By contrast if, for logistical reasons, a value of T' of 0.3 s is required, a (976, 960) code would be preferred, although tolerance to code choice is evident from these curves.

Problems

8.1   What is meant by *disparity* as it applies to binary codes and why is it desirable that the disparity should be kept small? What techniques other than disparity reduction can be used to overcome the problems caused by lack of a.c. coupling within the transmission path?

8.2   Lumped loading of a local telephone line (see section 2.9) is employed to improve its performance when handling voice signals. Such lines could be well suited to digital data transmission by removing the loading coils. However, it is frequently the case that the line may be required at different times for both voice and data communications. What forms of signalling could be applied to the task of transmitting data, under these circumstances; which would you choose, and why?

8.3   Compare paired selected ternary and 50 per cent duty cycle AMI as methods of preparing a binary signal for line transmission. Describe the operation of each by considering the effect of the two techniques on a statistically representative sequence of binary 1s and 0s (that is, a reasonably long sequence of 1s and 0s chosen randomly and such that the two digits are equiprobable).

8.4   In question 2.3 we saw that a non-ideal transfer-function amplitude characteristic introduced echo pairs which corrupted a received signal. If a channel has an amplitude characteristic

$$A(f) = 1 + a\cos(\pi f\tau) \quad -\tau^{-1} \leqslant f \leqslant +\tau^{-1}$$
$$= 0 \quad \text{elsewhere}$$

and a phase characteristic

$$\phi(f) = 2\pi f t_0$$

show that the channel output is given by the relation

$$v(t - t_0) + \frac{1}{2}av(t - t_0 + \tau/2) + \frac{1}{2}av(t - t_0 - \tau/2)$$

where $v(t)$ is the input signal. Sketch both the transfer function, and the output signal corresponding to a typical pulse-type input signal. Comment on the effect such a channel would have on a random-data wave. What steps can be taken to eliminate the effect of a non-ideal transfer function?

8.5   A channel with an ideal amplitude characteristic

$$A(f) = 1 \quad -\tau^{-1} \leqslant f \leqslant +\tau^{-1}$$
$$= 0 \quad \text{elsewhere}$$

has a phase characteristic exhibiting first-order phase distortion, thus

$$\phi(f) = 2\pi f t_0 - b\sin(\pi f\tau)$$

Show that such a channel produces an output signal

$$v(t - t_0) + \frac{1}{2}bv(t - t_0 + \tau/2) - \frac{1}{2}bv(t - t_0 - \tau/2)$$

assuming that b is much less than unity. Again, sketch the transfer characteristic of the channel and typical input- and output-pulse waveforms. What will be the effect of not constraining b to be small? What will be the effect of having a more highly non-linear phase characteristic than the one specified above?

8.6   What is inter-symbol interference and how may its severity be visually assessed? How is it minimised in a practical data-communication system? Describe a
form of signalling in which the presence of inter-symbol interference is to our
advantage.

8.7   Describe the differential PSK system and contrast its operation with that of
an ordinary PSK system. Which will have the greater noise immunity and why?

8.8   What kind of repeatering is used when digital data is transmitted through
the switched telephone-network and how does it affect system performance?
Compare with the repeatering used for PCM telephony.

9 The Integrated Services Digital Network

It has been remarked by more than one eminent commentator upon the contemporary scientific scene, that the most complex engineering entity yet created by mankind is the international telephone network. Although such an observation may seem at first sight to be a mere truism, closer consideration of its implications in terms of the future of the world community will rapidly dispel any such dismissive judgement. Current developments in network switching and signalling will lead to vastly enhanced communication capability not merely for voice-telephony, but for high-speed data transmission, improved information dispersion and retrieval and for remote-location data-telemetry. The social and economic consequences of accelerating growth and enhanced power within the international telephone network will inevitably be profound. The communication engineer must, therefore, be familiar with the basic structure of the network and the way in which it utilises and builds upon the various techniques described in the preceding chapters.

Although the student may look for, and find, a logic in the development of the telephone network from the time of its inception, he should be warned that this logic is not evidence of a master plan of sustained growth. The installation of plant (cables, switchgear, power supplies, modulation equipment and terminal equipment) on a national and international scale is very costly. Plant lifetimes of several decades may be necessary to justify an enormous capital expenditure. As the demand for extended services grows with time, more economical methods of utilising existing plant have to be devised. In conjunction with the relatively rapid development of the electronics industry, this had led to a somewhat confusing array of systems in which technological arguments are often outweighed by economic ones.

For example, the earliest automatic exchanges involved step-by-step (Strowger) switching. This technique, decimal-based and purely mechanical in operation, held sway for several decades. It involved a 'fixed wired-logic' and satisfactorily eliminated dependence upon labour-intensive manual exchanges. To accommodate more flexible control of message-handling, crossbar and reed switching systems were evolved during the 1960s and were used in the implementation of new automatic exchanges. At about the same period, consideration of the economics of line-plant usage led to the introduction of time-division multiplexing with pulse code modulation as a method of expanding the capacity of the junction network. With digital transmission expanding rapidly, the concept of the electronically-switched exchange became attractive from a logistical viewpoint. However, economic considerations weigh even more heavily in favour of such an approach. Thus, the two decades from 1960 to 1980 have seen microcircuit complexity (measured in terms of components per chip) rise by five or six *orders of magnitude*, while exhibiting an equally dramatic fall in cost per chip component. These factors inexorably point towards the concept of the *integrated services digital network*, in which all message-transfer is digital and all message-switching electronic and under computer control.

If this scenario is placed against the present structuring of information-interchange systems in many of the developed nations, its advantages become apparent. For example, we have seen that digital data are extensively handled within the public switched network on voice channels, by means of modem interfaces. However, the rapid escalation of the use of digital computers as data bases has led to the evolution of separate data networks, such as TELENET and TYMNET (U.S.A.), DATAROUTE (Canada), EURONET, TRANSPAC (France), PSS (U.K.), NPDN (Denmark, Finland, Norway and Sweden), DATEX (Germany) and, with the distinction of being the first operational example of this class of system, RETD (Spain). These networks involve the use of high data rates (typically 48 Kbit s^{-1}) by comparison with those used over the switched public network together with the concept of *packet switching*. Packet switching causes information to be transferred in blocks (packets) of 128 8-bit bytes. Each such block is preceded by an address byte which dictates its routeing through the packet-switched network. It will readily be appreciated that a unification of data-transfer systems such as these with PCM telephony, by means of an integrated services digital network, may in the future be expected to yield benefits of scale in the implementation of new plant and provision of advanced subscriber facilities.

9.1   A Perspective on Telephony[56,5]

Telephony consists of the conversion of voice signals into voltage fluctuations and the distribution of these signals by means of a suitable electrical transmission system. The received voltage fluctuations are then reconverted into an acoustical signal. Conversion to and from the acoustical state is performed by transducers, usually the earpiece and microphone of a standard telephone handset. The operation of the transducers is not our concern. Our interest lies in the nature of the transmission network and the processing of the signals conveyed within it. We shall begin our discussion with the simplest of telephone systems and illustrate the development both of the network and the signal processors contained within it, arriving finally at an outline description of the most advanced modern telephone systems, in which pulse code modulation is employed to convey many voice signals upon a single wire-pair or cable.

One feature of the organisation of any telephone system is the arrangement of message switching and routeing. The majority of line communication takes place on general utility, exchange-switched networks. Relatively rarely, wideband lines are used to connect two users directly. These, referred to as *leased* lines, have the advantage of minimising switching noise, increasing security and providing a permanent and reliable connection. The penalty is, of course, cost. Leased lines are usually employed as a method of linking digital computers to remote terminals or to other computers within a large network of machines.

We may think of the switched telephone network as an hierarchical structure, wherein the *international network* links together *national networks* which themselves consist of a *trunk network* linking many *local* or *junction networks*.

Local networks consist of *local exchanges* connected directly to the subscriber by means of suspended wire-pairs or buried multicore cable. The local exchange is responsible for the switching which serves to connect any two subscribers and provides a supply of power to both subscribers' handsets. Sometimes two local exchanges can be connected directly; sometimes they are connected through a third local exchange. If a third exchange is required, usually to make a medium-distance connection, it is referred to as a *tandem* exchange. Call routeing in these ways is referred to as establishing a *junction connection*, since it utilises only the subscribers' lines and *junction circuits*. Junction circuits are those cable connections which link local exchanges to each other and to those switching centres which act as interface exchanges between the local and the long-distance, or trunk network.

Trunk networks facilitate long-distance telephone calls. The link to the local networks is made by exchanges known as *group switching-centres*. Each group switching-centre is responsible for co-ordinating and dispersing signals from its dependent local exchanges. Long trunk-calls may pass through a higher echelon of routeing within the trunk network, being relayed by *transit switching-centres*.

Local networks and trunk networks together form the *national network*. The national network, in turn, is connected to other national networks by means of *international switching-centres*. The physical link between the various national networks depends on the geographical features separating the nations in question. Land lines, submarine cables, radio links and even satellite links are employed.

One reason for the clear division of the national network into local and trunk networks is the nature of cable usage within the two smaller categories. In the trunk network, two wire-pairs are used to convey a conversation, one wire-pair carrying the transmitted signal from one of the handsets, the other conveying the received signal for that same handset. This is known as *four-wire operation*. In contrast, both transmitted and received signals are conveyed on one wire-pair on junction circuits and subscribers' lines. This means that separation of these signals must take place both at the handset and at the group switching-centre, which has to perform two- to four-wire conversion. The junction circuits and subscribers lines are said to exhibit *two-wire operation*. Figure 9.1 illustrates the layout of a variety of typical telephone connections which are often encountered in practice. It is evident that two-wire operation is more economical of line plant than four-wire working. However, for long-distance transmission, when many repeater amplifiers are required, four-wire working permits the use of simpler circuitry and is relatively free from instability, as we shall see.

The very simplest telephone system, shown in figure 9.2*a*, illustrates the concept of four-wire working. It can, of course, be readily modified to yield a crude form of two-wire working, figure 9.2*b*, but this circuit suffers from the disadvantage that speech at either end appears directly in the earpiece of the same handset. This local speech signal is known as *sidetone* to distinguish it from the speech signal generated at the remote handset. Subjectively, too much sidetone is objectionable because it causes the speaker to lower his voice, thereby reducing the signal strength applied to the line. The problem of sidetone can be resolved by using the same method for coupling the four send- and receive-transducer wires to the two-wire subscriber's line as is used in performing four- to two-wire conversion and vice versa. Figure 9.3 shows the basic circuit required to achieve these functions. It is known as a *hybrid transformer* and functions in the following way. The

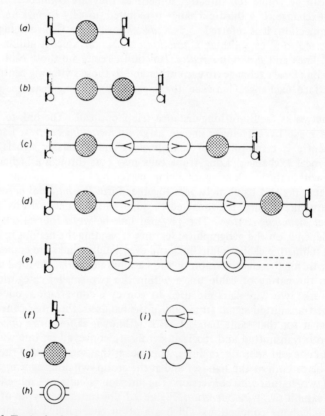

Figure 9.1 Typical telephone-network connections within the United Kingdom Subscriber Trunk Dialling (STD) *network, (a) local, (b) junction, (c) short trunk, (d) trunk, (e) national end of international connection. The symbols used to depict these connections are: (f) telephone handset, (g) local exchange offering two-wire switching, (h) international exchange offering four-wire switching, (i) group switching-centre offering either two or four-wire switching and two to four-wire conversion, (j) transit switching-centre offering four-wire switching*

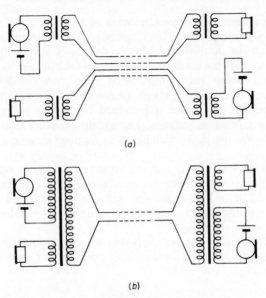

(a)

(b)

Figure 9.2 (a) Simple telephone systems involving the use of two wire-pairs, and (b) one wire-pair

line balance network, Z_0, is presumed to have the same impedance as the line. A signal v_s from the send side of a four-wire system will therefore divide equally between the coils L_1 and L_2. It will, as a consequence, induce equal voltages $v_s/2$ across coils L_3 and L_4. Since coils L_3, L_4, L_5 and L_6 are identical, this signal voltage will also be developed across L_5 and L_6. However, because L_5 is connected in a reversed manner, the voltages across L_7 and L_8 will be equal and opposite,

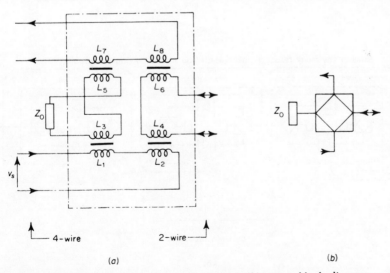

(a)   *(b)*

Figure 9.3 The hybrid transformer: (a) circuit, (b) system block-diagram

and will therefore cancel. Consequently, none of the voice signal emanating from the microphone will find its way to the earpiece providing the line-balance network is an exact match for the line itself. In practice, of course, a slight mismatch is inevitable and the result is a small amount of signal feedthrough to the receive side of the four-wire system. This contributes an 'echo' component to the received signal at both ends of the overall telephone connection. To summarise, then, half the four-wire transmit-side power is presented to the two-wire system and the other half to the balance impedance. The hybrid therefore introduces a −3 dB loss into the transmission path which has to be regained at some stage by repeater amplification.

A signal from the two-wire system can be shown, by similar reasoning, to split upon entering the hybrid in much the same way. In this case, half the two-wire power is dissipated in the balance network again and the other half is presented to the receive wires of the four-wire system. Thus again a −3 dB loss occurs in the hybrid transformer.

Repeatering in the four-wire system is very simply accomplished, as figure 9.4a shows. Conversion to four-wire operation can certainly be used to provide two-

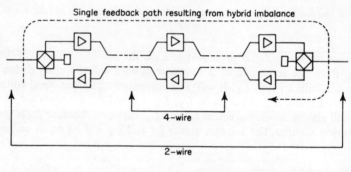

(a)

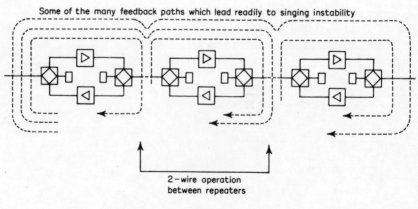

(b)

Figure 9.4 Repeatering: (a) four-wire trunk, (b) two-wire trunk

way repeatering for two-wire systems, figure 9.4*b*. However, the presence of the many return-path loops in the latter system leads to an increased probability of 'singing instability' (self-sustaining oscillation) taking place and disrupting normal communication. Thus two-wire operation is usually restricted to short-haul local connections between handset and exchange and on junction circuits.

The telephone systems depicted in figures 9.2*a* and 9.2*b* show power sources located at the transducers. In fact, this is not the way in which power is supplied in practical telephony systems. Instead, the telephone lines themselves are used to supply power to the handset from a battery at the local exchange. In order to achieve this, d.c. coupling to the exchange is used to permit power flow, while a.c. coupling is employed for signal transmission between handsets via the exchange, the necessary coupling at the exchange being achieved by a circuit known as a *transmission bridge*.

An important feature of the telephone networks depicted in figure 9.1 is that subscribers' lines are dedicated. In remote areas, shared, or 'party' lines may be employed for reasons of economy of line plant but these may be considered the exception, rather than the rule. In contrast, it is desirable that trunk lines between major switching-centres be shared by many signals. The sharing operation is known as *multiplexing* and its nature depends on the modulation methods employed at the exchange. Two principal forms of multiplexing are used within the telephone system. If the line network is instrumented for analogue signal transmission, individual baseband signals will each be modulated onto a carrier so that the baseband spectra may be stacked in frequency, a technique known as *frequency division multiplex*, FDM.

If the line network is instrumented for digital transmission (pulse code modulation) then coded samples, extracted synchronously from many baseband channels are interleaved in time. This technique is known as *time division multiplex*, TDM, and although it utilises the available line bandwidth less economically than FDM, it affords the possibility of cheaper terminal equipment on junction connections which formerly were not provided with a multiplex capability.

9.2 Frequency Division Multiplex Telephony

Single-sideband modulation is chosen for FDM in line-transmission systems employed for telephony because bandwidth is at a premium. The organisation of a fairly typical 960-channel system which utilises 4 MHz coaxial cable at the transmission medium is as follows. The basic voice bandwidth, complying with C.C.I.T.T. requirements, extends from 300 Hz to 3.4 kHz. A set of twelve subcarriers, with 4 kHz spacing between them is employed in the first stage of multiplexing. These carriers have frequencies 64, 68, . . . , 108 kHz. The lower sideband of each product-modulated subcarrier is extracted by means of a quartz-crystal sideband filter, figure 9.5. The set of twelve SSB signals obtained from the first twelve of the 960 voice-channels then form the first *group*.

In the same manner, the remaining 948 channels are split into sets of twelve and the members of each set are modulated to form a further 79 groups. The same subcarrier frequencies in the range 64 to 108 kHz are used to achieve this. The groups are then handled in much the same way, except that they are split into sets of five, yielding sixteen *supergroups*. In this case, the first five groups, each of which occupies a band of width 48 kHz between frequencies of 60 and 108 kHz,

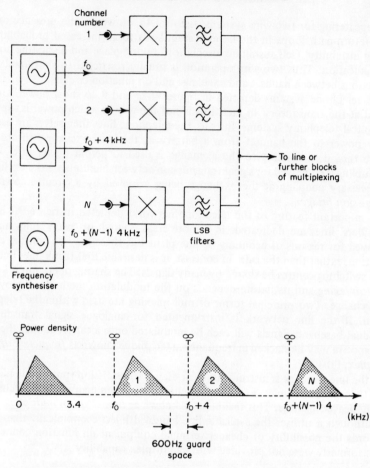

Figure 9.5 A typical FDM *telephone system*

are product-modulated onto carriers of frequencies 420, 468, . . . , 612 kHz. Again, only the lower sideband is retained. Because the group spectra possess no components below 60 kHz, these carrier frequencies result in the translation of the groups to lie in bands thus: 312 to 360 kHz, 360 to 408 kHz, . . . , and so on.

Finally the sixteen supergroups, each occupying a bandwidth of 240 kHz, are translated upon carriers of 612, 1116, . . . , 4340 kHz to establish the *mastergroup* which, for a line link provides the final transmitted signal.

De-multiplexing is performed by successive stages of bandpass filtering and product demodulation, to extract first the supergroups, then the groups and finally the individual voice-signals.

In both modulation and demodulation, during multiplexing, precise and stable carrier signals are required. These are derived by frequency synthesis from a crystal-controlled oscillator in a constant-temperature oven. Such frequency synthesisers are located at both terminal stations of any link. Phase lock is not necessary in the demodulation of SSB, as was pointed out in section 5.3, unless it is necessary to preserve the shape of a waveform. This is not the case with speech transmission since the human ear is to a large degree insensitive to phase distortion.

9.3   Pulse Code Modulation Telephony[24]

The use of single-sideband modulation and frequency division multiplexing, is an excellent, and in respect of bandwidth utilisation, an optimum solution to the problem of conveying many telephone messages on a single transmission line. However, there are important economic reasons for considering the use of PCM and TDM within the telephone system. In particular, multiplexing is not employed on some connections between exchanges. As system usage increases, it becomes necessary to increase the information-handling capacity of such connections. This may be done in three ways: more cable may be laid, conventional FDM equipment may be installed, or TDM with PCM may be used. If the required expansion is not massive, the first two ways will probably be uneconomical. PCM is more attractive both because much of the modulation and multiplexing equipment is common to all channels and because digital techniques are relatively cheap to implement. In contrast, the precision crystal-filter banks and modulators required for an FDM system are expensive items to construct. Another disadvantage with a standard FDM system is its relative inflexibility. It will only handle telephone bandwidth (300 Hz to 3.4 kHz) signals. In contrast, TDM systems offer the possibility that the PCM telephony signals may be interleaved with high-speed digital-data signals, as well as telegraph signals. Finally, the digital nature of plant and signals in a PCM system is such as to suggest and facilitate the use of digital computers or organise switching and routeing of signals.

Our study of the sampling theorem (section 6.1) has led us to the conclusion that the sampling rate for an analogue waveform must be at least twice the highest-frequency component within the waveform. In the case of a telephony signal, this indicates a rate in excess of 6.8 kHz. In practice there is universal agreement on a figure of 8 kHz. This value is just sufficient to make reconstruction filtering a non-critical operation. It is also a convenient frequency to use since it precludes interference with FDM equipment operating with carrier frequencies separated by multiples of 4 kHz.[43]

In the first commercial PCM systems, it was considered satisfactory to employ a non-redundant code of seven binary digits for PCM telephony. This permits a total of 128 quantising levels. As we saw in section 6.5 such a choice ensures a signal-to-quantising noise ratio of 40 dB for full-range signals. When signal compression is also used a subjectively acceptable operating noise-level results, even at low signal levels. Modern, high quality PCM systems being implemented both in Europe (CEPT 32) and the United States (D2) use eight binary digits and therefore 256 quantising levels.

Both the 128- and 256-level systems *transmit* an eight-digit binary codeword. In the 128-level systems, the extra digit alternates between binary states on each successive word and provides the means of extracting a word-synchronising signal. Other methods[44] are used to obtain synchronisation in the 256-level systems.

The number of analogue channels handled by the PCM system is (with the exception of CEPT 32) 24. In the American Bell D1 system, each 'frame' of 24 eight-digit words is preceded with a single-frame synchronising digit. Thus there are a total of

$$(8 \times 24) + 1 = 193 \text{ digits}$$

yielding a total digit rate of

$$193 \times 8 \times 10^3 = 1.544 \times 10^6 \text{ digits s}^{-1}$$

The United Kingdom 24-channel system does not use a frame-synchronising digit, and consequently has a digit rate of 1.536×10^6. The D2 system is designed for compatibility with the D1 system and utilises the same digit rate. The CEPT 32 system incorporates 32 time slots, as opposed to 24, although only 30 channels are actually handled. One of the time slots is used for frame synchronisation, the other for signalling purposes within the network. In this case the digit rate is 2.048×10^6.

For economic, rather than technological reasons, PCM systems are usually installed within existing telephony equipment designed for operation with analogue signals. Although the line systems may be modified by removing the loading coils necessary for speech transmission, the line will still be a.c. coupled. This is because the d.c. path is used to supply power to the regenerative repeaters on the line. Since a.c. coupling severely degrades a non-redundant PCM signal, it is common practice to convert from a two-level binary format to a three-level 'quasi-ternary' format. The method used to achieve this is known as 'alternate mark inversion', AMI, and this technique has been discussed at length in section 8.2. It is a signalling format which removes the d.c. level and reduces the low-frequency components in the PCM waveform, without requiring any additional signalling bandwidth.

9.4 Telephone Circuit Switching[57]

In the introductory paragraphs of this chapter, it was mentioned that early automatic exchanges involved the use of hard-wired logic to establish the 'programming' of exchange operation (although such terminology would not have been used at the time). These exchanges used analogue switching involving, usually, step-by-step rotary contactors. Typical of such contactors is the two-motion selector, figure 9.6a. Contact is established to one of one hundred switch-poles first by vertical and then by rotational translation of the wiper. Both translations are effected by electromagnetically activated rack and pawl assemblies exemplified by the mechanism illustrated in figure 9.6b. The electromagnet is actuated by dial-pulse sequences generated at the handset. When the first digit is dialled, a number of dial-pulses equal to the value of the digit passes to the selector. Each pulse racks the mechanism upwards by one tooth-position. Having thus established the required vertical displacement among the rows of switch-poles, the second dialled digit then actuates the rotary rack and pawl to effect rotational translation around the chosen row. Subsequent banks of selectors cater in similar fashion for the remaining dialled digits. This approach is referred to as *distributed control switching* and is characterised by the sequential setting of contactors by dialled digits in a rigidly defined manner. Although distributed control has held sway for many years, it is completely unsuited to the requirements of large, modern exchanges, which call for flexible

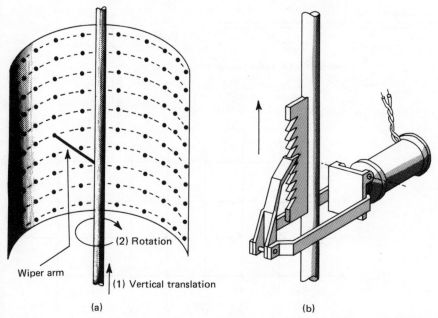

Wiper arm

(2) Rotation

(1) Vertical translation

(a)   (b)

Figure 9.6   The two-motion selector (a) and the rack and pawl mechanism for establishing vertical translation of the wiper (b)

structuring of exchange operation and efficient use of switching plant. An alternative philosophy is to be found in the concept of *common control switching* whereby, typically, an incoming directory number is register-stored and used to establish a 'best path' through a *switching matrix*.

In its simplest form, the switching matrix consists of an array of *crosspoint switches*. Such an array is illustrated in figure 9.7, in which a linear bilateral switch is depicted as interconnecting input and output lines. When such a switch is used as the crosspoint element, the entire array is referred to as an *analogue switch* and is capable of routeing analogue or digital (PCM) signals. A preferred approach, which we consider more fully later in this section, utilises digital logic gates to switch purely digital signals. In this case the switching matrix is referred to as a digital switch.

Within an analogue switch, the switch elements may be electromagnetic reed-relays, high-speed relays of conventional design or any of a variety of advanced crosspoint designs. To illustrate the development of the analogue switch, we will consider by way of example, the reed crosspoint element, which is shown in idealised form in figure 9.8. An activation coil surrounds the single-crosspoint reed-bank. This bank contains reed-switches for voice-path switching and an additional element providing a latching function. When the activation coil is energised, the ferrous-metal reed-blades become magnetised and draw together, effecting switch closure. This connects the speech-path but also energises, through the *holding* reed-switch, the holding coil. The activation relay may then be de-energised and the relay will remain closed. By using this holding principle, other relay-banks (crosspoints) in the matrix may be addressed to satisfy the requirements of other callers and thus make effective use of switching plant.

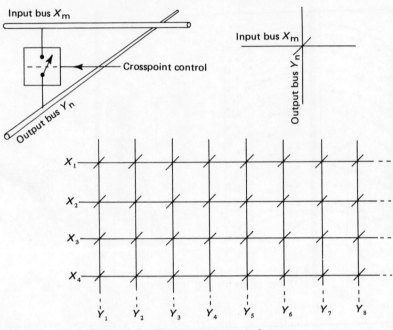

Figure 9.7   The crosspoint switch array

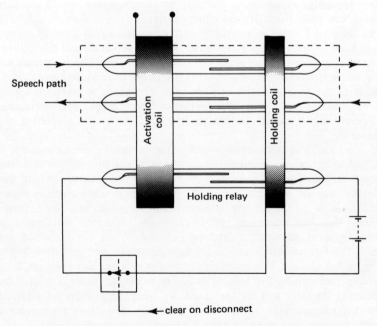

Figure 9.8   Reed-switch crosspoint element construction

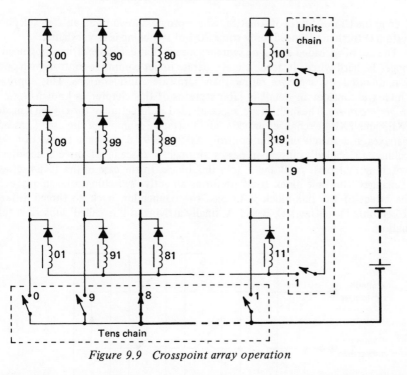

Figure 9.9   Crosspoint array operation

Figure 9.9 shows how the activation coils operate to provide switching within a matrix. Suppose, for example, that the switching matrix is addressed by the dialled digits '89'. The first received dial-pulse sequence actuates the '8' switch in the 'tens' chain of matrix-control relays. The second received dial-pulse sequence acts to close the '9' switch of the 'units' chain. A path is thus established which energises only the '89' activate coil, which in turn causes the '89' holding coil (not shown in figure 9.9 for the sake of clarity) to energise. The 'tens' and 'units' chain matrix-control switches may then be reopened and the connected path will hold automatically. The diodes shown in figure 9.9 prevent branching of the current beyond the required path. The number of line interconnections the matrix is capable of supplying is limited by the fact that only one crosspoint on each row or column may be activated at any one time.

Clearly, one problem associated with crosspoint switching in this way is the escalation of crosspoint elements as the square of the number of lines connected. To avoid this adverse tradeoff, large exchanges use cascaded switching matrixes. This approach makes recognition of the fact that only a relatively small proportion of users connected to an exchange will wish to pass calls through it at any given time. If too many callers do attempt to access the exchange, *call-blocking* (equivalently referred to as 'congestion') will occur.

Irrespective of the nature of the switching element used for the crosspoint, a switching matrix of the type shown in figure 9.7 is referred to as a *space-divided network*. The majority of exchanges have, in the past, used this network architecture, or one derived from it. They involve analogue switching and reflect the essentially analogue nature of the public telephone network at the present time.

Even in the United States of America, where progress towards an all-digit telephony system is further advanced, only some 30% of switching is as yet digital.

The use of cascaded analogue switches means that exchange-structuring need no longer be hard-wired. Instead, it may operate under computer control, with operation dictated by *software* rather than hardware considerations. This approach, which we consider in detail in later sections of this chapter, is known as *stored program control*. The multi-stage, space-divided architecture of the United Kingdom TXE3 and TXE4 exchanges provides an illustrative example of the use of cascaded matrixes and stored program control. As figure 9.10 shows, a connection from 'calling' to 'called' subscriber passes through a cascade of three space-divided switching matrixes: A, B and C to a link-block. In the case of the TXE4 series of exchanges, the link block itself performs an active switching role. In any event, the effect of the link-block is to pass the connection back, to thread different crosspoints in matrixes C, B and A, finally arriving at the 'called' subscriber termination.

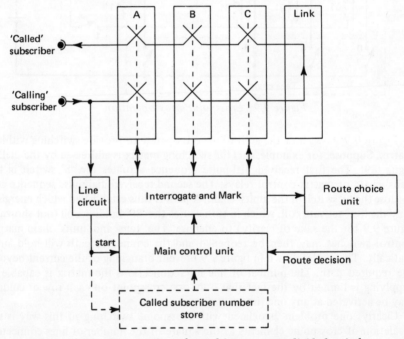

Figure 9.10   Organisation of a multistage, space-divided switch

Call connection begins when the caller lifts his handset and the handset cradle-switch causes the *line circuit* at the exchange to emit an 'initiate connection' signal for the main control unit, which is a special-purpose, programmable digital computer. Proceeding inwards, simultaneously, from 'caller' and 'called' subscriber terminations towards the link-block, the main control unit causes crosspoint testing (interrogation) to take place. This determines all inward routes topologically connected to these terminations which are not, themselves, in a 'busy' state. All possible routes are passed to the *route choice unit* which determines an optimum path. The main control unit then sets ('marks') the appropriate crosspoint switches within matrixes A, B and C and the call is connected.

An alternative approach to call-routeing involves the use of *time-divided networks* and is well suited to the operation of time-multiplexed transmission and the concept of an integrated services digital network. The advantages of making the transition from an analogue to a purely digital telephony system (thereby including trunk and international, as well as junction circuits in the PCM transmission of voice signals) are considerable. The digital approach offers

(1) Reduced installation size and power requirement and (consequent upon superior processing function density and reduced package count) easier setting-up and reduced maintenance requirements.

(2) Easier coding for privacy, security and transmission reliability.

(3) Enhanced versatility in terms of the variety and nature of the information sources which may be handled and the manner in which that handling takes place.

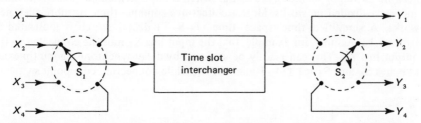

Figure 9.11   The time-divided network approach to implementing exchange switching

Operation of time-divided switching is illustrated in figure 9.11. Let us suppose that a hypothetical interconnection pattern, as indicated by table 9.1 is required, with input bus X_1 connected to output but Y_2 and so on. The function of the *time-slot interchanger* (TSI) is to *delay* PCM words on the input bus lines until they synchronise with the required PCM word-uptake for the output bus lines. Multiplex switches S_1 and S_2 operate with mutual synchronism. The TSI effects a one-step delay on PCM words entering input bus X_1 and two-step delays on the three remaining inputs. Here a 'step' is taken to correspond to the multiplexing

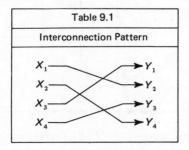

Table 9.1
Interconnection Pattern

switch pole-to-pole transition time. The time-sequencing of PCM word-exchange is thus

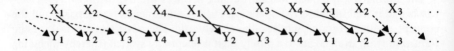

It is interesting to note that the functions of the multiplexing switches and the TSI can be usefully combined, with resulting economies in implementation of exchange systems, if a separate (non-shared) CODEC is dedicated to each termination.

If we consider time-divided switching from a practical standpoint, it becomes apparent that, when the number of terminations becomes large, memory access times within the TSI become prohibitively short. This means that time-divided switching is only appropriate in its basic form, or extended as a cascaded time–time (T–T) switch, for relatively small private branch exchanges making, perhaps, a few hundred connections. To satisfy the requirements of the much larger public-network switching facilities, the digital switch is implemented as a cascade of time- and space-divided networks. Most architectures combine three or more such networks. A simplified time–space–time (T–S–T) digital switch is illustrated in figure 9.12. Assume, for example, that the input bus X_1 must be connected to the output bus Y_3'. This can readily be achieved by delay-synchronising multiplexing switches S_1 and S_4 via TSI–1 and TSI–4, while connecting crosspoint switch C.

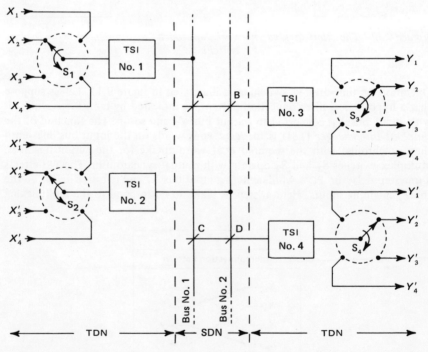

Figure 9.12   The time–space–time (T–S–T) architecture of a digital switch

In this case, however, the space-divided portion of the system must have a double-rate time-slot capability, by comparison with any of the TSI branches in the time-divided networks. If this provision is not made, it is possible that the prescribed connection may be blocked within the space-divided network by an existing connection calling for the closure of crosspoint switch A and thus demanding that C remains open.

The way in which the digital switch is incorporated into a public switched network exchange is shown in figure 9.13. Because the digital switch requires a PCM-format input, it interfaces directly with digital (PCM/TDM) trunk circuits. However, because transition from the present, basically analogue telephony system to the desired all-digital system must progress gradually, the digital switch must also be capable of handling connections which utilise analogue transmission media. The necessary interfacing is provided by standard FDM *terminal equipment*, which translates signals between the carrier trunk and voiceband lines and by the *voiceband interface* which converts voiceband signals to and from standard PCM format. Provision is also made for synchronism of data bit-streams appearing on dedicated data links by means of a *data-link interface*.

Several of the commercial digital switches at present in operation utilise the particularly popular T–S–T network architecture described above. Other architectures are, however, possible. The most obvious simple example is the S–T–S architecture used in an early, experimental digital switch implemented by the

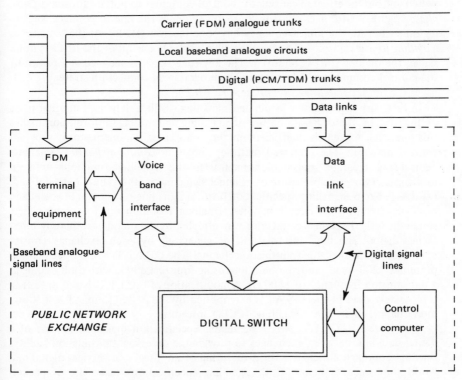

Figure 9.13   The public network exchange: use of the digital switch

then British Post Office. Operational systems with architectures which may be regarded as derivative from these two basic structures use multiple space stages to increase line-handling capability. Thus S–S–T–S–S and T–S–S–T architectures have been used in Japan, France, Italy and the U.S.A. in commercial equipment offering up to 60 000 line capacity. Worthy of note in this respect is the T–S–S–S–S–T architecture used in the NO. 4 ESS (Electronic Switching System) developed for the Bell System in the U.S.A. This digital switch has a capacity exceeding 100 000 terminals and is 24 channel PCM, T1 carrier compatible.

9.5 Telephony Signalling Procedures[58,59]

Signalling in a telephone network serves to establish the functions of line-acquisition, call-routeing, bell-ringing, monitoring the progress of the call, detecting line-clearance on termination of the call and finally calculating and recording the call-charge. In many telephone systems, signalling information and message information are conveyed upon the same transmission facility. This approach is referred to as *channel-associated signalling* and is exemplified by the signalling used on the wire-loop connecting subscriber to local exchange. In this situation, call-connection follows the sequence of operations illustrated in figure 9.14. In the *rest condition*, figure 9.14*a*, the subscriber's set is one of many connected, via an exchange *line-circuit* to the exchange control computer. Raising the handset actuates the cradle-switch and has the effect of causing the control computer to initiate the *instruction phase*, figure 9.14*b*. The control computer switches the line to connect, via the digital switch, to the multifrequency key-tone receiver (MFR). At the same time, a *dialling tone* is transmitted to the subscriber's set. On receipt of the first key-tone signal, the dialling tone is removed. The key-tone signal is decoded and passed to the control computer which, adopting its programmed connection strategy, establishes the third, *communication phase*, figure 9.14*c*.

In fact, although channel-associated signalling is still widely used in other parts of the system, the disparate nature of signalling and message information makes this approach extremely inefficient in the context of a modern stored-program control network. The preferred method, known as *common-channel* signalling, dedicates a separate transmission facility to the signalling functions between exchanges. Two principle common-channel signalling methods have been defined. C.C.I.T.T. No. 6 Signalling Specification involves signalling on a separate voiceband analogue circuit. This circuit handles signalling requirements for many callers simultaneously. Exchange connections are effected by data modems, thereby interfacing digital signalling information, as generated by each exchange control computer to the analogue transmission channel. The C.C.I.T.T. No. 6 Specification presumes 1200 baud modem operation, using four-phase PSK with dibit coding at a transmission frequency of 1800 Hz. A modification of C.C.I.T.T. No. 6 Specification, widely used in the U.S.A., is exemplified by the Bell System/AT & T 'Common Channel Interoffice Signalling' (CCIS) procedure.

By contrast, C.C.I.T.T. No. 7 Signalling Specification makes direct use of a digital data-link between exchanges to provide the necessary transmission facility. Such an approach anticipates the structuring of an integrated services digital network some decades hence. Both signalling specifications make use of packet-switching techniques in relaying signalling information (see section 9.8).

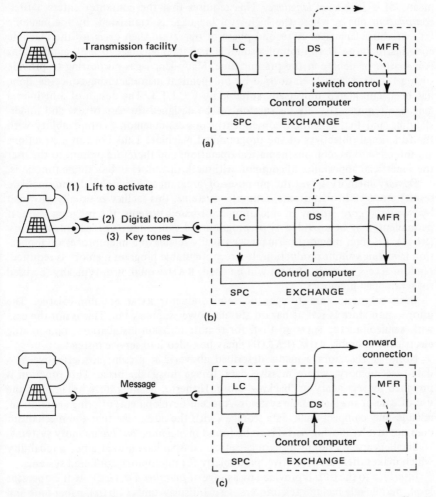

Figure 9.14 Channel-associated signalling in a local circuit: initiating a call. LC:
line-circuit; DS: *digital switch;* MFR: *multi-frequency (key-tone) receiver*

9.6 Stored Program Control

In this section, a precis of the technology associated with stored program control
(*SPC*) of telephone network switching is presented. We begin by reviewing the
operation and structure of the digital computer. Computer operation involves the
manipulation of binary number sequences in accordance with instruction steps
residing in computer memory, as a stored program. These manipulations are
performed in the *central processing unit* (CPU) of the computer, which consists
of arithmetic, logic and control steps. Instruction steps, like the numbers the
processing of which they determine, are retained in binary form and constitute a
program 'written' in *machine language*. Because machine language is an extremely
unwieldy method of interacting with the computer, program entry is made by

means of a *high-level language*. This requires that the computer enters a first, *compilation* phase, where the high-level language is 'translated' by the machine into machine language. A second phase of operation then *executes* the machine code instructions. Definition of a suitable high-level language for SPC applications is a matter of debate at the present time. Many languages purporting to provide such a function have been devised by independent manufacturing concerns; none has been considered universally suitable by C.C.I.T.T. The design of a high-level language requires that its instruction set be designed for ease of use and understanding and that it should consequently possess mnemonic comparability with the functional objectives of the programmed machine. Thus Fortran instructions are intended to execute mathematical operations and therefore present to the user the superficial appearance of common arithmetic operators and algebraic functions.

Primary memory serves the purposes of program and scratchpad (intermediate result) storage. In mainframe computer systems, this facility is usually provided by *magnetic core stores*. In microprocessor-based systems, the program store, if permanent, may be provided by preprogrammed semiconductor read-only memory (ROM). Program memory permanence usually relates to a microprocessor application involving volume production. If a reconfigurable program memory is required, random-access memory (RAM) will be used. RAM would also, typically, be used for scratchpad memories.

Both magnetic core-storage and semiconductor ROM are non-volatile. The information store is not at hazard should power supplies fail. This is not the case with semiconductor RAM so that, for remote location installations, non-volatile electrically-alterable ROM (EAROM) may be called into service instead.

None of the storage media described above is at present cost-effective as a data-base memory, where massive data-storage must take place. This function is provided by secondary or 'backing' store. Hitherto, backing store has implied the use of disc or magnetic tape systems. A recent development, offering economical, reliable and compact bulk data-storage (with the advantage that the mechanism does not involve moving parts) is to be found in *magnetic bubble* memory systems.

Smaller capacity floppy disks or cassette memories have now attained a reliability which makes their use attractive, particularly for microprocessor-based systems.

Interface to the CPU is provided by a range of *peripheral devices*. At the operator level, peripherals include teleprinters, visual display units (VDUs), paper tape and card readers and punches and line-printers. These provide the vehicle for program and data entry and for result presentation. When the computer is used in a control application, the interface will allow machine interaction and may include ADCs, DACs and various electromechanical actuators or electronic switches.

Let us now consider the reasons for moving towards a computer-based switching system architecture. The primary motivation is, as we have come to expect, economic. The ultimate objective of network evolution is the integrated services digital network, which may yet require some decades for its realisation. The principal economic factors which have to be balanced in deciding to opt for such a system are

(1) call-cost per mile of connection and
(2) the cost of setting up the call.

Although it remains true that analogue (FDM) trunk operation makes best use of line plant, relatively few calls are long-distance (inter-urban or international) so that setting-up costs predominate. (The ratio of urban to long-distance calls is about 15:1 in the North American subcontinent.) Setting-up costs are greatly reduced by digital switching and SPC exchange operation. Furthermore, these approaches improve upon the use of switching plant and reduce the probability of exchange overload and call-blocking. Rapidly reducing component costs and increasing component density in digital computing equipment thus favour the all-digital transmission system, despite line-plant usage inefficiencies over long-haul trunk circuits. In respect of this last comment, it is worth noting that the increased use of fibre-optic systems (see section 2.12) will engender a situation in which bandwidth is not at a premium, a factor which must also serve to persuade network planners of the attractiveness of the integrated services digital network.

The first stored-program control systems were introduced in the mid-1960s. At this time, digital processors were by nature mainframe machines and their use thus introduced a cost-penalty which suggested *mono-processor* architecture, figure 9.13. Monoprocessor architecture implies centralisation of control and carries further penalties in respect of hardware/software interdependence. Since software creation for SPC applications is a major manpower-intensive undertaking, it will be appreciated that even small hardware changes may lead to extensive and therefore costly software modifications.

As a consequence of the subsequent rapid growth of mini- and microprocessor-related systems, the ability to duplicate processor functions has led to more complex SPC architectures. Dual- and even triple-processor controllers have been used in an effort to improve reliability.

Such systems employ identical, replicated processors, operated in a variety of modes. One, figure 9.15, requires dual-synchronous operation, whereby the processors maintain mutual self-check by running identical programs in parallel. An alternative strategy is to retain one processor in *hot-standby* mode, ready to assume control in some few hundreds of milliseconds, when its companion exhibits a fault condition. A third option involves the use of load-sharing dual-processors. Triple-processor architecture requires that a dual-processor operating in synchronous mode is protected by a third processor in hot-standby mode.

'Single-level' multi-processor architecture, such as has been described above, is used to provide hardware redundancy to combat hardware failure in a system which (unlike, perhaps, a conventional batch-processing general-purpose computing

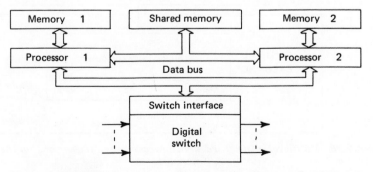

Figure 9.15   Dual-processor architecture for the control computer

system) is obviously not tolerant of critical-component failure. An entirely different approach takes us away from the direct multi-processor descendants of early mono-processor systems towards an heirarchical structure offering *distributed control*. Thus, we may conceive of multi-level, multi-processor architecture, such as is illustrated in figure 9.16. Level 1 control determines line-switching and other simple, repetitive operations. It involves the use of a multiplicity of microprocessors individually using a monoprocessor architecture with little, if any, software controllability. Failure of a single processor at level 1 results in the loss of but a few lines, at worst. Level 2 control may, again, involve no software flexibility. It might provide such functions as path-routeing strategy within the digital switch, call-processing and relay of signalling information. Failure at level 2 could, conceivably halt the entire exchange, suggesting the use of a multi-processor architecture. Level 3 control may be centralised and common to many exchanges, providing a range of software-flexible options enhancing the information-capacity of the network. By localising critical control functions (to levels 1 and 2) and centralising software-dominated supervisory control, a mono-processor architecture may be adopted for the supervisory computer. System organisation is such that total failure of the supervisory computer leads to degradation of service but not to network failure.

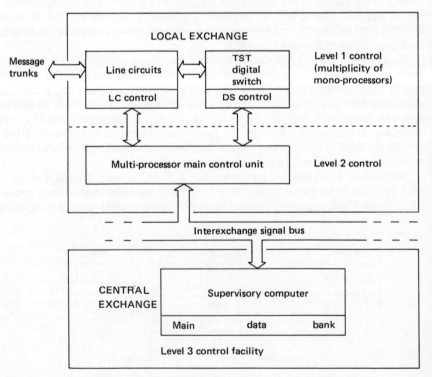

Figure 9.16 Multilevel, distributed multiprocessor architecture within the public network

9.7   SPC Software

Software consists of the 'written' instructions created by a computer-system programmer. These instructions are presented to the computer via interface hardware, such as card-readers or data-terminals, and determine its sequencing of data-manipulation. General-purpose computing systems involve the use of *high-level languages* as the principal means of interfacing man to machine. Such languages are mnemonically structured for ease of understanding and use. SPC software structuring, however, involves constraints not placed upon the general-purpose computer user. It must take into account the disparate requirements of network and exchange management (the 'vendor' who wishes to maximise profit), provision of advanced subscriber services (for the 'purchaser' who wishes to maximise usage and convenience) and software developability (for the 'programmer' who must interweave these requirements and who is subject also to the limitations imposed by the 'machinery').

Management involves information flow between the network administration and the network/exchange system. Information concerning system usage and system failures is presented to the administration and provides the basis from which system command, maintenance and evolution proceeds. These objectives must be achieved economically and effectively, through software structuring, and must allow for effective management without loss of grade of service.

Provision of advanced subscriber services is, from the user's viewpoint, a major feature of SPC exchange operation. Examples of such facilities are automatic call-transfer if a called number is engaged or does not reply, third-party calling (for consultation or conferencing) or caller identification by means of characteristic ringing tones. Resource facilities such as automatic credit-card calling, toll-free dialling or improved civilian emergency services also fall within this category. Consider, by way of example, the case of a national automobile breakdown rescue service. A 'distressed' calling member, dialling the emergency service, is connected not to an operator but to a network computer with access to a resource data-bank. His calling-location is automatically compared against the 'nearest-resource' directory which establishes the number of his nearest breakdown service. The network computer then effects the connection between the calling member and the breakdown service. In this way, a single entry-number possessed by many motorists becomes the key which unlocks a vast resource-directory, making available many exit-numbers. Resource-utilisation clearly favours data-bank centralisation since this simplifies the updating of national membership and resource files and command-sequencing files. We see, then, that subscriber service development takes place at the behest of the user and software-flexibility must reflect rapidly-changing user requirements.

Finally, from the standpoint of the system programmer, who must implement both management decisions and user requirements, software must be both reliable and easily extended without compounding complexity. Software evolution involves analysis of requirement, job specification, programming, testing, documentation, distribution and software maintenance. This complex sequence of operations has led to the development of a modular, heirarchical approach to the structuring of SPC software.

As we have noted in the previous section, early SPC systems used a mono-processor architecture. This involved the use of a costly general-purpose computer programmed in a language which was not of problem-specific design. For reasons of hardware economy, software targets emphasised minimisation of storage and reduction of call set-up time. These factors rapidly led to a situation in which software became unwieldy and difficult to understand, modify or extend. Annual generic software/hardward revisions increasingly involved software testing rather than software development, simply to ensure that existing software was not compromised by added material. Consequently, a new approach to software methodology, which would reintroduce *flexibility*, the predominant advantage of software over hardware, was sought. Further desirable features of this new methodology involved a 'transparency' of functional operation to software and, particularly, hardware revision, and the elimination of interdependence between incoming and outgoing trunk specification within software packages. Functional operation transparency, provided by the *virtual machine* concept, means that developments in hardware technology may be rapidly exploited to permit certain operations, previously defined in software terms, to be replaced by dedicated hardware. This feature is, of course, of considerable significance in the context of current microprocessor development. A virtual machine is a hypothetical processor 'called' by an SPC high-level language statement to execute some system function. Its actual nature and internal working (for example, whether it is lower-level software, or hardware, or a combination of both) is immaterial to the programmer, but input—output interactions are precisely defined. This black-box approach, further developed in the *finite message machine*, allows exchange implementation to take advantage of new technological developments with a minimum of disruption to the system at the time a revision is implemented. Finite message machines are modular software constructs in which an input message or messages leads to a precisely defined output message or message-set, much in the manner of a complex input—output 'look-up' table.

These advanced software concepts place the accent on modularisation and the use of *structured programming*. The structured program is written in independently designed, functional modules, each supported by its own data-base. Groups of modules, perhaps with replication of modules on a group-to-group basis to avoid inter-group sharing of modules, form *clusters*. The assembly of clusters then forms the structured program. This approach to programming is complemented by an analysis approach referred to as *top-down design*. In the context of SPC exchange programming, top-down design requires first the definition of a *universal call* followed by a functional decomposition of the universal call into logistically-useful *call-stages*, appropriate to a viable 'compartmentalisation' of tasks. The universal call, as defined for the Bell System/AT & T No. 4 ESS (Electronic Switching System) involves seven call events

(1) Origination (caller signals exchange by lifting handset and dialling or keying number)
(2) Digit reception (at exchange)
(3) Outgoing trunk selection
(4) Origination on the outgoing trunk
(5) Digit sending
(6) Receive answer
(7) Receive disconnect

The functional decomposition of this universal call divides the call into *setup, post-setup* and *clearing* phases, as is shown in figure 9.17, thus conveniently grouping the tasks required of the exchange system. A third level of decomposition draws apart incoming and outgoing trunk specification, removing module interdependence across the digital switch.

It might be thought that the replication of identical modules in different clusters is particularly inefficient in terms of hardware. This is indeed the case. However, hardware costs are now less significant than programming costs and the independence of clusters, one from another, allows for ease of redesign or replacement of individual modules.

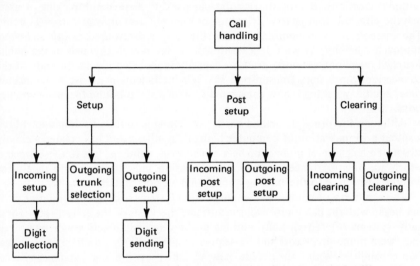

Figure 9.17   Functional decomposition of the 'universal call'

A useful feature of stored program control is the technique known as *map-in-memory*. Application of this method retains a record of the status of paths through the digital switch. In some systems, the use of map-in-memory allows the requirement for a holding path to be eliminated, with a consequent reduction of wiring cost and crosspoint complexity. It is an approach which also facilitates temporary interruption and rerouteing of a call-path, thereby enhancing SPC flexibility.

9.8   Packet Switching[60,61]

In this section we consider the development of data-carrying networks which, at the present time, operate in partial independence from the public switched telephony network. With the development of the integrated services digital network, it might be anticipated that a drawing together of resource facilities would take place. The extent and rapidity of such an occurrence is, however, a matter for speculation. Whatever developments shape the future of the integrated network, the methodologies at present evolving in the sphere of computer network synthesis will inevitably be profound. Our subject material is, then, the structuring of data-handling networks containing a plurality of computers linked by some communication facility (usually a line, radio or satellite link). Such networks (which may or may not be available for public use) are intended to offer

(1) high-capacity, high-efficiency data transfer
(2) access to exceptionally large data bases carrying mass information files or unusually specialised or complex software.

The vehicle used to realise these aims is referred to as *packet switching*, and involves assembling the user's data into addressed and protected blocks (the 'packets') for transmission through the network from one computer to another (or to a remote terminal location). By transferring data in packets, a time-multiplexing of users may be effected, leading to efficient use of each physical message-carrying circuit. The method is to be contrasted with the now less-favoured *circuit switching* approach whereby, as with data transmission over speech channels in the public switched telephony network, available capacity is allocated for the duration of the connection. Since data transmission is often inefficient in its use of connected time, circuit switching is now considered economically unsound for many applications.

Although the principle behind packet switching is simple, its development has inspired a formalisation of computer network synthesis and has created a closely structured language of interaction between network elements. It is to these aspects, which are of importance if network modification and extension is to take place without disruption to the existing system, that we now address ourselves.

The evolution of computer communication systems over the past quarter century began with the batch-processing mainframe machines of the early 1960s. These early systems offered virtually nothing in the way of interactive user interfaces; they were mono-processors and consequently involved only primitive communication capabilities. Within the decade, however, the provision of geographically local terminal equipment, presenting the user with a multi-access, time-sharing capability had greatly improved the ease of program development and use. During the 1970s, an extreme cost-penalty began to force a trend towards centralisation of the larger and more powerful mainframe machines. Network architecture then involved two alternatives. The first involved the use of leased-line connection of a large host computer to satellite computers at remote job-handling locations. The second, the use of modem connected, speech-grade circuits operating over the public switched telephone network. Towards the end of this decade, the falling cost and increasing power of microprocessors led to the development of so-called 'intelligent' terminals, with a processing capability of their own.

This scenario has led to two approaches to the visualisation of computer network synthesis. For example, the host computer linked to satellite machines, as described above, is known as a *top-down structuring* of the network. Such a strategy involves considerable initial capital investment and results in a system which is vulnerable in the event of host-computer failure. On the other hand, it may be an appropriate strategy to adopt if the *raison d'être* of the network is, perhaps, the provision of an extensive and centralised data base.

Alternatively, and offering initial economies in implementation, a 'bottom-up' structuring may be adopted. Here, all users are provided with 'intelligent' microcomputer terminals. As necessary, these may 'link in' to local minicomputers providing enhanced software and storage capabilities. At a later stage, the entire system may assume the superficial appearance of a 'top-down' structured network, with the addition of an overall, centralised host computer. However, it should be stressed that, with the bottom-up approach, the host computer need not be an ultimate target. For example, the first packet switched network design, evolved by the Rand Corporation for the United States Air Force (but never commissioned), called for a *fundamentally* distributed military data-communication system. This system was specifically required to be 'globally' unaffected by 'local' damage during a military exchange. Under such circumstances, the concepts of a centralised control facility might, indeed, be considered inappropriate.

Overlaying these two basic approaches (top-down or bottom-up) to computer network synthesis is a range of *network topologies*, some of which are shown in figure 9.18. Of them, the star topology is most readily representative of top-down structuring. The loop and multi-drop topologies offer less complicated network structures which are better suited to a bottom-up evolution. They may be developed into multimesh structures representative of the complex topologies encountered in modern packet switched data networks.

However the topology is organised, the potential for flexibility of structure at the hardware level (for both local and distributed sites) must be retained. This is effected by imagining a hypothetical computer-to-computer connection to be

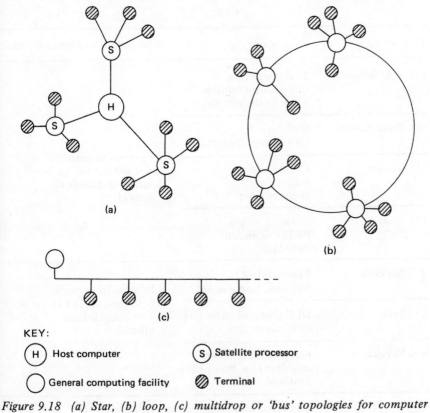

(a)

(b)

(c)

KEY:

(H) Host computer   (S) Satellite processor

(○) General computing facility   (⊘) Terminal

Figure 9.18 (a) Star, (b) loop, (c) multidrop or 'bus' topologies for computer networking

amenable to a 'dissection' into critical *levels* or *layers* of interaction. For example, the actual transmission medium between machines defines one fundamental level of interaction identified as an 'in-common' feature by both machines. Above this level, another 'in-common' feature is the keying format adopted for signalling. Higher still, both machines will recognise a common data-block structuring. Many other levels can be envisaged, to the point of inclusion of the 'users' of each machine. At this topmost level, two users may literally communicate with each other, via the computer network, yet remain unaware of the various parallel levels of commonality at work in their various computers. Notice that, by conceiving of the agglomeration of computers forming a network in this way, we open the way to an explicit definition of level function and level-to-level interaction.

These level-function and level-interaction definitions are referred to as *protocols*. The word 'protocol' derives from Greek roots which, literally translated render, evocatively, as 'first-glue'. Dissection of a computer network into operational levels is as shown in table 9.2. Levels 4 to 7 are shown in parentheses because, at this time, no standards exist. Currently (and at present universally, if we allow local or 'dialect' differences) packet switching protocols covering levels 1 to 3 derive from the C.C.I.T.T. X25 recommendation.

Above the *communication facility* (the 'common carrier', or actual physical

TABLE 9.2

Level or Layer	Function	Location and Standardisation
(7) Application	Text processing Information transfer Fiscal exchange, etc.	
(6) Presentation	Data format Encryption/decryption	External to network. Not subject to agreed standards at present.
(5) Session	File transfer Buffering Segmentation	
(4) Transport	Network access Packet or circuit switching	
3 Network	Flow control Network management	Internal to network. Governed by CCITT X25 Standard and others.
2 Link	DLC protocol, including error checking	
1 Physical	Electrical/mechanical interface (e.g. RS−232 protocol	
0 −	Communication facility (line, radio, etc.)	

medium for interconnection) *level 1* provides the *physical level* (or *layer*) *protocols*. This level of protocol is intended to govern the physical interface between (essentially) a computer data input/output port and (typically) a data modem. At the input/output port we expect to encounter data bytes (incoming or outgoing, as appropriate) suitably padded with address, flag and parity bytes. The actual protocols specify mechanical, electrical, functional and procedural characteristics of this interconnection. An example of a physical level protocol which will be familiar to most communication engineers is the RS 232 interface.

The level 2 *data link control* (DLC) *protocols* provide rules which allow a local terminal

(1) to determine that a remote terminal is in a 'ready' condition

(2) to signal a request for the remote to prepare to receive or, alternatively, to transmit data and

(3) to conduct a trans-link dialogue to advise retransmission in the event of errors being detected.

In order to achieve these objectives, the DLC may be 'character'- or 'bit'-oriented. A character-oriented DLC transmits control character groups (such as STX for 'start of text', ETX for 'end of text' or ACK for 'acknowledge') to establish trans-link dialogue. This approach evolved in the context of relatively low capacity, *half-duplex* links in which data transmission takes place in both directions, but only alternately. (In *simplex* links transmission is unidirectional.) For high-speed *full-duplex* links, which sustain simultaneous bi-directional transmission, the more recent bit-oriented approach is preferred. This is because a bit-oriented DLC offers data transparency, high efficiency (consequent upon its ability to format large data blocks) and high reliability (because of in-built cyclical error check coding). The structure of a typical bit-oriented DLC frame is shown in figure 9.19. Frame delimiting is provided by the eight-digit flag sequence 01111110.

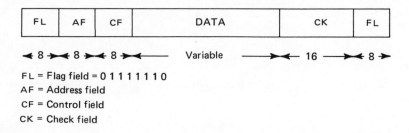

FL = Flag field = 0 1 1 1 1 1 1 0
AF = Address field
CF = Control field
CK = Check field

To prevent confusion with identical bit-sequences within the remainder of the frame, a technique known as *bit-stuffing* is used. Bit-stuffing merely inserts (stuffs) a zero after any run of five consecutive 1s, prior to transmission. This prevents the characteristic 'six 1s' sequence from ever occurring, except in the flag fields at the start and end of the frame. At the receive terminal, the frame is identified and buffered into store. The stuffed zeros can then be removed since, at this stage, the frame flags will have served their function and will have been 'stripped' from the received data. Bit stuffing is important because it allows the data field to assume any length (see section 8.12 for criteria concerning transmission efficiency and choice of block-size) and ensures that the user is provided with a completely transparent communication channel. Error detection is established by means of a cyclic code, typically using the C.C.I.T.T. V41 or CRC-16 generating polynomial (see section 7.4).

Level 3 network protocols establish flow-control through the network and provide network management rules. In a packet-switched network they are typically responsible for determining packet structure, addressing and routeing.

Level 4 to 7 protocols govern data control external to the network and establish further rules to the level of actual user-applications, as table 9.2 suggests.

Appendix I

This table should be used in conjunction with table 1.2.

TABLE AI A TABLE OF USEFUL FOURIER TRANSFORM PAIRS

Function	Time domain	$F(f)$	Frequency domain	
Unit step $f(t) = u(t)$ $= 1; 0 \leqslant t$ $= 0; t < 0$		$F(f) = 1/2\pi jf + \delta(0)/2$		Slope = 1, Delta function unrepresentable
Unit impulse $f(t) = \delta(0)$ $\delta(t) = 0; t \neq 0$ $\int_{-\infty}^{+\infty} \delta(t)dt = 1$	Area = 1	$F(f) = 1$		
D.C. level $f(t) = 1;$ all t		$F(f) = \delta(0)$ $\delta(f) = 0; f \neq 0$ $\int_{-\infty}^{+\infty} \delta(f)df = 1$	Area = 1	Cannot be represented on logarithmic scales
Rectangular pulse $f(t) = 1; -\frac{T}{2} \leqslant t \leqslant +\frac{T}{2}$ $= 0$ elsewhere	$-T/2 \quad +T/2$	$F(f) = T \text{ sinc}(fT)$ $\left[\text{sinc}(x) = \frac{\sin \pi x}{\pi x} \right]$		Slope = 1, $20 \log_{10} T$

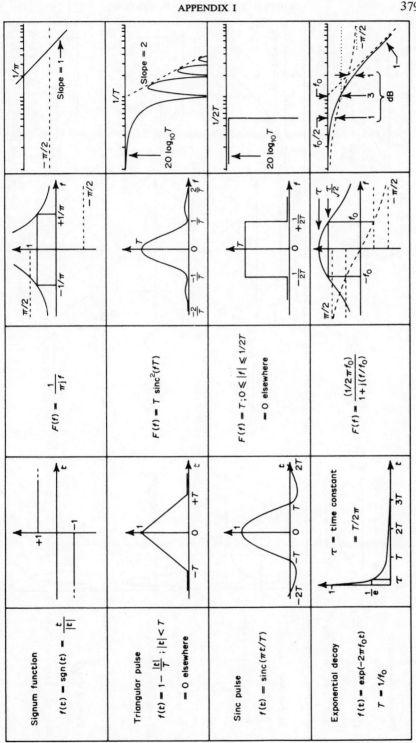

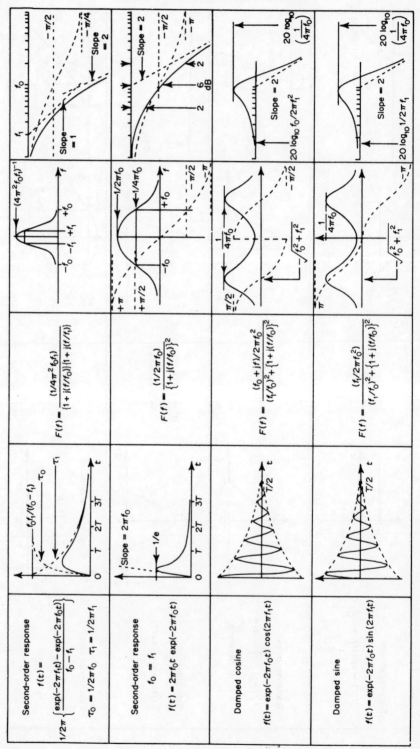

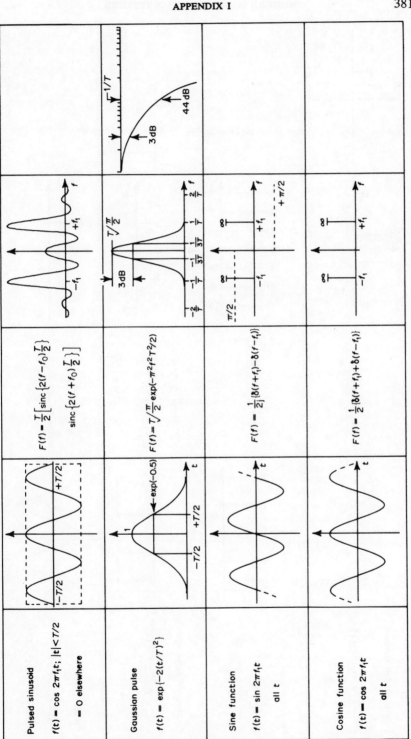

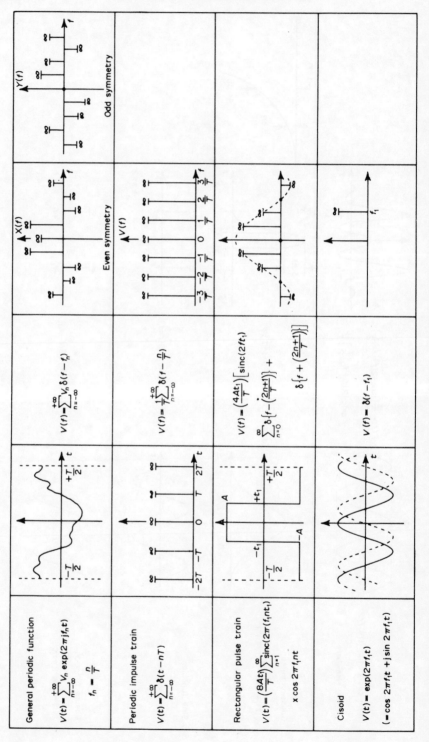

Appendix II

Mathematical Functions

(a) Integral Relationships

$$\int_{-\infty}^{+\infty} \mathrm{sinc}(kx)\,\mathrm{d}x = 1/k$$

$$\int_{-\infty}^{+\infty} \mathrm{sinc}^2(kx)\,\mathrm{d}x = 1/k$$

$$\int \sin^2(x)\,\mathrm{d}x = \frac{x}{2} - \frac{1}{2}\cos(x)\sin(x) + C$$

$$= \frac{x}{2} - \frac{1}{4}\sin(2x) + C$$

$$\int \cos^2(x)\,\mathrm{d}x = \frac{x}{2} + \frac{1}{2}\cos(x)\sin(x) + C$$

$$= \frac{x}{2} + \frac{1}{4}\sin(2x) + C$$

$$\int \sin(mx)\sin(nx)\,\mathrm{d}x = \frac{\sin\{(m-n)x\}}{2(m-n)} - \frac{\sin\{(m+n)x\}}{2(m+n)} + C \qquad (m \neq n)$$

$$\int \cos(mx)\cos(nx)\,\mathrm{d}x = \frac{\sin\{(m-n)x\}}{2(m-n)} + \frac{\sin\{(m+n)x\}}{2(m+n)} + C \qquad (m \neq n)$$

$$\int \sin(mx)\cos(nx)\,\mathrm{d}x = -\frac{\cos\{(m-n)x\}}{2(m-n)} - \frac{\cos\{(m+n)x\}}{2(m+n)} + C \qquad (m \neq n)$$

(b) Trigonometric Functions

$$\sin^2(A) + \cos^2(A) = 1$$

$$\sin^2(A) = \frac{1}{2}\{1 - \cos(2A)\}$$

$$\cos^2(A) = \frac{1}{2}\{1 + \cos(2A)\}$$

$$\cos(2A) = 1 - 2\sin^2(A)$$

$$= 2\cos^2(A) - 1$$

$$\sin(2A) = 2\sin(A)\cos(A)$$

$$\sin(A + B) = \sin(A)\cos(B) + \cos(A)\sin(B)$$

$$\sin(A - B) = \sin(A)\cos(B) - \cos(A)\sin(B)$$

$$\cos(A + B) = \cos(A)\cos(B) - \sin(A)\sin(B)$$

$$\cos(A - B) = \cos(A)\cos(B) + \sin(A)\sin(B)$$

$$\sin(A)\sin(B) = \frac{1}{2}\{\cos(A - B) - \cos(A + B)\}$$

$$\sin(A)\cos(B) = \frac{1}{2}\{\sin(A - B) + \sin(A + B)\}$$

$$\cos(A)\cos(B) = \frac{1}{2}\{\cos(A - B) + \cos(A + B)\}$$

$$\sin(A) + \sin(B) = 2\sin\left\{\frac{1}{2}(A + B)\right\}\cos\left\{\frac{1}{2}(A - B)\right\}$$

$$\sin(A) - \sin(B) = 2\sin\left\{\frac{1}{2}(A - B)\right\}\cos\left\{\frac{1}{2}(A + B)\right\}$$

$$\cos(A) + \cos(B) = 2\cos\left\{\frac{1}{2}(A + B)\right\}\cos\left\{\frac{1}{2}(A - B)\right\}$$

$$\cos(A) - \cos(B) = -2\sin\left\{\frac{1}{2}(A + B)\right\}\sin\left\{\frac{1}{2}(A - B)\right\}$$

Appendix III

Noise Sources and Their Effect within the Communication System[14,63]

In chapter 2 we saw that thermal and shot noise were two important and readily characterised sources of noise corruption in a communication system. In this appendix, we collate information pertinent to the evaluation of noise-behaviour. In so doing, we note that noise data provided by a manufacturer or derived from practical measurements is almost always expressed in terms of single-sided bandwidth (positive frequency only). By contrast, most theoretical analyses utilise double-sided noise power spectral densities. Which form of terminology is being used will be made clear at all relevant points in the following paragraphs.

(1) Our general noise process is a current or voltage waveform $n(t)$ superimposed upon a mean value I or V as appropriate. To determine the noise magnitude we 'measure' a time-averaged 'spread about the mean' in an implied single-sided measurement bandwidth B to obtain a mean-square noise voltage

$$\overline{n^2(t)} = 1/T \int_0^T n^2(t)\mathrm{d}t$$

The averaging epoch, T, must be chosen to be substantially greater than the reciprocal of the implied measurement bandwidth, B^{-1}, if the measurement is to be statistically representative.

(2) Thermal noise generated by a metallic, non-reactive resistor of value R, at temperature T ($\mathrm{K} \equiv {}^\circ\mathrm{C} + 273$) is given over a *single-sided* bandwidth B Hz by

$$\overline{n^2(t)} = 4kTBR \text{ volt}^2$$

where k is Boltzmann's constant ($\cong 1.38 \times 10^{-23}\ J\,K^{-1}$). By way of example, consider an FM receiver input stage with a bandwidth of 150 kHz, accepting signals from an antenna with a 50 Ω radiation resistance and presume this radiation resistance to represent also the source of thermal noise at the front-end input. Calculation yields an r.m.s. noise input of 0.35 μV, a value which reflects the need to receive signals of at least a few μV in amplitude, if the signal-to-noise ratio is to exceed the detection threshold.

(3) The noise generated ((2) above) has gaussian statistics (equation 2.1 applies with $p_a \equiv \overline{n^2(t)}$) and is spectrally white over the bandwidth B. The *double-sided* noise power spectral density used for theoretical studies is

$$P(f) = \overline{n^2(t)}/2B = 2kTR$$

(4) For practical resistor materials, it is necessary to note the following deviation from ideal performance. An 'excess' noise component, with magnitude proportional to current flow through the resistor (and referred to as 'current-noise') is evident. This noise component has a '$1/f$' spectrum (see also section (9) below) and thus, *per frequency decade*, contributes equal mean-square noise voltage. (That is, the frequency decade from 1 Hz to 10 Hz contributes exactly the same mean-square noise voltage as that from 1 MHz to 10 MHz.) The 'current-noise' excess contribution $\overline{n_c^2(t)}$ adds to the thermal noise component $\overline{n^2(t)}$ to yield a total noise contribution $\overline{n_t^2(t)} = \overline{n^2(t)} + \overline{n_c^2(t)}$. The current noise contribution is calculated by reference to manufacturers' published specifications of the 'microvolt per volt' index, which gives the number of microvolts r.m.s. current-noise generated in a frequency decade when the d.c. bias across the resistor material is V_{dc}. We write, for the index, $(\mu V/V)$ and calculate the mean-square current-noise over an arbitrary frequency band f_1 to f_2 as

$$\overline{n_c^2(t)} = V_{dc}^2 \times (\mu V/V)^2 \times \log_{10}(f_2/f_1)$$

Typical current noise indexes are quoted in table A.III. It is generally the case that thermal noise dominates at high frequencies, where communication processes are inherently narrowband, a condition of operation which makes $\log_{10}(f_2/f_1)$ (and hence the current-noise contribution) small.

TABLE A.III

Resistor Material	$(\mu V/V)$ Current-noise Index
Carbon composition	$2 + \log_{10}(R/1000)$
High-stability carbon film	~ 1.0
Metal glaze	~ 0.1
Metal oxide	~ 0.1
Metal film	$0.25-0.5$

(5) For an impedance component Z, the component terminal mean-square noise voltage in an incremental single-sided band of width δf is

$$\delta(\overline{n^2(t)}) = 4kTRe\{Z\}\delta f$$

The reason for expressing the noise power $\delta(\overline{n^2(t)})$ in incremental fashion is that $Re\{Z\}$ may well be frequency dependent. The *double-sided* noise power spectral density is then 'coloured' and is given as

$$P(f) = 2kTRe\{Z\}$$

For example, consider the case of a resistance with significant self-capacitance,

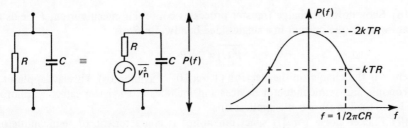

Figure A.III.1   Thermal noise power spectral density for a reactive component

figure AIII.1. For such a component, we readily calculate

$$Re\{Z\} = R/(1 + 4\pi^2 C^2 R^2)$$

so that the power spectral density has the form shown on the figure and is given (double-sided) by

$$P(f) = 2kTR/(1 + 4\pi^2 C^2 R^2)$$

In general, the total noise output in a single-sided band extending from f_1 to f_2 is

$$\overline{n^2(t)} = \int_{f_1}^{f_2} 4kTRe\{Z\}df$$

Often, the nature of $Re\{Z\}$ is such as to present a power spectral density (such as that derived above for the capacitive resistor) which is of low-pass form. It should be noted that

$$\int_{f_1}^{f_2} (1 + (f/f_0)^2)^{-1}df = [f_0 \arctan(f/f_0)]_{f_1}^{f_2}$$

and that, if $f_1 = 0$ and $f_2 = \infty$ the integral equates to $\pi f_0/2$. Thus the *total* mean-square voltage viewed at the open-circuit component terminals is $2kT\pi f_0$.

(6) In more general terms, filtering of a noise power spectral density $P_1(f)$ by a transfer function $H(f)$ yields an output noise power spectral density (given by equation 1.49)

$$P_2(f) = P_1(f)|H(f)|^2$$

(7) Equivalent noise bandwidth, B_n, is the bandwidth of a rectangular filter passing the same noise as a filter with transfer function $H(f)$. If f_m is the frequency at which $H(f)$ is a maximum, then

$$B_n = \frac{\int_{-\infty}^{+\infty} |H(f)|^2 df}{2|H(f_m)|^2}$$

Some cases of interest are listed here:

(7.1) First order lowpass filter: $f_0 = 1/2\pi CR$; $H(f_m = 0) = 1$; $B_n = f_0\pi/2$
(7.2) Gaussian lowpass filter: (see section 1.17.5 for definition) $B_n = 1.5f_0$
(7.3) Single tuned circuit: $B_n = B\pi/2$ where B is the -3 dB bandwidth and the centre frequency response modulus is scaled to unity.

(8) Shot noise in charge transfer processes conveying mean current I yields a mean-square noise current in a single-sided bandwidth B of

$$\overline{i^2(t)} = 2eIB$$

where e is the charge on the electron (1.6×10^{-19} coulombs). This law applies to thermionic and semiconductor devices and includes in the latter category, photodiodes as used in fibre-optic applications.

(9) Flicker noise (or $1/f$ spectrum noise) is characteristic of semiconductor devices. It is additional to and uncorrelated with shot noise and is of greatest significance at low frequencies. It is not usually important in a communication context and will therefore not be considered further.

(10) Spot noise value is quoted by manufacturers for low-noise amplifiers and semiconductor devices. It is a root-mean-square voltage or current scaled to a 1 Hz normalization bandwidth. It is therefore expressed in 'volts per root Hertz' and is denormalised to give r.m.s. noise voltage in a single-sided bandwidth B by multiplication with $B^{1/2}$. Assumptions are made that the noise is spectrally white, over the amplifier or device nominal operational bandwidth and that the noise so characterised is gaussian. For amplifiers, spot noise value is referred to the *input* and is thus an r.m.s. *output* noise voltage divided by the (probably large) amplifier gain.

(11) Noise figure, NF, for an amplifier is given as

$$NF = 10 \log_{10} \left\{ (S/N)_{\text{out}} / (S/N)_{\text{in}} \right\}$$

where S is signal power, N is noise power and 'in' and 'out' refer to signal-to-noise power ratios at amplifier input and output, respectively. If several amplifiers are connected in cascade, and the kth amplifier has noise figure NF_k and gain G_k, the overall noise figure is

$$NF = NF_1 + G_1^{-1}(NF_2 - 1) + (G_1 G_2)^{-1}(NF_3 - 1) + \ldots$$
$$+ (G_1 G_2 \ldots G_{k-1})^{-1}(NF_k - 1)$$

If all stages are of similar performance in respect of noise figure and each stage gain is reasonably large, then the first stage noise performance dominates. To maximise the noise figure and hence optimise performance the noise contribution added by the first amplifier should be minimised and its gain should be made large.

Bibliography

(A) *General reference texts covering communication engineering as a whole, or specific areas in great detail*
1. P. F. Panter, *Modulation, Noise and Spectral Analysis*, McGraw-Hill, New York (1965)
2. D. Middleton, *Introduction to Statistical Communication Theory*, McGraw-Hill, New York (1960)
3. F. E. Terman, *Radio Engineers' Handbook*, McGraw-Hill, New York (1943)
4. D. H. Hamsher, *Communication System Engineering Handbook*, McGraw-Hill, New York (1967)
5. D. L. Richards, *Telecommunication by Speech*, Butterworth, London (1973)
6. M. Schwartz, W. R. Bennet and S. Stein, *Communication Systems and Techniques*, McGraw-Hill, New York (1966)

(B) *Books mainly on Fourier Transforms, Spectral Analysis or Filtering*
7. R. Bracewell, *The Fourier Transform and its Application*, McGraw-Hill, New York (1965)
8. R. D. Stuart, *An Introduction to Fourier Analysis*, Science Paperbacks (Associated Book Publishers Ltd), London (1966)
9. P. A. Lynn, *The Analysis and Processing of Signals*, Macmillan, London (1973)
10. G. R. Cooper and C. D. McGillem, *Methods of Signal and System Analysis*, Holt Rinehart Winston, New York (1967)
11. E. A. Guillemin, *Synthesis of Passive Networks*, Wiley, New York (1957)
12. P. R. Geffe, *Simplified Modern Filter Design*, Iliffe, London (1964)

(C) *Books mainly on Noise Processes and the Communication Channel*
13. A. W. Drake, *Fundamentals of Applied Probability Theory*, McGraw-Hill, New York (1967)

14. R. King, *Electrical Noise*, Chapman and Hall, London (1966)
15. J. J. Freeman, *Principles of Noise*, Wiley, New York (1958)
16. A. Piquenard, *Radio Wave Propagation*, Macmillan, London (1974)
17. T. Moreno, *Microwave Transmission Design Data*, Dover, New York (1958)

(D) *Books on the Modulation of Sinusoids*
18. D. G. Tucker, *Modulators and Frequency Changers*, Macdonald, London (1953)
19. D. G. Tucker, *Circuits With Periodically Time Varying Parameters*, Macdonald, London (1964)
20. J. P. Froelich, *Information Transmittal and Communicating Systems*, Holt Rinehart Winston, New York (1969)
21. J. Fagot and P. Magne, *Frequency Modulation Theory*, Pergamon, London (1961)
22. A. J. Viterbi, *Principles of Coherent Communication*, McGraw-Hill, New York (1966)
23. E. W. Pappenfus, W. B. Breune and E. O. Schoenike, *Single Sideband Principles and Circuits*, McGraw-Hill, New York (1964)

(E) *Books on Digital Systems and Techniques*
24. K. W. Cattermole, *Principles of Pulse Code Modulation*, Iliffe, London (1969)
25. G. C. Hartley, *et al.*, *Pulse Code Modulation in Communication Networks*, I.E.E. Monograph, Series 1, Cambridge (1967)
26. D. F. Hoeschele, *Analog-to-Digital/Digital-to-Analog Conversion Techniques*, Wiley, New York (1968)
27. W. W. Peterson and E. J. Weldon, *Error Correcting Codes*, (2nd Edition) M.I.T. Press, Cambridge, Mass. (1972)
28. W. R. Bennet and J. R. Davey, *Data Transmission*, McGraw-Hill, New York (1965)

(F) *More Specific References*
29. M. Abramowitz and I. A. Stegun, *Handbook of Mathematical Functions*, Dover, New York (1965)
30. R. H. Barker, Group Synchronisation of Binary Digital Systems, *Communication Theory*, (ed. W. Jackson) Butterworth, London (1953), pp. 273–8
31. N. M. Blackman, *Noise and its Effect on Communication*, McGraw-Hill, New York (1966), pp. 104–13
32. M. Dishal, Gaussian Response Filter Design, *Elect. Commun.*, **36** (1959), pp. 3–26
33. D. W. Hagelbarger, Recurrent Codes; Easily Mechanised Burst Correcting Binary Codes, *Bell Syst. tech. J.*, **38** (1959), 969–84
34. R. W. Hamming, Error Detecting and Error Correcting Codes, *Bell Syst. tech. J.*, **29** (1950), 147–60
35. R. Harrison, Analysis of the Statistics and Threshold of the Phase Locked Loop. *Proc. Instn elect. Engrs*, **116** (1969), 43–52

36. F. G. Jenks and D. C. Hannon, A Comparison of the Merits of Phase and Frequency Modulation for Medium Speed Serial Binary Digital Transmission Over Telephone Lines, *J. Br. Instn Radio Engrs*, **24** (1962), 21–36

37. P. R. Keller, An Automatic Error Correction System for Unidirectional HF Teleprinter Circuits, *Point to Point Telecomm.*, **7** (1963), pp. 14–29

38. G. A. Korn, *Random Process Simulation and Measurement*, McGraw-Hill, New York (1966), pp. 83–94

39. J. Millman and H. Taub, *Pulse, Digital and Switching Waveforms*, McGraw-Hill, New York (1965)

40. E. C. Posner, Combinatorial Structures in Planetary Reconnaisance. *Error Correcting Codes*, (ed. H. B. Mann), Wiley, New York (1968)

41. H. J. Pushman, Spectral Density Distribution of Signals for Binary Data Transmission. *J. Br. Instn Radio Engrs*, **25** (1963), 155–65

42. S. O. Rice, Noise in FM Receivers, *Proceedings of the Symposium on Time Series Analysis*, (ed. Rosenblatt), Wiley, New York (1963), pp. 395–414

43. D. L. Richards, Transmission Performance of Telephone Networks Containing PCM links. *Proc. Instn elect. Engrs*, **115** (1968), 1245–58

44. W. C. Sain, Pulse Code Modulation Systems in North America. *Electl Commun.*, **48** (1973), 59–68

45. J. G. Spencer, The Design of Receivers for the Pilot Tone Stereophonic System. *B.B.C. Research Department Technological Report*, No. G-092 (1964/31)

46. E. D. Sunde. Pulse Transmission by AM, PM and FM in the Presence of Phase Distortion. *Bell Syst. tech. J.*, **40** (1961), pp. 353–422

47. J. M. Wosencraft and I. M. Jacobs, *Principles of Communication Engineering*, Wiley, New York (1965)

48. J. G. Lawton, Theoretical Error Rates of Differentially Coherent Binary and Kineplex Data Transmission Systems. *Proc. Instn Radio Engrs*, **47** (1969) No. 2, 333–4

49. M. Schwartz, W. R. Bennet and S. Stein, *Communication Systems and Techniques*, McGraw-Hill, New York (1966), 297–8

50. R. Gold, Optimal Binary Sequences for Spread Spectrum Multiplexing. *IEEE Trans Information Theory*, **IT–13** (1967), 619–21

51. D. V. Sarawate and M. B. Pursley, Crosscorrelation Properties of Pseudo-random and Related Sequences. *Proc. IEEE*, **68** (1980), 593–619

52. R. C. Dixon, *Spread Spectrum Systems*, Wiley, New York (1961)

53. W. D. T. Davies, Generation and Properties of Maximal Length Sequences, *Control*, **10** (1966), 302–4, 364–5, 431–4

54. F. de Jaeger and M. Christians, A Fast Automatic Equaliser for Data Links. *Philips Tech. Rev.*, **37** (1977), 10–24

55. Special Section on Combined Modulation and Encoding, *IEEE Trans Commun.*, **COM–27** (1979), No. 3

56. J. G. Pearce, *Telecommunication Switching*, Plenum Press, New York (1981)

57. Special Issue on Digital Switching, *IEEE Trans Commun.*, **COM–27** (1979), No. 7

58. Special Section on Digital Subscriber Lines and Digital Telephones, *IEEE Trans Commun.*, **COM–29** (1981), No. 11

59. Special Section on the Thrust of Electronic Systems in the Subscriber Loop Plant, *IEEE Trans Commun.*, **COM–28** (1980), No. 7
60. Special Issue on Packet Communication, *Proc. IEEE*, **66** (1978), No. 11
61. Special Issue on Computer Network Architectures and Protocols, *IEEE Trans Commun.*, **COM–28** (1980), No. 4
62. Special Issue on Optical Fibre Communication, *Proc. IEEE*, **68** (1980), No. 10
63. Y. Netzer, The Design of Low Noise Amplifiers, *Proc. IEEE*, **69** (1981), No. 6, 728–41

Index